Pattern Discovery Using Sequence Data Mining:
Applications and Studies

Pradeep Kumar
Indian Institute of Management Lucknow, India

P. Radha Krishna
Infosys Lab, Infosys Limited, India

S. Bapi Raju
University of Hyderabad, India

Information Science
REFERENCE

Senior Editorial Director:	Kristin Klinger
Director of Book Publications:	Julia Mosemann
Editorial Director:	Lindsay Johnston
Acquisitions Editor:	Erika Carter
Development Editor:	Joel Gamon
Production Editor:	Sean Woznicki
Typesetters:	Jennifer Romanchak, Lisandro Gonzalez
Print Coordinator:	Jamie Snavely
Cover Design:	Nick Newcomer

Published in the United States of America by
Information Science Reference (an imprint of IGI Global)
701 E. Chocolate Avenue
Hershey PA 17033
Tel: 717-533-8845
Fax: 717-533-8661
E-mail: cust@igi-global.com
Web site: http://www.igi-global.com

Library of Congress Cataloging-in-Publication Data

Pattern discovery using sequence data mining : applications and studies / Pradeep Kumar, P. Radha Krishna, and S. Bapi Raju, editors.
       p. cm.
  Summary: "This book provides a comprehensive view of sequence mining techniques, and present current research and case studies in Pattern Discovery in Sequential data authored by researchers and practitioners"-- Provided by publisher.
  Includes bibliographical references and index.
  ISBN 978-1-61350-056-9 (hardcover) -- ISBN 978-1-61350-058-3 (print & perpetual access) -- ISBN 978-1-61350-057-6 (ebook) 1. Sequential pattern mining. 2. Sequential processing (Computer science) I. Kumar, Pradeep, 1977- II. Radha Krishna, P. III. Raju, S. Bapi, 1962-
  QA76.9.D343P396 2012
  006.3'12--dc22
                                     2011008678

British Cataloguing in Publication Data
A Cataloguing in Publication record for this book is available from the British Library.

All work contributed to this book is new, previously-unpublished material. The views expressed in this book are those of the authors, but not necessarily of the publisher.

List of Reviewers

Manish Gupta, *University of Illinois at Urbana, USA*
Chandra Sekhar, *Indian Institute of Technology Madras, India*
Arnab Bhattacharya, *Indian Institute of Technology Kanpur, India*
Padmaja T Maruthi, *University of Hyderabad, India*
T. Ravindra Babu, *Infosys Technologies Ltd, India*
Pratibha Rani, *International Institute of Information Technology Hyderabad, India*
Nita Parekh, *International Institute of Information Technology Hyderabad, India*
Anass El-Haddadi, *IRIT, France*
Pinar Senkul, *Middle East Technical University, Turkey*
Jessica Lin, *George Mason University, USA*
Pradeep Kumar, *Indian Institute of Management Lucknow, India*
Raju S. Bapi, *University of Hyderabad, India*
P. Radha Krishna, *Infosys Lab, Infosys Limited, India*

Table of Contents

Preface

A huge amount of data is collected every day in the form of sequences. These sequential data are valuable sources of information not only to search for a particular value or event at a specific time, but also to analyze the frequency of certain events or sets of events related by particular temporal/sequential relationship. For example, DNA sequences encode the genetic makeup of humans and all other species, and protein sequences describe the amino acid composition of proteins and encode the structure and function of proteins. Moreover, sequences can be used to capture how individual humans behave through various temporal activity histories such as weblog histories and customer purchase patterns. In general there are various methods to extract information and patterns from databases, such as time series approaches, association rule mining, and data mining techniques.

The objective of this book is to provide a concise state-of-the-art in the field of sequence data mining along with applications. The book consists of 14 chapters divided into 3 sections. The first section provides review of state-of-art in the field of sequence data mining. Section 2 presents relatively new techniques for sequence data mining. Finally, in section 3, various application areas of sequence data mining have been explored.

Chapter 1, *Approaches for Pattern Discovery Using Sequential Data Mining*, by Manish Gupta and Jiawei Han of University of Illinois at Urbana-Champaign, IL, USA, discusses different approaches for mining of patterns from sequence data. Apriori based methods and the pattern growth methods are the earliest and the most influential methods for sequential pattern mining. There is also a vertical format based method which works on a dual representation of the sequence database. Work has also been done for mining patterns with constraints, mining closed patterns, mining patterns from multi-dimensional databases, mining closed repetitive gapped subsequences, and other forms of sequential pattern mining. Some works also focus on mining incremental patterns and mining from stream data. In this chapter, the authors have presented at least one method of each of these types and discussed advantages and disadvantages.

Chapter 2, *A Review of Kernel Methods Based Approaches to Classification and Clustering of Sequential Patterns, Part I: Sequences of Continuous Feature Vectors*, was authored by Dileep A. D., Veena T., and C. Chandra Sekhar of Department of Computer Science and Engineering, Indian Institute of Technology Madras, India. They present a brief description of kernel methods for pattern classification and clustering. They also describe dynamic kernels for sequences of continuous feature vectors. The chapter also presents a review of approaches to sequential pattern classification and clustering using dynamic kernels.

Chapter 3 is *A Review of Kernel Methods Based Approaches to Classification and Clustering of Sequential Patterns, Part II: Sequences of Discrete Symbols* by Veena T., Dileep A. D., and C. Chandra Sekhar of Department of Computer Science and Engineering, Indian Institute of Technology Madras, India. The authors review methods to design dynamic kernels for sequences of discrete symbols. In their chapter they have also presented a review of approaches to classification and clustering of sequences of discrete symbols using the dynamic kernel based methods.

Chapter 4 is titled, *Mining Statistically Significant Substrings Based on the Chi-Square Measure*, contributed by Sourav Dutta of IBM Research India along with Arnab Bhattacharya Dept. of Computer Science and Engineering, Indian Institute of Technology, Kanpur, India. This chapter highlights the challenge of efficient mining of large string databases in the domains of intrusion detection systems, player statistics, texts, proteins, et cetera, and how these issues have emerged as challenges of practical nature. Searching for an unusual pattern within long strings of data is one of the foremost requirements for many diverse applications. The authors first present the current state-of-art in this area and then analyze the different statistical measures available to meet this end. Next, they argue that the most appropriate metric is the chi-square measure. Finally, they discuss different approaches and algorithms proposed for retrieving the top-k substrings with the largest chi-square measure. The local-maxima based algorithms maintain high quality while outperforming others with respect to the running time.

Chapter 5 is *Unbalanced Sequential Data Classification Using Extreme Outlier Elimination and Sampling Techniques*, by T. Maruthi Padmaja along with Raju S. Bapi from University of Hyderabad, Hyderabad, India and P. Radha Krishna, Infosys Lab, Infosys Technologies Ltd, Hyderabad, India. This chapter focuses on problem of predicting minority class sequence patterns from the noisy and unbalanced sequential datasets. To solve this problem, the atuhors proposed a new approach called extreme outlier elimination and hybrid sampling technique.

Chapter 6 is *Quantization Based Sequence Generation and Subsequence Pruning for Data Mining Applications* by T. Ravindra Babu and S. V. Subrahmanya of E-Comm. Research Lab, Education and Research, Infosys Technologies Limited, Bangalore, India, along with M. Narasimha Murty, Dept. of Computer Science and Automation, Indian Institute of Science, Bangalore, India. This chapter has highlighted the problem of combining data mining algorithms with data compaction used for data compression. Such combined techniques lead to superior performance. Approaches to deal with large data include working with a representative sample instead of the entire data. The representatives should preferably be generated with minimal data scans, methods like random projection, et cetera.

Chapter 7 is *Classification of Biological Sequences* by Pratibha Rani and Vikram Pudi of International Institute of Information Technology, Hyderabad, India, and it discusses the problem of classifying a newly discovered sequence like a protein or DNA sequence based on their important features and functions, using the collection of available sequences. In this chapter, the authors study this problem and present two techniques Bayesian classifiers: RBNBC and REBMEC. The algorithms used in these classifiers incorporate repeated occurrences of subsequences within each sequence. Specifically, RBNBC (Repeat Based Naive Bayes Classifier) uses a novel formulation of Naive Bayes, and the second classifier, REBMEC (Repeat Based Maximum Entropy Classifier) uses a novel framework based on the classical Generalized Iterative Scaling (GIS) algorithm.

Chapter 8, *Applications of Pattern Discovery Using Sequential Data Mining*, by Manish Gupta and Jiawei Han of University of Illinois at Urbana-Champaign, IL, USA, presents a comprehensive review of applications of sequence data mining algorithms in a variety of domains like healthcare, education, Web usage mining, text mining, bioinformatics, telecommunications, intrusion detection, et cetera.

Chapter 9, *Analysis of Kinase Inhibitors and Druggability of Kinase-Targets Using Machine Learning Techniques*, by S. Prashanthi, S. Durga Bhavani, T. Sobha Rani, and Raju S. Bapi of Department of Computer & Information Sciences, University of Hyderabad, Hyderabad, India, focuses on human kinase drug target sequences since kinases are known to be potential drug targets. The authors have also presented a preliminary analysis of kinase inhibitors in order to study the problem in the protein-ligand space in future. The identification of druggable kinases is treated as a classification problem in which druggable kinases are taken as positive data set and non-druggable kinases are chosen as negative data set.

Chapter 10, *Identification of Genomic Islands by Pattern Discovery*, by Nita Parekh of International Institute of Information Technology, Hyderabad, India addresses a pattern recognition problem at the genomic level involving identifying horizontally transferred regions, called genomic islands. A horizontally transferred event is defined as the movement of genetic material between phylogenetically unrelated organisms by mechanisms other than parent to progeny inheritance. Increasing evidence suggests the importance of horizontal transfer events in the evolution of bacteria, influencing traits such as antibiotic resistance, symbiosis and fitness, virulence, and adaptation in general. Considerable effort is being made in their identification and analysis, and in this chapter, a brief summary of various approaches used in the identification and validation of horizontally acquired regions is discussed.

Chapter 11, *Video Stream Mining for On-Road Traffic Density Analytics*, by Rudra Narayan Hota of Frankfurt Institute for Advanced Studies, Frankfurt, Germany along with Kishore Jonna and P. Radha Krishna, Infosys Lab, Infosys Technologies Limited, India, addresses the problem of estimating computer vision based traffic density using video stream mining. The authors present an efficient approach for traffic density estimation using texture analysis along with Support Vector Machine (SVM) classifier, and describe analyzing traffic density for on-road traffic congestion control with better flow management.

Chapter 12, *Discovering Patterns in Order to Detect Weak Signals and Define New Strategies*, by Anass El Haddadi of Université de Toulouse, IRIT UMR France Bernard Dousset, Ilham Berrada of Ensias, AL BIRONI team, Mohamed V University – Souissi, Rabat, Morocco presents four methods for discovering patterns in the competitive intelligence process: "correspondence analysis," "multiple correspondence analysis," "evolutionary graph," and "multi-term method." Competitive intelligence activities rely on collecting and analyzing data in order to discover patterns from data using sequence data mining. The discovered patterns are used to help decision-makers considering innovation and defining business strategy.

Chapter 13, *Discovering Patterns for Architecture Simulation by Using Sequence Mining*, by Pınar Senkul (Middle East Technical University, Computer Engineering Dept., Ankara, Turkey) along with Nilufer Onder (Michigan Technological University, Computer Science Dept., Michigan, USA), Soner Onder (Michigan Technological University, Computer Science Dept., Michigan, USA), Engin Maden (Middle East Technical University, Computer Engineering Dept., Ankara, Turkey) and Hui Meen Nyew (Michigan Technological University, Computer Science Dept., Michigan, USA), discusses the problem of designing and building high performance systems that make effective use of resources such as space and power. The design process typically involves a detailed simulation of the proposed architecture followed by corrections and improvements based on the simulation results. Both simulator development and result analysis are very challenging tasks due to the inherent complexity of the underlying systems. They present a tool called Episode Mining Tool (EMT), which includes three temporal sequence mining algorithms, a preprocessor, and a visual analyzer.

Chapter 14 is called *Sequence Pattern Mining for Web Logs* by Pradeep Kumar, Indian Institute of Management, Lucknow, India, Raju S. Bapi, University of Hyderabad, India and P. Radha Krishna,

Infosys Lab, Infosys Technologies Limited, India. In their work, the authors utilize a variation to the AprioriALL Algorithm, which is commonly used for the sequence pattern mining. The proposed variation adds up the measure Interest during every step of candidate generation to reduce the number of candidates thus resulting in reduced time and space cost.

This book can be useful to academic researchers and graduate students interested in data mining in general and in sequence data mining in particular, and to scientists and engineers working in fields where sequence data mining is involved, such as bioinformatics, genomics, Web services, security, and financial data analysis.

Sequence data mining is still a fairly young research field. Much more remains to be discovered in this exciting research domain in the aspects related to general concepts, techniques, and applications. Our fond wish is that this collection sparks fervent activity in sequence data mining, and we hope this is not the last word!

Pradeep Kumar
Indian Institute of Management Lucknow, India

P. Radha Krishna
Infosys Lab, Infosys Limited, India

S. Bapi Raju
University of Hyderabad, India

Section 1
Current State of Art

Chapter 1
Applications of Pattern Discovery Using Sequential Data Mining

Manish Gupta
University of Illinois at Urbana-Champaign, USA

Jiawei Han
University of Illinois at Urbana-Champaign, USA

ABSTRACT

Sequential pattern mining methods have been found to be applicable in a large number of domains. Sequential data is omnipresent. Sequential pattern mining methods have been used to analyze this data and identify patterns. Such patterns have been used to implement efficient systems that can recommend based on previously observed patterns, help in making predictions, improve usability of systems, detect events, and in general help in making strategic product decisions. In this chapter, we discuss the applications of sequential data mining in a variety of domains like healthcare, education, Web usage mining, text mining, bioinformatics, telecommunications, intrusion detection, et cetera. We conclude with a summary of the work.

HEALTHCARE

Patterns in healthcare domain include the common patterns in paths followed by patients in hospitals, patterns observed in symptoms of a particular disease, patterns in daily activity and health data. Works related to these applications are discussed in this sub-section.

DOI: 10.4018/978-1-61350-056-9.ch001

Patterns in patient paths: The purpose of the French Diagnosis Related Group's information system is to describe hospital activity by focusing on hospital stays. (Nicolas, Herengt & Albuisson, 2004) propose usage of sequential pattern mining for patient path analysis across multiple healthcare institutions. The objective is to discover, to classify and to visualize frequent patterns among patient path. They view a patient path as a sequence of sets. Each set in the sequence is a hospitalization instance. Each element in a hospitalization can be any symbolic data gathered by the PMSI (medical data source). They used the SLPMiner system (Seno & Karypis, 2002) for mining the patient path database in order to find frequent sequential patterns among the patient path. They tested the model on the 2002 year of PMSI data at the Nancy University Hospital and also propose an interactive tool to perform inter-institutional patient path analysis.

Patterns in dyspepsia symptoms: Consider a domain expert, who is an epidemiologist and is interested in finding relationships between symptoms of dyspepsia within and across time points. This can be done by first mining patterns from symptom data and then using patterns to define association rules. Rules could look like ANOREX2=0 VOMIT2=0 NAUSEA3=0 AN-OREX3=0 VOMIT3=0 $\Rightarrow$ DYSPH2=0 where each symptom is represented as <symptom>N=V (time=N and value=V). ANOREX (anorexia), VOMIT (vomiting), DYSPH (dysphagia) and NAUSEA (nausea) are the different symptoms. However, a better way of handling this is to define subgroups as a set of symptoms at a single time point. (Lau, Ong, Mahidadia, Hoffmann, Westbrook, & Zrimec, 2003) solve the problem of identifying symptom patterns by implementing a framework for constraint based association rule mining across subgroups. Their framework, Apriori with Subgroup and Constraint (ASC), is built on top of the existing Apriori framework. They have identified four different types of phase-wise constraints for subgroups: constraint across subgroups, constraint on subgroup, constraint on pattern content and constraint on rule. A constraint across subgroups specifies the order of subgroups in which they are to be mined. A constraint on subgroup describes the intra-subgroup criteria of the association rules. It describes a minimum support for subgroups and a set of constraints for each subgroup. A constraint on pattern content outlines the inter-subgroup criteria on association

rules. It describes the criteria on the relationships between subgroups. A constraint on rule outlines the composition of an association rule; it describes the attributes that form the antecedents and the consequents, and calculates the confidence of an association rule. It also specifies the minimum support for a rule and prunes away item-sets that do not meet this support at the end of each subgroup-merging step. A typical user constraint can look like [1,2,3][1, a=A1&n<=2][2, a=B1&n<=2][3, v=1][rule, (s1 s2) $\Rightarrow$ s3]. This can be interpreted as: looking at subgroups 1, 2 and 3, from subgroup 1, extract patterns that contain the attribute A1 (a=A1) and contain no more than 2 attributes (n<=2); from subgroup 2, extract patterns that contain the attribute B1 (a=B1) and contain no more than 2 attributes (n<=2); then from subgroup 3, extract patterns with at least one attribute that has a value of 1 (v=1). Attributes from subgroups 1 and 2 form the antecedents in a rule, and attributes from subgroup 3 form the consequents ([rule, (s1 s2) $\Rightarrow$ s3]). Such constraints are easily incorporated into the Apriori process by pruning away more candidates based on these constraints.

They experimented on a dataset with records of 303 patients treated for dyspepsia. Each record represented a patient, the absence or presence of 10 dyspepsia symptoms at three time points (initial presentation to a general practitioner, 18 months after endoscopy screening, and 8–9 years after endoscopy) and the endoscopic diagnosis for the patient. Each of these symptoms can have one of the following three values: symptom present, symptom absent, missing (unknown). At each of the three time points, a symptom can take any of these three possible values. They show that their approach leads to interesting symptom pattern discovery.

Patterns in daily activity data: There are also works, which investigate techniques for using agent-based smart home technologies to provide at-home automated assistance and health monitoring. These systems first learn patterns from at-home health and activity data. Further, for any new test cases, they identify behaviors that do not conform to normal behavior and report them as predicted anomalous health problems.

EDUCATION

In the education domain, work has been done to extract patterns from source code and student teamwork data.

Patterns in source code: A coding pattern is a frequent sequence of method calls and control statements to implement a particular behavior. Coding patterns include copy-and-pasted code, crosscutting concerns (parts of a program which rely on or must affect many other parts of the system) and implementation idioms. Duplicated code fragments and crosscutting concerns that spread across modules are problematic in software maintenance. (Ishio, Date, Miyake, & Inoue, 2008) propose a sequential pattern mining approach to capture coding patterns in Java programs. They define a set of rules to translate Java source code into a sequence database for pattern mining, and apply PrefixSpan algorithm to the sequence database. They define constraints for mining source code patterns. A constraint for control statements could be: If a pattern includes a LOOP/IF element, the pattern must include its corresponding element generated from the same control statement. They classify sub-patterns into pattern groups. As a case study, they applied their tool to six open-source programs and manually investigated the resultant patterns.

They identify about 17 pattern groups which they classify into 5 categories:

1. A boolean method to insert an additional action: <Boolean method>, <IF>, <action-method>, <END-IF>
2. A boolean method to change the behavior of multiple methods: <Boolean method>, <IF>, <action-method>, <END-IF>
3. A pair of set-up and clean-up: <set-up method>, <misc action>, …, <clean-up method>
4. Exception Handling: Every instance is included in a try-catch statement.
5. Other patterns.

They have made this technique available as a tool: Fung(http://sel.ist.osaka-u.ac.jp/~ishio/fung/)

Patterns in student team-work data: (Kay, Maisonneuve, Yacef, & Zaïane, 2006) describe data mining of student group interaction data to identify significant sequences of activity. The goal is to build tools that can flag interaction sequences indicative of problems, so that they can be used to assist student teams in early recognition of problems. They also want tools that can identify patterns that are markers of success so that these might indicate improvements during the learning process. They obtain their data using TRAC which is an open source tool designed for use in software development projects. Students collaborate by sharing tasks via the TRAC system. These tasks are managed by a "Ticket" system; source code writing tasks are managed by a version control system called "SVN"; students communicate by means of collaborative web page writing called "Wiki". Data consist of events where each event is represented as Event = {EventType, ResourceId, Author, Time} where: EventType is one of T (for Ticket), S (for SVN), W (for Wiki). One such sequence is generated for each of the group of students.

The original sequence obtained for each group was 285 to 1287 long. These event sequences were then broken down into several "sequences" of events using a per session approach or a per resource approach. In breakdown per session approach, date and the resourceId are omitted and a sequence is of form: (iXj) which captures the number of i consecutive times a medium X was used by j different authors, e.g., <(2T1), (5W3), (2S1),(1W1)>. In breakdown per resource approach, sequence is of form <iXj, t> which captures the number of i different events of type X, the number j of authors, and the number of days over which t the resource was modified, e.g., <10W5, 2>. In a follow-up paper (Perera, Kay, Yacef, & Koprinska, 2007), they have a third approach, breakdown by task where every sequence is of the form (i,X,A) which captures the number of consecutive events (i) occurring on a particular TRAC medium (X), and the role of the author (A).

Patterns observed in group sessions: Better groups had many alternations of SVN and Wiki events, and SVN and Ticket events whereas weaker groups had almost none. The best group also had the highest proportion of author sessions containing many consecutive ticket events (matching their high use of ticketing) and SVN events (suggesting they committed their work to the group repository more often).

A more detailed analysis of these patterns revealed that the best group used the Ticket more than the Wiki, whereas the weakest group displayed the opposite pattern. The data suggested group leaders in good groups were much less involved in technical work, suggesting work was being delegated properly and the leader was leading rather than simply doing all the work. In contrast, the leaders of the poorer groups either seemed to use the Wiki (a less focused medium) more than the tickets, or be involved in too much technical work.

Patterns observed in task sequences: The two best groups had the greatest percentage support for the pattern (1,t,L)(1,t,b), which were most likely tickets initiated by the leader and accepted by another team member. The fact this occurred more often than (1,t,L)(2,t,b), suggests that the better groups were distinguished by tasks being performed on the Wiki or SVN files before the ticket was closed by the second member. Notably, the weakest group had higher support for this latter pattern than the former. The best group was one of the only two to display the patterns (1,t,b)(1,s,b) and (1,s,b)(1,t,b) – the first likely being a ticket

being accepted by a team member and then SVN work relating to that task being completed and the second likely being work being done followed by the ticket being closed. The close coupling of task-related SVN and Wiki activity and Ticket events for this group was also shown by relatively high support for the patterns (1,t,b)(1,t,b)(1,t,b), (1,t,b)(1,s,b)(1,t,b) and (1,t,b)(1,w,b)(1,t,b). The poorest group displayed the highest support for the last pattern, but no support for the former, again indicating their lack of SVN use in tasks.

Patterns observed in resource sequences: The best group had very high support for patterns where the leader interacted with group members on tickets, such as (L,1,t)(b,1,t)(L,1,t). The poorest group in contrast lacked these interaction patterns, and had more tickets which were created by the Tracker rather than the Leader, suggestive of weaker leadership. The best group displayed the highest support for patterns such as (b,3,t) and (b,4,t), suggestive of group members making at least one update on tickets before closing them. In contrast, the weaker groups showed support mainly for the pattern (b,2,t), most likely indicative of group members accepting and closing tickets with no update events in between.

Web Usage Mining

The complexity of tasks such as Web site design, Web server design, and of simply navigating through a Web site has been increasing continuously. An important input to these design tasks is the analysis of how a Web site is being used. Usage analysis includes straightforward statistics, such as page access frequency, as well as more sophisticated forms of analysis, such as finding the common traversal paths through a Web site. Web Usage Mining is the application of pattern mining techniques to usage logs of large Web data repositories in order to produce results that can be used in the design tasks mentioned above. However, there are several preprocessing tasks that must be performed prior to applying data mining algorithms to the data collected from server logs.

Transaction identification from web usage data: (Cooley, Mobasher, & Srivastava, 1999) present several data preparation techniques in order to identify unique users and user sessions. Also, a method to divide user sessions into semantically meaningful transactions is defined. Each user session in a user session file can be thought of in two ways; either as a single transaction of many page references, or a set of many transactions each consisting of a single page reference. The goal of transaction identification is to create meaningful clusters of references for each user. Therefore, the task of identifying transactions is one of either dividing a large transaction into multiple smaller ones or merging small transactions into fewer larger ones. This process can be extended into multiple steps of merge or divide in order to create transactions appropriate for a given data mining task. Both types of approaches take a transaction list and possibly some parameters as input, and output a transaction list that has been operated on by the function in the approach in the same format as the input. They consider three different ways of identifying transactions based on: Reference Length (time spent when visiting a page), Maximal Forward Reference (set of pages in the path from the first page in a user session up to the page before a backward reference is made) and Time Window.

By analyzing this information, a Web Usage Mining system can determine temporal relationships among data items such as the following Olympics Web site examples:

- 9.81% of the site visitors accessed the Atlanta home page followed by the Sneakpeek main page.
- 0.42% of the site visitors accessed the Sports main page followed by the Schedules main page.

Patterns for customer acquisition: (Buchner & Mulvenna, 1998) propose an environment that allows the discovery of patterns from trading related web sites, which can be harnessed for electronic commerce activities, such as personalization, adaptation, customization, profiling, and recommendation.

The two essential parts of customer attraction are the selection of new prospective customers and the acquisition of the selected potential candidates. One marketing strategy to perform this exercise, among others, is to find common characteristics in already existing visitors' information and behavior for the classes of profitable and non-profitable customers. The authors discover these sequences by extending GSP so it can handle duplicates in sequences, which is relevant to discover navigational behavior.

```
A found sequence looks as the
  following:
{ecom.infm.ulst.ac.uk/, ecom.infm.
ulst.ac.uk/News_Resources.html, ecom.
infm.ulst.ac.uk/Journals.html, ecom.
infm.ulst.ac.uk/, ecom.infm.ulst.
ac.uk/search.htm} Support = 3.8%;
Confidence = 31.0%
```

The discovered sequence can then be used to display special offers dynamically to keep a customer interested in the site, after a certain page sequence with a threshold support and/or confidence value has been visited.

Patterns to Improve Web Site Design

For the analysis of visitor navigation behavior in web sites integrating multiple information systems (multiple underlying database servers or archives), (Berendt, 2000) proposed the web usage miner (WUM), which discovers navigation patterns subject to advanced statistical and structural constraints. Experiments with a real web site that integrates data from multiple databases, the German SchulWeb (a database of German-language school magazines), demonstrate the appropriateness of WUM in discovering navigation patterns and show how those discoveries can help in assessing and improving the quality of the site design i.e. conformance of the web site's structure to the intuition of each group of visitors accessing the site. The intuition of the visitors is indirectly reflected in their navigation behavior, as represented in their browsing patterns. By comparing the typical patterns with the site usage expected by the site designer, one can examine the quality of the site and give concrete suggestions for its improvement. For instance, repeated refinements of a query may indicate a search environment that is not intuitive for some users. Also, long lists of results may signal that sufficiently selective search options are lacking, or that they are not understood by everyone.

A session is a directed list of page accesses performed by a user during her/his visit in a site. Pages of a session are mapped onto elements of a sequence, whereby each element is a pair comprised of the page and a positive integer. This integer is the occurrence of the page in the session, taking the fact into account that a user may visit the same page more than once during a single session. Further, they also define generalized sequences which are sequences with length constraints on gaps. These constraints are expressed in a mining language MINT.

The patterns that they observe are as follows. Searches reaching a 'school' entry are a dominant sub-pattern. 'State' lists of schools are the most popular lists. Schools are rarely reached in short searches.

Pattern Discovery for Web Personalization

Pattern discovery from usage data can also be used for Web personalization. (Mobasher, Dai, Luo, & Nakagawa, 2002) find that more restrictive patterns, such as contiguous sequential patterns (e.g.,

frequent navigational paths) are more suitable for predictive tasks, such as Web pre-fetching, which involve predicting which item is accessed next by a user), while less constrained patterns, such as frequent item-sets or general sequential patterns are more effective alternatives in the context of Web personalization and recommender systems.

Web usage preprocessing ultimately results in a set of n page-views, $P = \{p_1, p_2 \dots p_n\}$, and a set of m user transactions, $T = \{t_1, t_2 \dots t_m\}$. Each transaction t is defined as an l-length sequence of ordered pairs: $t = <(p_t^1, w(p_t^1)), (p_t^2, w(p_t^2)), \dots, (p_t^l, w(p_t^l))>$ where $w(p_t^i)$ is the weight associated with page-view p_t^i. Contiguous sequential patterns (CSPs -- patterns in which the items appearing in the sequence must be adjacent with respect to the underlying ordering) are used to capture frequent navigational paths among user trails. General sequential patterns are used to represent more general navigational patterns within the site.

To build a recommendation algorithm using sequential patterns, the authors focus on frequent sequences of size $|w| + 1$ whose prefix contains an active user session w. The candidate page-views to be recommended are the last items in all such sequences. The recommendation values are based on the confidence of the patterns. A simple trie structure is used to store both the sequential and contiguous sequential patterns discovered during the pattern discovery phase. The recommendation algorithm is extended to generate all k^{th} order recommendations as follows. First, the recommendation engine uses the largest possible active session window as an input for recommendation engine. If the engine cannot generate any recommendations, the size of active session window is iteratively decreased until a recommendation is generated or the window size becomes 0.

The CSP model can do better in terms of precision, but the coverage levels, in general, may be too low when the goal is to generate as many good recommendations as possible. On the other hand, when dealing with applications such as Web pre-fetching in which the primary goal is to predict the user's immediate next actions (rather than providing a broader set of recommendations), the CSP model provides the best choice. This is particularly true in sites with many dynamically generated pages, where often a contiguous navigational path represents a semantically meaningful sequence of user actions each depending on the previous actions.

TEXT MINING

Pattern mining has been used for text databases to discover trends, for text categorization, for document classification and authorship identification. We discuss these works below.

Trends in Text Databases

(Lent, Agrawal, & Srikant, 1997) describe a system for identifying trends in text documents collected over a period of time. Trends can be used, for example, to discover that a company is shifting interests from one domain to another. Their system mines these trends and also provides a method to visualize them.

The unit of text is a word and a phrase is a list of words. Associated with each phrase is a history of the frequency of occurrence of the phrase, obtained by partitioning the documents based upon their timestamps. The frequency of occurrence in a particular time period is the number of documents that contain the phrase. A trend is a specific subsequence of the history of a phrase that satisfies the users' query over the histories. For example, the user may specify a shape query like a spike query to find those phrases whose frequency of occurrence increased and then decreased. In this trend analysis, sequential pattern mining is used for phrase identification.

A transaction ID is assigned to each word of every document treating the words as items in the data mining algorithms. This transformed data is then mined for dominant words and phrases, and

the results saved. The user's query is translated into a shape query and this query is then executed over the mined data yielding the desired trends. The results of the mining are a set of phrases that occur frequently in the underlying documents and that match a query supplied by the user. Thus, the system has three major steps: Identifying frequent phrases using sequential patterns mining, generating histories of phrases and finding phrases that satisfy a specified trend.

1-phrase is a list of elements where each element is a phrase. k-phrase is an iterated list of phrases with k levels of nesting. <<(IBM)><(data mining)>> is a 1-phrase, which can mean that IBM and "data mining" should occur in the same paragraph, with "data mining" being contiguous words in the paragraph.

A word in a text field is mapped to an item in a data-sequence or sequential pattern and a phrase to a sequential pattern that has just one item in each element. Each element of a data sequence in the sequential pattern problem has some associated timestamp relative to the other elements in the sequence thereby defining an ordering of the elements of a sequence. Sequential pattern algorithms can now be applied to the transaction ID labeled words to identify simple phrases from the document collection.

User may be interested in phrases that are contained in individual sentences only. Alternatively, the words comprising a phrase may come from sequential sentences so that a phrase spans a paragraph. This generalization can be accommodated by the use of distance constraints that specify a minimum and/or maximum gap between adjacent words of a phrase. For example, the first variation described above would be constrained by specifying a minimum gap of one word and a maximum gap of one sentence. The second variation would have a minimum gap of one sentence and a maximum gap of one paragraph. For this latter example, one could further generalize the notion from a single word from each sentence to a set of words from each sentence by using a sliding transaction time window within sentences. The generalizations made in the GSP algorithm for mining sequential patterns allow a one-to-one mapping of the minimum gap, maximum gap, and transaction window to the parameters of the algorithm.

Basic mapping of phrases to sequential patterns is extended by providing a hierarchical mapping over sentences, paragraphs, or even sections of a text document. This extended mapping helps in taking advantage of the structure of a document to obtain a richer set of phrases. Where a document has completely separate sections, phrases that span multiple sections can also be mined, thereby discovering a new set of relationships. This enhancement of the GSP algorithm can be implemented by changing the Apriori-like candidate generation algorithm, to consider both phrases and words as individual elements when generating candidate k-phrases. The manner in which these candidates are counted would similarly change.

Patterns for Text Categorization

(Jaillet, Laurent, & Teisseire, 2006) propose usage of sequential patterns in the SPaC method (Sequential Patterns for Classification) for text categorization. Text categorization is the task of assigning a boolean value to each pair (document, category) where the value is true if the document belongs to the particular category. SPaC method consists of two steps. In the first step, sequential patterns are built from texts. In the second step, sequential patterns are used to classify texts.

The text consists of a set of sentences. Each sentence is associated with a timestamp (its position in the text). Finally the set of words contained in a sentence corresponds to the set of items purchased by the client in the market basket analysis framework. This representation is coupled with a stemming step and a stop-list. Sequential patterns are extracted using a different support applied for each category C_i. The support of a frequent pattern is the number of texts containing the sequence of

words. E.g., the sequential pattern < (data) (information) (machine)> means that some texts contain words 'data' then 'information' then 'machine' in three different sentences. Once sequential patterns have been extracted for each category, the goal is to derive a categorizer from the obtained patterns. This is done by computing, for each category, the confidence of each associated sequential pattern. To solve this problem, a rule R is generated in the following way:

$R:<s_1 ... s_p> \Rightarrow C_i$; confidence(R)=(#texts from C_i matching $<s_1 ... s_p>$)/(#texts matching $<s_1 ... s_p>$).

Rules are sorted depending on their confidence level and the size of the associated sequence. When considering a new text to be classified, a simple categorization policy is applied: the K rules having the best confidence level and being supported are applied. The text is then assigned to the class mainly obtained within the K rules.

Patterns for XML Document Classification

(Garboni, Masseglia, & Trousse, 2005) present a supervised classification technique for XML documents which is based on structure only. Each XML document is viewed as an ordered labeled tree, represented by its tags only. After a cleaning step, each predefined cluster is characterized in terms of frequent structural subsequences. Then the XML documents are classified based on the mined patterns of each cluster.

Documents are characterized using frequent sub-trees which are common to at least x% (the minimum support) documents of the collection. The system is provided a set of training documents each of which is associated with a category. Frequently occurring tags common to all clusters are removed. In order to transform an XML document to a sequence, the nodes of the XML tree are mapped into identifiers. Then each identifier is associated with its depth in the tree. Finally a depth-first exploration of the tree gives the corresponding sequence. An example sequential pattern looks like <(0 movie), (1 title), (1 url), (1 CountryOfProduction), (2 item), (2 item), (1 filmography), (3 name)>. Once the whole set of sequences (corresponding to the XML documents of a collection) is obtained, a traditional sequential pattern extraction algorithm is used to extract the frequent sequences. Those sequences, once mapped back into trees, will give the frequent sub-trees embedded in the collection.

They tested several measures in order to decide which class each test document belongs to. The two best measures are based on the longest common subsequence. The first one computes the average matching between the test document and the set of sequential patterns and the second measure is a modified measure, which incorporates the actual length of the pattern compared to the maximum length of a sequential pattern in the cluster.

Patterns to Identify Authors of Documents

(Tsuboi, 2002) aims at identifying the authors of mailing list messages using a machine learning technique (Support Vector Machines). In addition, the classifier trained on the mailing list data is applied to identify the author of Web documents in order to investigate performance in authorship identification for more heterogeneous documents. Experimental results show better identification performance when features of not only conventional word N-gram information but also of frequent sequential patterns extracted by a data mining technique (PrefixSpan) are used.

They applied PrefixSpan to extract sequential word patterns from each sentence and used them as author's style markers in documents. The sequential word patterns are sequential patterns where item and sequence correspond to word and sentence, respectively.

Sequential pattern is $<w_1 * w_2 * ... * w_l>$ where w_i is a word and l is the length of pattern. $*$ is any

sequence of words including empty sequence. These sequential word patterns were introduced for authorship identification based on the following assumption. Because people usually generate words from the beginning to the end of a sentence, how one orders words in a sentence can be an indicator of author's writing style. As word order in Japanese (they study a Japanese corpus) is relatively free, rigid word segments and non-contiguous word sequences may be a particularly important indicator of the writing style of authors.

While N-grams (consecutive word sequences) fail to account for non-contiguous patterns, sequential pattern mining methods can do so quite naturally.

BIOINFORMATICS

Pattern mining is useful in the bioinformatics domain for predicting rules for organization of certain elements in genes, for protein function prediction, for gene expression analysis, for protein fold recognition and for motif discovery in DNA sequences. We study these applications below.

Pattern Mining for Bio-Sequences

Bio-sequences typically have a small alphabet, a long length, and patterns containing gaps (i.e., "don't care") of arbitrary size. A long sequence (especially, with a small alphabet) often contains long patterns. Mining frequent patterns in such sequences faces a different type of explosion than in transaction sequences primarily motivated in market-basket analysis. (Wang, Xu, & Yu, 2004) study how this explosion affects the classic sequential pattern mining, and present a scalable two-phase algorithm to deal with this new explosion.

Biosequence patterns have the form of $X_1 * ... * X_n$ spanning over a long region, where each X_i is a short region of consecutive items, called a segment, and * denotes a variable length gap corresponding to a region not conserved in the evolution. The presence of * implies that pattern matching is more permissible and involves the whole range in a sequence. The support of a pattern is the percentage of the sequences in the database that contain the pattern. Given a minimum segment length min_len and a minimum support min_sup, a pattern $X_1 * ... * X_n$ is frequent if $|X_i|>=$min_len for $1<=i<=n$ and the support of the pattern is at least min_sup. The problem of mining sequence patterns is to find all frequent patterns.

The Segment Phase first searches short patterns containing no gaps (X_i), called segments. This phase is efficient. This phase finds all frequent segments and builds an auxiliary structure for answering position queries. GST (generalized suffix tree) is used to find: (1) The frequent segments of length min_len, B_i, called base segments, and the position lists for each B_i, s:p_1, p_2... where $p_j<p_j+1$ and each <s, p_j> is a start position of B_i. (2) All frequent segments of length>min_len. Note that position lists for such frequent segments are not extracted. This information about the base segments and their positions is then stored in an index, Segment to Position Index.

The Pattern Phase searches for long patterns ($X_1 * ... * X_n$) containing multiple segments separated by variable length gaps. This phase grows rapidly one segment at a time, as opposed to one item at a time. This phase is time consuming. The purpose of two phases is to exploit the information obtained from the first phase to speed up the pattern growth and matching and to prune the search space in the second phase.

Two types of pruning techniques are used. Consider a pattern P', which is a super-pattern of P:

- **Pattern Generation Pruning:** If P*X fails to be a frequent pattern, so does P'*X. So, we can prune P'*X.
- **Pattern Matching Pruning**: If P*X fails to occur before position i in sequence s, so does P'*X. So, we only need to examine

the positions after i when matching P'*X against s.

Further to deal with the huge size of the sequences, they introduce compression based querying. In this method, all positions in a non-coding region are compressed into a new item ε that matches no existing item except *. A non-coding region contains no part of a frequent segment. Each original sequence is scanned once, each consecutive region not overlapping with any frequent segment is identified and collapsed into the new item ε. For a long sequence and large min_len and min_sup, a compressed sequence is typically much shorter than the original sequence.

On real life datasets like DNA and protein sequences submitted from 2002/12, 2003/02, they show the superiority of their method compared to PrefixSpan with respect to execution time and the space required.

Patterns in Genes for Predicting Gene Organization Rules

In eukaryotes, rules regarding organization of cis-regulatory elements are complex. They sometimes govern multiple kinds of elements and positional restrictions on elements. (Terai & Takagi, 2004) propose a method for detecting rules, by which the order of elements is restricted. The order restriction is expressed as element patterns. They extract all the element patterns that occur in promoter regions of at least the specified number of genes. Then, significant patterns are found based on the expression similarity of genes with promoter regions containing each of the extracted patterns. By applying the method to Saccharomyces cerevisiae, they detected significant patterns overlooked by previous methods, thus demonstrating the utility of sequential pattern mining for analysis of eukaryotic gene regulation. Several types of element organization exist, those in which (1) only the order of elements is important, (2) order and distance both are important and (3) only the combination of elements is important. In this case, pattern support is the number of genes containing the pattern in their promoter region. Minimum length of the patterns may vary with the species. They use Apriori algorithm to perform mining.

Each element typically has a length of 10–20 base pairs. Therefore, two elements sometimes overlap one another. In this study, any two elements overlapping each other are not considered to be ordered elements, because they use elements defined by computational prediction. Most of these overlapping sites may have no biological meaning; they may simply be false-positive hits during computational prediction of elements. The decision of how to treat such overlapping elements is reflected in the count stage −if a pattern consisting of element A followed by and overlapping with B should not be considered as <A,B>, we can exclude genes containing such elements when counting the support of <A,B>. This is an interesting tweak in counting support, specific to this problem.

Patterns for Predicting Protein Sequence Function

(Wang, Shang, & Li, 2008) present a novel method of protein sequence function prediction based on sequential pattern mining. First, known function sequence dataset is mined to get frequent patterns. Then, a classifier is built using the patterns generated to predict function of protein sequences. They propose the usage of joined frequent patterns based and joined closed frequent patterns based sequential pattern mining algorithms for mining this data. First, the joined frequent pattern segments are generated. Then, longer frequent patters can be obtained by combining the above segments. They generate closed patterns only. The purpose of producing closed patterns is to use them to construct a classifier for protein function prediction. So using non-redundant patterns can improve the accuracy of classification.

Patterns for Analysis of Gene Expression Data

(Icev, 2003) introduces a sequential pattern mining based technique for the analysis of gene expression. Gene expression is the effective production of the protein that a gene encodes. They focus on the characterization of the expression patterns of genes based on their promoter regions. The promoter region of a gene contains short sequences called motifs to which gene regulatory proteins may bind, thereby controlling when and in which cell types the gene is expressed. Their approach addresses two important aspects of gene expression analysis: (1) Binding of proteins at more than one motif is usually required, and several different types of proteins may need to bind several different types of motifs in order to confer transcriptional specificity. (2) Since proteins controlling transcription may need to interact physically, the order and spacing in which motifs occur can affect expression. They use association rules to address the combinatorial aspect. The association rules have the ability to involve multiple motifs and to predict expression in multiple cell types. To address the second aspect, association rules are enhanced with information about the distances among the motifs, or items that are present in the rule. Rules of interest are those whose set of motifs deviates properly, i.e. set of motifs whose pair-wise distances are highly conserved in the promoter regions where these motifs occur.

They define the cvd of a pair of motifs with respect to a collection (or item-set) I of motifs as the ratio between the standard deviation and the mean of the distances between the motifs in those promoter regions that contain all the motifs in I.

Given a dataset of instances D, a minimum support min_sup, a minimum confidence min_conf, and a maximum coefficient of variation of distances (max-cvd), they find all distance-based association rules from D whose support and confidence are >= the min_sup and min_conf thresholds and such that the cvd's of all the pairs of items in the rule are <= the maximum cvd threshold. Their algorithm to mine distance-based association rules from a dataset of instances extends the Apriori algorithm.

In order to obtain distance-based association rules, one could use the Apriori algorithm to mine all association rules whose supports and confidences satisfy the thresholds, and then annotate those rules with the cvd's of all the pair of items present in the rule. Only those rules whose cvd's satisfy the max-cvd threshold are returned. They call this algorithm to mine distance-based association rules, Naïve distance-Apriori.

Distance-based Association Rule Mining (DARM) algorithm first generates all the frequent item-sets that satisfy the max-cvd constraint (cvd-frequent item-sets), and then generates all association rules with the required confidence from those item-sets. Note that the max-cvd constraint is a non-monotonic property. An item-set that does not satisfy this constraint may have supersets that do. However, they define the following procedure that keeps under consideration only frequent item-sets that deviate properly in an interesting manner.

Let n be the number of promoter regions (instances) in the dataset. Let I be a frequent item-set, and let S be the set of promoter regions that contain I. I is then said to deviate properly if either:

1. I is cvd-frequent. That is, the cvd over S of each pair of motifs in I is <= max-cvd, or
2. For each pair of motifs $P \in I$, there is a subset S' of S with cardinality >= $\lceil min\_sup*n \rceil$ such that the cvd over S' of P is <= max-cvd.

The k-level of item-sets kept by the DARM algorithm is the collection of frequent item-sets of cardinality k that deviate properly. Those item-sets are used to generate the (k+1)-level. Once, all the frequent item-sets that deviate properly have been generated, distance-based association rules are constructed from those item-sets that satisfy the max-cvd constraint. As is the case with the Apriori algorithm, each possible split of such an item-set

into two parts, one for the antecedent and one for the consequent of the rule, is considered. If the rule so formed satisfies the min_conf constraint, then the rule is added to the output. These rules are then used for building a classification/predictive model for gene expression.

Patterns for Protein Fold Recognition

Protein data contain discriminative patterns that can be used in many beneficial applications if they are defined correctly. (Exarchos, Papaloukas, Lampros, & Fotiadis, 2008) use sequential pattern mining for sequence-based fold recognition. Protein classification in terms of fold recognition plays an important role in computational protein analysis, since it can contribute to the determination of the function of a protein whose structure is unknown. Fold means 3D structure of a protein. They use cSPADE (Zaki, Sequence mining in categorical domains: incorporating constraints, 2000), for the analysis of protein sequence. Sequential patterns were generated for each category (fold) separately. A $pattern_i$ extracted from $fold_i$, indicates an implication (rule) of the form $pattern_i$ $\Rightarrow fold_i$. A maximum gap constraint is also used.

When classifying an unknown protein to one of the folds, all the extracted sequential patterns from all folds are examined to find which of them are contained in the protein. For a pattern contained in a protein, the score of this protein with respect to this fold is increased by: $score_a^i$=(length of the $pattern_a^i$-k)/(number of patterns in $fold^i$) where 'i' represents a fold, 'a' represents a pattern of a fold. Here, the length is the size of the pattern with gaps. $Pattern_a^i$ is the ath pattern of the ith fold and k is a value employed to assign the minimum score, to the minimal pattern. It should be mentioned that if a pattern is contained in a protein sequence more than once, it receives the same score as if it was contained only once. The scores for each fold are summed and the new protein is assigned to the fold exhibiting the highest sum.

The score of a protein with respect to a fold is calculated based on the number of sequential patterns of this fold contained in the protein. The higher the number of patterns of a fold contained in a protein, the higher the score of the protein for this fold.

A classifier uses the extracted sequential patterns to classify proteins in the appropriate fold category. For training and evaluating the proposed method they used the protein sequences from the Protein Data Bank and the annotation of the SCOP database. The method exhibited an overall accuracy of 25% (random would be 2.8%) in a classification problem with 36 candidate categories. The classification performance reaches up to 56% when the five most probable protein folds are considered.

Patterns for Protein Family Detection

In another work on protein family detection (protein classification), (Ferreira & Azevedo, 2005) use the number and average length of the relevant subsequences shared with each of the protein families, as features to train a Bayes classifier. Priors for the classes are set using the number of patterns and average length of the patterns in the corresponding class.

They Identify Two Types of Patterns

Rigid Gap Patterns (only contain gaps with a fixed length) and Flexible Gap Patterns (allow a variable number of gaps between symbols of the sequence). Frequent patterns are mined with the constraint of minimum length. Apart from this, they also support item constraints (restricts set of other symbols that can occur in the pattern), gap constraints (minGap and maxGap), duration or window constraints which defines the maximum distance (window) between the first and the last event of the sequence patterns.

Protein sequences of the same family typically share common subsequences, also called motifs.

These subsequences are possibly implied in a structural or biological function of the family and have been preserved through the protein evolution. Thus, if a sequence shares patterns with other sequences it is expected that the sequences are biologically related. Considering the two types of patterns, rigid gap patterns reveal better conserved regions of similarity. On the other hand, flexible gap patterns have a greater probability of occur by chance, having a smaller biological significance. Since the protein alphabet is small, many small patterns that express trivial local similarity may arise. Therefore, longer patterns are expected to express greater confidence in the sequences similarity.

Patterns in DNA Sequences

Large collections of genomic information have been accumulated in recent years, and embedded in them is potentially significant knowledge for exploitation in medicine and in the pharmaceutical industry. (Guan, Liu, & Bell, 2004) detect strings in DNA sequences which appear frequently, either within a given sequence (e.g., for a particular patient) or across sequences (e.g., from different patients sharing a particular medical diagnosis). Motifs are strings that occur very frequently. Having discovered such motifs, they show how to mine association rules by an existing rough-sets based technique.

TELECOMMUNICATIONS

Pattern mining can be used in the field of telecommunications for mining of group patterns from mobile user movement data, for customer behavior prediction, for predicting future location of a mobile user for location based services and for mining patterns useful for mobile commerce. We discuss these works briefly in this sub-section.

Patterns in Mobile User Movement Data

(Wang, Lim, & Hwang, 2006) present a new approach to derive groupings of mobile users based on their movement data. User movement data are collected by logging location data emitted from mobile devices tracking users. This data is of the form $D = (D_1, D_2... D_M)$, where D_i is a time series of tuples $(t, (x, y, z))$ denoting the x, y and z coordinates of user u_i at time t. A set of consecutive time points $[t_a, t_b]$ is called a valid segment of G (where G is a set of users) if all the pair of users are within dist max_dis for time $[t_a, t_b]$, at least one pair of users has distance greater than max_dis before time t_a, at least one pair of users has distance greater than max_dis after time t_b and $t_b - t_a + 1 \geq$ min_dur. Given a set of users G, thresholds max_dis and min_dur, these form a group pattern, denoted by P = <G,max_dis,min_dur>, if G has a valid segment. Thus, a group pattern is a group of users that are within a distance threshold from one another for at least a minimum duration.

In a movement database, a group pattern may have multiple valid segments. The combined length of these valid segments is called the weight-count of the pattern. Thus the significance of the pattern is measured by comparing its weight-count with the overall time duration.

Since weight represents the proportion of the time points a group of users stay close together, the larger the weight is, the more significant (or interesting) the group pattern is. Furthermore, if the weight of a group pattern exceeds a threshold min_wei, it is called a valid group pattern, and the corresponding group of users a valid group.

To mine group patterns, they first propose two algorithms, namely AGP (based on Apriori) and VG-growth (based on FP-growth). They show that when both the number of users and logging duration are large, AGP and VG-growth are inefficient for the mining group patterns of size two. Therefore, they propose a framework that summarizes user movement data before group pattern mining.

In the second series of experiments, they show that the methods using location summarization reduce the mining overheads for group patterns of size two significantly.

Patterns for Customer Behavior Prediction

Predicting the behavior of customers is challenging, but important for service oriented businesses. Data mining techniques are used to make such predictions, typically using only recent static data. (Eichinger, Nauck, & Klawonn) propose the usage of sequence mining with decision tree analysis for this task. The combined classifier is applied to real customer data and produces promising results.

They Use Two Sequence Mining Parameters

maxGap, the maximum number of allowed extra events in between a sequence and maxSkip, the maximum number of events at the end of a sequence before the occurrence of the event to be predicted.

They use an Apriori algorithm to detect frequent patterns from a Sequence tree and hash table based data structure. This avoids multiple database scans, which are otherwise necessary after every generation of candidate sequences in Apriori based algorithms.

The frequent sequences are combined with decision tree based classification to predict customer behavior.

Patterns for Future Location Prediction of Mobile Users

Future location prediction of mobile users can provide location-based services (LBSs) with extended resources, mainly time, to improve system reliability which in turn increases the users' confidence and the demand for LBSs. (Vu, Ryu, & Park, 2009) propose a movement rule-based Location

Prediction method (RLP), to guess the user's future location for LBSs. They define moving sequences and frequent patterns in trajectory data. Further, they find out all frequent spatiotemporal movement patterns using an algorithm based on GSP algorithm. The candidate generating mechanism of the technique is based on that of GSP algorithm with an additional temporal join operation and a different method for pruning candidates. In addition, they employ the clustering method to control the dense regions of the patterns. With the frequent movement patterns obtained from the preceding subsection, the movement rules are generated easily.

Patterns for Mobile Commerce

To better reflect the customer usage patterns in the mobile commerce environment, (Yun & Chen, 2007) propose an innovative mining model, called mining mobile sequential patterns, which takes both the moving patterns and purchase patterns of customers into consideration. How to strike a compromise among the use of various knowledge to solve the mining on mobile sequential patterns, is a challenging issue. They devise three algorithms for determining the frequent sequential patterns from the mobile transaction sequences.

INTRUSION DETECTION

Sequential pattern mining has been used for intrusion detection to study patterns of misuse in network attack data and thereby detect sequential intrusion behaviors and for discovering multistage attack strategies.

Patterns in Network Attack Data

(Wuu, Hung, & Chen, 2007) have implemented an intrusion pattern discovery module in Snort network intrusion detection system which applies data mining technique to extract single intrusion

patterns and sequential intrusion patterns from a collection of attack packets, and then converts the patterns to Snort detection rules for on-line intrusion detection. Patterns are extracted both from packet headers and the packet payload. A typical pattern is of the form "A packet with DA port as 139, DgmLen field in header set to 48 and with content as 11 11". Intrusion behavior detection engine creates an alert when a series of incoming packets match the signatures representing sequential intrusion scenarios.

Patterns for Discovering Multi-Stage Attack Strategies

In monitoring anomalous network activities, intrusion detection systems tend to generate a large amount of alerts, which greatly increase the workload of post-detection analysis and decision-making. A system to detect the ongoing attacks and predict the upcoming next step of a multistage attack in alert streams by using known attack patterns can effectively solve this problem. The complete, correct and up to date pattern rule of various network attack activities plays an important role in such a system. An approach based on sequential pattern mining technique to discover multistage attack activity patterns is efficient to reduce the labor to construct pattern rules. But in a dynamic network environment where novel attack strategies appear continuously, the novel approach proposed by (Li, Zhang, Li, & Wang, 2007) to use incremental mining algorithm shows better capability to detect recently appeared attack. They remove the unexpected results from mining by computing probabilistic score between successive steps in a multistage attack pattern. They use GSP to discover multistage attack behavior patterns. All the alerts stored in database can be viewed as a global sequence of alerts sorted by ascending DetectTime timestamp. Sequences of alerts describe the behavior and actions of attackers. Multistage attack strategies can be found by analyzing this alert sequence. A sequential pattern is a collection of alerts that occur relatively close to each other in a given order frequently. Once such patterns are known, the rules can be produced for describing or predicting the behavior of the sequence of network attack.

OTHER APPLICATIONS

Apart from the different domains mentioned above, sequential pattern mining has been found useful in a variety of other domains. We briefly mention works in some of such areas in this sub-section. Besides the works mentioned below, there are some applications that may need to classify sequence data, such as based on sequence patterns. An overview on research in sequence classification can be found in (Xing, Pei & Keogh).

Patterns in Earth Science Data

The earth science data consists of time series measurements for various Earth science and climate variables (e.g. soil moisture, temperature, and precipitation), along with additional data from existing ecosystem models (e.g. Net Primary Production). The ecological patterns of interest include associations, clusters, predictive models, and trends. (Potter, Klooster, Torregrosa, Tan, Steinbach, & Kumar) discuss some of the challenges involved in preprocessing and analyzing the data, and also consider techniques for handling some of the spatio-temporal issues. Earth Science data has strong seasonal components that need to be removed prior to pattern analysis, as Earth scientists are primarily interested in patterns that represent deviations from normal seasonal variation such as anomalous climate events (e.g., El Nino) or trends (e.g., global warming). They de-seasonalize the data and then compute variety of spatio-temporal patterns. Rules learned from the patterns look like (WP-Hi) $\Rightarrow$ (Solar-Hi) $\Rightarrow$ (NINO34-Lo) $\Rightarrow$ (Temp-Hi) $\Rightarrow$ (NPP-Lo) where

WP, Solar etc are different earth science parameters with values Hi (High) or Lo (Low).

Patterns for Computer Systems Management

Predictive algorithms play a crucial role in systems management by alerting the user to potential failures. (Vilalta, Apte, Hellerstein, Ma, & Weiss, 2002) focus on three case studies dealing with the prediction of failures in computer systems: (1) long-term prediction of performance variables (e.g., disk utilization), (2) short-term prediction of abnormal behavior (e.g., threshold violations), and (3) short-term prediction of system events (e.g., router failure). Empirical results show that predictive algorithms based on mining of sequential patterns can be successfully employed in the estimation of performance variables and the prediction of critical events.

Patterns to Detect Plan Failures

(Zaki, Lesh, & Mitsunori, 1999) present an algorithm to extract patterns of events that predict failures in databases of plan executions: Plan-Mine. Analyzing execution traces is appropriate for planning domains that contain uncertainty, such as incomplete knowledge of the world or actions with probabilistic effects. They extract causes of plan failures and feed the discovered patterns back into the planner. They label each plan as "good" or "bad" depending on whether it achieved its goal or it failed to do so. The goal is to find "interesting" sequences that have a high confidence of predicting plan failure. They use SPADE to mine such patterns.

TRIPS is an integrated system in which a person collaborates with a computer to develop a high quality plan to evacuate people from a small island. During the process of building the plan, the system simulates the plan repeatedly based on a probabilistic model of the domain, including predicted weather patterns and their effect on vehicle performance.

The system returns an estimate of the plan's success. Additionally, TRIPS invokes PlanMine on the execution traces produced by simulation, in order to analyze why the plan failed when it did. The system runs PlanMine on the execution traces of the given plan to pinpoint defects in the plan that most often lead to plan failure. It then applies qualitative reasoning and plan adaptation algorithms to modify the plan to correct the defects detected by PlanMine.

Patterns in Automotive Warranty Data

When a product fails within a certain time period, the warranty is a manufacturer's assurance to a buyer that the product will be repaired without a cost to the customer. In a service environment where dealers are more likely to replace than to repair, the cost of component failure during the warranty period can easily equal three to ten times the supplier's unit price. Consequently, companies invest significant amounts of time and resources to monitor, document, and analyze product warranty data. (Buddhakulsomsiri & Zakarian, 2009) present a sequential pattern mining algorithm that allows product and quality engineers to extract hidden knowledge from a large automotive warranty database. The algorithm uses the elementary set concept and database manipulation techniques to search for patterns or relationships among occurrences of warranty claims over time. The sequential patterns are represented in a form of IF–THEN association rules, where the IF portion of the rule includes quality/warranty problems, represented as labor codes, that occurred in an earlier time, and the THEN portion includes labor codes that occurred at a later time. Once a set of unique sequential patterns is generated, the algorithm applies a set of thresholds to evaluate the significance of the rules and the rules that pass these thresholds are reported in the solution.

Significant patterns provide knowledge of one or more product failures that lead to future product fault(s). The effectiveness of the algorithm is illustrated with the warranty data mining application from the automotive industry.

Patterns in Alarm Data

Increasingly powerful fault management systems are required to ensure robustness and quality of service in today's networks. In this context, event correlation is of prime importance to extract meaningful information from the wealth of alarm data generated by the network. Existing sequential data mining techniques address the task of identifying possible correlations in sequences of alarms. The output sequence sets, however, may contain sequences which are not plausible from the point of view of network topology constraints. (Devitt, Duffin, & Moloney, 2005) presents the Topographical Proximity (TP) approach which exploits topographical information embedded in alarm data in order to address this lack of plausibility in mined sequences. Their approach is based on an Apriori approach and introduces a novel criterion for sequence selection which evaluates sequence plausibility and coherence in the context of network topology. Connections are inferred at run-time between pairs of alarm generating nodes in the data and a Topographical Proximity (TP) measure is assigned based on the strength of the inferred connection. The TP measure is used to reject or promote candidate sequences on the basis of their plausibility, i.e. the strength of their connection, thereby reducing the candidate sequence set and optimizing the space and time constraints of the data mining process.

Patterns for Personalized Recommendation System

(Romero, Ventura, Delgado, & Bra, 2007) describe a personalized recommender system that uses web mining techniques for recommending a student which (next) links to visit within an adaptable educational hypermedia system. They present a specific mining tool and a recommender engine that helps the teacher to carry out the whole web mining process. The overall process of Web personalization based on Web usage mining generally consists of three phases: data preparation, pattern discovery and recommendation. The first two phases are performed off-line and the last phase on-line. To make recommendations to a student, the system first, classifies the new students in one of the groups of students (clusters). Then, it only uses the sequential patterns of the corresponding group to personalize the recommendations based on other similar students and his current navigation. Grouping of students is done using k-means. They use GSP to get frequent sequences for each of the clusters. They mine rules of the form readme⇒install, welcome⇒install which are intuitively quite common patterns for websites.

Patterns in Atmospheric Aerosol Data

EDAM (Exploratory Data Analysis and Management) is a joint project between researchers in Atmospheric Chemistry and Computer Science at Carleton College and the University of Wisconsin-Madison that aims to develop data mining techniques for advancing the state of the art in analyzing atmospheric aerosol datasets.

The traditional approach for particle measurement, which is the collection of bulk samples of particulates on filters, is not adequate for studying particle dynamics and real-time correlations. This has led to the development of a new generation of real-time instruments that provide continuous or semi-continuous streams of data about certain aerosol properties. However, these instruments have added a significant level of complexity to atmospheric aerosol data, and dramatically increased the amounts of data to be collected, managed, and analyzed. (Ramakrishnan, et al., 2005) experiment

with a dataset consisting of samples from aerosol time-of-flight mass spectrometer (ATOFMS).

A mass spectrum is a plot of signal intensity (often normalized to the largest peak in the spectrum) versus the mass-to-charge (m/z) ratio of the detected ions. Thus, the presence of a peak indicates the presence of one or more ions containing the m/z value indicated, within the ion cloud generated upon the interaction between the particle and the laser beam. In many cases, the ATOFMS generates elemental ions. Thus, the presence of certain peaks indicates that elements such as Na+ (m/z = +23) or Fe+ (m/z = +56) or O- (m/z = -16) ions are present. In other cases, cluster ions are formed, and thus the m/z observed represents that of a sum of the atomic weights of various elements.

For many kinds of analysis, what is significant in each particle's mass spectrum is the composition of the particle, i.e., the ions identified by the peak labels (and, ideally, their proportions in the particle, and our confidence in having correctly identified them). While this representation is less detailed than the labeled spectrum itself, it allows us to think of the ATOFMS data stream as a time-series of observations, one per observed particle, where each observation is a set of ions (possibly labeled with some additional details). This is precisely the market-basket abstraction used in e-commerce: a time-series of customer transactions, each recording the items purchased by a customer on a single visit to a store. This analogy opens the door to applying a wide range of association rule and sequential pattern algorithms to the analysis of mass spectrometry data. Once these patterns are mined, they can be used to extrapolate to periods where filter-based samples were not collected.

Patterns in Individuals' Time Diaries

Identifying patterns of activities within individuals' time diaries and studying similarities and deviations between individuals in a population is of interest in time use research. So far, activity patterns in a population have mostly been studied either by visual inspection, searching for occurrences of specific activity sequences and studying their distribution in the population, or statistical methods such as time series analysis in order to analyze daily behavior. (Vrotsou, Ellegård, & Cooper) describe a new approach for extracting activity patterns from time diaries that uses sequential data mining techniques. They have implemented an algorithm that searches the time diaries and automatically extracts all activity patterns meeting user-defined criteria of what constitutes a valid pattern of interest. Amongst the many criteria which can be applied are: a time window containing the pattern, and minimum and maximum number of people that perform the pattern. The extracted activity patterns can then be interactively filtered, visualized and analyzed to reveal interesting insights using the VISUAL-TimePAcTS application. To demonstrate the value of this approach they consider and discuss sequential activity patterns at a population level, from a single day perspective, with focus on the activity "paid work" and some activities surrounding it.

An activity pattern in this paper is defined as a sequence of activities performed by an individual which by itself or together with other activities, aims at accomplishing a more general goal/project. When analyzing a single day of diary data, activity patterns identified in a single individual (referred to as an individual activity pattern) are unlikely to be significant but those found amongst a group or population (a collective activity pattern) are of greater interest. Seven categories of activities that they consider are: care for oneself, care for others, household care, recreation/reflection, travel, prepare/procure food, work/school. {"cook dinner"; "eat dinner"; "wash dishes"} is a typical pattern. They also incorporate a variety of constraints like min and max pattern duration, min and max gap between activities, min and max number of occurrences of the pattern and min and max number of people (or a percentage

of the population) that should be performing the pattern. The sequential mining algorithm that they have used for the activity pattern extraction is an "AprioriAll" algorithm which is adapted to the time diary data.

Two stage classification using patterns: (Exarchos, Tsipouras, Papaloukas, & Fotiadis, 2008) present a methodology for sequence classification, which employs sequential pattern mining and optimization, in a two-stage process. In the first stage, a sequence classification model is defined, based on a set of sequential patterns and two sets of weights are introduced, one for the patterns and one for classes. In the second stage, an optimization technique is employed to estimate the weight values and achieve optimal classification accuracy. Extensive evaluation of the methodology is carried out, by varying the number of sequences, the number of patterns and the number of classes and it is compared with similar sequence classification approaches.

CONCLUSION

We presented selected applications of the sequential pattern mining methods in the fields of healthcare, education, web usage mining, text mining, bioinformatics, telecommunications, intrusion detection, etc. We envision that the power of sequential mining methods has not yet been fully exploited. We hope to see many more strong applications of these methods in a variety of domains in the years to come.

REFERENCES

Berendt, B. A. (2000). Analysis of navigation behaviour in web sites integrating multiple information systems. *The VLDB Journal*, *9*(1), 56–75. doi:10.1007/s007780050083

Buchner, A. G., & Mulvenna, M. D. (1998). Discovering Internet marketing intelligence through online analytical web usage mining. *SIGMOD Record, 27*(4), 54–61. doi:10.1145/306101.306124

Buddhakulsomsiri, J., & Zakarian, A. (2009). Sequential pattern mining algorithm for automotive warranty data. *Journal of Computers and Industrial Engineering, 57*(1), 137–147. doi:10.1016/j.cie.2008.11.006

Chen, Y.-L., & Huang, T. C.-K. (2008). A novel knowledge discovering model for mining fuzzy multi-level sequential patterns in sequence databases. *Data & Knowledge Engineering, 66*(3), 349–367. doi:10.1016/j.datak.2008.04.005

Cooley, R., Mobasher, B., & Srivastava, J. (1999). Data preparation for mining World Wide Web browsing patterns. *Knowledge and Information Systems, 1*(1), 5–32.

Devitt, A., Duffin, J., & Moloney, R. (2005). Topographical proximity for mining network alarm data. *MineNet '05: Proceedings of the 2005 ACM SIGCOMM workshop on Mining network data* (pp. 179-184). Philadelphia, PA: ACM.

Eichinger, F., Nauck, D. D., & Klawonn, F. (n.d.). *Sequence mining for customer behaviour predictions in telecommunications.*

Exarchos, T. P., Papaloukas, C., Lampros, C., & Fotiadis, D. I. (2008). Mining sequential patterns for protein fold recognition. *Journal of Biomedical Informatics, 41*(1), 165–179. doi:10.1016/j.jbi.2007.05.004

Exarchos, T. P., Tsipouras, M. G., Papaloukas, C., & Fotiadis, D. I. (2008). A two-stage methodology for sequence classification based on sequential pattern mining and optimization. *Data & Knowledge Engineering, 66*(3), 467–487. doi:10.1016/j.datak.2008.05.007

Ferreira, P. G., & Azevedo, P. J. (2005). Protein sequence classification through relevant sequence mining and bayes classifiers. *Proc. 12th Portuguese Conference on Artificial Intelligence (EPIA)* (pp. 236-247). Springer-Verlag.

Garboni, C., Masseglia, F., & Trousse, B. (2005). *Sequential pattern mining for structure-based XML document classification.* Workshop of the INitiative for the Evaluation of XML Retrieval.

Guan, J. W., Liu, D., & Bell, D. A. (2004). Discovering motifs in DNA sequences. *Fundam. Inform., 59*(2-3), 119–134.

Icev, A. (2003). *Distance-enhanced association rules for gene expression.* BIOKDD'03, in conjunction with ACM SIGKDD.

Ishio, T., Date, H., Miyake, T., & Inoue, K. (2008). Mining coding patterns to detect crosscutting concerns in Java programs. *WCRE '08: Proceedings of the 2008 15th Working Conference on Reverse Engineering* (pp. 123-132). Washington, DC: IEEE Computer Society.

Jaillet, S., Laurent, A., & Teisseire, M. (2006). Sequential patterns for text categorization. *Intelligent Data Analysis, 10*(3), 199–214.

Kay, J., Maisonneuve, N., Yacef, K., & Zaïane, O. (2006). *Mining patterns of events in students' teamwork data.* In Educational Data Mining Workshop, held in conjunction with Intelligent Tutoring Systems (ITS), (pp. 45-52).

Kum, H.-C., Chang, J. H., & Wang, W. (2006). Sequential Pattern Mining in Multi-Databases via Multiple Alignment. *Data Mining and Knowledge Discovery, 12*(2-3), 151–180. doi:10.1007/s10618-005-0017-3

Kum, H.-C., Chang, J. H., & Wang, W. (2007). Benchmarking the effectiveness of sequential pattern mining methods. *Data & Knowledge Engineering, 60*(1), 30–50. doi:10.1016/j.datak.2006.01.004

Kuo, R. J., Chao, C. M., & Liu, C. Y. (2009). Integration of K-means algorithm and AprioriSome algorithm for fuzzy sequential pattern mining. *Applied Soft Computing, 9*(1), 85–93. doi:10.1016/j.asoc.2008.03.010

Lau, A., Ong, S. S., Mahidadia, A., Hoffmann, A., Westbrook, J., & Zrimec, T. (2003). Mining patterns of dyspepsia symptoms across time points using constraint association rules. *PAKDD '03: Proceedings of the 7th Pacific-Asia conference on Advances in knowledge discovery and data mining* (pp. 124-135). Seoul, Korea: Springer-Verlag.

Laur, P.-A., Symphor, J.-E., Nock, R., & Poncelet, P. (2007). Statistical supports for mining sequential patterns and improving the incremental update process on data streams. *Intelligent Data Analysis, 11*(1), 29–47.

Lent, B., Agrawal, R., & Srikant, R. (1997). Discovering trends in text databases. *Proc. 3rd Int. Conf. Knowledge Discovery and Data Mining, KDD* (pp. 227-230). AAAI Press.

Li, Z., Zhang, A., Li, D., & Wang, L. (2007). Discovering novel multistage attack strategies. *ADMA '07: Proceedings of the 3rd international conference on Advanced Data Mining and Applications* (pp. 45-56). Harbin, China: Springer-Verlag.

Lin, N. P., Chen, H.-J., Hao, W.-H., Chueh, H.-E., & Chang, C.-I. (2008). Mining strong positive and negative sequential patterns. *W. Trans. on Comp., 7*(3), 119–124.

Mannila, H., Toivonen, H., & Verkamo, I. (1997). Discovery of frequent episodes in event sequences. *Data Mining and Knowledge Discovery, 1*(3), 259–289. doi:10.1023/A:1009748302351

Masseglia, F., Poncelet, P., & Teisseire, M. (2003). Incremental mining of sequential patterns in large databases. *Data & Knowledge Engineering, 46*(1), 97–121. doi:10.1016/S0169-023X(02)00209-4

Masseglia, F., Poncelet, P., & Teisseire, M. (2009). Efficient mining of sequential patterns with time constraints: Reducing the combinations. *Expert Systems with Applications, 36*(2), 2677–2690. doi:10.1016/j.eswa.2008.01.021

Mendes, L. F., Ding, B., & Han, J. (2008). Stream sequential pattern mining with precise error bounds. *Proc. 2008 Int. Conf. on Data Mining (ICDM'08),* Italy, Dec. 2008.

Mobasher, B., Dai, H., Luo, T., & Nakagawa, M. (2002). Using sequential and non-sequential patterns in predictive Web usage mining tasks. *ICDM '02: Proceedings of the 2002 IEEE International Conference on Data Mining* (pp. 669-672). Washington, DC: IEEE Computer Society.

Nicolas, J. A., Herengt, G., & Albuisson, E. (2004). Sequential pattern mining and classification of patient path. *MEDINFO 2004: Proceedings Of The 11th World Congress On Medical Informatics.*

Parthasarathy, S., Zaki, M., Ogihara, M., & Dwarkadas, S. (1999). Incremental and interactive sequence mining. In *Proc. of the 8th Int. Conf. on Information and Knowledge Management (CIKM'99).*

Perera, D., Kay, J., Yacef, K., & Koprinska, I. (2007). *Mining learners' traces from an online collaboration tool. Proceedings of Educational Data Mining workshop* (pp. 60–69). CA, USA: Marina del Rey.

Pinto, H., Han, J., Pei, J., Wang, K., Chen, Q., & Dayal, U. (2001). Multi-dimensional sequential pattern mining. *CIKM '01: Proceedings of the Tenth International Conference on Information and Knowledge Management* (pp. 81-88). New York, NY: ACM.

Potter, C., Klooster, S., Torregrosa, A., Tan, P.-N., Steinbach, M., & Kumar, V. (n.d.). *Finding spatio-temporal patterns in earth science data.*

Ramakrishnan, R., Schauer, J. J., Chen, L., Huang, Z., Shafer, M. M., & Gross, D. S. (2005). The EDAM project: Mining atmospheric aerosol datasets: Research articles. *International Journal of Intelligent Systems, 20*(7), 759–787. doi:10.1002/int.20094

Romero, C., Ventura, S., Delgado, J. A., & Bra, P. D. (2007). *Personalized links recommendation based on data mining un adaptive educational hypermedia systems.* Creating New Learning Experiences on a Global Scale. Second European Conference on Technology Enhanced Learning, EC-TEL 2007 (pp. 293-305). Crete, Greece: Springer.

Seno, M., & Karypis, G. (2002). SLPMiner: An algorithm for finding frequent sequential patterns using length-decreasing support constraint. In *Proceedings of the 2nd IEEE International Conference on Data Mining (ICDM)*, (pp. 418-425).

Srikant, R., & Agrawal, R. (1996)... *Advances in Database Technology EDBT, 96*, 3–17.

Terai, G., & Takagi, T. (2004). Predicting rules on organization of cis-regulatory elements, taking the order of elements into account. *Bioinformatics (Oxford, England), 20*(7), 1119–1128. doi:10.1093/bioinformatics/bth049

Tsuboi, Y. (2002). *Authorship identification for heterogeneous documents.*

Vilalta, R., Apte, C. V., Hellerstein, J. L., Ma, S., & Weiss, S. M. (2002). Predictive algorithms in the management of computer systems. *IBM Systems Journal, 41*(3), 461–474. doi:10.1147/sj.413.0461

Vrotsou, K., Ellegård, K., & Cooper, M. (n.d.). *Exploring time diaries using semi-automated activity pattern extraction.*

Vu, T. H., Ryu, K. H., & Park, N. (2009). A method for predicting future location of mobile user for location-based services system. *Computers & Industrial Engineering, 57*(1), 91–105. doi:10.1016/j.cie.2008.07.009

Wang, J. L., Chirn, G., Marr, T., Shapiro, B., Shasha, D., & Zhang, K. (1994). Combinatorial pattern discovery for scientific data: Some preliminary results. *Proc. ACM SIGMOD Int'l Conf. Management of Data*, (pp. 115-125).

Wang, K., Xu, Y., & Yu, J. X. (2004). Scalable sequential pattern mining for biological sequences. *CIKM '04: Proceedings of the Thirteenth ACM International Conference on Information and Knowledge Management* (pp. 178-187). Washington, DC: ACM.

Wang, M., Shang, X.-Q., & Li, Z.-H. (2008). Sequential pattern mining for protein function prediction. *ADMA '08: Proceedings of 4th International Conference on Adv Data Mining and Applications* (pp. 652-658). Chengdu, China: Springer-Verlag.

Wang, Y., Lim, E.-P., & Hwang, S.-Y. (2006). Efficient mining of group patterns from user movement data. *Data & Knowledge Engineering, 57*(3), 240–282. doi:10.1016/j.datak.2005.04.006

Wong, P. C., Cowley, W., Foote, H., Jurrus, E., & Thomas, J. (2000). Visualizing sequential patterns for text mining. *Proc. IEEE Information Visualization, 2000* (pp. 105-114). Society Press.

Wuu, L.-C., Hung, C.-H., & Chen, S.-F. (2007). Building intrusion pattern miner for Snort network intrusion detection system. *Journal of Systems and Software, 80*(10), 1699–1715. doi:10.1016/j.jss.2006.12.546

Xing, Z., Pei, J., & Keogh, E. (2010). A brief survey on sequence classification. *SIGKDD Explorations Newsletter, 12*(1), 40–48. doi:10.1145/1882471.1882478

Yun, C. H., & Chen, M. S. (2007). Mining mobile sequential patterns in a mobile commerce environment. *IEEE Transactions on Systems, Man, and Cybernetics*, 278–295.

Yun, U. (2008). A new framework for detecting weighted sequential patterns in large sequence databases. *Knowledge-Based Systems*, *21*(2), 110–122. doi:10.1016/j.knosys.2007.04.002

Zaki, M. J. (2001). SPADE: An efficient algorithm for mining frequent sequences. *Machine Learning*, *42*(1-2), 31–60. doi:10.1023/A:1007652502315

Zaki, M. J., Lesh, N., & Mitsunori, O. (1999). PlanMine: Predicting plan failures using sequence mining. *Artificial Intelligence Review*, *14*(6), 421–446. doi:10.1023/A:1006612804250

ADDITIONAL READING

Adamo, J.-M. (2001). *Data Mining for Association Rules and Sequential Patterns: Sequential and Parallel Algorithms*. Secaucus, NJ, USA: Springer-Verlag New York, Inc. doi:10.1007/978-1-4613-0085-4

Alves, R., & Rodriguez-Baena, D. S., Aguilar-Ruiz, & S., J. (2009). Gene association analysis: a survey of frequent pattern mining from gene expression data. *Briefings in Bioinformatics*, 210–224.

Han, J., & Kamber, M. (2006). *Data Mining: Concepts and Techniques* (2nd ed.). Morgan Kaufmann Publishers.

Li, T.-R., Xu, Y., Ruan, D., & Pan, W.-m. Sequential pattern mining. In R. Da, G. Chen, E. E. Kerre, & G. Wets, *Intelligent data mining: techniques and applications* (pp. 103-122). Springer.

Lu, J., Adjei, O., Chen, W., Hussain, F., & Enachescu, C. (n.d.). *Sequential Patterns Mining*.

Srinivasa, R. N. (2005). Data mining in e-commerce: A survey. *Sadhana*, 275–289. doi:10.1007/BF02706248

Teisseire, M., Poncelet, P., Scientifique, P., Besse, G., Masseglia, F., & Masseglia, F. (2005). *Sequential pattern mining: A survey on issues and approaches. Encyclopedia of Data Warehousing and Mining, nformation Science Publishing* (pp. 3–29). Oxford University Press.

Yang, L. (2003). Visualizing frequent itemsets, association rules, and sequential patterns in parallel coordinates. *ICCSA'03: Proceedings of the 2003 international conference on Computational science and its applications* (pp. 21-30). Montreal, Canada: Springer-Verlag.

Zhao, Q., & Bhowmick, S. S. (2003). Sequential Pattern Matching: A Survey.

Chapter 2
A Review of Kernel Methods Based Approaches to Classification and Clustering of Sequential Patterns, Part I:
Sequences of Continuous Feature Vectors

Dileep A. D.
Indian Institute of Technology, India

Veena T.
Indian Institute of Technology, India

C. Chandra Sekhar
Indian Institute of Technology, India

ABSTRACT

Sequential data mining involves analysis of sequential patterns of varying length. Sequential pattern analysis is important for pattern discovery from sequences of discrete symbols as in bioinformatics and text analysis, and from sequences or sets of continuous valued feature vectors as in processing of audio, speech, music, image, and video data. Pattern analysis techniques using kernel methods have been explored for static patterns as well as sequential patterns. The main issue in sequential pattern analysis using kernel methods is the design of a suitable kernel for sequential patterns of varying length. Kernel functions designed for sequential patterns are known as dynamic kernels. In this chapter, we present a brief description of kernel methods for pattern classification and clustering. Then we describe dynamic kernels for sequences of continuous feature vectors. We then present a review of approaches to sequential pattern classification and clustering using dynamic kernels.

DOI: 10.4018/978-1-61350-056-9.ch002

INTRODUCTION TO SEQUENTIAL PATTERN ANALYSIS USING KERNEL METHODS

Classification and clustering of patterns extracted from sequential data are important for pattern discovery using sequence data mining. Pattern discovery from bio-sequences involves classification and clustering of discrete symbol sequences. Pattern discovery from multimedia data such as audio, speech and video data involves classification and clustering of continuous valued feature vector sequences. Classification and clustering of sequential patterns of varying length have been challenging tasks in pattern recognition. Conventional methods for classification of sequential patterns use discrete hidden Markov models (HMMs) for discrete sequences, and continuous density HMMs for continuous feature vector sequences. Conventional methods for clustering of sequential patterns use distance measures such as edit distance for discrete sequences and dynamic time warping based distance for continuous feature vector sequences. During the past 15 years, kernel methods based approaches such as support vector machines and kernel K-means clustering have been explored for classification and clustering of static patterns and sequential patterns. Kernel methods have been shown to give a good generalization performance. This Chapter presents a review of kernel methods based approaches to classification and clustering of sequential patterns.

Kernel methods for pattern analysis involve performing a nonlinear transformation from the input feature space to a higher dimensional feature space induced by a Mercer kernel function, and then constructing an optimal linear solution in the kernel feature space. Support vector machine for two class pattern classification constructs an optimal hyperplane corresponding to the maximum margin separating hyperplane in the kernel feature space (Burges, 1998). Kernel K-means clustering gives an optimal nonlinear separation of clusters in the input feature space by minimizing the trace of the within-cluster scatter matrix for the clusters formed in the kernel feature space (Girolami, 2002; Satish, 2005). The choice of the kernel function used in the kernel methods is important for their performance. Several kernel functions have been proposed for static patterns. Kernel methods for sequential pattern analysis adopt one of the following two strategies: (1) Convert a sequential pattern into a static pattern and then use a kernel function defined for static patterns, and (2) Design and use a kernel function for sequential patterns. Kernel functions designed for sequential data are referred to as dynamic kernels or sequence kernels (Wan & Renals, 2002). Examples of dynamic kernels for continuous feature vector sequences are Gaussian mixture model (GMM) supervector kernel (Campbell et al., 2006*b*) and intermediate matching kernel (Boughorbel et al., 2005). Fisher kernel (Jaakkola et al,. 2000) is used for both the discrete observation symbol sequences and sequences of continuous feature vectors. This Chapter discusses the issues in designing dynamic kernels for continuous feature vector sequences and then presents a review of dynamic kernels proposed in the literature.

Dynamic kernels for continuous feature vector sequences belong to the following two main categories: (1) Kernels such as Fisher kernels that capture the sequence information in the feature vector sequences, and (2) Kernels such as GMM supervector kernels and intermediate matching kernels that consider the feature vector sequences as sets of feature vectors. The kernels belonging to the first category have been explored for classification of units of speech such as phonemes, syllables and words in speech recognition. The kernels belonging to the second category have been explored for tasks such as speaker identification and verification, speech emotion recognition and image classification. This chapter presents a review of dynamic kernels based approaches to classification and clustering of sequential patterns.

The organization of the rest of the chapter is as follows: The next section describes the kernel methods for pattern analysis. The SVM based approach to pattern classification and kernel based approaches to pattern clustering are presented in this section. Then the design of dynamic kernels for sequential patterns is presented in the third section. This section also describes the dynamic kernels for continuous feature vector sequences. Finally, we present a review of kernel methods based approaches to sequential pattern analysis.

KERNEL METHODS FOR PATTERN ANALYSIS

In this section we describe different approaches using kernel methods for patterns analysis. We first describe the support vector machines (SVMs) for pattern classification, and then present the kernel K-means clustering and support vector clustering methods for pattern clustering.

Support Vector Machines for Pattern Classification

The SVM (Burges, 1998; Cristianini & Shawe-Taylor, 2000; Sekhar et al., 2003) is a linear two-class classifier. An SVM constructs the maximum margin hyperplane (optimal hyperplane) as a decision surface to separate the data points of two classes. The margin of a hyperplane is defined as the minimum distance of training points from the hyperplane. We first discuss the construction of an optimal hyperplane for linearly separable classes. Then we discuss the construction of an optimal hyperplane for linearly nonseparable classes, *i.e.*, some training examples of the classes cannot be classified correctly. Finally, we discuss building an SVM for nonlinearly separable classes by constructing an optimal hyperplane in a high dimensional feature space corresponding to a nonlinear transformation induced by a kernel function.

Optimal Hyperplane for Linearly Separable Classes

Suppose the training data set consists of L examples, $\left\{ \mathbf{x}_i, y_i \right\}_{i=1}^{L}$, $\mathbf{x}_i \in \mathbb{R}^d$ and $y_i \in \{+1, -1\}$, where $\mathbf{x}_i$ is ith training example and y_i is the corresponding class label. Figure 1 illustrates the construction of an optimal separating hyperplane for linearly separable classes in the two-dimensional input space of $\mathbf{x}$.

A hyperplane is specified as $\mathbf{w}^t\mathbf{x} + b = 0$, where $\mathbf{w}$ is the parameter vector and b is the bias. A separating hyperplane that separates the data points of two linearly separable classes satisfies the following constraints:

$$y_i(\mathbf{w}^t\mathbf{x}_i + b) > 0 \text{ for } i = 1, 2,..., L \qquad (1)$$

The distance between the nearest example and the separating hyperplane, called the margin, is given by $1/\|\mathbf{w}\|$. The problem of finding the optimal separating hyperplane that maximizes the margin is the same as the problem of minimizing the Euclidean norm of the parameter vector $\mathbf{w}$. For reducing the search space of $\mathbf{w}$, the constraints that the optimal separating hyperplane must satisfy are specified as follows:

Figure 1. Illustration of constructing the optimal hyperplane for linearly separable classes

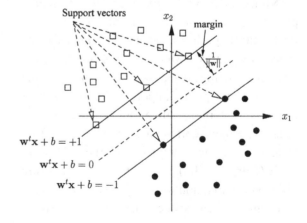

$$y_i(\mathbf{w}^t\mathbf{x}_i + b) \geq 1 \text{ for } i = 1, 2, \ldots, L \qquad (2)$$

The learning problem of finding the optimal separating hyperplane is a constrained optimization problem stated as follows: Given the training data set, find the values of $\mathbf{w}$ and b such that they satisfy the constraints in (2) and the parameter vector $\mathbf{w}$ minimizes the following cost function:

$$J(\mathbf{w}) = \frac{1}{2}\|\mathbf{w}\|^2 \qquad (3)$$

The constrained optimization problem is solved using the method of Lagrangian multipliers. The primal form of the Lagrangian objective function is given by

$$\mathcal{L}_p(\mathbf{w}, b, \boldsymbol{\alpha}) = \frac{1}{2}\|\mathbf{w}\|^2 - \sum_{i=1}^{L}\alpha_i\left[y_i\left(\mathbf{w}^t\mathbf{x}_i + b\right) - 1\right] \qquad (4)$$

where the non-negative variables α_i are called Lagrange multipliers. The saddle point of the Lagrangian objective function provides the solution for the optimization problem. The solution is determined by first minimizing the Lagrangian objective function with respect to $\mathbf{w}$ and b, and then maximizing with respect to $\boldsymbol{\alpha}$. The two conditions of optimality due to minimization are

$$\frac{\partial \mathcal{L}_p(\mathbf{w}, b, \boldsymbol{\alpha})}{\partial \mathbf{w}} = \mathbf{0} \qquad (5)$$

$$\frac{\partial \mathcal{L}_p(\mathbf{w}, b, \boldsymbol{\alpha})}{\partial b} = 0 \qquad (6)$$

Application of optimality conditions gives

$$\mathbf{w} = \sum_{i=1}^{L}\alpha_i y_i\mathbf{x}_i \qquad (7)$$

$$\sum_{i=1}^{L}\alpha_i y_i = 0 \qquad (8)$$

Substituting the expression for $\mathbf{w}$ from (7) in (4) and using the condition in (8), the dual form of Lagrangian objective function can be derived as a function of Lagrangian multipliers $\boldsymbol{\alpha}$, as follows:

$$\mathcal{L}_d(\boldsymbol{\alpha}) = \sum_{i=1}^{L}\alpha_i - \frac{1}{2}\sum_{i=1}^{L}\sum_{j=1}^{L}\alpha_i\alpha_j y_i y_j\mathbf{x}_i^t\mathbf{x}_j \qquad (9)$$

The optimum values of Lagrangian multipliers are determined by maximizing the objective function $L_d(\boldsymbol{\alpha})$ subject to the following constraints:

$$\sum_{i=1}^{L}\alpha_i y_i = 0 \qquad (10)$$

$$\alpha_i \geq 0 \text{ for } i = 1, 2, \ldots, L \qquad (11)$$

This optimization problem is solved using quadratic programming methods (Kaufman, 1999). The data points for which the values of the optimum Lagrange multipliers are not zero are the support vectors. For these data points the distance to the optimal hyperplane is minimum. Hence, the support vectors are the training data points that lie on the margin, as illustrated in Figure 1. For the optimum Lagrange multipliers $\left\{\alpha_j^*\right\}_{j=1}^{L_s}$, the optimum parameter vector $\mathbf{w}^*$ is given by

$$\mathbf{w}^* = \sum_{j=1}^{L_s}\alpha_j^* y_j\mathbf{x}_j \qquad (12)$$

where L_s is the number of support vectors. The discriminant function of the optimal hyperplane in terms of support vectors is given by

$$D(\mathbf{x}) = \mathbf{w}^{*t}\mathbf{x} + b^* = \sum_{j=1}^{L_s} \alpha_j^* y_j \mathbf{x}^t \mathbf{x}_j + b^* \qquad (13)$$

where b^* is the optimum bias.

However, the data for most of the real world tasks are not linearly separable. Next we present a method to construct an optimal hyperplane for linearly non-separable classes.

Optimal Hyperplane for Linearly Non-Separable Classes

The training data points of the linearly non-separable classes cannot be separated by a hyperplane without classification error. In such cases, it is desirable to find an optimal hyperplane that minimizes the probability of classification error for the training data set. A data point is non-separable when it does not satisfy the constraint in (2). This corresponds to a data point that falls either within margin or on the wrong side of the separating hyperplane as illustrated in Figure 2.

For linearly non-separable classes, the constraints in (2) are modified by introducing the nonnegative slack variables ξ_i as follows:

$$y_i(\mathbf{w}^t\mathbf{x}_i + b) \geq 1 - \xi_i \text{ for } i = 1, 2, \ldots, L \qquad (14)$$

Figure 2. Illustration of constructing the optimal hyperplane for linearly nonseparable classes

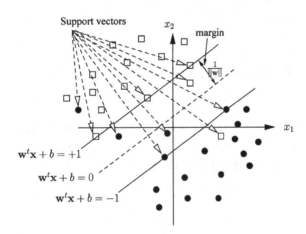

The slack variable ξ_i is a measure of the deviation of a data point $\mathbf{x}_i$ from the ideal condition of separability. For $0 \leq \xi_i \leq 1$, the data point falls inside the region of separation, but on the correct side of the separating hyperplane. For $\xi_i > 1$, the data point falls on the wrong side of the separating hyperplane. The support vectors are those particular data points that satisfy the constraint in (14) with equality sign. The cost function for linearly non-separable classes is given as

$$J(\mathbf{w}, \boldsymbol{\xi}) = \frac{1}{2}\|\mathbf{w}\|^2 + C\sum_{i=1}^{L}\xi_i \qquad (15)$$

where C is a user-specified positive parameter that controls the trade-off between the complexity of the classifier and the number of non-separable data points. Using the method of Lagrange multipliers to solve the constrained optimization problem as in the case of linearly separable classes, the dual form of the Lagrangian objective function can be obtained as follows (Haykin, 1999):

$$\mathcal{L}_d(\boldsymbol{\alpha}) = \sum_{i=1}^{L}\alpha_i - \frac{1}{2}\sum_{i=1}^{L}\sum_{j=1}^{L}\alpha_i\alpha_j y_i y_j \mathbf{x}_i^t \mathbf{x}_j \qquad (16)$$

subject to the constraints:

$$\sum_{i=1}^{L}\alpha_i y_i = 0 \qquad (17)$$

$$0 \leq \alpha_i \leq C \text{ for } i = 1, 2, \ldots, L \qquad (18)$$

It may be noted that the maximum value that the Lagrangian multipliers α_i can take is C for the linearly non-separable classes. For the optimum Lagrange multipliers $\left\{\alpha_j^*\right\}_{j=1}^{L_s}$, the optimum parameter vector $\mathbf{w}^*$ is given by

$$\mathbf{w}^* = \sum_{j=1}^{L_s}\alpha_j^* y_j \mathbf{x}_j \qquad (19)$$

where L_s is the number of support vectors. The discriminant function of the optimal hyperplane for an input vector $\mathbf{x}$ is given by

$$D(\mathbf{x}) = \mathbf{w}^{*t}\mathbf{x} + b^* = \sum_{j=1}^{L_s} \alpha_j^* y_j \mathbf{x}^t \mathbf{x}_j + b^* \qquad (20)$$

where b^* is the optimum bias.

Support Vector Machine for Nonlinearly Separable Classes

For nonlinearly separable classes, an SVM is built by mapping the input vector $\mathbf{x}_i$, $i = 1, 2, \ldots, L$ into a high dimensional feature vector $\mathbf{\Phi}(\mathbf{x}_i)$ using a nonlinear transformation $\mathbf{\Phi}$, and constructing an optimal hyperplane defined by $\mathbf{w}^t\mathbf{\Phi}(\mathbf{x}) + b = 0$ to separate the examples of two classes in the feature space $\mathbf{\Phi}(\mathbf{x})$. This is based on Cover's theorem which states that an input space where the patterns are nonlinearly separable may be transformed into a feature space where the patterns are linearly separable with a high probability, provided two conditions are satisfied (Haykin, 1999). The first condition is that the transformation is nonlinear and the second condition is that the dimensionality of the feature space is high enough. The concept of support vector machine for pattern classification is illustrated in Figure 3. It is seen that the nonlinearly separable data points $\mathbf{x}_i = [x_{i1}, x_{i2}]^t$, $i = 1, 2, \ldots, L$ in a two-dimensional input space are

mapped onto three-dimensional feature vectors $\mathbf{\Phi}(\mathbf{x}_i) = [x_{i1}^2, x_{i2}^2, \sqrt{2}x_{i1}x_{i2}]^t$, $i = 1, 2, \ldots, L$ where they are linearly separable.

For the construction of the optimal hyperplane in the high dimensional feature space $\mathbf{\Phi}(\mathbf{x})$, the dual form of the Lagrangian objective function in (16) takes the following form:

$$\mathcal{L}_d(\boldsymbol{\alpha}) = \sum_{i=1}^{L} \alpha_i - \frac{1}{2}\sum_{i=1}^{L}\sum_{j=1}^{L} \alpha_i \alpha_j y_i y_j \mathbf{\Phi}(\mathbf{x}_i)^t \mathbf{\Phi}(\mathbf{x}_j)$$

$$(21)$$

subject to the constraints:

$$\sum_{i=1}^{L} \alpha_i y_i = 0 \qquad (22)$$

$$0 \leq \alpha_i \leq C \text{ for } i = 1, 2, \ldots, L \qquad (23)$$

For the optimal $\boldsymbol{\alpha}^*$, the optimal parameter vector $\mathbf{w}^*$ is given by

$$\mathbf{w}^* = \sum_{j=1}^{L_s} \alpha_j^* y_j \mathbf{\Phi}(\mathbf{x}_j) \qquad (24)$$

where L_s is the number of support vectors. The discriminant function of the optimal hyperplane for an input vector $\mathbf{x}$ is defined as

Figure 3. Illustration of nonlinear transformation used in building an SVM for nonlinearly separable classes

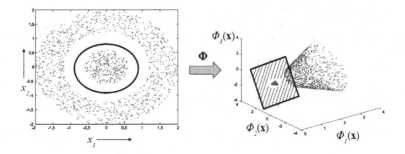

$$D(\mathbf{x}) = \mathbf{w}^{*t}\boldsymbol{\Phi}(\mathbf{x}) + b^* = \sum_{j=1}^{L_s} \alpha_j^* y_j \boldsymbol{\Phi}(\mathbf{x})^t \boldsymbol{\Phi}(\mathbf{x}_j) + b^*$$

(25)

$$L_d(\boldsymbol{\alpha}) = \sum_{i=1}^{L} \alpha_i - \frac{1}{2}\sum_{i=1}^{L}\sum_{j=1}^{L} \alpha_i \alpha_j y_i y_j K(\mathbf{x}_i, \mathbf{x}_j)$$

(28)

Solving (21) involves computation of the innerproduct operation $\boldsymbol{\Phi}(\mathbf{x}_i)^t\boldsymbol{\Phi}(\mathbf{x}_j)$. Evaluation of innerproducts in a high dimensional feature space is avoided by using an innerproduct kernel, $K(\mathbf{x}_i, \mathbf{x}_j)$, defined as $K(\mathbf{x}_i, \mathbf{x}_j) = \boldsymbol{\Phi}(\mathbf{x}_i)^t\boldsymbol{\Phi}(\mathbf{x}_j)$ (Scholkopf et al., 1999). A valid innerproduct kernel $K(\mathbf{x}_i, \mathbf{x}_j)$ for two pattern vectors $\mathbf{x}_i$ and $\mathbf{x}_j$ is a symmetric function for which the following Mercer's condition holds good:

$$\int K(\mathbf{x}_i, \mathbf{x}_j)g(\mathbf{x}_i)g(\mathbf{x}_j)d\mathbf{x}_i d\mathbf{x}_j \geq 0 \qquad (26)$$

for all $g(\mathbf{x}_i)$ such that

$$\int g^2(\mathbf{x}_i)d\mathbf{x}_i < \infty \qquad (27)$$

The objective function in (21) and the discriminant function of the optimal hyperplane in (25) can now be specified using the kernel function as follows:

$$D(\mathbf{x}) = \mathbf{w}^{*t}\boldsymbol{\Phi}(\mathbf{x}) + b^* = \sum_{j=1}^{L_s} \alpha_j^* y_j K(\mathbf{x}, \mathbf{x}_j) + b^*$$

(29)

The architecture of a support vector machine for two-class pattern classification that implements the discriminant function of the hyperplane in (29) is given in Figure 4. The number of hidden nodes corresponding to the number of support vectors, and the training examples corresponding to the support vectors are determined by maximizing the objective function in (28) using a given training data set and for a chosen kernel function.

Some commonly used innerproduct kernel functions are as follows:

Polynomial kernel: $K(\mathbf{x}_i, \mathbf{x}_j) = (a\mathbf{x}_i^t\mathbf{x}_j + c)^p$
Sigmoidal kernel: $K(\mathbf{x}_i, \mathbf{x}_j) = \tanh(a\mathbf{x}_i^t\mathbf{x}_j + c)$
Gaussian kernel: $K(\mathbf{x}_i, \mathbf{x}_j) = \exp(-\delta\|\mathbf{x}_i - \mathbf{x}_j\|^2)$

Here, $\mathbf{x}_i$ and $\mathbf{x}_j$ are vectors in the d-dimensional input pattern space, a and c are constants, p is the

Figure 4. Architecture of a support vector machine for two-class pattern classification. The class of the input pattern $\mathbf{x}$ is given by the sign of the discriminant function $D(\mathbf{x})$. The number of hidden nodes corresponds to the number of support vectors L_s. Each hidden node computes the innerproduct kernel function $K(\mathbf{x}, \mathbf{x}_i)$ on the input pattern $\mathbf{x}$ and a support vector $\mathbf{x}_i$.

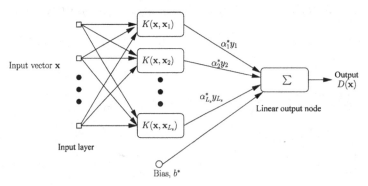

degree of the polynomial and δ is a nonnegative constant used for numerical stability in Gaussian kernel function. The dimensionality of the feature space is $(p+d)!/(p!\ d!)$ for the polynomial kernel (Cristianini & Shawe-Taylor, 2000). The feature spaces for the sigmoidal and Gaussian kernels are of infinite dimension. The kernel functions involve computations in the d-dimensional input space and avoid the innerproduct operations in the high dimensional feature space.

The best choice of the kernel function for a given pattern classification problem is still a research issue (Burges, 1998). The suitable kernel function and its parameters are chosen empirically. The complexity of a two-class support vector machine is a function of the number of support vectors (L_s) determined during its training. Multiclass pattern classification problems are generally solved using a combination of two-class SVMs. Therefore, the complexity of a multiclass pattern classification system depends on the number of SVMs and the complexity of each SVM used. In the next subsection, we present the commonly used approaches to multiclass pattern classification using SVMs.

Multiclass Pattern Classification Using SVMs

Support vector machines are originally designed for two-class pattern classification. Multiclass pattern classification problems are commonly solved using a combination of two-class SVMs and a decision strategy to decide the class of the input pattern (Allwein et al., 2001). Each SVM has the architecture given in Figure 4 and is trained independently. Now we present the two approaches to decomposition of the learning problem in multiclass pattern classification into several two-class learning problems so that a combination of SVMs can be used. The training data set $\{(\mathbf{x}_i, c_i)\}$ consists of L examples belonging to T classes. The class label $c_i \in \{1, 2, ..., T\}$. For the sake of simplicity,

we assume that the number of examples for each class is the same, *i.e.*, $L_t = L/T$.

One-Against-the-Rest Approach

In this approach, an SVM is constructed for each class by discriminating that class against the remaining (T-1) classes. The classification system based on this approach consists of T SVMs. All the L training examples are used in constructing an SVM for each class. In constructing the SVM for the class t the desired output y_i for a training example $\mathbf{x}_i$ is specified as follows:

$$y_i = \begin{cases} +1, & \text{if } c_i = t \\ -1, & \text{if } c_i \neq t \end{cases} \tag{30}$$

The examples with the desired output $y_i = +1$ are called *positive* examples. The examples with the desired output $y_i = -1$ are called *negative* examples. An optimal hyperplane is constructed to separate L_t positive examples from $L(T$-1$)/T$ negative examples. The much larger number of negative examples leads to an imbalance, resulting in the dominance of negative examples in determining the decision boundary (Kressel & Ulrich, 1999). The extent of imbalance increases with the number of classes and is significantly high when the number of classes is large. A test pattern $\mathbf{x}$ is classified by using the *winner-takes-all* strategy that uses the following decision rule:

$$\text{Class label for x} = \arg_t \max D_t\ (x) \tag{31}$$

where $D_t(\mathbf{x})$ is the discriminant function of the SVM constructed for the class t.

One-Against-One Approach

In this approach, an SVM is constructed for every pair of classes by training it to discriminate the two classes. The number of SVMs used in this approach is $T(T$-1$)/2$. An SVM for a pair of classes s and t is constructed using $2L_t$ training examples belonging to the two classes only. The desired output y_i for a training example $\mathbf{x}_i$ is specified as follows:

$$y_i = \begin{cases} +1, & \text{if } c_i = s \\ -1, & \text{if } c_i = t \end{cases} \qquad (32)$$

The small size of the set of training examples and the balance between the number of positive and negative examples lead to a simple optimization problem to be solved in constructing an SVM for a pair of classes. When the number of classes is large, the proliferation of SVMs leads to a complex classification system.

The *maxwins* strategy is commonly used to determine the class of a test pattern $\mathbf{x}$ in this approach. In this strategy, a majority voting scheme is used. If $D_{st}(\mathbf{x})$, the value of the discriminant function of the SVM for the pair of classes s and t, is positive, then the class s wins a vote. Otherwise, the class t wins a vote. Outputs of SVMs are used to determine the number of votes won by each class. The class with the maximum number of votes is assigned to the test pattern. When there are multiple classes with the same maximum number of votes, the class with the maximum value of the total magnitude of discriminant functions (TMDF) is assigned. The total magnitude of discriminant functions for the class s is defined as follows:

$$\text{TMDF} = \sum_t \left| D_{st}(\mathbf{x}) \right| \qquad (33)$$

where the summation is over all t with which the class s is paired. The maxwins strategy needs evaluation of discriminant functions of all the SVMs in deciding the class of a test pattern.

The SVM based classifiers have been successfully used in various applications like image categorization, object categorization, text classification, handwritten character recognition, speech recognition (Sekhar et al., 2003), speaker recognition and verification, and speech emotion recognition.

Kernel Methods for Pattern Clustering

In this subsection we the describe kernel K-means clustering and support vector clustering methods for clustering in the kernel feature space.

Kernel K-means Clustering

The commonly used K-means clustering method gives a linear separation of data, as illustrated in Figure 5, and is not suitable for separation of nonlinearly separable data. In this subsection, the criterion for partitioning the data into clusters in the input space using the K-means clustering algorithm is first presented. Clustering in the kernel feature space is then realised using the K-means clustering algorithm (Girolami, 2002; Satish, 2005).

Consider a set of L data points in the input space, $\left\{ \mathbf{x}_i \right\}_{i=1}^L$, $\mathbf{x}_i \in \mathbf{R}^d$. Let the number of clusters to be formed is Q. The criterion used by the K-means clustering method in the input space for grouping the data into Q clusters is to minimize the trace of the within-cluster scatter matrix, $\mathbf{S}_w$, defined as follows (Girolami, 2002):

$$\mathbf{S}_w = \frac{1}{L} \sum_{q=1}^Q \sum_{i=1}^L z_{qi} (\mathbf{x}_i - \boldsymbol{\mu}_q)(\mathbf{x}_i - \boldsymbol{\mu}_q)^t \qquad (34)$$

where $\boldsymbol{\mu}_q$ is the center of the qth cluster, C_q, and z_{qi} is the membership of data point $\mathbf{x}_i$ to the cluster C_q. The membership value $z_{qi} = 1$, if $\mathbf{x}_i \in C_q$ and 0 otherwise. The number of points in the qth cluster is given as L_q defined by

$$L_q = \sum_{i=1}^L z_{qi} \qquad (35)$$

Figure 5. *Illustration of K-means clustering in input space. (a) Scatter plot of the data in clusters separable by a circular shaped curve in a 2-dimensional space. Inner cluster belongs to cluster 1 and the outer cluster belongs to cluster 2. (b) Linear separation of data obtained using K-means clustering in the input space.*

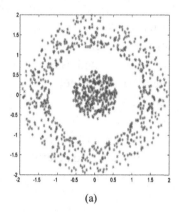
(a)

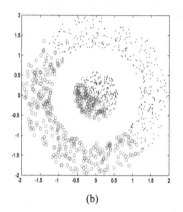
(b)

The center of the cluster C_q is given as μ_q defined by

$$\mu_q = \frac{1}{L_q} \sum_{i=1}^{L} z_{qi} x_i \qquad (36)$$

The optimal clustering of the data points involves determining the $Q \times L$ indicator matrix, **Z**, with the elements as z_{qi}, that minimizes the trace of the matrix $\mathbf{S}_w$. This method is used in the K-means clustering algorithm for linear separation of the clusters. For nonlinear separation of clusters of data points, the input space is transformed into a high dimensional feature space using a smooth and continuous nonlinear mapping, **Φ**, and the clusters are formed in the feature space. The optimal partitioning in the feature space is based on the criterion of minimizing the trace of the within-cluster scatter matrix in the feature space, S_w^Φ. The feature space scatter matrix is given by

$$S_w^\Phi = \frac{1}{L} \sum_{q=1}^{Q} \sum_{i=1}^{L} z_{qi} \left(\Phi(x_i) - \mu_q^\Phi \right) \left(\Phi(x_i) - \mu_q^\Phi \right)^t \qquad (37)$$

where μ_q^Φ, the center of the qth cluster in the feature space, is given by

$$\mu_q^\Phi = \frac{1}{L_q} \sum_{i=1}^{L} z_{qi} \Phi(x_i) \qquad (38)$$

The trace of the scatter matrix S_w^Φ can be computed using the innerproduct operations as given below:

$$Tr(S_w^\Phi) = \frac{1}{L} \sum_{q=1}^{Q} \sum_{i=1}^{L} z_{qi} \left(\Phi(x_i) - \mu_q^\Phi \right)^t \left(\Phi(x_i) - \mu_q^\Phi \right) \qquad (39)$$

When the feature space is explicitly represented, as in the case of mapping using polynomial kernels, the K-means clustering algorithm can be used to minimise the trace given in the above equation. However, for Mercer kernels such as Gaussian kernels with implicit mapping used for transformation, it is necessary to express the trace in terms of kernel function. The Mercer kernel function in the input space corresponds to the inner-product operation in the feature space, i.e., $K_{ij} = K(\mathbf{x}_i, \mathbf{x}_j) = \Phi(\mathbf{x}_i)^t\Phi(\mathbf{x}_j)$. The trace of $\mathbf{S}_w^\Phi$ can be rewritten as

$$
\begin{aligned}
Tr(S_w^\Phi) &= \frac{1}{L}\sum_{q=1}^{Q}\sum_{i=1}^{L}z_{qi}K_{ii} - \frac{1}{L}\sum_{q=1}^{Q}\sum_{i=1}^{L}z_{qi}\sum_{j=1}^{L}\frac{z_{qj}}{L_q}K_{ij}\\
&= \frac{1}{L}\sum_{q=1}^{Q}\sum_{i=1}^{L}z_{qi}\left[K_{ii} - \frac{1}{L_q}\sum_{j=1}^{L}z_{qj}K_{ij}\right]\\
&= \frac{1}{L}\sum_{q=1}^{Q}\sum_{i=1}^{L}z_{qi}D_{qi}
\end{aligned}
$$
(40)

where

$$
D_{qi} = K_{ii} - \frac{1}{L_q}\sum_{j=1}^{L}z_{qj}K_{ij}
$$
(41)

The term D_{qi} is the penalty associated with assigning $\mathbf{x}_i$ to the qth cluster in the feature space. For explicit mapping kernels such as the polynomial kernel function, the feature space representation is explicitly known. Polynomial kernel is given by $K(\mathbf{x}, \mathbf{x}_i) = (a\mathbf{x}^t\mathbf{x}_i + c)^p$, where a and c are constants, and p is the degree of polynomial kernel. The vector $\Phi(\mathbf{x})$ in the feature space of the polynomial kernel corresponding to the input space vector $\mathbf{x}$ includes the monomials upto order p of elements in $\mathbf{x}$. For a polynomial kernel, D_{qi} may take a negative value because the magnitude of K_{qj} can be greater than that of K_{ii}. To avoid D_{qi} taking negative values, K_{ij}, in the equation for D_{qi} is replaced with the normalized value $\hat{K}_{ij}$ defined as

$$
\hat{K}_{ij} = \frac{|K_{ij}|}{\sqrt{K_{ii}}\sqrt{K_{jj}}}
$$
(42)

From Cauchy-Schwarz inequality, $K_{ij} \leq \sqrt{K_{ii}}\sqrt{K_{jj}}$. It follows that for the polynomial kernel $\hat{K}_{ii} = 1$ and $\hat{K}_{ij} \leq \hat{K}_{ii}$, and D_{qi} is defined as:

$$
D_{qi} = \hat{K}_{ii} - \frac{1}{L_q}\sum_{j=1}^{L}z_{qj}\hat{K}_{ij}
$$
(43)

For implicit mapping kernels such as the Gaussian kernel function, the explicit feature space representation is not known. A Gaussian kernel is defined as $K(\mathbf{x}, \mathbf{x}_i) = \exp(-\delta\|\mathbf{x} - \mathbf{x}_i\|^2)$, where δ is the kernel width parameter. For Gaussian kernel, D_{qj} takes a nonnegative value because $K_{ii} = 1$ and $K_{ij} \leq K_{ii}$.

In the kernel K-means clustering, the optimization problem is to determine the indicator matrix $\mathbf{Z}^*$ such that

$$
Z^* = \arg\min_{Z} Tr(S_w^\Phi)
$$
(44)

An iterative method for solving this optimization problem is given in (Girolami, 2002). The clusters obtained for the ring data using the kernel K-means clustering method are shown in Figure 6.

Figure 6. Nonlinear separation of data obtained using the kernel K-means clustering method for the ring data plotted in Figure 5(a).

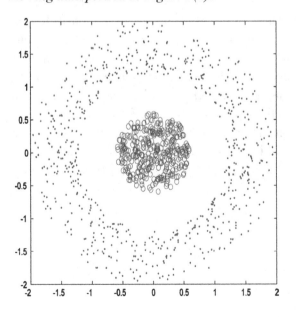

Support Vector Clustering

Support vector clustering (Ben-Hur et al., 2001) is a clustering method that follows the support vector data description technique. Here, data points are mapped by means of a Gaussian kernel to a high dimensional feature space, where a search for the minimal enclosing sphere is performed. This sphere, when mapped back to data space, can form several contours, each enclosing a separate cluster of points.

Consider a set of L data points in the input space, $\left\{x_i\right\}_{i=1}^{L}$, $\mathbf{x}_i \in \mathbf{R}^d$. Using a nonlinear transformation $\mathbf{\Phi}$ from the input space to a high dimensional feature space, the smallest enclosing sphere of radius R is found in the feature space. This is described by the constraints as given below:

$$\| \mathbf{\Phi}(\mathbf{x}_i) - \mathbf{a}\|^2 \leq R^2, \text{ for } i = 1, 2, ..., L \qquad (45)$$

where $\mathbf{a}$ is the center of the sphere. Soft constraints are incorporated by adding slack variables ζ_i as follows:

$$\| \mathbf{\Phi}(\mathbf{x}_i) - \mathbf{a}\|^2 \leq R^2 + \zeta_i, \text{ for } i = 1, 2, ..., L \qquad (46)$$

with $\zeta_i \geq 0$. This constrained optimization problem is solved using the method of Lagrangian multipliers. The primal form of the Lagrangian objective function is given by

$$L_p = R^2 - \sum_{i=1}^{L}\alpha_i\left(R^2 + \zeta_i - \left\|\Phi(x_i) - a\right\|^2\right) - \sum_{i=1}^{L}\beta_i\zeta_i + C\sum_{i=1}^{L}\zeta_i \qquad (47)$$

where $\alpha_i \geq 0$ and $\beta_i \geq 0$ are the Lagrange multipliers, C is a constant, and $C\sum_{i=1}^{L}\zeta_i$ is a penalty term. Setting to zero the derivative of L_p with respect to R, $\mathbf{a}$ and ζ_i, respectively, leads to

$$\sum_{i=1}^{L}\alpha_i = 1 \qquad (48)$$

$$a = \sum_{i=1}^{L}\alpha_i\Phi(x_i) \qquad (49)$$

$$\alpha_i = C - \beta_i \qquad (50)$$

Using these relations, the variables R, $\mathbf{a}$ and ζ_i may be eliminated from the Lagrangian objective function giving rise to the Wolf dual, that is expressed solely in terms of α_i, as follows:

$$L_d = \sum_{i=1}^{L}\alpha_i\left\|\Phi(x_i)\right\|^2 - \sum_{i=1}^{L}\sum_{j=1}^{L}\alpha_i\alpha_j\Phi(x_i)^t\Phi(x_j) \qquad (51)$$

subject to the following constraints:

$$\sum_{i=1}^{L}\alpha_i = 1 \qquad (52)$$

$$0 \leq \alpha_i \leq C \text{ for } i = 1, 2, ..., L \qquad (53)$$

The objective function in (51) can now be specified using the kernel function as follows:

$$L_d = \sum_{i=1}^{L}\alpha_i K(x_i, x_i) - \sum_{i=1}^{L}\sum_{j=1}^{L}\alpha_i\alpha_j K(x_i, x_j) \qquad (54)$$

This optimization problem is solved using a quadratic programming method to determine the optimum center of the sphere $\mathbf{a}$ in the feature space. Like in SVM, the set of points whose corresponding Lagrange multipliers are non-zero become support vectors. Further, the support vectors whose Lagrange multipliers are at C are called bounded support vectors and the rest of them are called unbounded support vectors. Geometrically, the unbounded support vectors lie on the surface of the sphere, bounded support vectors lie outside the sphere and the remaining points lie inside the sphere.

Let $Z(\mathbf{x})$ be the distance of $\mathbf{\Phi}(\mathbf{x})$ to the center of the sphere $\mathbf{a}$ is given by

$$Z^2(\mathbf{x}) = \| \mathbf{\Phi}(\mathbf{x}) - \mathbf{a} \|^2 \qquad (55)$$

From equations (55) and (49) we have,

$$Z^2(x) = K(x,x) - 2\sum_{i=1}^{L} \alpha_i K(x_i, x) - \sum_{i=1}^{L}\sum_{j=1}^{L} \alpha_i \alpha_j K(x_i, x_j) \qquad (56)$$

Then, the radius of the sphere R can be determined by computing $Z(\mathbf{x}_i)$, where $\mathbf{x}_i$ is a unbounded support vector.

The sphere in the feature space when mapped back to the input space leads to the formation of a set of contours which are interpreted as cluster boundaries. To identify the points that belong to different clusters, a geometric approach involving $Z(\mathbf{x})$ and based on the following observation is used: Given a pair of data points that belong to different clusters, any path that connects them must exit from the sphere in feature space. Therefore, such a path contains a segment of points $\mathbf{v}$ such that $Z(\mathbf{v}) > R$. This leads to the following definition of the adjacency $\mathbf{A}_{ij}$ between a pairs of points $\mathbf{x}_i$ and $\mathbf{x}_j$ with $\mathbf{\Phi}(\mathbf{x}_i)$ and $\mathbf{\Phi}(\mathbf{x}_j)$ being present in or on the sphere in feature space shown in Box 1.

Clusters are now defined as the connected components of the graph induced by the adjacency matrix $\mathbf{A}$. Bounded support vectors are unclassified by this procedure since their feature space images lie outside the enclosing sphere. One may decide either to leave them unclassified, or to assign them to the cluster that they are closest.

In this section, we presented the kernel methods for classification and clustering of patterns.

Though the methods are described for static patterns with each example represented as a vector in d-dimensional input space, these methods can also be used for patterns with each example represented as a non-vectorial type structure. However, it is necessary to design a Mercer kernel function for patterns represented using a non-vectorial type structure so that the kernel methods can be used for analysis of such patterns. Kernel functions have been proposed for different types of structured data such as strings, sets, texts, graphs, images and time series data. In the next section, we present dynamic kernels for sequential patterns represented as sequences of continuous feature vectors.

DESIGN OF DYNAMIC KERNELS FOR CONTINUOUS FEATURE VECTOR

Sequences

Continuous sequence data is represented in the form of a sequence of continuous feature vectors. Examples of continuous sequence data are speech data, handwritten character data, video data and time series data such as weather forecasting data, financial data, stock market data and network traffic data. Short-time spectral analysis of the speech signal of an utterance gives a sequence of continuous feature vectors. Short-time analysis of speech signal involves performing spectral analysis on each frame of about 20 milliseconds duration and representing each frame by a real valued feature vector. These feature vectors correspond to the observations. The speech signal of an

Box 1.

$$A_{ij} = \begin{cases} 1, & \text{if } Z(v) \leq R, \text{ for all } v \text{ on the line segment connecting } x_i \text{ and } x_j \\ 0, & \text{otherwise} \end{cases} \qquad (57)$$

utterance with M number of frames is represented as $\mathbf{X} = \mathbf{x}_1 \mathbf{x}_2 \ldots \mathbf{x}_m \ldots \mathbf{x}_M$, where $\mathbf{x}_m$ is a vector of real valued observations for frame m. The duration of utterances belonging to a class varies from one utterance to another. Hence, the number of frames also differs from one utterance to another. This makes the number of observations to vary. In the tasks such as speech recognition, duration of the data is short and there is a need to model the temporal dynamics and correlations among the features. This requires the sequence information present in the data to be preserved. In such cases, a speech utterance is represented as a sequence of feature vectors. On the other hand, in the tasks such as speaker identification, spoken language identification, and speech emotion recognition, the duration of the data is long and preserving sequence information is not critical. In such cases, a speech signal is represented as a set of feature vectors. In the handwritten character data also, each character is represented as a sequence of feature vectors. In the video data, each video clip is considered as a sequence of frames and a frame may be considered as an image. Each image can be represented by a feature vector. Since the sequence information present among the adjacent frames is to be preserved, a video clip data is represented as a sequence of feature vectors. An image can also be represented as a set of local feature vectors.

The main issue in designing a kernel for sequences of continuous feature vectors is to handle the varying length nature of sequences. Dynamic kernels for sequences of continuous feature vectors are designed in three ways. In the first approach, a sequence of feature vectors is mapped onto a vector in a fixed dimension feature space and a kernel is defined in that space (Campbell et al., 2006a; Lee et al., 2007). The second approach involves in kernelizing a suitable distance measure used to compare two sequences of feature vectors (Campbell et al., 2006b; Jing et al., 2003; Moreno et al., 2004; You et al., 2009a). In the third approach, matching based technique is considered

for designing the kernel between two sequences of feature vectors (Boughorbel et al., 2005; Grauman & Darrell, 2007). In this Section, we describe different dynamic kernels such as generalized linear discriminant sequence kernel (Campbell et al., 2006a), the probabilistic sequence kernel (Lee et al., 2007), Kullback-Leibler divergence based kernel (Moreno et al., 2004), GMM supervector kernel (Campbell et al., 2006b), Bhattacharyya distance based kernel (You et al., 2009a), earth mover's distance kernel (Jing et al,. 2003), intermediate matching kernel (Boughorbel et al., 2005), and pyramid match kernel (Grauman & Darrell, 2007) used for sequences or sets of continuous feature vectors.

Generalized Linear Discriminant Sequence Kernel

Generalized linear discriminant sequence (GLDS) kernel (Campbell et al., 2006a) uses an explicit expansion into a kernel feature space defined by the polynomials of degree p. Let $\mathbf{X} = \mathbf{x}_1 \mathbf{x}_2 \ldots \mathbf{x}_m \ldots \mathbf{x}_M$, where $\mathbf{x}_m \in \mathbb{R}^d$ be a set of M feature vectors. The GLDS kernel is derived by considering polynomials as the generalized linear discriminant functions (Campbell et al., 2002). A feature vector $\mathbf{x}_m$ is represented in a higher dimensional space $\boldsymbol{\Psi}$ as a polynomial expansion $\boldsymbol{\Psi}(\mathbf{x}_m) = [\psi_1(\mathbf{x}_m), \psi_2(\mathbf{x}_m), \ldots, \psi_r(\mathbf{x}_m)]^t$. The expansion $\boldsymbol{\Psi}(\mathbf{x}_m)$ includes all monomials of elements of $\mathbf{x}_m$ upto and including degree p. The set of feature vectors $\mathbf{X}$ is represented as a fixed dimensional vector $\boldsymbol{\Phi}(\mathbf{X})$ which is obtained as follows:

$$\Phi^{GLDS}(X) = \frac{1}{M} \sum_{m=1}^{M} \Psi(x_m) \qquad (58)$$

The GLDS kernel between two examples $\mathbf{X} = \mathbf{x}_1 \mathbf{x}_2 \ldots \mathbf{x}_M$ and $\mathbf{Y} = \mathbf{y}_1 \mathbf{y}_2 \ldots, \mathbf{y}_N$ is given as

$$K^{GLDS}(X,Y) = \left(\frac{1}{M}\sum_{m=1}^{M}\Psi(x_m)\right)^t S^{-1}\left(\frac{1}{N}\sum_{n=1}^{N}\Psi(y_n)\right) \tag{59}$$

Let L be the total number of examples in the training data set which includes the data belonging to two classes. The correlation matrix $\mathbf{S}$ is defined as follows:

$$S = \frac{1}{L}R^t R \tag{60}$$

where $\mathbf{R}$ is the matrix whose rows are the polynomial expansions of the feature vectors in the training set. When the correlation matrix $\mathbf{S}$ is a diagonal matrix, the GLDS kernel is given as

$$K^{GLDS}(X,Y) = \left(\frac{1}{M}\sum_{m=1}^{M}S^{-\frac{1}{2}}\Psi(x_m)\right)^t \left(\frac{1}{N}\sum_{n=1}^{N}S^{-\frac{1}{2}}\Psi(y_n)\right) \tag{61}$$

When the identity matrix is considered for $\mathbf{S}$, the GLDS kernel in (61) turns out to be

$$\begin{aligned}K^{GLDS}(X,Y) &= \frac{1}{M}\frac{1}{N}\sum_{m=1}^{M}\sum_{n=1}^{N}\Psi(x_m)^t\Psi(y_n)\\ &= \frac{1}{M}\frac{1}{N}\sum_{m=1}^{M}\sum_{n=1}^{N}k(x_m,y_n)\end{aligned} \tag{62}$$

where $k(\mathbf{x}_m, \mathbf{y}_n)$ is the polynomial kernel function of degree p between $\mathbf{x}_m$ and $\mathbf{y}_n$.

Probabilistic Sequence Kernel

Probabilistic sequence kernel (PSK) (Lee et al. 2007) maps a set of feature vectors onto a probabilistic feature vector obtained using generative models like Gaussian mixture models (GMMs). The GMM is a linear superposition of Q Gaussian components, used to obtain the parameterized density estimation of the given data. The set of parameters, $\boldsymbol{\theta} = \{\pi_q, \boldsymbol{\mu}_q, \boldsymbol{\Sigma}_q\}$, $q = 1, 2,..., Q$ is estimated from the training data using maximum likelihood (ML) method. The models for each class are trained independently. The universal background model (UBM) is a large GMM trained using the training data of all the classes to represent the class independent distribution of data. A class-specific GMM is obtained by adapting the UBM to the data of that class. Maximum a posteriori (MAP) method is commonly used for the adaptation.

The PSK uses the UBM with Q mixtures (Reynolds et al., 2000) and the class-specific GMM obtained by adapting UBM. The likelihood of a feature vector $\mathbf{x}$ being generated by the $2Q$-mixture GMM that includes the UBM and class-specific GMM is given as

$$p(x) = \sum_{q=1}^{2Q} p(x\,|q)P(q) \tag{63}$$

where $P(q)$ denotes the mixture weight and $p(\mathbf{x}|q) = N(\mathbf{x}|\boldsymbol{\mu}_q, \boldsymbol{\Sigma}_q)$. The normalized Gaussian basis function for the qth component is defined as

$$\psi_q(x) = \frac{p(x\,|q)P(q)}{\sum_{q'=1}^{2Q} p(x\,|q')P(q')} \tag{64}$$

A feature vector $\mathbf{x}$ is represented in a higher dimensional space as a vector of normalized Gaussian basis functions, $\boldsymbol{\Psi}(\mathbf{x}) = [\psi_1(\mathbf{x}), \psi_2(\mathbf{x}),..., \psi_{2Q}(\mathbf{x})]^t$. Since the element $\psi_q(\mathbf{x})$ indicates the probabilistic alignment of $\mathbf{x}$ to the qth component, $\boldsymbol{\Psi}(\mathbf{x})$ is called as the probabilistic alignment vector. A set of feature vectors $\mathbf{X} = \mathbf{x}_1\mathbf{x}_2... \mathbf{x}_M$ is represented as a fixed dimensional vector $\boldsymbol{\Phi}(\mathbf{X})$ in the higher dimensional space, as given by

$$\Phi^{PSK}(X) = \frac{1}{M}\sum_{m=1}^{M}\Psi(x_m) \tag{65}$$

The PSK between two examples $\mathbf{X} = \mathbf{x}_1\mathbf{x}_2...$ $\mathbf{x}_M$ and $\mathbf{Y} = \mathbf{y}_1\mathbf{y}_2..., \mathbf{y}_N$ is given as

$$K^{PSK}(X,Y) = \left(\frac{1}{M}\sum_{m=1}^{M}\Psi(x_m)\right)^{t} S^{-1}\left(\frac{1}{N}\sum_{n=1}^{N}\Psi(y_n)\right)$$

(66)

where $\mathbf{S}$ is the correlation matrix as in (60), except that it is obtained using the probabilistic alignment vectors.

Kullback-Leibler Divergence Based Kernel

A kernel function computes a measure of similarity between a pair of examples. One way of designing a kernel is to first find a suitable distance metric for the pair of examples, and then kernelize that distance metric. Deriving a suitable distance metric for two varying length sequences is a non-trivial task. Kullback-Leibler (KL) divergence (Kullback & Leibler, 1951) can be used to compare two distributions $p(\mathbf{x})$ and $g(\mathbf{x})$ defined over the space of $\mathbf{x}$ as follows,

$$D^{KL}\left(p(x)\|g(x)\right) = \int p(x) \ \log \ \frac{p(x)}{g(x)}dx$$

(67)

This KL divergence is not symmetric. A symmetric version of KL divergence between two distributions is given by

$$D^{KL}\left(p(x)\|g(x)\right) =$$
$$\int p(x) \ \log \ \frac{p(x)}{g(x)}dx + \int g(x) \ \log \ \frac{g(x)}{p(x)}dx$$

(68)

The KL divergence based kernel (Moreno et al., 2004) between the two sequences $\mathbf{X}$ and $\mathbf{Y}$ whose elements are in the space of $\mathbf{x}$ is obtained by exponentiating the symmetric KL divergence as follows:

$$K^{KLD}(X,Y) = e^{-\delta \ D^{KL}(p_X(x)\|p_Y(x))}$$

(69)

where δ is a constant used for numerical stability. The KL divergence between two Gaussian distributions (Moreno et al., 2004), $p_\mathbf{X}(\mathbf{x}) = \mathrm{N}(\mathbf{x}|\boldsymbol{\mu}_\mathbf{X}, \boldsymbol{\Sigma}_\mathbf{X})$ and $p_\mathbf{Y}(\mathbf{x}) = \mathrm{N}(\mathbf{x}|\boldsymbol{\mu}_\mathbf{Y}, \boldsymbol{\Sigma}_\mathbf{Y})$, is given by Equation 70 in Box 2.

There is no closed form expression for the KL divergence between two GMMs. In (Moreno et al., 2004), the Monte Carlo method is used to compute the KL divergence between two GMMs.

The KLD kernel does not satisfy the Mercer property. However, in (Campbell et al., 2006b) a GMM supervector kernel that uses KL divergence to compare the GMM supervectors of two sequences of feature vectors is introduced. The GMM supervector kernel is explained in the next subsection.

GMM Supervector Kernel

The GMM supervector (GMMSV) kernel (Campbell et al., 2006b) performs a mapping of a set of feature vectors onto a higher dimensional vector corresponding to a GMM supervector. An UBM is built using the training examples of all the classes. An example-specific GMM is built for each example by adapting only the means of the UBM using the data of that example. An example is represented by a supervector obtained by stacking the mean vectors of the components of

Box 2.

$$D^{KL}\left(p_X(x)\|p_Y(x)\right) = tr(\Sigma_X\Sigma_Y^{-1}) + tr(\Sigma_Y\Sigma_X^{-1}) - 2d + tr\left((\Sigma_X^{-1} + \Sigma_Y^{-1})(\mu_X - \mu_Y)(\mu_X - \mu_Y)^t\right)$$

(70)

the example-specific GMM. A GMM supervector kernel is designed using a distance measure between the supervectors of two examples. In (Campbell et al., 2006b), the distance measure between the GMM supervectors is obtained by the approximation to KL divergence between the two GMMs.

Let $p(x) = \sum_{q=1}^{Q} \pi_q N(x \,|\, \mu_q \Sigma_q)$ be the probability density function represented by the UBM with Q components. Let $p_X(x) = \sum_{q=1}^{Q} \pi_q N(x \,|\, \mu_q^{(X)} \Sigma_q)$ and $p_Y(x) = \sum_{q=1}^{Q} \pi_q N(x \,|\, \mu_q^{(Y)} \Sigma_q)$ be the example-specific GMMs obtained by adapting only the means of the UBM to the examples $\mathbf{X} = \mathbf{x}_1 \mathbf{x}_2 ... \mathbf{x}_M$ and $\mathbf{Y} = \mathbf{y}_1 \mathbf{y}_2 ..., \mathbf{y}_N$ respectively. The examples $\mathbf{X}$ and $\mathbf{Y}$ are now represented by the suprevector of adapted mean vectors of the components as

$$\Psi(X) = \left[\mu_1^{(X)}, \mu_2^{(X)}, \ ... \ , \mu_Q^{(X)}\right]^t \qquad \text{and}$$

$\Psi(Y) = \left[\mu_1^{(Y)}, \mu_2^{(Y)}, \ ... \ , \mu_Q^{(Y)}\right]^t$ respectively. When only mean vector adaptation is considered, an approximation for the distance between two GMMs is considered by bounding the KL divergence with the log-sum inequality as seen in Equation 71 in Box 3.

For diagonal covariance matrices, the closed form expression for the distance between two example-specific GMMs is given by

$$D(\Psi(X), \Psi(Y)) =$$
$$\frac{1}{2}\sum_{q=1}^{Q} \pi_q \left(\mu_q^{(X)} - \mu_q^{(Y)}\right)^t \Sigma_q^{-1} \left(\mu_q^{(X)} - \mu_q^{(Y)}\right) \qquad (72)$$

The distance in (72) is symmetric and can be used for kernel computation. The resulting GMMSV kernel is given as

$$K^{GMMSV}(X, Y) = \sum_{q=1}^{Q} \pi_q \left(\mu_q^{(X)}\right)^t \Sigma_q^{-1} \left(\mu_q^{(Y)}\right) \tag{73}$$

$$= \sum_{q=1}^{Q} \left(\sqrt{\pi_q} \Sigma_q^{-1/2} \mu_q^{(X)}\right)^t \left(\sqrt{\pi_q} \Sigma_q^{-1/2} \mu_q^{(Y)}\right) \tag{74}$$

It is seen that the GMMSV kernel is linear in the GMM supervectors. The feature space of the GMMSV kernel represents a diagonal scaling using $\sqrt{\pi_q \Sigma_q}$ of the GMM supervector, i.e., $\Phi(X) = \sum_{q=1}^{Q} \sqrt{\pi_q} \Sigma_q^{-1/2} \mu_q^{(X)}$. Hence the resulting kernel satisfies the Mercer property. In (Campbell et al. 2006b), only the adapted means are considered in forming a supervector. However, significant information is present in the covariance terms. In (Campbell, 2008), the covariance terms are also considered to compute the kernel. An example-specific GMM is built for each example by adapting both the means and covariance matrices of the UBM using the data of that example. Here the symmetric KL divergence is used as the distance measure between the two GMMs. The supervector kernel for the two sets of feature vectors $\mathbf{X}$ and $\mathbf{Y}$ is given by Equation 75 in Box 4 where Σ_q is the diagonal covariance matrix of qth component of UBM, $\Sigma_q^{(X)}$ and $\Sigma_q^{(Y)}$ are the diagonal covariance matrices of qth adapted components corresponding to $\mathbf{X}$ and $\mathbf{Y}$.

Box 3.

$$\boxed{D^{KL}\left(p_X(x) \,\|\, p_Y(x)\right) \leq \sum_{q=1}^{Q} \pi_q D^{KL}\left(N(x \,|\, \mu_q^{(X)}\Sigma_q) \,\|\, N(x \,|\, \mu_q^{(Y)}\Sigma_q)\right)} \qquad (71)$$

Box 4.

$$K^{COVSV}(X,Y) = \sum_{q=1}^{Q}\left(\sqrt{\pi_q}\Sigma_q^{-\frac{1}{2}}\mu_q^{(X)}\right)^t\left(\sqrt{\pi_q}\Sigma_q^{-\frac{1}{2}}\mu_q^{(Y)}\right) + \sum_{q=1}^{Q}\frac{\pi_q}{2}tr\left(\Sigma_q^{(X)}\Sigma_q^{-2}\Sigma_q^{(Y)}\right) \tag{75}$$

One way of obtaining the kernel function is exponentiating a distance metric (Shawe-Taylor & Cristianini, 2004). In (Dehak et al., 2007), a nonlinear GMM supervector kernel is introduced. It is seen that the distance in (72) is symmetric and satisfies the Mercer property. The nonlinear GMM supervector (NLGMMSV) kernel is obtained as

$$K^{NLGMMSV}(X,Y) = e^{-\delta\ D(\Psi(X),\Psi(Y))} \tag{76}$$

where δ is a constant used for numerical stability.

Bhattacharyya Distance Based Kernel

An alternative measure of similarity between two distributions is the Bhattacharyya affinity measure (Bhattacharyya, 1943; Kailath, 1967). The Bhattacharyya distance between two probability distributions $p(\mathbf{x})$ and $g(\mathbf{x})$ defined over $\mathbf{x}$ is given by

$$B\left(p(x)\|g(x)\right) = \int \sqrt{p(x)}\sqrt{g(x)}\ dx \tag{77}$$

Let $p(x) = N(x|\mu^{(p)},\Sigma^{(p)})$ and $g(x) = N(x|\mu^{(g)},\Sigma^{(g)})$ be two Gaussian distributions. The closed form expression for Bhattacharyya distance (You et al., 2009b) between $p(\mathbf{x})$ and $g(\mathbf{x})$ is given by Equation 78 in Box 5.

This can be extended to compare two distributions represented as GMMs. Let

$$p_X(x) = \sum_{q=1}^{Q}\pi_q^{(X)}N(x|\mu_q^{(X)},\Sigma_q^{(X)}) \quad \text{and}$$

$$p_Y(x) = \sum_{q=1}^{Q}\pi_q^{(Y)}N(x|\mu_q^{(Y)},\Sigma_q^{(Y)}) \quad \text{be the GMMs}$$

for the examples $\mathbf{X} = \mathbf{x}_1\mathbf{x}_2...\mathbf{x}_M$ and $\mathbf{Y} = \mathbf{y}_1\mathbf{y}_2...,\mathbf{y}_N$ respectively. The closed form expression for Bhattacharyya distance between $p_X(\mathbf{x})$ and $p_Y(\mathbf{x})$ is given using the log-sum inequality as shown in Equation 79 in Box 6.

The Bhattacharyya distance measure is symmetric and the corresponding kernel gram matrix is shown to be positive semidefinite in (Kondor & Jebara, 2003). Hence it can be used as a kernel function.

In (You et al. 2009b), the Bhattacharyya mean distance is used to represent the similarity between two GMMs. Let $p(x) = \sum_{q=1}^{Q}\pi_q N(x|\mu_q,\Sigma_q)$ be the UBM with Q components and

Box 5.

$$B\left(p(x)\|g(x)\right) = \frac{1}{8}\left(\mu^{(p)} - \mu^{(g)}\right)^t\left(\frac{\Sigma^{(p)} + \Sigma^{(g)}}{2}\right)^{-1}\left(\mu^{(p)} - \mu^{(g)}\right) + \frac{1}{2}\ln\frac{\left|\dfrac{\Sigma^{(p)} + \Sigma^{(g)}}{2}\right|}{\sqrt{\left|\Sigma^{(p)}\right|\left|\Sigma^{(g)}\right|}} \tag{78}$$

Box 6.

$$B\left(p_X(x)\middle\|p_Y(x)\right) = \frac{1}{8}\sum_{q=1}^{Q}\left[\left(\mu_q^{(X)} - \mu_q^{(Y)}\right)^t \left(\frac{\Sigma_q^{(X)} + \Sigma_q^{(Y)}}{2}\right)^{-1} \left(\mu_q^{(X)} - \mu_q^{(Y)}\right)\right]$$

$$+ \frac{1}{2}\sum_{q=1}^{Q}\ln\frac{\left|\dfrac{\Sigma_q^{(X)} + \Sigma_q^{(Y)}}{2}\right|}{\sqrt{\left|\Sigma_q^{(X)}\right|\left|\Sigma_q^{(Y)}\right|}} - \frac{1}{2}\sum_{q=1}^{Q}\ln\left(\pi_q^{(X)}\pi_q^{(Y)}\right) \tag{79}$$

$p_X(x) = \sum_{q=1}^{Q}\pi_q^{(X)}N(x\middle|\mu_q^{(X)},\Sigma_q^{(X)})$ be the GMM obtained by adapting the UBM to the example **X**. The GMM-UBM mean interval (GUMI) vector $\Phi_q(\mathbf{X})$ is obtained from the approximation of Bhattacharyya mean distance between the qth component of the adapted GMM $p_X(\mathbf{x})$ and the corresponding qth component of the UBM $p(\mathbf{x})$ as follows:

$$\Phi_q(X) = \left(\frac{\Sigma_q^{(X)} + \Sigma_q}{2}\right)^{-\frac{1}{2}} \left(\mu_q^{(X)} - \mu_q\right) \tag{80}$$

The GUMI supervector is obtained by concatenating the GUMI vectors of different components as

$$\Phi^{GUMI}(X) = \left[\Phi_1(X)^t, \Phi_2(X)^t, \ldots, \Phi_Q(X)^t\right]^t \tag{81}$$

The GUMI kernel is defined as the innerproduct of the GUMI supervectors of a pair of examples, and is given by

$$K^{GUMI}(X,Y) = \Phi^{GUMI}(X)^t \Phi^{GUMI}(Y) \tag{82}$$

In the GUMI kernel, the supervector is obtained from the Bhattacharyya mean distance between a

GMM and an UBM. However, significant information is present in covariance terms. In (You et al., 2009a), the covariance terms are also considered to obtain the GUMI supervector. It is shown in (You et al., 2009a) that a GUMI vector is obtained by concatenating the mean vector and the variance vector. The GUMI vector using the covariance terms for the qth component is given by

$$\Phi^{COV}(X) = \begin{bmatrix} \left(\dfrac{\Sigma_q^{(X)} + \Sigma_q}{2}\right)^{-\frac{1}{2}} \left(\mu_q^{(X)} - \mu_q\right) \\ diag\left(\left(\dfrac{\Sigma_q^{(X)} + \Sigma_q}{2}\right)^{\frac{1}{2}} \left(\mu_q^{(X)}\right)^{-\frac{1}{2}}\right) \end{bmatrix} \tag{83}$$

The supervector is obtained by concatenating the GUMI vectors using the covariance terms of the different components as

$$\Phi^{COVGUMI}(X) = \left[\Phi_1^{COV}(X)^t, \Phi_2^{COV}(X)^t, \ldots, \Phi_Q^{COV}(X)^t\right]^t \tag{84}$$

Now the modified Bhattacharyya distance based kernel is obtained as

$$K^{COVGUMI}(X,Y) = \Phi^{COVGUMI}(X)^t \Phi^{COVGUMI}(Y) \tag{85}$$

Earth Mover's Distance Kernel

Earth mover's distance (EMD) (Rubner et al., 2000) is a distance metric that computes a similarity measure between two multidimensional distributions. The EMD is computed based on the transportation problem (Hitchcock, 1941). Let $\mathbf{X} = \mathbf{x}_1 \mathbf{x}_2 ... \mathbf{x}_M$ and $\mathbf{Y} = \mathbf{y}_1 \mathbf{y}_2 ..., \mathbf{y}_N$ be the two sets of feature vectors. In (Rubner et al., 2000), feature vectors of each of the examples are clustered into a fixed number of clusters. Let the example $\mathbf{X}$ be represented using S clusters as $P_X = \{(p_1, w_{p_1}), (p_2, w_{p_2}), ... , (p_S, w_{p_S})\}$ and the example $\mathbf{Y}$ be represented with T number of clusters as $R_Y = \{(r_1, w_{r_1}), (r_2, w_{r_2}), ... , (r_T, w_{r_T})\}$. Here $\mathbf{p}_s$ and $\mathbf{r}_t$ are the cluster representatives, and w_{p_s} and w_{r_t} are the corresponding cluster weights. The EMD metric between the two examples is based on considering one set of clusters as piles of earth and another set of clusters as holes in the ground, and then finding the least work necessary to fill the holes with the earth in the piles. The EMD between the two sets of clusters P and R is defined as

$$D^{EMD}\left(P_X, R_Y\right) = \frac{\sum_{s=1}^{S}\sum_{t=1}^{T} f_{st} d_{ground}(p_s, r_t)}{\sum_{s=1}^{S}\sum_{t=1}^{T} f_{st}} \quad (86)$$

where $d_{ground}(.)$ denotes a ground distance metric quantifying the distance between the two clusters and $f_{st} \geq 0$ are selected so as to minimize the numerator in (86) subject to the following constraints:

$$\sum_{t=1}^{T} f_{st} \leq w_{p_s} \quad 1 \leq s \leq S$$

$$\sum_{s=1}^{S} f_{st} \leq w_{r_t} \quad 1 \leq t \leq T \quad (87)$$

$$\sum_{s=1}^{S}\sum_{t=1}^{T} f_{st} = \min\left(\sum_{s=1}^{S} w_{p_s}, \sum_{t=1}^{T} w_{r_t}\right)$$

This formulation is solved using a linear programming technique to obtain the EMD between the two sets of clusters P_X and R_Y. In (Jing et al., 2003), a valid kernel is obtained by exponentiating the EMD. The EMD kernel for two sequences $\mathbf{X}$ and $\mathbf{Y}$ is defined as

$$K^{EMD}(X, Y) = e^{-\delta \ D^{EMD}(P_X, R_Y)} \quad (88)$$

where δ is a constant used for numerical stability.

Intermediate Matching Kernel

The intermediate matching kernel (IMK) (Boughorbel et al., 2005) is used for the examples represented as sets of local feature vectors. The core of the IMK is the set of virtual feature vectors. The two sets of local feature vectors are matched using an intermediate set of virtual feature vectors. The role of every virtual feature vector is to select a local feature vector each from the pair of examples to be matched. A kernel is then computed on the selected pairs of local feature vectors. An IMK is computed by adding the kernels obtained from the pair of local feature vectors selected using each virtual feature vector. Consider a pair of examples $\mathbf{X} = \mathbf{x}_1 \mathbf{x}_2 ... \mathbf{x}_M$ and $\mathbf{Y} = \mathbf{y}_1 \mathbf{y}_2 ..., \mathbf{y}_N$ that need to be matched. Let $\mathbf{V} = \{\mathbf{v}_1, \mathbf{v}_2, ..., \mathbf{v}_Q\}$ be the set of virtual feature vectors extracted from the training data of all the classes. The feature vectors in $\mathbf{X}$ and $\mathbf{Y}$ that are closest to $\mathbf{v}_q$ are selected for matching. The measure of closeness is given by Euclidean distance. The feature vectors x_q^* and y_q^* in $\mathbf{X}$ and $\mathbf{Y}$ that are closest to $\mathbf{v}_q$ are obtained as follows:

$$x_q^* = \arg\min_{x \in X} \|x - v_q\| \quad and \quad y_q^* = \arg\min_{y \in Y} \|y - v_q\| \quad (89)$$

A basic kernel $K(x_q^*, y_q^*) = \exp\left(-\delta \|x_q^* - y_q^*\|^2\right)$ is computed for each of the Q pairs of selected local feature vectors. Here δ is a constant scaling term used for numerical stability. An IMK is computed as the sum of all the Q basic kernel values and is given as

$$K^{IMK}(X,Y) = \sum_{q=1}^{Q} K(x_q^*, y_q^*) \qquad (90)$$

In (Boughorbel et al., 2005), the set of the centers of clusters formed from the training data of all classes is considered as the set of virtual feature vectors. It is intuitive that the cluster centers indicate the centers of highly informative regions. The pairs of local feature vectors from a pair of examples that are closest to these centers are selected for building the IMK. A better representation for the set of virtual feature vectors can be provided by considering additional information. In (Dileep & Sekhar, 2011), the set of components of the UBM is used as the set of virtual feature vectors.

Set of Components of UBM as Set of Virtual Feature Vectors:

In this approach, the set of components of the UBM built using the training data of all the classes is used as the set of virtual feature vectors. This representation for the set of virtual feature vectors makes use of the mean vector, covariance matrix, and the mixture coefficient for each component. The UBM is a large GMM of Q components built using the training data of all the classes. The feature vectors from the pair of examples $\mathbf{X}$ and $\mathbf{Y}$ that are closest to the component q are selected for matching. The responsibility term is considered as a measure of closeness of a feature vector to the component q. The responsibility of the component q of UBM for the feature vector $\mathbf{x}$, $\gamma_q(\mathbf{x})$, is given by

$$\gamma_q(x) = \frac{\pi_q N(x|\mu_q, \Sigma_q)}{\sum_{j=1}^{Q} \pi_j N(x|\mu_j, \Sigma_j)} \qquad (91)$$

where π_q is the mixture coefficient of the component q, $N(\mathbf{x}|\boldsymbol{\mu}_q, \boldsymbol{\Sigma}_q)$ is the normal density for the component q with mean $\boldsymbol{\mu}_q$ and covariance $\boldsymbol{\Sigma}_q$. The feature vectors x_q^* and y_q^* in $\mathbf{X}$ and $\mathbf{Y}$ that are closest to the component q of UBM are given by

$$x_q^* = \arg \max_{x \in X} \gamma_q(x) \quad and \quad y_q^* = \arg \max_{y \in Y} \gamma_q(y) \qquad (92)$$

A basic kernel $K(x_q^*, y_q^*) = \exp\left(-\delta \left\| x_q^* - y_q^* \right\|^2\right)$ is computed between every pair of selected feature vectors. An intermediate matching kernel (IMK) is computed as the sum of all the Q basic kernel values as in (90).

Pyramid Match Kernel

In certain cases as in images, the range of values for each of the features is uniformly the same. Let the range be 0 to D. In such cases, each example can be represented by a histogram. For example, pixels in a colour image consist of three colour components, where each colour component has a fixed range 0 to 255. An image can be considered as a set of 3-dimensional feature vectors and represented by colour histogram formed using 3-dimensional bins. In pyramid match kernel (PMK) (Grauman & Darrell, 2007) a set of feature vectors is mapped onto a multiresolution histogram that is also called as a histogram pyramid. The histogram pyramids are then compared by computing a weighted histogram intersection that defines an implicit correspondence between the multiresolution histograms.

In PMK, the feature representation is based on a multiresolution histogram or pyramid, which is computed by binning the feature vector of an example into discrete regions of increasingly larger size. The set of feature vectors $\mathbf{X} = \mathbf{x}_1, \mathbf{x}_2 ..., \mathbf{x}_m, ... \mathbf{x}_M$, $\mathbf{x}_m \in R^d$, is represented as a vector of concatenated histograms, $\mathbf{\Psi}(\mathbf{X}) = [H_0(\mathbf{X})^t, H_1(\mathbf{X})^t, ..., H_{J-1}(\mathbf{X})^t]^t$. The number of levels, J is $\lceil \log_2 D \rceil + 1$ and the resolution of histogram at each level is different.

$H_j(\mathbf{X})$ is the jth histogram vector formed using d-dimensional bins of side 2^j, and $H_j(\mathbf{X})$ has the dimension $r_j = \left(\dfrac{D}{2^j}\right)^d$.

Let $\mathbf{X} = \mathbf{x}_1\mathbf{x}_2\ldots\mathbf{x}_M$ and $\mathbf{Y} = \mathbf{y}_1\mathbf{y}_2\ldots, \mathbf{y}_N$ be the two sets of feature vectors. The similarity between $\mathbf{X}$ and $\mathbf{Y}$ is defined as the weighted sum of the number of matches found at each level of pyramids formed by $\Psi(\mathbf{X})$ and $\Psi(\mathbf{Y})$. Let $H_j^{(i)}(\mathbf{X})$ and $H_j^{(i)}(\mathbf{Y})$ be the number of feature vectors in the ith bin of the histograms $H_j(\mathbf{X})$ and $H_j(\mathbf{Y})$ respectively. The number of matches in the ith bin of the histogram at the level j is obtained as

$$S_j^{(i)} = \min\left(H_j^{(i)}(\mathbf{X}), H_j^{(i)}(\mathbf{Y})\right) \qquad (93)$$

The total number of matches at level j is obtained as

$$S_j = \sum_{i=1}^{r_j} S_j^{(i)} \qquad (94)$$

The number of new matches, A_j at the level j is calculated by computing the difference between the number of matches at levels j and j-1 as follows:

$$A_j = S_j - S_{j-1} \qquad (95)$$

The number of new matches found at each level in the pyramid is weighted according to the size of that histogram bin. The weight at the level j is given by $w_j = \dfrac{1}{d2^j}$. Thus, the PMK for $\mathbf{X}$ and $\mathbf{Y}$ is defined as

$$K^{\mathrm{PMK}}(\mathbf{X},\mathbf{Y}) = \sum_{j=0}^{J-1} w_j A_j \qquad (96)$$

The normalized PMK for two sequences $\mathbf{X}$ and $\mathbf{Y}$ is obtained as

$$\hat{K}^{\mathrm{PMK}}(\mathbf{X},\mathbf{Y}) = \frac{K^{\mathrm{PMK}}(\mathbf{X},\mathbf{Y})}{\sqrt{K^{\mathrm{PMK}}(\mathbf{X},\mathbf{X})}\sqrt{K^{\mathrm{PMK}}(\mathbf{Y},\mathbf{Y})}} \qquad (97)$$

In this section, we presented the different methods for designing dynamic kernels for sequences of continuous feature vectors. The generalized linear discriminant sequence kernel for a pair of patterns is defined by computing the average of polynomial expansions of feature vectors in each pattern as an explicit mapping of that pattern, and then computing the inner product between the explicit mappings of two patterns. This method is computationally intensive when the lengths of pattern are high. Methods for designing the probabilistic sequence kernel, Kullback-Leibler divergence kernel, GMM supervector kernel, Bhattacharyya distance based kernel, and earth movers distance kernel involve building a probabilistic model for each of the sequential patterns. These methods are suitable for long patterns considered as sets of feature vectors. The intermediate matching kernel is designed by matching the feature vectors in two patterns with elements of a set of virtual feature vectors. The choice of a suitable set of virtual feature vector is important in the design of intermediate matching kernel. The pyramid matching kernel is designed by computing the multiresolution histogram representations of two patterns and then matching the histograms at different levels.

In the next section we present a review of kernel method based approaches to sequential pattern analysis.

REVIEW OF KERNEL METHOD BASED APPROACHES TO CLASSIFICATION AND CLUSTERING OF CONTINUOUS FEATURE VECTOR SEQUENCES

A speech utterance, an image, an audio clip, a video clip or time series data such as handwritten character data, sensor recordings in a chemical plant, stock market data, and network traffic data are all represented as sequences of continuous feature vectors. In this section, we present pattern analysis tasks such as classification and clustering of sequence of continuous feature vectors using dynamic kernels.

Sequential pattern analysis tasks such as speaker recognition, speech emotion recognition and spoken language identification involve dynamic kernels on sequences of continuous feature vectors corresponding to speech utterances. Every such continuous feature vector corresponds to features obtained by the spectral analysis of a frame of the speech signal. For all these tasks an example is represented as a set of feature vectors. The task of speaker recognition corresponds to either speaker identification or speaker verification (Campbell et al., 2006a). Speaker identification involves identifying a speaker among a known set of speakers based on the speech utterance produced by the speaker. Speaker verification involves whether to accept or reject the claim of a speaker based on a speech utterance and is used in a voice based authentication system. The GLDS kernel is used for speaker recognition in (Campbell, 2002; Campbell et al., 2006a). The KL-divergence based kernel is used for speaker verification in (Dehak & Chollet, 2006). The GMM supervector kernel was used for speaker verification in (Campbell et al., 2006c,b). Here the distance between the two GMM supervectors is computed as the KL divergence between the respective GMMs. Bhattacharyya distance is an alternative measure of distance between two distributions. The Bhattacharyya distance based kernel is used for speaker recognition in (You et al., 2009b). The continuous feature vectors are transformed using the kernel Fisher discriminant analysis and the Bhattacharyya distance based kernel is used for speaker recognition in (Chao et al., 2005). An approach for speaker verification based on the probabilistic sequence kernel is proposed in (Lee et al., 2007). Dileep and Sekhar

(2011) used the intermediate matching kernel for speaker identification task. Spoken language recognition involves determining the language of an utterance from a set of known languages. Here an utterance is represented as a set of feature vectors. The GLDS kernel (Campbell et al., 2006a) and covariance kernel (Campbell, 2008) are used for language recognition using SVMs. Speech emotion recognition involves identifying the emotion with which a given speech utterance is produced among a set of predefined emotions. The GMM supervector kernel (Campbell et al., 2006c) was used for speech emotion recognition in (Hu et al., 2007). Kernel based clustering was used by Satish (2005) in order to discritize the continuous feature vectors so as to make use of discrete HMMs in the kernel feature space for speech recognition tasks involving the recognition of confusable classes of subword units. A similar approach was also used for a task in handwritten character recognition (Satish, 2005).

Local feature vectors extracted from an image used to represent an image as a set of feature vectors and dynamic kernels are used for tasks such as image retrieval and object detection. In content-based image retrieval (CBIR) all the images in the database that are relevant to a user's query are retrieved. Understanding the user's intention is an issue to be addressed in a CBIR system. In order to address this issue, CBIR systems use the relevance feedback mechanism where the user's intention is understood iteratively based on the feedback provided by the user. Dynamic kernels can be used for matching the query image and the set of images in a database. In the relevance feedback based CBIR system, dynamic kernel based SVMs are used for identifying the relevant and irrelevant images for the query. For example, the EMD kernel based SVM was used in (Jing et al., 2003) for the relevance feedback approach based CBIR. Object recognition is required in a CBIR system in order to obtain a better understanding of the content of an image. Object recognition involves categorizing a given object image or a region in an image to one of the priorly known object categories. An object image or a region in an image is represented using a set of local features. In (Boughorbel et al., 2005), the IMK was used for SVM based object recognition. Multiple resolution features are considered for object recognition using the pyramid match kernel in (Grauman & Darrell, 2005; 2007).

We presented the dynamic kernel based approaches for sequential pattern analysis of speech and image data. The dynamic kernels for sequences of continuous feature vectors presented in this chapter can also be used for variable length multimedia sequence data. The term multimedia refers to the diversity of modalities (for example images, video, text, music, speech) and also to the complex, compound (multimodal) data sets (for example a video with an accompanying sound track and closed caption) (Hanjalic et al., 2008). The KL divergence based kernel was used for SVM based classification of multimedia data in (Moreno et al., 2004).

SUMMARY

In this chapter, we presented a review of approaches to sequential pattern classification and clustering using kernel methods. The focus is on design of suitable kernel functions for different types of sequential patterns. We presented the methods for design of dynamic kernels for sequences of continuous valued feature vectors. Three categories of methods for designing dynamic kernels are as follows: (1) Construct a higher-dimensional representation using an explicit mapping for each of the sequential patterns and then compute an inner product between the higher-dimensional representations, (2) Construct a probabilistic model for distribution of the data of each of the sequential patterns and then compute a kernel function using a measure of similarity between the distributions, (3) Match the sequen-

tial patterns of the different lengths using a fixed size set of virtual feature vectors and construct a kernel using the matching parts of patterns. The generalized linear discriminant sequence kernel and probabilistic sequence kernel for sequences of continuous feature vectors belong to the first category. The GMM supervector kernel, Bhattacharyya distance based kernel and earth mover's distance kernel belong to the second category. The intermediate matching kernel belongs to the third category. Pyramid match kernel matches the multiresolution histograms of sequential patterns. It may be noted that all these dynamic kernels for continuous feature patterns consider a pattern as a set of feature vectors rather than as a sequence of feature vectors. In other words, the sequence information in the patterns is not considered in the method used for design of the dynamic kernel. Fisher kernel for discrete symbol sequences uses the sequence information in the patterns. The score-space kernel (Smith & Gales, 2002) extends the Fisher kernel for sequences of continuous feature vectors. Dynamic kernels for sequences of continuous valued feature vectors have been explored for several tasks speech and audio processing, image processing and video processing. Kernel methods using dynamic kernels have been shown to be effective for sequential patterns analysis in these tasks.

REFERENCES

Allwein, E. L., Schapire, R. E., & Singer, Y. (2001). Reducing multiclass to binary: A unifying approach for margin classifiers. *Journal of Machine Learning Research*, *1*, 113–141. doi:10.1162/15324430152733133

Ben-Hur, A., Horn, D., Siegelmann, H., & Vapnik, V. (2001). Support vector clustering. *Journal of Machine Learning Research*, *2*, 125–137. doi:10.1162/15324430260185565

Bhattacharyya, A. (1943). On a measure of divergence between two statistical populations defined by their probability distributions. *Bulletin of the Calcutta Mathematical Society, 35*, 99–109.

Boughorbel, S., Tarel, J. P., & Boujemaa, N. (2005). The intermediate matching kernel for image local features. In *Proceedings of the International Joint Conference on Neural Networks*, (pp. 889–894). Montreal, Canada.

Burges, C. J. C. (1998). A tutorial on support vector machines for pattern recognition. *Data Mining and Knowledge Discovery, 2*(2), 121–167. doi:10.1023/A:1009715923555

Campbell, W. (2008). A covariance kernel for SVM language recognition. In *Proceedings of International Conference on Acoustics, Speech and Signal Processing, 2008 (ICASSP 2008)*, (pp. 4141–4144). Las Vegas, Nevada, USA.

Campbell, W., Assaleh, K., & Broun, C. (2002). Speaker recognition with polynomial classifiers. *IEEE Transactions on Speech and Audio Processing, 10*(4), 205–212. doi:10.1109/TSA.2002.1011533

Campbell, W., Sturim, D. E., Reynolds, D. A., & Solomonoff, A. (2006c). *SVM based speaker verification using a GMM supervector kernel and NAP variability compensation*. In IEEE International Conference on Acoustics, Speech and Signal Processing, 2006. ICASSP 2006, vol. 1, (pp. 97–100).

Campbell, W. M. (2002). *Generalized linear discriminant sequence kernels for speaker recognition*. In IEEE International Conference on Acoustics, Speech, and Signal Processing, 2002, ICASSP '02, vol. 1, (pp. 161–164). Orlando, Florida, USA.

Campbell, W. M., Campbell, J. P., Reynolds, D. A., Singer, E., & Torres-Carrasquillo, P. A. (2006a). Support vector machines for speaker and language recognition. *Computer Speech &. Language, 20*(2-3), 210–229.

Campbell, W. M., Sturim, D. E., & Reynolds, D. A. (2006b). Support vector machines using GMM supervectors for speaker verification. *IEEE Signal Processing Letters, 13*(5), 308–311. doi:10.1109/LSP.2006.870086

Chao, Y.-H., Wang, H.-M., & Chang, R.-C. (2005). GMM-based Bhattacharyya kernel Fher discriminant analysis for speaker recognition. In *IEEE International Conference on Acoustics, Speech and Signal Processing, 2005, ICASSP 2005*, Vol. 1, (pp. 649–652). Philadelphia, PA, USA.

Cristianini, N., & Shawe-Taylor, J. (2000). *An introduction to support vector machines and other kernel-based learning methods. The Edinburgh building*. Cambridge, UK: Cambridge University Press.

Dehak, N., & Chollet, G. (2006). *Support vector GMMs for speaker verification*. In IEEE Odyssey 2006: The Speaker and Language Recognition Workshop, (pp. 1–4).

Dehak, R., Dehak, N., Kenny, P., & Dumouchel, P. (2007). Linear and non linear kernel GMM supervector machines for speaker verification. In *Proceedings of INTERSPEECH*, (pp. 302–305). Antwerp, Belgium.

Dileep, A. D., & Sekhar, C. C. (2011). Speaker recognition using intermediate matching kernel based support vector machines pairwise classification and support vector machines. In Neustein, A., & Patil, H. (Eds.), *Speaker forensics: New developments in voice technology to combat crime and detect threats to homeland security*.

Girolami, M. (2002). Mercer kernel-based clustering in feature space. *IEEE Transactions on Neural Networks*, *13*(3), 780–784. doi:10.1109/TNN.2002.1000150

Grauman, K., & Darrell, T. (2005). *The pyramid match kernel: Discriminative classification with sets of image features*. In Tenth IEEE International Conference on Computer Vision, 2005. ICCV 2005, vol. 2, (pp. 1458–1465).

Grauman, K., & Darrell, T. (2007). The pyramid match kernel: Efficient learning with sets of features. *Journal of Machine Learning Research*, *8*, 725–760.

Hanjalic, A., Lienhart, R., Ma, W.-Y., & Smith, J. R. (2008). The holy grail of multimedia information retrieval: So close or yet so far away? *Proceedings of the IEEE*, *96*(4), 541–547. doi:10.1109/JPROC.2008.916338

Haykin, S. (1999). *Neural networks: A comprehensive foundation* (2nd ed.). Upper Saddle River, NJ: Prentice-Hall.

Hitchcock, F. L. (1941). The distribution of a product from several sources to numerous localities. *Journal of Mathematics and Physics*, *20*, 224–230.

Hu, H., Xu, M.-X., & Wu, W. (2007). *GMM supervector based SVM with spectral features for speech emotion recognition*. In IEEE International Conference on Acoustics, Speech and Signal Processing, 2007, ICASSP 2007, vol. 4, (pp. 413–416). Honolulu, Hawaii, USA.

Jaakkola, T., Diekhans, M., & Haussler, D. (2000). A discriminative framework for detecting remote protein homologies. *Journal of Computational Biology*, *7*(1-2), 95–114. doi:10.1089/10665270050081405

Jing, F., Li, M., Zhang, H.-J., & Zhang, B. (2003). Support vector machines for region-based image retrieval. In *Proceedings of the 2003 International Conference on Multimedia and Expo*, (pp. 21–24). Washington DC, USA.

Kailath, T. (1967). The divergence and Bhattacharyya distance measures in signal selection. *IEEE Transactions on Communication Technology*, *15*(1), 52–60. doi:10.1109/TCOM.1967.1089532

Kaufman, L. (1999). Solving the quadratic programming problem arising in support vector classification. In Scholkopf, B., Burges, C., & Smola, A. (Eds.), *Advances in kernel methods: Support vector learning* (pp. 147–167). Cambridge, MA: MIT Press.

Kondor, R., & Jebara, T. (2003). A kernel between sets of vectors. In *Proceedings of International Conference on Machine Learning, (ICML 2003)*. Washington DC, USA.

Kressel, U. H.-G. (1999). Pairwise classification and support vector machines. In Scholkopf, B., Burges, C., & Smola, A. (Eds.), *Advances in kernel methods: Support vector learning* (pp. 255–268). Cambridge, MA: MIT Press.

Kullback, S., & Leibler, R. A. (1951). On information and sufficiency. *Annals of Mathematical Statistics*, *22*(1), 79–86. doi:10.1214/aoms/1177729694

Lee, K.-A., You, C. H., Li, H., & Kinnunen, T. (2007). A GMM-based probabilistic sequence kernel for speaker verification. In *Proceedings of INTERSPEECH*, (pp. 294–297). Antwerp, Belgium.

Moreno, P. J., Ho, P. P., & Vasconcelos, N. (2004). A Kullback-Leibler divergence based kernel for SVM classification in multimedia applications. In Thrun, S., Saul, L., & Schölkopf, B. (Eds.), *Advances in Neural Information Processing Systems 16*. Cambridge, MA: MIT Press.

Reynolds, D. A., Quatieri, T. F., & Dunn, R. B. (2000). Speaker verification using adapted Gaussian mixture models. *Digital Signal Processing*, *10*(1-3), 19–41. doi:10.1006/dspr.1999.0361

Rubner, Y., Tomasi, C., & Guibas, L. J. (2000). The earth mover's distance as a metric for image retrieval. *International Journal of Computer Vision, 40*(2), 99–121. doi:10.1023/A:1026543900054

Satish, D. S. (2005). *Kernel based clustering and vector quantization for pattern classification*. Master of Science thesis, Indian Institute of Technology Madras, Chennai.

Scholkopf, B., Mika, S., Burges, C., Knirsch, P., Muller, K.-R., Ratsch, G., & Smola, A. (1999). Input space versus feature space in kernel-based methods. *IEEE Transactions on Neural Networks, 10*(5), 1000–1017. doi:10.1109/72.788641

Sekhar, C. C., Takeda, K., & Itakura, F. (2003). Recognition of subword units of speech using support vector machines. In *Recent research developments in electronics and communication* (pp. 101–136). Trivandrum, Kerala, India: Transworld Research Network.

Shawe-Taylor, J., & Cristianini, N. (2004). *Kernel methods for pattern analysis*. Cambridge, UK: Cambridge University Press. doi:10.1017/CBO9780511809682

Smith, N., & Gales, M. (2002). Speech recognition using SVMs. In *Proceedings of the 2002 Conference on Advances in Neural Information Processing Systems*, (pp. 1197–1204). Cambridge, MA: MIT Press.

Wan, V., & Renals, S. (2002). Evaluation of kernel methods for speaker verification and identification. In *Proceedings of IEEE International Conference on Acoustics, Speech and Signal Processing*, (pp. 669-672). Orlando, Florida, US.

You, C. H., Lee, K. A., & Li, H. (2009a). A GMM supervector kernel with the Bhattacharyya distance for SVM based speaker recognition. In *Proceedings of IEEE International Conference on Acoustics, Speech and Signal Processing*, (pp. 4221–4224). Taipei, Taiwan.

You, C. H., Lee, K. A., & Li, H. (2009b). An SVM kernel with GMM-supervector based on the Bhattacharyya distance for speaker recognition. *IEEE Signal Processing Letters, 16*(1), 49–52. doi:10.1109/LSP.2008.2006711

Chapter 3
A Review of Kernel Methods Based Approaches to Classification and Clustering of Sequential Patterns, Part II:
Sequences of Discrete Symbols

Veena T.
Indian Institute of Technology, India

Dileep A. D.
Indian Institute of Technology, India

C. Chandra Sekhar
Indian Institute of Technology, India

ABSTRACT

Pattern analysis tasks on sequences of discrete symbols are important for pattern discovery in bioinformatics, text analysis, speech processing, and handwritten character recognition. Discrete symbols may correspond to amino acids or nucleotides in biological sequence analysis, characters in text analysis, and codebook indices in processing of speech and handwritten character data. The main issues in kernel methods based approaches to pattern analysis tasks on discrete symbol sequences are related to defining a measure of similarity between sequences of discrete symbols, and handling the varying length nature of sequences. We present a review of methods to design dynamic kernels for sequences of discrete symbols. We then present a review of approaches to classification and clustering of sequences of discrete symbols using the dynamic kernel based methods.

DOI: 10.4018/978-1-61350-056-9.ch003

INTRODUCTION

Kernel methods for pattern classification and clustering were presented in the previous chapter. We also explained the design of dynamic kernels for sequences of continuous feature vectors. In this chapter, we present a review on the design of dynamic kernels for discrete symbol sequences.

A discrete symbol sequence comprises of a sequence of symbols, belonging to an alphabet $\sum$, observed or recorded during a process. For example, in coin tossing experiment, the observations being either head (H) or tail (T) may result in a discrete observation sequence $HHTHTTH$. Here the alphabet $\sum$ is a set of two symbols $\{H, T\}$ and the length of the observation sequence is seven. The discrete observation sequence obtained in another coin tossing experiment may be $THHHTTHHT$ resulting in a sequence of different length. One major issue in handling discrete symbol sequences is that the observation sequences are of varying length in nature. This applies to any sequence data. A major source of discrete symbol sequences is the biological sequences such as protein sequences, DNA sequences and RNA sequences. The DNA sequences are strings over four nucleotides, represented by the alphabet $\sum=\{A,C,G,T\}$. The RNA sequences are strings over the alphabet $\sum=\{A,C,G,U\}$. The symbols in the alphabet for DNA and RNA correspond to the following nucleotides: A(adenine), C(cytosine), G(guanine), T(thymine), and U(uracil). The positions of occurrence of these nucleotides in the chain molecule of DNA or RNA signify the functioning of that DNA or RNA. An example DNA sequence of length 50 is *ATAATAAAAAATAAAAATA-AAAAAAATTAAAAAATATTAAAAAATAAAAA*. Protein sequences are strings over an alphabet of 20 amino acids which are the building blocks of proteins. The kinds of amino acids occurring, their frequency of occurrence and their relative positions of occurrence in a protein sequence influence the functionality of a protein. An example of a protein sequence is *MGTPTLAQPVVTGM-*

FLDPCH. Discrete symbol sequences are also used to analyze text data.

A paragraph is considered as a sequence of words. In text analysis, words are the observation symbols derived from a vocabulary of all the words. Discrete observation sequences are also derived by vector quantization of the continuous feature vector sequences extracted from speech data and online handwritten character data. Pattern analysis tasks involving discrete symbol sequences are classification and clustering. In order to use kernel methods for these tasks, it is necessary to address the issue of handling the varying length nature of sequences. In some approaches, an explicit feature map (Ding & Dubchak, 2001; Jaakkola et al., 2000; Leslie et al., 2002; Leslie & Kuang, 2003; Liao & Noble, 2002; Lodhi et al., 2002; Logan et al., 2001) is used to obtain a fixed length representation for each of the varying length sequences. In some other approaches, a kernel is designed directly from the varying length sequences (Saigo et al., 2004; Tsuda et al., 2002; Vert et al., 2004; Watkins, 1999). Kernels designed using any of these two methods are called as dynamic kernels for discrete symbol sequences.

The organization of the rest of the chapter is as follows: The next section describes the methods for the design of dynamic kernels for discrete symbol sequences. Then a review of kernel methods based approaches to sequential pattern analysis involving discrete symbol sequences is presented.

DESIGN OF DYNAMIC KERNELS FOR DISCRETE SYMBOL SEQUENCES

The main issue in designing a kernel for discrete observation symbol sequence is to handle the varying length nature of the sequences. The varying length sequences of discrete observation symbols may be explicitly mapped onto a fixed dimensional feature vector and then the kernel is computed as an innerproduct in that fixed dimensional space.

Instead of obtaining an explicit feature map, kernel between a pair of discrete symbol sequences can also be computed implicitly either by defining a function or an operation between the pair of sequences. In this section we present the design of various dynamic kernels for discrete symbol sequences.

Consider two discrete symbol sequences, $\mathbf{P} = p_1 p_2 \cdots p_m \cdots p_M$ and $\mathbf{Q} = q_1 q_2 \cdots q_n \cdots q_N$ of lengths M and N respectively defined over an alphabet Σ. A dynamic kernel between the sequences

$\mathbf{P}$ and $\mathbf{Q}$ is defined as

$$K(\mathbf{P},\mathbf{Q}) = \langle \Phi(\mathbf{P}), \Phi(\mathbf{Q}) \rangle \qquad (1)$$

Where $\Phi(\mathbf{P})$ and $\Phi(\mathbf{Q})$ correspond to an implicit or explicit feature map for $\mathbf{P}$ and $\mathbf{Q}$ respectively and $\langle .,. \rangle$ denotes the inner product operation. The kernel function $K(\mathbf{P},\mathbf{Q})$ represents a measure of similarity between the two sequences. For example, in Figure 1, the feature map $\Phi(.)$ maps variable length sequences of symbols to points in a fixed dimensional space. The transformation is expected to increase the discrimination between the families of sequences. In this section, we present the feature maps $\Phi(.)$ designed for different dynamic kernels.

Pairwise Comparison Kernel

A common task involving discrete symbol sequences is to assign a sequence to a family of sequences.

For example, protein homology detection process involves understanding the structure and functionality of an unannotated protein and assigning it to a family of proteins whose structure is known and with which the given protein is similar. This requires detecting similarities among sequences. Pairwise comparison kernel (Liao & Noble, 2002; 2003) uses an empirical feature map that maps a discrete symbol sequence to a fixed dimension vector of pairwise similarity scores. Empirical feature map (Tsuda, 1998) involves representing an object by measures of its similarity to the reference objects. The empirical feature map used by the pairwise comparison kernel represents a sequence by a set of scores indicating how similar the sequence is to the reference sequences.

Let $\mathbf{P} = p_1 p_2 \cdots p_m \cdots p_M$ be a discrete observation sequence. Let $P = \{\mathbf{P}_1, \mathbf{P}_2, \ldots, \mathbf{P}_r, \ldots, \mathbf{P}_R\}$ be the set of reference sequences used for mapping. Pairwise comparison score based feature map for $\mathbf{P}$ is given by $\Phi^{\text{pair-comparison}}(\mathbf{P}) = \left(\varphi_r(P) \right)_{r=1}^{R}$ (2)

Figure 1. Illustration of a feature map for variable length sequences

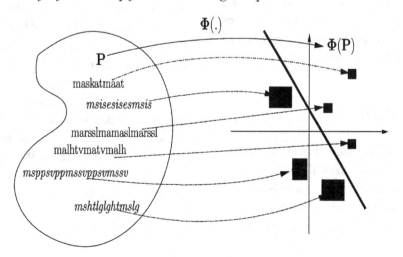

Where $\varphi_r(\mathbf{P})$ denotes the similarity score between the sequence $\mathbf{P}$ and the reference sequence $\mathbf{P}_r$. The similarity score $\varphi_r(\mathbf{P})$ is computed using any of the string similarity metrics such as, edit distance based measures, city block distance, Needleman-Wunsch algorithm (Needleman & Wunsch, 1970), or Smith-Waterman dynamic programming algorithm (Smith & Waterman, 1981). In (Liao & Noble, 2002; 2003), Smith-Waterman dynamic programming algorithm is used for computing the similarity between two sequences. Pairwise comparison kernel for two sequences $\mathbf{P}$ and $\mathbf{Q}$ using this empirical feature map is defined as

$$K^{\text{pair-comparison}}(\mathbf{P},\mathbf{Q})= \left\langle \Phi^{pair-comparison}(P), \Phi^{pair-comparison}(Q) \right\rangle \quad (3)$$

The pairwise comparison score based feature map uses the information present in various families of sequences. It differs from the other aggregate statistics based approaches such as profiles (Gribskov et al., 1990) and hidden Markov models (HMMs) (Baldi et al., 1994, Krogh et al., 1994) in that it captures the discriminatory information between the families of sequences. The discriminatory information between the families of sequences was also considered in the Fisher score based feature map (Jaakkola et al., 1999, 2000). This involves modeling the aggregate statistics for a family of sequences by training a HMM. Pairwise comparison score based feature map is simpler when compared to the Fisher score based feature map because it does not need training of HMMs.

Composition Kernel

A composition kernel defines a feature map of a sequence that characterizes the composition of various discrete observation symbols or their properties. The feature map is defined as

$$\Phi^{\text{composition}}(\mathbf{P})=(\varphi_r(\mathbf{P}))_{p\epsilon\Sigma} \quad (4)$$

where $\varphi_r(\mathbf{P})$ is the number of occurrences of the symbol p in the sequence $\mathbf{P}$. For example, a feature map for a protein sequence may be a 20-dimensional vector that contains the frequency of occurrence of each amino acid. For a protein sequence $\mathbf{P}=MGTPTLAQPVVTGMFLDPCHTWTVM$, the feature map $\Phi^{\text{composition}}(\mathbf{P})$ is $[1\ 1\ 1\ 0\ 1\ 2\ 1\ 0\ 0\ 2\ 3\ 0\ 3\ 1\ 0\ 0\ 5\ 3\ 1\ 0]^T$. Significant amount of information present in the sequence is neglected in the composition feature map of (4). The composition feature map of (4) can be enhanced by appending additional features as follows:

$$\Phi^{\text{composition}}(\mathbf{P})=\left(\varphi_r(\mathbf{P})\right)_{p\epsilon\Sigma}, \left(\left(\varphi_s(P)\right)_{s=1}^{m}\right) \quad (5)$$

where $\left(\varphi_s(P)\right)_{s=1}^{m}$ correspond to m features representing the structural or physico-chemical or sequence information. In (Ding & Dubchak, 2001), $\left(\varphi_s(P)\right)_{s=1}^{m}$ comprises of 5 sets of features related to structural and physico-chemical properties of the amino acids present in a given protein sequence. The 5 sets of features with 21 features in each set contain the information about the following: (1) predicted secondary structure, (2) hydrophobicity, (3) normalized van der Waals volume, (4) polarity, and (5) polarizability. A protein sequence is mapped onto a 125-dimensional feature vector consisting of 5 sets of features along with the 20 compositional features. In (Wang et al., 2004; Zhang et al., 2003), sequence information is used as the m features. Every amino acid symbol in the protein sequence is represented by a numerical index so as to obtain a numerical sequence, $\mathbf{H}=h_1 h_2 \dots h_n \dots h_N$ corresponding to the discrete symbol sequence $\mathbf{P}=p_1 p_2 \dots p_n \dots p_N$. An autocorrelation function defined as follows is used to obtain the m features:

$$r_j = \frac{1}{N-j} \sum_{i=1}^{N-j} h_i h_{i+j} \qquad j = 1,2,\cdots,m$$

$$(6)$$

The composition kernel for two sequences **P** and **Q** is given by

$$K^{composition}(P,Q) = \left\langle \Phi^{composition}(P), \Phi^{composition}(Q) \right\rangle$$

$$(7)$$

The composition kernel that uses the feature maps corresponding to the frequencies of occurrence of symbols and sequencing information is called as physico-chemical kernel in (Zhang et al., 2003). In the next subsection, we describe the spectrum kernel for strings defined as a composition kernel based on substrings.

Spectrum Kernel

Spectrum kernel is a string kernel based on the sequence similarity. The sequence similarity is computed using k-mers that correspond to substrings of k contiguous symbols occurring in a sequence. Figure 2 illustrates all possible 3-mers for a given sequence.

The similarity score for two sequences is related to the number of common k-mers. The k-spectrum of a sequence is defined as the set of all possible k-length substrings in the sequence (Les-

lie et al., 2002). The feature map based on k-mers for a sequence is given by

$$\Phi_k^{spectrum}(P) = (\varphi_u(P))_{u \in \Sigma^k}$$

$$(8)$$

where $\varphi_u(P)$ is the frequency of occurrence of a k-mer **u** in **P**. The spectrum kernel for two sequences **P** and **Q** is computed as

$$K_k^{spectrum}(P,Q) = \left\langle \Phi_k^{spectrum}(P), \Phi_k^{spectrum}(Q) \right\rangle \qquad (9)$$

The computation of spectrum kernel function between two given sequences is illustrated in Figure 3.

The k-spectrum feature map, $\Phi_k^{spectrum}(P)$, results in a high dimensional sparse feature vector. For example, when $k = 5$ and the size of the alphabet is 20, each feature vector consists of 5^{20} elements. However, the spectrum kernel can be computed implicitly using data structures such as trie or suffix trees, without obtaining an explicit feature map. The k-spectrum feature map proposed in (Leslie et al., 2002) considers an equal weight for every k-mer. Weighted sum of k-mers is proposed in (Vishwanathan & Smola, 2003) that uses different weights for different k-mers. Spectrum kernel computes a measure of similarity between the sequences by considering the exact match between the k-mers. Many problems involving the sequence similarity computation need to consider some amount of mismatch between the

Figure 2. The k-mers and their frequencies of occurrence for a given sequence using k = 3

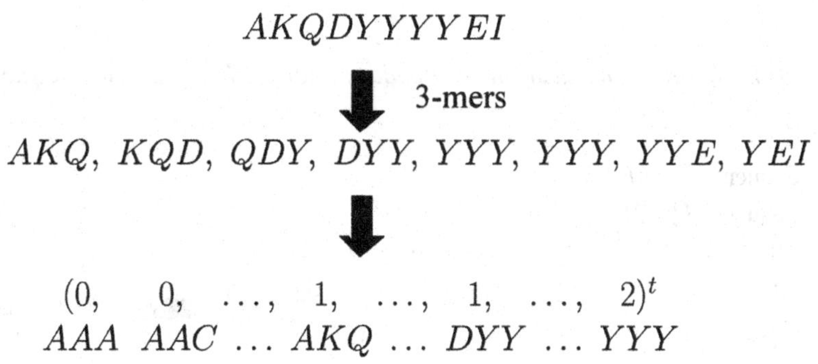

$$AKQDYYYYEI$$

⬇ 3-mers

$$AKQ, \; KQD, \; QDY, \; DYY, \; YYY, \; YYY, \; YYE, \; YEI$$

⬇

$$(0, \quad 0, \quad \ldots, \quad 1, \quad \ldots, \quad 1, \quad \ldots, \quad 2)^t$$
$$AAA \quad AAC \; \ldots \; AKQ \; \ldots \; DYY \; \ldots \; YYY$$

Figure 3. Illustration of computing the spectrum kernel function between two sequences for k = 2

Sequence P: *ABAAC*
Sequence Q: *CBACACA*

2-mers:	AA	AB	AC	BA	BB	BC	CA	CB	CC	
$\Phi_2^{spectrum}(P)$	1	1	1	1	0	0	0	0	0	$\Longrightarrow K_2^{spectrum}(P, Q) = 3$
$\Phi_2^{spectrum}(Q)$	0	0	2	1	0	0	2	1	0	

k-mers of the two sequences. For example, in molecular biology, proteins of a family may not match exactly due to mutations. With some extent of mismatch tolerated, all of them are considered to be similar and belonging to the same family. In the next subsection, we describe the mismatch kernel to compute a measure of similarity between sequences when there are some mismatches.

Mismatch Kernel

Mismatch kernel is a generalization of a spectrum kernel. The value of the spectrum kernel function computed between a pair of sequences is high when many common *k*-mers are present in both the sequences. This notion is generalized in the mismatch kernel (Leslie et al., 2003; 2004). If there are many number of *k*-length substrings that mismatch by at most *l* symbols and occur commonly between a pair of sequences, then the measure of similarity between them is high. For example, consider a 5-mer *VTWTA* that would match with the sequences such as *VTATA*, *VCWTA*, or *VTWTK* when *l* = 1. For a given *k*-mer, all the *k*-length substrings that differ from it by at most *l* symbols form a (*k*, *l*) neighborhood for the *k*-mer.

For a *k*-mer, $\mathbf{u} = u_1 u_2 \dots u_k$, the (*k*, *l*) neighborhood is the set of all *k*-length subsequences $\mathbf{v} \in \Sigma^k$ that mismatch from $\mathbf{u}$ by at most *l* symbols. For a *k*-mer $\mathbf{u}$, the feature map is defined as

$$\Psi_{(k,l)}^{mismatch}(u) = \left(\Psi_v(u) \right)_{v \in \Sigma^k} \tag{10}$$

where $\Psi_v(\mathbf{u}) = 1$ if $\mathbf{v}$ belongs to the (*k*, *l*) neighborhood of $\mathbf{u}$ and $\Psi_v(\mathbf{u}) = 0$ otherwise. Mismatch feature map for a sequence $\mathbf{P}$ is obtained by summing the feature vectors from the feature maps of all the *k*-mers as given below:

$$\Phi_{(k,l)}^{mismatch}(\mathbf{P}) = \sum_{\mathbf{u} \in \mathbf{P}} \Psi_{(k,l)}^{mismatch}(\mathbf{u}) \tag{11}$$

The (*k*, *l*) mismatch kernel for two sequences $\mathbf{P}$ and $\mathbf{Q}$ is computed as

$$K_{(k,l)}^{mismatch}(P, Q) = \left\langle \Phi_{(k,l)}^{mismatch}(P), \Phi_{(k,l)}^{mismatch}(Q) \right\rangle \tag{12}$$

An illustration of computation of the mismatch kernel between two sequences is given in Figure 4.

Figure 4. An illustration for the computation of mismatch kernel between two sequences P and Q for k = 3 and l = 1

Sequence P: *ABAABAA*
Sequence Q: *BBABABA*

3-mers:	AAA	AAB	ABA	ABB	BAA	BAB	BBA	BBB	
$\Phi_{(3,1)}^{mismatch}(P)$	5	1	2	2	2	3	2	0	$\Longrightarrow K_{(3,1)}^{mismatch}(P, Q) = 37$
$\Phi_{(3,1)}^{mismatch}(Q)$	2	1	3	2	2	2	3	3	

A specific case of mismatch kernel when $l = 0$ is the spectrum kernel. The mismatch feature map proposed in (Leslie et al., 2003;2004) is extended using other kinds of inexact string matching that involve restricted gaps (restricted gappy kernel), probabilistic substitutions (substitution kernel) or wildcards (wildcard kernel) in (Leslie & Kuang, 2003). Explicit mismatch feature map involves considering all possible k-mers and results in high dimensional feature vectors. However, the mismatch kernel function between the two sequences, $K_{(k,l)}^{\text{mismatch}}(P,Q)$, can be computed implicitly using data structures like tries.

String Subsequence Kernel or Gappy N-Gram Kernel

String kernels such as spectrum kernel and mismatch kernels consider two sequences to be similar if they share many common substrings, where a substring is a contiguous sequence of symbols. In this section, we present a string kernel that considers two sequences to be similar when they have many common subsequences, where a subsequence is a non-contiguous sequence of symbols. For example, the pattern *car* occurs as a subsequence in both the sequences *card* and *custard*. The string subsequence feature map (Lodhi et al., 2002) maps a string into a feature vector whose dimension is equal to the number of all possible subsequences of a particular length. However, in order to compensate for the non-continuities while matching, a decay factor $\lambda \in (0,1)$ is used to weigh each feature.

Given an alphabet Σ, a string $\mathbf{P}$ is a finite length sequence of symbols from Σ denoted by

$\mathbf{P} = p_1 p_2 \ldots p_{|\mathbf{P}|}$, where $|\mathbf{P}|$ is the length of the string $\mathbf{P}$. Then a subsequence $\mathbf{u}$ of $\mathbf{P}$ is defined as follows: $\mathbf{u}$ is a subsequence of $\mathbf{P}$, if there exist indices $\mathbf{i} = (i_1, i_2, \ldots, i_{|\mathbf{u}|})$, with $1 \leq i_1 \leq \ldots \leq i_{|\mathbf{u}|} \leq |\mathbf{P}|$, such that $u_j = \mathbf{P}_{i_j}$, for $j = 1, 2, \ldots, |\mathbf{u}|$, or $\mathbf{u} = \mathbf{P}[\mathbf{i}]$. The length $l(\mathbf{i})$ of the subsequence in $\mathbf{P}$ is $i_{|\mathbf{u}|} - i_1 + 1$ The set of all strings of length k is denoted by Σ^k. The string subsequence feature map is defined as

$$\Phi_k^{\text{subsequence}}(P) = (\varphi_u(P))_{u \in \Sigma^k} \tag{13}$$

where $\varphi_u(P)$ is given by

$$\varphi_u(P) = \sum_{i:u=P[i]} \lambda^{l(i)} \tag{14}$$

The subsequence kernel for two sequences $\mathbf{P}$ and $\mathbf{Q}$ is given by,

$$\begin{aligned} K_k^{\text{subsequence}}(P,Q) &= \left\langle \Phi_k^{\text{subsequence}}(\mathbf{P}), \Phi_k^{\text{subsequence}}(\mathbf{Q}) \right\rangle \\ &= \sum_{u \in \Sigma^k} \left\langle \varphi_u(P), \varphi_u(Q) \right\rangle \\ &= \sum_{u \in \Sigma^k} \sum_{i:u=P[i]} \sum_{j:u=Q[j]} \lambda^{l(i)+l(j)} \end{aligned}$$

$$(15)$$

For example, the two sequences *DIARY* and *DAILY* are mapped onto a 15-dimensional feature space by considering the subsequences of length 2 as shown in Table 1.

It is seen that the features are weighted by a decay factor proportional to the length of the subsequences. For example for the feature *DA*, the weight used for the string *DIARY* is λ^3, whereas for the string *DAILY*, the weight factor is λ^2. The value of subsequence kernel between the two sequences *DIARY* and *DAILY* for $k = 2$

Table 1.

	DL	DI	DA	DR	DY	IA	IR	IY	IL	AR	AY	AL	AI	RY	LY
$\Phi_2^{\text{subsequence}}(DIARY)$	0	λ^2	λ^3	λ^4	λ^5	λ^2	λ^3	λ^4	0	λ^2	λ^3	0	0	λ^2	0
$\Phi_2^{\text{subsequence}}(DAILY)$	λ^4	λ^3	λ^2	0	λ^5	0	0	λ^3	λ^2	0	λ^4	λ^3	λ^2	0	λ^2

is, $K_2^{\text{subsequence}}(DIARY,DAILY)=2\lambda^{5+2}\lambda^7+\lambda^{10}$. String subsequence kernel was proposed as a measure of similarity between two text documents. The text documents are considered as long sequences of words. This representation is better than the bag-of-words representation (Salton et al. 1975), where the sequential information between the words in the text document is neglected. String subsequence kernel for two sequences is computed as the inner product between the explicit feature maps corresponding to the two sequences. Since the explicit feature map results in a high dimensional feature vector, whose dimension is given by the total number of k-mers possible for a given alphabet, computation of the kernel function becomes impractical even for small values of k. However, the kernel formulation is shown to be of recursive nature in (Lodhi et al., 2002), so that the dynamic programming based approaches can be used for efficient computation.

Term Frequency Log Likelihood Ratio Kernel

The string kernels such as spectrum kernel and subsequence kernel map a discrete symbol sequence onto a feature space corresponding to the frequency of occurrence of certain patterns like k-mers or subsequences of length k. In case of term frequency log likelihood ratio based feature map, probabilities of occurrence of k-mers are considered (Campbell et al., 2004a,b; 2007). Given a sequence $\mathbf{P}=p_1 p_2...p_n...p_N$, let the K k-mers occurring in $\mathbf{P}$ be denoted as $u_1^P, u_2^P,...,u_k^P$. For example, given the sequence $ABCABC$, the 2-mers in the sequence are given by AB, BC, CA, AB, BC. Let the unique k-mers occurring in a corpus be $\mathbf{u}_j$, $j=1,2,...,D$. Here the corpus comprises of all the sequences available in the training data set. Let L denote the total number of k-mers occurring in the corpus. The probability of observing a k-mer $\mathbf{u}_j$ in a sequence $\mathbf{P}$ is given by

$$p(\mathbf{u}_j|\mathbf{P})=\frac{n_j^P}{K} \tag{16}$$

where n_j^P is the frequency of occurrence of $\mathbf{u}_j$ in $\mathbf{P}$. The probability of occurrence of $\mathbf{u}_j$ in the corpus is given by

$$p(\mathbf{u}_j)=\frac{n_j}{L} \tag{17}$$

where n_j is the frequency of occurrence of $\mathbf{u}_j$ in the corpus. The feature map used by the term frequency log likelihood ratio (TFLLR) kernel is given by

$$\Psi_k^{TFLLR}(P) = \left(p(u_j|P)\right)_{j=1}^{D} \tag{18}$$

The elements of the feature vector in (18) correspond to the term frequencies. Here 'term' refers to a k-mer. In order to normalize the elements of the feature vector in (18), every element in the feature vector is weighted using the corresponding term frequencies in the corpus. This is explained below along with the description of the TFLLR kernel.

The TFLLR kernel considers a sequence $\mathbf{P}$ to be similar to a sequence $\mathbf{Q}$ if the probability of occurrence of k-mers of $\mathbf{P}$ in $\mathbf{Q}$ is high. The probability of occurrence of the k-mers of $\mathbf{P}$ in $\mathbf{Q}$ is computed using the likelihood ratio given below:

$$\text{Likelihood ratio score} = \prod_{i=1}^{K} \frac{p(u_i^P|Q)}{p(u_i^P)} \tag{19}$$

where $p(\mathbf{u}_i^P|\mathbf{Q})$ denotes the probability of a k-mer of $\mathbf{P}$, u_i^P also occurring in $\mathbf{Q}$. The TFLLR kernel is obtained by considering the log of the likelihood ratio (19) and normalizing it by the number of observations in $\mathbf{P}$ as follows:

$$K_k^{TFLLR}(P,Q) = \frac{1}{K} \sum_{i=1}^{K} \log \frac{p(u_i^P | Q)}{p(u_i^P)} \qquad (20)$$

Expressing in terms of unique k-mers in the corpus, the TFLLR kernel function can be written as

$$K_k^{TFLLR}(P,Q) = \sum_{j=1}^{D} \frac{n_j^P}{K} \log \frac{p(u_j | Q)}{p(u_j)} \qquad (21)$$

From (16) it follows that

$$K_k^{TFLLR}(P,Q) = \sum_{j=1}^{D} p(u_j | P) \log \frac{p(u_j | Q)}{p(u_j)} \qquad (22)$$

Linearizing the log function in (22) using $\log(x) \approx x - 1$,

$$
\begin{aligned}
K_k^{TFLLR}(P,Q) &\approx \sum_{j=1}^{D} p(u_j | P) \frac{p(u_j | Q)}{p(u_j)} - \sum_{j=1}^{D} p(u_j | P) \\
&= \sum_{j=1}^{D} p(u_j | P) \frac{p(u_j | Q)}{p(u_j)} - 1 \\
&= \sum_{j=1}^{D} \frac{p(u_j | P)}{\sqrt{p(u_j)}} \frac{p(u_j | Q)}{\sqrt{p(u_j)}} - 1
\end{aligned}
\qquad (23)
$$

From (23) it is seen that the elements of the feature vector in (18) are weighted using the factor $1/\sqrt{p(u_j)}$. Hence the TFLLR feature map is

$$\Phi_k^{TFLLR}(P) = \left(\varphi_j(P) \right)_{j=1}^{D} \qquad (24)$$

where $\varphi_j(P) = \dfrac{p(u_j | P)}{\sqrt{p(u_j)}}$. The TFLLR kernel between two sequences **P** and **Q** is computed as

$$K_k^{TFLLR}(P,Q) = \left\langle \Phi_k^{TFLLR}(P), \Phi_k^{TFLLR}(Q) \right\rangle. \qquad (25)$$

Motif Kernels

Pattern analysis tasks involving discrete symbol sequences need to compute a measure of similarity between two sequences. Kernels such as pairwise comparison kernel, composition kernel, spectrum kernel, subsequence kernel and TFLLR kernel compute a measure of similarity by considering common patterns in the two sequences. However, there are situations where the pattern analysis tasks need to be carried out even when the sequences have low similarity or share only a few common patterns. In molecular biology, remote homology detection involves protein homology detection even when the sequence similarities are low. Though the sequences are globally dissimilar, certain portions in protein sequences that represent the information regarding the protein's functionality are found to be similar in homologous proteins. These highly conserved regions in protein sequences that are functionally important are known as motifs. Protein sequence motifs are used to compute a measure of similarity between protein sequences. Protein sequences that share many number of motifs are considered as similar sequences. Motifs are constructed from multiple sequence alignments of related sequences. Motifs can be represented as discrete sequence motifs (Ben-Hur & Brutlag, 2003) or position specific scoring matrices (PSSMs) (Logan et al., 2001). Given a protein sequence, substrings of the same length as that of the motifs called 'blocks' are considered and are scored against the set of all available motifs.

A discrete sequence motif is defined as follows. A motif is a sequence of elements where an element is a symbol in the alphabet Σ, or a substitution group, or a wild card character *. A substitution group is a subset of Σ. For example, consider the motif **m** = $[AS$ $]$ $*DKF[FILMV]$

**[FILMV] ***L[AS T], with length $|\mathbf{m}|$ =14. Here [AS], [FILMV], and [AS T] are substitution groups. A sequence $\mathbf{P} = p_1 p_2 ... p_N$ is said to contain a motif $\mathbf{m} = m_1 m_2 ... m_{|\mathbf{m}|}$ at a position i, if one of the following properties is satisfied for every $j = 1, 2, ..., |\mathbf{m}|$:

1. $p_{i+j-1} = m_j$, if $m_j \in \Sigma$
2. $p_{i+j-1} \in S$, if $m_j \in S$, where S is a substitution group
3. $p_{i+j-1} \in \Sigma$ if $m_j = *$

An illustration of a discrete sequence motif of length 14 is shown in Figure 5 along with four protein blocks of the same length which are compared with the motif. The first two blocks $\mathbf{b}_1$ and $\mathbf{b}_2$ match with the motif whereas the blocks $\mathbf{b}_3$ and $\mathbf{b}_4$ do not match with the motif. The elements in blocks $\mathbf{b}_3$ and $\mathbf{b}_4$ that do not match with the corresponding elements in $\mathbf{m}$ are shown in bold.

A sequence $\mathbf{P}$ is mapped onto the fixed dimension motif feature space as

$$\Phi^{motif}(P) = \left(\varphi_m(P) \right)_{m \in M} \tag{26}$$

where M is the set of all motifs and $\varphi_m(\mathbf{P})$ is the frequency of occurrence of the motif $\mathbf{m}$ in $\mathbf{P}$. Motif kernel for two sequences $\mathbf{P}$ and $\mathbf{Q}$ is defined as

$$K^{motif}(P,Q) = \left\langle \Phi^{motif}(P), \Phi^{motif}(Q) \right\rangle \tag{27}$$

A motif can also be represented as a position specific scoring matrix (PSSM) (Logan et al.

2001). The PSSMs are used to map the sequences onto the motif feature space. A motif is represented by a $T \times L$ matrix, $\mathbf{M}_{PSSM}$, where each of the T rows corresponds to a symbol from the alphabet. For protein motifs, each of the T rows corresponds to an amino acid. Here L corresponds to the length of the motif and a column corresponds to a position in the motif. An element in the matrix $\mathbf{M}_{PSSM}(a_t, pos_l)$ represents the probability of occurrence of tth amino acid, a_t, at l^{th} position, pos_l, in the motif.

As a large number of motifs are considered, the dimension of motif feature vector space is high. Motif kernel computation between two sequences involves computation of inner product between such high dimensional feature vectors, that is computationally intensive. However, the motif kernel can be computed implicitly by storing the motifs in data structures such as tries.

Marginalised Kernels

String kernels such as spectrum kernel, mismatch kernel and subsequence kernel consider the frequency of occurrence of certain patterns called k-mers in a given sequence to obtain a measure of similarity between two sequences. The composition kernel uses such frequency based features to obtain a measure of similarity between sequences. Instead of using the frequency of occurrence based features, term frequency log likelihood ratio kernel considers the probability of occurrence of a pattern for mapping a sequence to a fixed dimension feature vector. However, none of these approaches for feature mapping consider the context information associated with the sym-

Figure 5. Matching a discrete sequence motif with four protein blocks

	i	$i+1$	$i+2$	$i+3$	$i+4$	$i+5$	$i+6$	$i+7$	$i+8$	$i+9$	$i+10$	$i+11$	$i+12$	$i+13$
Elements of a motif $\mathbf{m}$:	[AS]	*	D	K	F	[FILMV]	*	*	[FILMV]	*	*	*	L	[AST]
Protein blocks														
$\mathbf{b}_1$:	A	A	D	K	F	L	I	F	M	A	A	A	L	T
$\mathbf{b}_2$:	S	V	D	K	F	V	A	V	I	T	S	A	L	S
$\mathbf{b}_3$:	D	A	D	K	F	V	A	F	L	M	M	V	L	T
$\mathbf{b}_4$:	A	A	**K**	**F**	**D**	F	L	L	M	A	S	T	L	S

bols in the sequence. The context information corresponds to the circumstances under which a discrete symbol is observed. Some discrete symbols observed in two different contexts may have different meanings. For example, consider the following two text sentences where words are the discrete observation symbols: 'I purchased a book' and 'I am planning to book a ticket'. The word 'book' has a different meaning depending on the context of its appearance. For processing text sequences, say in text classification, considering the context information is useful. Biological sequences such as DNA sequences are also context sensitive. The DNA sequences have coding and noncoding regions that have different statistical properties. A particular residue occurring in a coding region has a different meaning when it occurs in a non-coding region. The coding and non-coding regions provide the context information that is hidden from the discrete observation symbols. In a generative perspective, we can consider an observation symbol being emitted by a hidden state corresponding to the context. Figure 6 shows a discrete symbol sequence **P** and the corresponding hidden state sequence **H** with the states representing the coding and non-coding regions of DNA.

Marginalized kernels (Tsuda et al. 2002) consider the context information in the form of the hidden state information for computing a measure of similarity between sequences. First, a joint kernel is defined as a measure of similarity between sequences assuming that the hidden state sequence is available. However, the information about hidden state sequence is not available. The marginalized kernel takes the expectation of the joint

kernel with respect to the hidden state sequence. The posterior distribution of the hidden state sequence is estimated using the probabilistic models such as HMMs.

Let $\mathbf{P} = p_1 p_2 \ldots p_n \ldots p_N$ and $\mathbf{Q} = q_1 q_2 \ldots q_m \ldots q_M$ be two sequences on an alphabet Σ. Let $\mathbf{H_P} = h_1 h_2 \ldots h_n \ldots h_N$ and $\mathbf{H_Q} = h_1 h_2 \ldots h_m \ldots h_M$ be the corresponding sequences of hidden states. Here, h_i corresponds to a hidden state such that $h_i \in H$, where H is the set of hidden states. A combined sequence $\mathbf{Z_P}$ can be written as, $\mathbf{Z_P} = z_1 z_2 \ldots z_n \ldots z_N = \{p_1, h_1\} \{p_2, h_2\} \ldots \{p_n, h_n\} \ldots \{p_N, h_N\}$. The hidden state sequence information is used in defining the joint kernel $K^{\text{joint}}(\mathbf{Z_P}, \mathbf{Z_Q})$. The marginalized kernel is derived from the joint kernel by taking the expectation with respect to hidden state sequence as follows:

$$K^{\text{marginalized}}(Z_P, Z_Q) = \sum_{H_P} \sum_{H_Q} p(H_P | P) p(H_Q | Q) K^{\text{joint}}(Z_P, Z_Q) \qquad (28)$$

The posterior distribution, $p(\mathbf{H_P}|\mathbf{P})$, is estimated using the probabilistic models such as HMMs. An important example of a marginalized kernel is the marginalized count kernel that incorporates the context information into a count kernel. Given the two sequences **P** and **Q**, a count kernel is defined as

$$K^{\text{count}}(P,Q) = \sum_{k \in \Sigma} C_k(\mathbf{P}) C_k(\mathbf{Q}) \qquad (29)$$

where $C_k(\mathbf{P})$ is the frequency of occurrence of the symbol k in the sequence **P**, normalized by the length of the sequence. The count kernel is extended to the combined sequences $\mathbf{Z_P}$ and $\mathbf{Z_Q}$ as

Figure 6. Illustration of a biological sequence with context information in the form of hidden states corresponding to coding (1) and non-coding (2) regions

H: 1   2   2   1   2   2   1   2   2

P: *A   C   G   G   T   T   C   A   A*

$$K_{combined}^{count}(Z_P, Z_Q) = \sum_{k \in \Sigma} \sum_{l \in H} C_{kl}(Z_P) C_{kl}(Z_Q)$$

$$(30)$$

where $C_{kl}(\mathbf{Z_P})$ is the number of instances in which a discrete observation symbol k is observed by being in the state l. The marginalized count kernel is derived from the joint count kernel as

$$K^{marginalized-count}(P,Q) = \sum_{k \in \Sigma} \sum_{l \in H} \psi_{kl}(P) \psi_{kl}(Q) \quad (31)$$

where $\psi_{kl}(P) = \sum_{H_P} p(H_P|P) C_{kl}(Z_P)$. If HMMs are used to model the distribution of the sequences, then the posterior probability of the hidden state sequence $p(\mathbf{H_p}|\mathbf{P})$ is computed in an efficient manner using the forward-backward algorithm. The marginalized count kernel enhances the count kernels by considering the context information. However, the adjacency relationships between symbols are totally ignored while computing the measure of similarity between the sequences. In order to consider the adjacency relationships between the symbols, the second order marginalized count kernels are proposed in (Tsuda et al., 2002). It is also shown that the Fisher kernel (Jaakkola et al., 2000) is a special case of marginalized kernel. In the next subsection, we present the Fisher kernel.

Fisher Kernel

Fisher kernel (Jaakkola et al., 2000) for discrete symbol sequences is designed using a global discrete hidden Markov model (DHMM) built using the training examples of all the classes. Let the set of parameters of the global DHMM be θ. Let the number of parameters of the global DHMM be R. The log-likelihood of a discrete symbol sequence $\mathbf{P}$ is given by

$$L_\theta(P) = \ln p(P|\theta) \quad (32)$$

where $p(\mathbf{P}|\boldsymbol{\theta})$, the probability of the global DHMM generating the discrete symbol sequence $\mathbf{P}$, is computed using the forward method or the backward method (Rabiner & Juang, 1993). The Fisher score vector corresponds to the gradient vector of the log-likelihood and is given by

$$g_\theta(P) = \left(\frac{\partial \mathcal{L}_\theta(P)}{\partial \theta_i} \right)_{i=1}^R \quad (33)$$

The Fisher information matrix I_θ is given by

$$I_\theta = \frac{1}{L} \sum_{l=1}^L \left(g_\theta(P_l) \right) \left(g_\theta(P_l) \right)^t \quad (34)$$

where L is the number of training examples used to build the global DHMM.

The Fisher kernel for two sequences of discrete symbols, $\mathbf{P}$ and $\mathbf{Q}$ is given by

$$K^{Fisher}(\mathbf{P}, \mathbf{Q}) = \left(g_\theta(\mathbf{P}) \right)^t \mathbf{I}_\theta^{-1} \left(g_\theta(\mathbf{Q}) \right) \quad (35)$$

Pair HMM Kernel

A pair hidden Markov model (pHMM) (Watkins, 1999) shown in Figure 7 is an HMM that generates two symbol sequences, $\mathbf{P}$ and $\mathbf{Q}$, simultaneously. The two sequences need not be of the same length.

A pHMM consists of a set of states $\mathbf{S}$ comprising of four subsets of states, a START state and an END state. The subset $\mathbf{S^{PQ}}$ includes the states that emit two symbols simultaneously, one for the sequence $\mathbf{P}$ and one for the sequence $\mathbf{Q}$. The subsets $\mathbf{S^P}$ and $\mathbf{S^Q}$ include the states that emit one symbol only for the sequences $\mathbf{P}$ and $\mathbf{Q}$ respectively. The subset $\mathbf{S^{-1}}$ includes the states that emit no symbols. The pHMM defines a joint probability distribution over pairs of discrete symbol sequences of finite length. The joint probability $p(\mathbf{P},\mathbf{Q})$ of two sequences, $\mathbf{P}$ and $\mathbf{Q}$, is related to the score obtained by global alignment of two

Figure 7. Pair hidden Markov model (pHMM) for generation of two sequences **P** *and* **Q** *simultaneously*

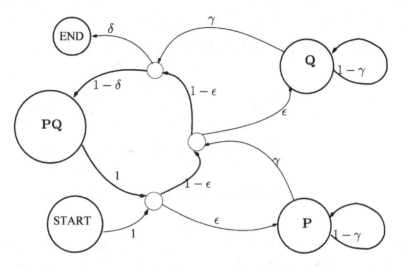

sequences (Haussler, 1999; Needleman & Wunsch, 1970; Watkins, 1999). Haussler (1999) showed that the joint probability $p(\mathbf{P},\mathbf{Q})$ obtained using a pHMM corresponds to the value of a valid string kernel. However, the joint probability values obtained are too small to be considered as the kernel function values. In situations where a family of sequences may not get aligned globally and still they have some localized similarity, global alignment based schemes such as pHMM may be of little use. For example, homologous proteins may have little global similarity. In such cases, local similarity measures like Smith-Waterman score (Smith & Waterman, 1981) are useful. In the next subsection, we present a convolution kernel that uses the local alignment between sequences.

Local Alignment Kernel

Local alignment kernel is based on alignment of sequences and is obtained by convolving simple kernels. Haussler (1999) has shown that convolution of two string kernels is a string kernel. Given two string kernel functions, K_1 and K_2, the convolution of the two kernels, $K_1 * K_2$, is given as

$$K(\mathrm{P},\mathrm{Q}) = K_1 * K_2 = \sum_{\mathrm{P}_1.\mathrm{P}_2=\mathbf{P},\,\mathrm{Q}_1.\mathrm{Q}_2=\mathbf{Q}} K_1(\mathrm{P}_1,\mathrm{Q}_1)$$
$$K_2(\mathrm{P}_2,\mathrm{Q}_2) \tag{36}$$

where $\mathbf{P}_1.\mathbf{P}_2$ denotes the concatenation of two substrings $\mathbf{P}_1$ and $\mathbf{P}_2$ to form the string $\mathbf{P}$. A string can be expressed as a concatenation of two strings in many ways. For example the string *S EQUENCE* can be expressed as *S EQ.UENCE, S EQU.ENCE, S E.QUENCE, S EQUEN.CE*, etc. While computing the kernel function in (36), all the possible ways of concatenation are considered in the summation. Given any two sequences **P** and **Q**, an alignment (with gaps) π of $n \geq 0$ positions between them is specified by a pair of n-tuples (Vert et al. 2004):

$$\pi = \left(\left(\pi_P(1), \cdots, \pi_P(n) \right), \left(\pi_Q(1), \cdots, \pi_Q(n) \right) \right) \tag{37}$$

that satisfies

$$1 \leq \pi_P(1) < \pi_P(2) < \cdots < \pi_P(n) \leq |P|$$

$$1 \leq \pi_Q(1) < \pi_Q(2) < \cdots < \pi_Q(n) \leq |Q|$$

Figure 8. Illustration for one possible alignment of two sequences **P** *and* **Q**

Sequence **P**: $GCGCATGGATTGAGCGAB$

Sequence **Q**: $TGCGCCATTGATGACCA$

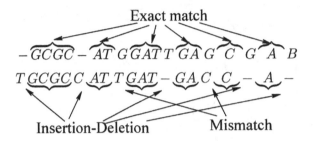

where $|\mathbf{P}|$ and $|\mathbf{Q}|$ are the lenghts of sequences **P** and **Q** respectively. An example for one possible alignment for two sequences is shown in Figure 8. The alignment can be represented as a pair of 15-tuples as $\pi=((\pi_\mathbf{P}),(\pi_\mathbf{Q}))$, where $\pi_\mathbf{P} = (1, 2, 3, 4, 5, 6, 7, 8, 9, 10, 12, 13, 14, 15, 17)$ and $\pi_\mathbf{Q} =$

$(2, 3, 4, 5, 7, 8, 9, 10, 11, 12, 13, 14, 15, 16, 17)$.

It is seen that the symbols in the two sequences get aligned either to exactly match or to have mismatches. It is also seen that some insertions or deletions are required in order to align the two sequences. Few possible alignments between two sequences *HAWGEG* and *AGEHV* are given in Figure 9. It is seen that the number of symbols aligned varies from one alignment to another. It is also seen that for the same number of symbols aligned, the combination of the alignment varies.

For a given alignment of *n* symbols between two sequences **P** and **Q**, the local alignment kernel is defined as the convolution of three basic kernels, $K_0(\mathbf{P},\mathbf{Q})$, $K_{ai}^{\beta}(P,Q)$, and $K_{gi}^{\beta}(P,Q)$ as shown in Figure 10. The first basic kernel is defined as

$$K_0(P,Q)=1 \tag{38}$$

It is used to compare the parts of the two sequences that do not contribute to the local align-

ment. The other two basic kernels, $K_{ai}^{\beta}(P,Q)$, and $K_{gi}^{\beta}(P,Q)$ are used to compute a measure of similarity between the *n* symbols aligned with possible gaps. For every aligned position π (*i*), for $i = 1,..., n$, the kernel $K_{ai}^{\beta}(P,Q)$ is defined as

$$K_{ai}^{\beta}(P,Q) = e^{\beta S\left(P\left(\pi_P(i)\right), Q\left(\pi_Q(i)\right)\right)} \tag{39}$$

where $P(\pi_\mathbf{p}(i))$ indicates the ith aligned symbol in **P**, $\beta \geq 0$ is a parameter whose value decides the positive definiteness of the kernel matrix and **S**

Figure 9. Illustration of multiple alignments between two sequences

Sequence **P**:	*HAWGEG*	
Sequence **Q**:	*AGEHV*	
π^1	$AWGE$ $A - GE$	$|\pi^1| = 3$
π^2	$AWGE$ $AG - E$	$|\pi^2| = 3$
π^3	$HAWGE$ $A - G - E$	$|\pi^1| = 3$
π^4	$HAWGE - G$ $A - GEHV-$	$|\pi^1| = 4$

Figure 10. Illustration of the computation of the local alignment kernel for two sequences

Sequence **P**: $GCGCATGGATTGAGCGAB$

Sequence **Q**: $TGCGCCATTGATGACCA$

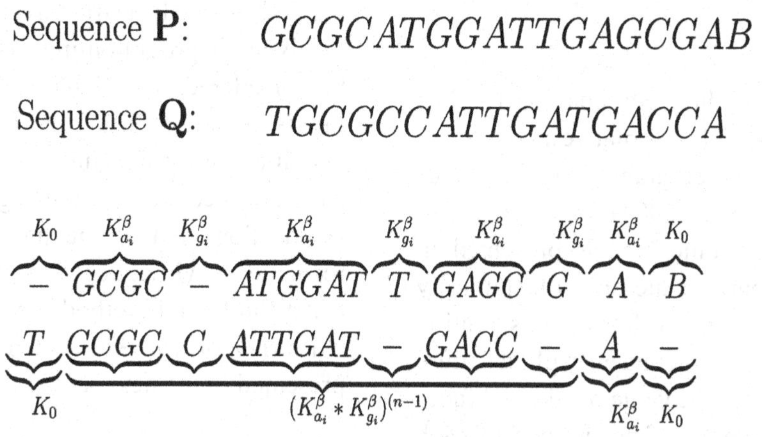

is the substitution matrix. Substitution matrix contains values proportional to the probability that a symbol in one sequence possibly gets substituted to the same or another symbol in the other sequence in order to get aligned with the other sequence. Substitution matrices are constructed by assessing a large and diverse sample of verified pairwise alignments of sequences. A substitution matrix used for protein sequence alignments is of size 20×20. The elements of the matrix denote the probability of one amino acid mutating to another amino acid. Though some of the amino acids mutate, the two proteins remain homologous.

In order to consider the possible gaps between the n aligned symbols, the kernel $K_{gi}^{\beta}(P,Q)$ is defined as

$$K_{gi}^{\beta}(P,Q) = e^{\beta\left(g\left(\pi_P(i+1)-\pi_P(i)\right)+g\left(\pi_Q(i+1)-\pi_Q(i)\right)\right)} \quad (40)$$

where g: N → R is a gap penalty function such that $g(0) = 0$. The gap penalty function may be a regular gap penalty function that adds a constant penalty for every insertion or deletion operation, or an affine gap penalty function given as $g(l) = d + e(l-1)$. Here l indicates the length of the gap, d indicates a gap opening cost and e indicates the gap extension cost. Affine gap penalty increases the kernel value when there are extended gaps rather than having multiple fragments of gaps.

For an alignment of n symbols between the sequences, **P** and **Q**, a kernel is obtained by convolving the three basic kernels, $K_0(\mathbf{P},\mathbf{Q})$, $K_{ai}^{\beta}(P,Q)$ and $K_{gi}^{\beta}(P,Q)$ as Equation 41 in Box 1.

This kernel gives a measure of similarity between the two sequences **P** and **Q** when n symbols are exactly aligned. The convolution operation sums up the contribution of all possible decompositions of the sequences **P** and **Q** or all possible alignments of **P** and **Q**. In order to consider alignments of different number of symbols as shown in Figure 9, the local alignment kernel for two sequences, **P** and **Q** is defined as

Box 1.

$$K_n^{\beta}(P,Q) = K_0(P,Q) * \left(K_{ai}^{\beta}(P,Q) * K_{gi}^{\beta}(P,Q)\right)^{(n-1)} K_0(P,Q) * \left(K_{ai}^{\beta}(P,Q) * K_{gi}^{\beta}(P,Q)\right)^{(n-1)} \quad (41)$$

$$K_\beta^{local-alignment}(P,Q) = \sum_{i=0}^{\infty} K_i^\beta(P,Q) \qquad (42)$$

The complexity of direct computation of (42) is exponential in $|\mathbf{P}|$ and $|\mathbf{Q}|$. Alternative methods that make use of dynamic programming approaches are proposed (Vert et al., 2004).

Each of the dynamic kernels presented in this section computes a measure of similarity between two sequences of discrete observation symbols either by constructing an explicit feature map or by computing the value of a kernel function directly. Frequency of occurrence of each of groups of symbols such as k-mers is used to construct the feature map in the spectrum kernel, the composition kernel, the mismatch kernel, and the subsequence kernel. The mismatch kernel differs from the spectrum kernel in that, it tolerates mismatches between sequences. The subsequence kernel is based on the subsequences present in the sequences, with the non-continuities penalized using appropriate decay factors. The pairwise comparison kernel uses an empirical feature map for mapping a sequence onto a fixed dimensional feature vector. Each element of the feature vector corresponds to the similarity of the given sequence to one of the reference sequences. The TFLLR kernel uses the probabilities of occurrence of k-mers in the sequences. If the probability of k-mers from one sequence occurring in the other sequence is high, then the measure of similarity between the two sequences computed using the TFLLR kernel is high. The pair HMM kernel gives a high value of a measure of similarity between two sequences, if their joint probability computed using a pair HMM is high. In biological sequences, it is common that the two sequences that may not be similar globally, may still belong to the same family of sequences. The two sequences may have same locally conserved regions that are similar. These characteristics of sequences are used in the motif kernel and the local alignment kernel. Although the computation is intensive for many

dynamic kernels presented in this section, faster methods using data structures such as tries or using dynamic programming based techniques can be considered. The dynamic kernels presented in this section are used for tasks such as protein classification, protein function prediction, protein structure prediction, text categorization, speaker verification, and online handwritten character recognition. A brief description of the approaches using the kernel methods for classification and clustering of sequences of discrete symbols is presented in the next section.

REVIEW OF KERNEL METHODS BASED APPROACHES TO CLASSIFICATION AND CLUSTERING OF DISCRETE SEQUENCES

Various kinds of discrete symbol sequences are biological sequences (for example proteins, DNA, RNA etc.), text data and the sequences obtained from tokenizing the continuous feature vector sequences extracted from speech signal data or handwritten character data. In this section we present approaches used for classification of discrete symbol sequences using the dynamic kernels.

Protein sequences are strings over an alphabet of 20 symbols that correspond to the amino acids which are the building blocks of proteins. Dynamic kernels are used for pattern analysis tasks such as protein classification, protein function prediction and protein structure prediction. Protein classification involves assigning an unannotated protein sequence to a category of proteins based on the sequence similarity between a pair of sequences. Spectrum feature map was used to map an unannotated protein sequence to a fixed dimension feature vector, in (Leslie et al., 2002). Since exact sequence similarity is very rare to occur in biological sequences like proteins, some degree of mismatch was tolerated in the feature map of (Leslie et al., 2003; 2004). The mismatches tolerated in biological sequences correspond to the mutations happening in the cell. The notion of mismatch was extended to restricted gaps, substitutions and wildcard characters in (Leslie & Kuang, 2003). The composition feature map involving frequency of occurrence of the amino acids as well as the autocorrelation coefficients is used in (Wang et al., 2004) to predict the type of the membrane proteins. Protein function prediction involves detecting the functionality of any unannotated protein by analyzing their amino acid sequences. Protein homology prediction is a process of detecting the functionality of a protein where the given protein sequence is compared with a family of protein sequences of known functionality. Difficulty in homology prediction is that there is less similarity between the sequences in terms of overall composition. However, the proteins in a family might have been generated from a common source and undergone multiple mutation cycles. The common functionality exhibited by the proteins in a family despite the differences in sequence similarities may be attributed to the remote source of common origin in the evolutionary hierarchy. Protein homology prediction is appropriately called as remote homology prediction. A dynamic kernel based on Fisher feature map was used for remote homology prediction by Jaakkola et al. (1999; 2000). Here, the statistical distribution of the protein sequences of a family is modeled using a HMM and the gradient of the log likelihood of an unannotated protein sequence in the HMM parameter space gives the Fisher feature map. The dimension of the feature vector is equal to the number of parameters of the HMM. The Fisher kernel needs a HMM to be trained for each family of proteins in order to obtain the statistics of that family. Liao ans Noble (2002; 2003) used the pairwise comparison kernel for remote homology prediction by mapping a protein sequence onto a fixed dimension feature vector of pairwise similarity scores of the sequence with a set of reference protein sequences. The set of reference protein sequences consists of protein sequences belonging to all the known families.

A 125-dimensional feature vector consisting of both the amino acid composition as well as the physico-chemical properties of the protein sequence is used for protein function prediction in (Cai et al., 2003). Though there is less global similarity between the sequences in a family of proteins with common functionality, there are certain regions in the sequences that are similar which correspond to the common functionality. These locally conserved regions of protein sequences are used as protein sequence motifs by Ben-Hur and Brutlag (2003) and Logan et al. (2001). Blocks of an unannotated protein sequence are matched against every motif in the set of motifs to verify the presence of a motif and the protein sequence is mapped onto a fixed dimensional feature vector of frequency of occurrence of motifs. Local sequence similarities among a family of proteins are utilized in the local lignment kernel (Saigo et al., 2004; Vert et al., 2004) for remote homology prediction. Protein structure prediction involves predicting the protein fold structure or quaternary structure of proteins using only the primary sequence. Structure prediction helps in predicting the functionality, understanding the cellular function, and discovery of new drugs and therapies. It is found that structurally similar proteins have less sequence similarities. However, considerable information regarding the structure is available in the primary sequence. Composition kernel was used in (Ding & Dubchak, 2001; Hua & Sun, 2001; Park & Kanehisa, 2003; Zhang et al., 2003) for protein structure prediction. Classification of bacterial gyrB amino acid sequence is carried out using marginalised kernel in (Tsuda et al., 2002). Spectrum and motif kernels were used to predict protein-protein interactions by Ben-Hur and Noble (2005). Understanding such interactions is useful to learn the functionality of proteins as proteins perform their functions by interacting with the other proteins.

Text data comprises of a sequence of words belonging to a language. Dynamic kernels are used for categorizing text documents and identification of the language of the written text. For categorizing text documents, Lodhi et al. (2002) considered a text document as a long sequence of symbols by concatenating the words in their order of occurrence. A sequence corresponding to a document is mapped onto a fixed dimension feature vector using the string subsequence feature map and classified using a SVM based classifier. Language of the text is identified using the spectrum kernel in (Kruengkrai et al., 2005). Every text is represented as a string of bytes and the spectrum kernel is computed using suffix trees.

The TFLLR kernel is used for speaker verification in (Campbell et al., 2004*a,b*, 2007; Stoicke et al. 2008). Speaker verification involves either to accept or reject the claim made by a speaker based an utterance given by the speaker. The speech signal of an utterance is first converted into a sequence of tokens such as words or phonemes. The sequence of tokens is classified using the TFLLR kernel based SVM classifier. The sequence corresponding to the speech signal of an utterance is tokenized in order to make use of high-level features like idiolects. This corresponds to the observation that every speaker has an unique way of language usage in terms of the words used and the order in which the words are used.

Online handwritten character recognition (OHCR) refers to the task of identifying characters in a script. A stroke based OHCR for an Indian language script, Telugu, is proposed in (Jayaraman, 2008). A character is written as a sequence of strokes, where a stroke is defined as the trajectory of pen from a pen-down event to a pen-up event. The number of strokes is different for different characters. A stroke is represented as a sequence of discrete symbols corresponding to the structural or segmental features, resulting in a varying length representation. An SVM based classification approach is used to classify a stroke to a known category using the string subsequence kernel. A character is recognized as combination of strokes using ternary search trees (TSTs). Time series data corresponding to measurements done

in a chemical process is tokenized and classified using the pHMM kernel and the string subsequence kernel in (Ruping, 2001).

CONCLUSION

In this chapter, we presented a review on the design of dynamic kernels for the sequences of discrete observation symbols. The focus is on design of suitable kernel functions for different kinds of discrete symbol sequences. Two categories of methods for designing dynamic kernels for discrete symbol sequences are as follows: (1) Construct a higher-dimensional representation using an explicit mapping for each of the discrete symbol sequences and then compute an innerproduct between the higher-dimensional representations, (2) Compute the kernel function without explicitly mapping the discrete symbol sequences onto higher-dimensional feature space. Most of the dynamic kernels presented in this chapter such as, the pairwise comparison kernel, the composition kernel, the spectrum kernel, the mismatch kernel, the string subsequence kernel, and the motif kernel belong to the first category. Instead of explicitly mapping the discrete symbol sequence onto a higher-dimensional feature space, the TFLLR kernel is computed based on the probability of occurrence of the features of one discrete symbol sequence in the other discrete symbol sequence. All these dynamic kernels for discrete symbol sequences do not consider the sequence information. The local alignment kernel, the pair HMM kernel, the marginalized kernel, and the Fisher kernel consider the sequence information. In addition to the sequence information, the marginalized kernel also considers the context information. The Fisher kernel is a special case of the marginalized kernel. Dynamic kernels for sequences of discrete symbols have been explored for several tasks in bioinformatics, text analysis, speaker verification, and handwritten character recognition. Kernel methods using dynamic kernels have been shown to be effective for sequential patterns analysis in these tasks.

REFERENCES

Baldi, P., Chauvin, Y., Hunkapiller, T., & McClure, M. A. (1994). Hidden Markov models of biological primary sequence information. *Proceedings of the National Academy of Sciences of the United States of America, 91*(3), 1059–1063. doi:10.1073/pnas.91.3.1059

Ben-Hur, A., & Brutlag, D. (2003). Remote homology detection: A motif based approach. *Bioinformatics (Oxford, England), 19*, i26–i33. doi:10.1093/bioinformatics/btg1002

Ben-Hur, A., & Noble, W. S. (2005). Kernel methods for predicting protein-protein interactions. *Bioinformatics (Oxford, England), 21*(1), i38–i46. doi:10.1093/bioinformatics/bti1016

Cai, C. Z., Wang, W. L., Sun, L. Z., & Chen, Y. Z. (2003). Protein function classification via support vector machine approach. *Mathematical Biosciences, 185*(1), 111–122. doi:10.1016/S0025-5564(03)00096-8

Campbell, W. M., Campbell, J. P., Gleason, T. P., Reynolds, D. A., & Shen, W. (2007). Speaker verification using support vector machines and high-level features. *IEEE Transactions on Audio Speech and Language Processing, 15*(7), 2085–2094. doi:10.1109/TASL.2007.902874

Campbell, W. M., Campbell, J. P., Reynolds, D. A., Jones, D. A., & Leek, T. R. (2004a). *High-level speaker verification with support vector machines*. In IEEE International Conference on Acoustics, Speech, and Signal Processing, vol. 1, (pp. I–73–76). Montreal, Quebec, Canada.

Campbell, W. M., Campbell, J. P., Reynolds, D. A., Jones, D. A., & Leek, T. R. (2004b). Phonetic speaker recognition with support vector machines. In *Advances in neural information processing systems*, (pp. 1377–1384). Vancouver, Canada.

Ding, C. H. Q., & Dubchak, I. (2001). Multi-class protein fold recognition using support vector machines and neural networks. *Bioinformatics (Oxford, England), 17*(4), 349–358. doi:10.1093/bioinformatics/17.4.349

Gribskov, M., Luthy, R., & Eisenberg, D. (1990). Profile analysis. *Methods in Enzymology, 183*, 146–159. doi:10.1016/0076-6879(90)83011-W

Haussler, D. (1999). *Convolution kernels on discrete structures* (Tech. Rep. No.UCSC-CRL-99-10). University of California at Santa Cruz: Department of Computer Science.

Hua, S., & Sun, Z. (2001). A novel method of protein secondary structure prediction with high segment overlap measure: Support vector machine approach. *Journal of Molecular Biology, 308*, 397–407. doi:10.1006/jmbi.2001.4580

Jaakkola, T., Diekhans, M., & Haussler, D. (1999). *Using the Fisher kernel method to detect remote protein homologies*. In Seventh International Conference on Intelligent Systems for Molecular Biology, (pp. 149–158). Menlo Park, CA.

Jaakkola, T., Diekhans, M., & Haussler, D. (2000). A discriminative framework for detecting remote protein homologies. *Journal of Computational Biology, 7*(1-2), 95–114. doi:10.1089/10665270050081405

Jayaraman, A. (2008). *Modular approach to online handwritten character recognition of Telugu script*. Master's thesis, Department of CSE, IIT Madras, Chennai-36.

Krogh, A., Brown, M., Mian, I. S., Sjolander, K., & Haussler, D. (1994). Hidden Markov models in computational biology: Applications to protein modeling. *Journal of Molecular Biology, 235*, 1501–1531. doi:10.1006/jmbi.1994.1104

Kruengkrai, C., Srichaivattana, P., Sornlertlamvanich, V., & Isahara, H. (2005). *Language identification based on string kernels*. In IEEE International Symposium on Communications and Information Technology, 2005. ISCIT 2005., vol. 2, (pp. 926–929).

Leslie, C., Eskin, E., Cohen, A., Weston, J., & Noble, W. S. (2004). Mismatch string kernels for discriminative protein classification. *Bioinformatics (Oxford, England), 20*, 467–476. doi:10.1093/bioinformatics/btg431

Leslie, C., Eskin, E., & Noble, W. S. (2002). The spectrum kernel: A string kernel for SVM protein classification. In The Pacific Symposium on Biocomputing, (pp. 564–575). River Edge, NJ.

Leslie, C., Eskin, E., Weston, J., & Noble, W. S. (2003). Mismatch string kernels for SVM protein classification. In Becker, S., Thrun, S., & Obermayer, K. (Eds.), *Advances in neural information processing* (pp. 1417–1424). Cambridge, MA: MIT Press.

Leslie, C., & Kuang, R. (2003). Fast kernels for inexact string matching. In B. Scholkopf & M. Warmth (Ed.), *16th Annual Conference on Learning Theory and 7th Annual Workshop on Kernel Machines*, vol. 2777, (pp. 114–128). Heidelberg, Germany: Springer Verlag

Liao, L., & Noble, W. S. (2002). *Combining pairwise sequence similarity and support vector machines for remote protein homology detection*. In Sixth Annual International Conference on Computational Molecular Biology, (pp. 225–232). Washington, DC, USA.

Liao, L., & Noble, W. S. (2003). Combining pairwise sequence similarity and support vector machines for detecting remote protein evolutionary and structural relationships. *Journal of Computational Biology, 10*(6), 857–868. doi:10.1089/106652703322756113

Lodhi, H., Saunders, C., Shawe-Taylor, J., Christianini, N., & Watkins, C. (2002). Text classification using string kernels. *Journal of Machine Learning Research, 2*, 419–444. doi:10.1162/153244302760200687

Logan, B., Moreno, P., Suzek, B., Weng, Z., & Kasif, S. (2001). *A study of remote homology detection (Tech. Rep. No. CRL 2001/05)*. Cambridge, MA: Compaq Computer Corporation, Cambridge Research Laboratory.

Needleman, S. B., & Wunsch, C. D. (1970). A general method applicable to the search for similarities in the amino acid sequences of two proteins. *Journal of Molecular Biology, 48*, 443–453. doi:10.1016/0022-2836(70)90057-4

Park, K.-J., & Kanehisa, M. (2003). Prediction of protein sub-cellular locations by support vector machines using compositions of amino acids and amino acid pairs. *Bioinformatics (Oxford, England), 19*(13), 1656–1663. doi:10.1093/bioinformatics/btg222

Rabiner, L., & Juang, B.-H. (1993). *Fundamentals of speech recognition*. United States: Prentice Hall.

Ruping, S. (2001). SVM kernels for time series analysis. In Klinkenberg, R., Ruping, S., Fick, A., Henze, N., Horzog, C., Molitor, R., & Schroder, O. (Eds.), *LLWA 01-Tagungsband der G1-Workshop-Woche Lemen-Lehren Wissen-Adaptivitet* (pp. 43–50).

Saigo, H., Vert, J.-P., Ueda, N., & Akutsu, T. (2004). Protein homology detection using string alignment kernels. *Bioinformatics (Oxford, England), 20*(11), 1682–1689. doi:10.1093/bioinformatics/bth141

Salton, G., Wong, A., & Yang, C. (1975). A vector space model for automatic indexing. *Communications of the ACM, 18*(11), 613–620. doi:10.1145/361219.361220

Smith, N., & Gales, M. (2002). Speech recognition using SVMs. In *Proceedings of the 2002 Conference on Advances in Neural Information Processing Systems*, (pp. 1197–1204). Cambridge, MA: MIT Press.

Smith, T. F., & Waterman, M. S. (1981). Identification of common molecular subsequences. *Journal of Molecular Biology, 147,* 195–197. doi:10.1016/0022-2836(81)90087-5

Stoicke, A., Kajarekar, S., & Ferrer, L. (2008). *Nonparametric feature normalization for SVM-based speaker verification.* In IEEE International Conference on Acoustics, Speech, and Signal Processing 2008, ICASSP 2008, (pp. 1577–1580). Las Vegas, NV.

Tsuda, K. (1998). *Support vector classifier with asymmetric kernel functions.* In European Symposium on Artificial Neural Networks, (pp. 183–188). Bruges, Belgium.

Tsuda, K., Kin, T., & Asai, K. (2002). Mariginalized kernels for biological sequences. *Bioinformatics (Oxford, England), 18,* S268–S275. doi:10.1093/bioinformatics/18.suppl_1.S268

Vert, J.-P., Saigo, H., & Akutsu, T. (2004). Local alignment kernels for biological sequences. In Scholkopf, B., Tsuda, K., & Platt, J. (Eds.), *Kernel methods in computational biology* (pp. 131–154). Cambridge, MA: MIT Press.

Vishwanathan, S. V. N., & Smola, A. J. (2003). Fast kernels for string and tree matching. In Becker, S., Thrun, S., & Obermayer, K. (Eds.), *Advances in neural information processing* (pp. 569–576). Cambridge, MA: MIT Press.

Wang, M., Yang, J., Liu, G.-P., Xu, Z.-J., & Chou, K.-C. (2004). Weighted-support vector machines for predicting membrane protein types based on pseudo-amino acid composition. *Protein Engineering, Design & Selection, 17*(6), 509–516. doi:10.1093/protein/gzh061

Watkins, C. (1999). *Dynamic alignment kernels* (Tech. Rep. No. CSD-TR-98-11). Royal Holloway, London, UK: University of London, Department of Computer Science.

Zhang, S.-W., Pan, Q., Zhang, H.-C., Zhang, Y.-L., & Wang, H.-Y. (2003). Classification of protein quaternary structure with support vector machine. *Bioinformatics (Oxford, England), 19*(18), 2390–2396. doi:10.1093/bioinformatics/btg331

Section 2
Techniques

Chapter 4
Mining Statistically Significant Substrings Based on the Chi-Square Measure

Sourav Dutta
IBM Research Lab, India

Arnab Bhattacharya
Indian Institute of Technology Kanpur, India

ABSTRACT

With the tremendous expansion of reservoirs of sequence data stored worldwide, efficient mining of large string databases in various domains including intrusion detection systems, player statistics, texts, and proteins, has emerged as a practical challenge. Searching for an unusual pattern within long strings of data is one of the foremost requirements for many diverse applications. Given a string, the problem is to identify the substrings that differ the most from the expected or normal behavior, i.e., the substrings that are statistically significant (or, in other words, less likely to occur due to chance alone). We first survey and analyze the different statistical measures available to meet this end. Next, we argue that the most appropriate metric is the chi-square measure. Finally, we discuss different approaches and algorithms proposed for retrieving the top-k substrings with the largest chi-square measure.

INTRODUCTION

Detection or identification of statistically significant sequences or mining interesting patterns from a given string has lately emerged as an important area of study (Denise et al., 2001; Ye & Chen, 2001). In such applications, we are given an input string composed of symbols from an alphabet set with a probability distribution defining the chance of occurrence of each symbol, and the aim is to find those portions of the string that deviate most from their expected nature, and are thus potent sources of hidden pattern and information. Such

DOI: 10.4018/978-1-61350-056-9.ch004

solutions come handy in automated monitoring systems, such as in a cluster of sensors sensing the ambient temperature for possible fire alert, or a network server sniffing the network for intrusion detection. Also, text analysis of blogs, stock market trend deciphering, detection of protein mutation and the identification of good and bad career patches of a sports icon can be few of the target applications. It is such diverse utility that makes the study and development of this field challenging and necessary.

STATISTICAL MODELS AND TOOLS

Establishing a relationship of the empirical or observed results of an experiment to factors affecting the system or to pure chance calls for various statistical models and measures. In such scenarios, an observation is deemed statistically significant if its presence cannot be attributed to randomness alone. The literature hosts a number of statistical models to capture the uniqueness of such observations such as *p-value* and *z-score*. In the next few sections, we discuss different important statistical tools that are used for this purpose.

Before venturing forward, we provide a formal definition of the problem.

Problem 1. Given a string S of length l comprising symbols from the alphabet set Σ of cardinality m, and with a given probability distribution P modeling the chance of occurrence of each symbol in Σ, the problem is to efficiently identify and extract the top-k substrings that exhibit the largest deviation from the expected nature, i.e., the substrings that are most statistically significant.

It is this measure of deviation of a sequence that we will capture by using various statistical models. In the remainder of the chapter, we interchangeably use the term string with sequence and substring with subsequence.

Hypothesis Testing and P-value

Given an observation sample X (in this case a substring), with an associated score of $S(X)$, the *p-value* of X is defined as the probability of obtaining a random sample with score $S(X)$ or greater under the same probability model (Bejerano et al., 2004; Regnier & Vandenbogaert, 2006). For each such observation, we test the null hypothesis H_0 that the substring is drawn from the given probability model P against the alternate hypothesis H_1 that the subsequence is not drawn from the same probability distribution. The p-value measures the chance of rejecting the null hypothesis; in other words, the less the p-value, the less likely it is that the null hypothesis is true.

Figure 1 shows an example. For a particular score S, the shaded area represents the chance of having a sample with a score greater than the one under consideration. In other words, the p-value is the value of the cumulative density function (cdf) measured at S subtracted from the total probability, i.e.,

$$pvalue(S) = 1 - cdf(S).$$

If the probability density function (pdf) of the scores is known, it is relatively simpler to compute the p-value of a particular score using the above formula. However, in most real situations, the pdf is hard to estimate or can be non-parametric. The accurate computation of the p-value then needs all the possible outcomes to be listed, their scores

Figure 1. Computing the p-value of X with score S

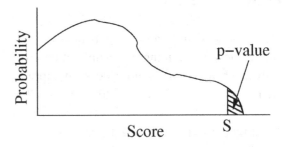

computed, and the number of outcomes having scores more than S counted. Since the number of possible outcomes is large, and is exponential in most cases, computing the p-value in such a manner is practically infeasible.

To alleviate this problem, various branch-and-bound techniques have been proposed (Bejerano et al., 2004). In systems where such accuracy in measurement is not a necessity and a small factor of error can be tolerated, an approximation of the p-value can be calculated using other statistical tools (Rahmann, 2003).

Z-Score

The *z-score* (Regnier & Vandenbogaert, 2006) or the *standard score* also measures the deviation exhibited by a sample from its expected value. It measures the number of standard deviations that an observation differs from the mean value. The z-score for an observation X with score S is given by,

$$Z(S) = \frac{S - \mu_x}{\sigma_x}$$

where μ_x and σ_x represent the mean and standard deviation of the population respectively.

The z-score is suitable if data about the entire population of the observations is known. If data about only a sample is at hand, this measure is known as the *Student's t-measure*.

It has been shown that between the z-score and the p-value, the latter is far more precise in evaluating the statistical significance, i.e., the deviation of a substring (Denise et al., 2001). This follows from the observation that the p-value actually computes all the possible outcomes and accurately predicts the chance of the particular outcome, whereas the z-score simply provides an approximation using the mean and variance of the population, without considering the probability at all the points on the probability distribution curve.

Log-Likelihood Ratio (G^2)

A statistical testing tool that is being increasingly used is the *log-likelihood ratio* (G^2) (Read & Cressie, 1988). This measure quantifies the significance of the result of an experiment based on the deviation of the observed sample from the given theoretical distribution. It takes into consideration the expected outcome and the observed outcome for all possibilities.

For an experiment having k possible outcomes (here, a string is composed of characters from an alphabet of size k), the G^2 value is calculated as

$$G^2 = 2 \sum_{i=1}^{k} \left(O_i \ln \left[\frac{O_i}{E_i} \right] \right)$$

where O_i and E_i are the observed and expected outcomes of the various possibilities respectively. For a string, the outcomes are measured by the observed and expected counts of the k different characters.

It is interesting to note that the log-likelihood ratio statistic G^2 follows a distribution approximating the *chi-square* distribution (Read & Cressie, 1988; Read & Cressie, 1989). In fact, the G^2 distribution is also characterized by the *degrees of freedom* as the chi-square distribution discussed later. However, G^2 suffers from the problem of instability of logarithm values when the expected or observed counts are too small and approach 0.

Hotelling's T^2 Measure

The *Hotelling's T^2 measure* is a generalization of the Student's t-measure (Hotelling, 1947). It takes into account the multivariate distribution of the various outcomes to identify the abnormal patterns. It measures the difference between the mean of two observed group of outcomes, or in other words, the distance of each observation from the centre of the given test dataset. Hotelling's T^2 measure is calculated as

$$T^2 = n(\vec{x} - \mu)^T C^{-1}(\vec{x} - \mu)$$

where n is the number of observations, $\bar{x}$ is a column vector of observations of size k (where k is the alphabet size), μ indicates the corresponding means and C is the covariance matrix of size $k \times k$. However, measuring T^2 is computationally very intensive and is thus impractical.

Chi-Square Measure (x^2)

The *chi-square* distribution (x^2) is widely used to compute the goodness-of-fit of a set of observations to the theoretical model describing a null hypothesis. In most situations, the x^2 distribution provides a good approximation of the p-value (Read & Cressie, 1988). However, when the sample size is small or the null model is highly uneven, it is better to compute the actual p-value. In such situations, the chi-square distribution tends to degenerate into the normal distribution, and the approximation to the p-value is lost. The *Pearson's chi-square measure* is based on the chi-square distribution and uses frequency of occurrences of an outcome to test the fit of a model by comparing it with the set of theoretical frequencies of the events. The events are assumed to be mutually exclusive and independent.

The Pearson's chi-square measure for a string of length l and an alphabet set Σ of size m is measured as

$$x^2 = \sum_{i=1}^{m} \frac{(O_i - E_i)^2}{E_i}$$

where O_i is the observed frequency of occurrence of symbol $\sigma_{i \in \Sigma}$ and E_i is the expected frequency. If p_i denotes the probability of occurrence of the symbol σ_i (where $\sum_{i=1}^{m} p_i = 1$), the expected frequency E_i is given by $p_i \times l$.

The chi-square distribution is characterized by the *degrees of freedom*, which in the case of a string is one less than the cardinality of the alphabet set. Thus, the chi-square values of all substrings follow the same distribution and can be easily compared. Further, the chi-square distribution is well-behaved; this implies that the chi-square value is anti-monotonic with the p-value, i.e., larger the deviation of a subsequence from the expected, greater is its x^2 value, lower is the p-value, and the more significant it is. The substring with the highest score is considered to be the most statistically significant substring.

However, if the expected frequencies of the outcomes are small, the approximation of chi-square measure to the actual p-value becomes low. In other cases, even for multinomial models, the x^2 statistic approximates the importance of a string more closely than the G^2 measure (Read & Cressie, 1988; Read & Cressie, 1989). In time-series databases, categorizing a pattern as surprising based on its frequency of occurrence alone and mining it efficiently using suffix trees has been proposed in (Keogh et al., 2002), but the x^2 measure seems to provide a better parameter for judging whether a pattern is indeed interesting. As the chi-square measure provides the best way of efficiently approximating the p-value for measuring the significance of an experimental observation, in this chapter, we use it as the tool for computing the statistical significance of a substring.

ALGORITHMS

In this section we look at the various existing algorithms and heuristics to efficiently mine the most statistically significant substring using the chi-square measure. The objective is to extract the top-k substrings with the highest x^2 values.

Naïve Algorithm

The simplest procedure to identify the substring having the maximum x^2 value involves extracting all the substrings from the given input string and individually computing their chi-square values. The algorithm then returns the substring(s) having the maximum or top-k scores (using a heap of k elements) as the result.

As an example, consider the following scenario.

Example 1. Assume an alphabet set $\Sigma=\{a,b\}$, and the probabilities of occurrence for the symbols: $p_a=0.2, p_b=0.8$. Consider the string $S=aaaabbba$.

Consider the substring a The observed frequencies for a and b are 1 and 0 respectively, while the expected frequencies are 0.2×1 and 0.8×1 respectively. The chi-square value, therefore, is:

$$x^2(a) = \frac{(1-0.2)^2}{0.2} + \frac{(0-0.8^2}{0.8} = 4$$

Consider another substring aab. The chi-square value can be similarly computed to be

$$x^2(aab) = \frac{(2-0.6)^2}{0.6} + \frac{(1-2.4)^2}{2.4} \approx 4.1$$

Considering all such possible substrings, the most significant substring is found to be *aaaa* with the corresponding chi-square value as 16.

This simple approach, however, is computationally expensive. For a string of length n, we obtain $O(n^2)$ substrings and hence the runtime complexity of this algorithm is $O(n^2)$. (The time complexity, more precisely, is $O(n^2m)$ where m is the size of the alphabet set, as the computation of x^2 requires measuring the frequencies of m symbols. However, for a given string, m is fixed. Therefore, it can be treated as a constant and we do not include it in the complexity analysis any further.) For long strings (n in the order of thousands), the quadratic complexity renders the algorithm impractical, especially for real-time applications. In the subsequent sections we look at more efficient algorithms and heuristics.

Blocking Algorithm and its Variants

The *blocking algorithm* (Agarwal, 2009) reduces the practical running time of the naïve algorithm, although its theoretical runtime remains $O(n^2)$ for a string of length n. The algorithm initially partitions the string into blocks consisting of identical symbols lying adjacent to each other in the input string.

As an example, consider the string $S=aaaabbba$ given in Example 1. After "block"-ing identical adjacent symbols, the string becomes $S'=a_1b_2a_3$ where the bold face indicates blocks. The first block a_1 represents the first four a's in the original string, the next block b_2 represents the three b's and the final a_3 represents the single a. In most cases, this step significantly reduces the length of the input string.

The naïve algorithm is now run on this "block"-ed string and the substring with the highest chi-square value is returned as the answer. Note that while the number of substrings is reduced in this manner, the computation of the chi-square value for each substring takes into account the frequency of the symbol in each block (it is not taken as 1).

The above algorithm is optimal (Agarwal, 2009), the proof of which hinges on the following fact: if the most significant substring selects a symbol in a block, then it must select the entire block associated with the symbol. In other words, either a block is completely selected in the most significant substring, or it is not selected at all. There is no substring that selects the symbols of a block partially and has a x^2 value greater than the two extreme alternatives – the substring that selects the entire block and the substring that does not select the block at all. Referring to Example 1, it can be verified that the substring *aaaab* has a x^2 value (11.25) which is not greater than both

Box 1.

$$\sum_{i=1,i\neq e}^{m} \frac{(p_i(l_{sub}+1) - \theta_{i,sub+1})^2}{p_i(l_{sub}+1)} + \frac{(p_e(l_{sub}+1) - \theta_{e,sub+1})^2}{p_e(l_{sub}+1)} \geq \sum_{i=1,i\neq e}^{m} \frac{(p_i(l_{sub} - \theta_{i,sub})^2}{p_i l_{sub}} + \frac{(p_e l_{sub} - \theta_{e,sub})^2}{p_e l_{sub}}$$

the possibilities (*aaaabbb* with x^2=6.03 and *aaaan*with x^2=16).

While the full proof is given in (Agarwal, 2009), we provide a sketch of the idea. Consider the current substring to be *sub* with length l_{sub} and the adjacent block of length *n* to be composed of the symbol $\sigma_e \in \Sigma$. Suppose that appending the first σ_e of the block to *sub* increases the x^2 value of the new substring. Given that $x^2_{sub+1} \geq x^2_{sub}$, denoting the observed frequencies by θ, we have the equation in Box 1.

By algebraic manipulations of the above equation, we can show that $x^2_{sub+j} \geq x^2_{sub+j-1} \geq \ldots \geq x^2_{sub+2} \geq x^2_{sub+1}$ for any *j*. Hence, by including the entire block the x^2 value of the substring will increase.

The practical running time of the blocking algorithm is considerably less than the naïve one. However, in the worst case, adjacent symbols at all positions of the input string may be dissimilar, and there will be no benefit. The expected number of blocks for an alphabet where the probability distribution of occurrences of the symbols tend to be uniform, is *O(n)* for a string of length *n*. Thus, the running time remains *O(n²)*.

An interesting optimization of the blocking algorithm was proposed in (Agarwal, 2009) for binary alphabets. It was shown that the most significant substring must start and end with the same symbol, i.e., for the above example, the possibilities are restricted to a_1,b_2,a_3, and a_1,b_2,a_3 only. The two other substrings $a_1 b_2$ and $b_2 a_3$ cannot have the largest x^2 value.

A heap variant of the above algorithms was also proposed in (Agarwal, 2009). However, it suffers from high theoretical and practical running time costs and is not discussed any further.

Local Maxima-Based Algorithms

A recent method proposed in (Dutta and Bhattacharya, 2010) works on a similar strategy as that of the blocking algorithm. It too initially partitions the input string, but instead of constructing blocks based on adjacent identical symbols, it constructs *local maxima*. A local maximum is defined as a substring such that while traversing through it the inclusion of the next symbol *does not decrease* the x^2 score. In other words, when the inclusion of the next symbol decreases the current x^2 value, the present local maximum ends. The next local maximum begins at this symbol position. The first local maximum starts at the beginning of the string, and the last one finishes at the end.

Consider Example 1. The first substring *a* has a x^2 value of 4. Inclusion of the next character increases the x^2 value of *aa* to 8. Thus, the local maximum extends to *aa*. Continuing in this fashion, we notice that $x^2(aaaa)=16$ and $x^2(aaaab)=11.25$. Therefore, the first local maxima is *aaaa*. Repeating this procedure for the entire string *S*, all the local maxima present, namely, *aaaa.*, *bbb* and *a* are found. Note that they need not be equivalent to the blocks.

The *global maximum*, i.e., the string with the maximum x^2 score may obviously start from anywhere within the input string and not necessarily from the starting positions of the local maxima. So, after identifying the local maxima, the method finds the suffix within each of the maxima having the largest x^2 score. The suffix may be the whole local maximum itself (as it is in the case in Example 1). The starting positions of these suffixes are stored in a list *A*. These positions form the potential starting positions for the global maximum.

To find the potential ending positions, the string is reversed and the same procedure is repeated. The starting position of the suffixes of the reversed string are stored in another list B. These positions form the potential ending positions for the global maximum.

It was conjectured in (Dutta & Bhattacharya, 2010) that the starting and ending positions of the global maximum are in A and B respectively. Based on this conjecture, two heuristics are proposed: All Pair Refined Local Maxima Search (ARLM) and Approximate Greedy Maximum Maxima Search (AGMM).

All-Pair Refined Local Maxima Search (ARLM)

The All-Pair Refined Local Maxima Search (ARLM) algorithm examines all combinations of starting and ending positions, and finds the combination with the largest x^2 value. A starting and ending position is combined to form a substring extending from the symbol at the starting position to the symbol at the ending position. It is ensured that the combination is valid, i.e., the starting position is not later than the ending position.

Approximate Greedy Maximum Maxima Search (AGMM)

The Approximate Greedy Maximum Maxima Search (AGMM) algorithm uses the same two lists A and B, but in a different manner. Instead of considering all possible combinations of starting and ending positions, the AGMM algorithm first finds the suffix with the largest x^2 value and uses only that corresponding starting position. The other starting positions are pruned. This position is combined with all the ending positions to find the substring with the largest x^2 value. Since the starting and ending positions are similar, the same is repeated by finding the ending position

with the largest x^2 value and then combining only that with all the starting positions. The substring thus found is declared as the most statistically significant substring.

The above two algorithms has been further optimized by first "block"-ing the string before extracting the local maxima (Dutta & Bhattacharya, 2010). Since the blocks can be treated as indivisible portions of the string for the purposes of x^2 measure, the above optimization works.

Runtime Analysis

In this section, we analyze the runtime performance of the two local maxima-based algorithms. For a string of length n, all the local maxima present can be extracted in a single pass of the input string in $O(n)$ time. In the worst case, each symbol may form a local maxima by itself, and so the number of local maxima is also n, and in general, is $O(n)$. However, practically the number of local maxima has been found to be much less, depending on the probabilities of occurrence of the symbols. The number of local maxima d has been shown to be less than n (Dutta & Bhattacharya, 2010).

The number of suffixes and the sizes of the lists A and B are, therefore, $O(d)$ as well. Since ARLM examines all possible combinations, the runtime of ARLM is $O(d^2+n)$. AGMM, however, only combines the maximum with all the ending positions (and reverse); so, the running time is $O(d+n)$. Since d is $O(n)$, ARLM is essentially a quadratic-time algorithm (although with a lower practical running time) while AGMM is strictly a linear-time algorithm.

EXPERIMENTAL RESULTS

In this section we look at the different experimental results, performed on multiple datasets, real as well as synthetic, to assess the performance of the various procedures and heuristics discussed (Agarwal, 2009, Dutta & Bhattacharya, 2010).

The heap variant of the blocking algorithm has not been compared with as it is practically infeasible due to large memory and runtime requirements. The results shown are based on two parameters, (1) the number of blocks or local maxima found (whichever is applicable), and (2) accuracy of the results. The accuracy of an algorithm is measured using the *approximation ratio*, i.e., the ratio of the x^2 value of the answer returned by it to that of the optimal.

Real Datasets

No results were reported on real datasets on blocking algorithm by (Agarwal, 2009). Experiments on real datasets for local maxima-based algorithms were, however, carried out by Dutta and Bhattacharya (2010). The authors used the innings-by-innings runs scored by Sachin Tendulkar in one-day internationals (ODI) (425 records as on November 2009, available from http://stats.cricinfo.Com/ci/engine/player/35320.html?class =2;template=results;type=batting;view=innings). The runs were quantized into five symbols, namely, 0-9 (poor), 10-24 (bad), 25-49 (average), 50-99 (good) and 100+ (excellent). The probability of occurrence of each of the symbols was calculated empirically as the ratio of the number of innings with that score to the total number of innings to obtain the probability distribution. The ARLM and AGMM algorithms were then run to obtain the substrings with the highest x^2 value. These were identified as the good and bad patches in his career.

The findings have been summarized in Table 1 which shows that his best career patch was in the latter half of 1998 with an average of above 84. Referring to cricket databases, it was found that this period included his run in Sharjah that many pundits believe to be his best. Moreover, in this period, he scored 8 centuries within 7 months. While the best patch of a sportsperson is clearly a matter of subjective opinion, the analysis shows that the top performances can be identified by using the x^2 measure. During his bad patch for nearly the whole of 1992, Sachin struggled with his form and did not have a single score of even 40.

For the cricket dataset, the local maxima-based algorithms, AGMM and ARLM, required the least amount of time to find the substring with the largest x^2 values when compared to the blocking and naïve algorithms (Dutta & Bhattacharya, 2010). This gain in time comes from the lesser number of *local maxima* constructed with respect to the number of substrings or blocks in the naïve and the blocking algorithms respectively. For Sachin's data, the number of local maxima found was 281 as compared to 319 blocks. The accuracy (or approximation ratio) for ARLM and AGMM was 1 for the top-1 query, i.e., they found the substring with the largest x^2 value. With increasing values of k for the top-k query, the approximation ratio initially drops to around 0.98 before increasing again to almost 1.

Experiments on a much larger real dataset were run by (Dutta & Bhattacharya, 2010) to analyze the difference in running times of the algorithms. The data was that of number of user clicks (nearly a million) encountered on the front page of msnbc.com (available from http://archive.ics.uci.edu/ml/datasets/MSNBC.com+Anonymous+Web+Data). The results shown in Table 2 established the advantage of ARLM over the blocking algorithm. As expected, since it is a linear algorithm, AGMM was about an order of magnitude faster than the others.

Table 1. Results of x^2 analysis on Sachin Tendulkar's batting career

Form	Date	Average
Best patch	From 22nd April, 1998 to 13th November, 1998	84.31
Worst patch	From 15th March, 1992 to 19th December, 1992	21.89

Table 2. Results for dataset of number of user clicks (containing 989819 records). The naïve algorithm consumed too much memory and did not finish in 75 hours.

Algorithm	Running time	Number of blocks or local maxima
Naïve	75+ hrs	989819
Blocking	52 hrs	835412
ARLM	40 hrs	759921
AGMM	3 hrs	759921

Synthetic Datasets

To study the scalability of the various algorithms with the different parameters, experiments on synthetic datasets were conducted by (Dutta & Bhattacharya, 2010). The synthetic datasets used were randomly generated using a uniform distribution. Chunks of data from a different distribution (in this case, geometric) were inserted randomly to perturb the original data and simulate the deviations encountered in real applications. The parameters tested with were: (1) length of the input string, (2) size of the alphabet, and (3) number of top-k values to be reported.

The results indicate that the number of "blocks" were approximately from 0.70 to 0.85 of the total length of the string while the number of local maxima were between 0.65 and 0.75 of the total length. Consequently, the local maxima-based algorithms were faster. The scalability of AGMM was the best as it was a linear algorithm. ARLM, while theoretically has a running time which is quadratic with the length of the string, showed a better scalability. The running time increased with the size of the alphabet and the number of top-k values.

The approximation ratio of the local maxima-based heuristics always remained 1 for top-1 query. Even for values of k up to 50, the accuracy never dropped below 0.96. More detailed results and analysis be found in (Dutta and Bhattacharya, 2010).

CONCLUSION

This chapter aims at tackling the problem of efficiently mining statistically significant substrings present in an input string. Such interesting pattern detection is applicable in many applications ranging from intrusion detection to protein mutation. We discussed various statistical tools that can be used to model a substring as "statistically significant". Given the setting, we found that the *chi-square* measure is best suited for this purpose, the reason being the fact that it is computationally simple, and yet, it provides a high approximation of the p-value as compared to the other measures.

We discussed various existing algorithms in the literature from naïve to blocking to local maxima-based ones for finding the substrings with the largest x^2 values. The local maxima-based algorithms, ARLM and AGMM, reported the best running time and the best approximation ratio.

Finally, we would like to mention that the field is ready for richer analyses, including finding heuristics with guaranteed approximation ratio, and randomized algorithms. Moreover, the problem can be extended to a two-dimensional setting for spatial data mining applications, or more generally, to a graph.

REFERENCES

Agarwal, S. (2009). *On finding the most statistically significant substring using the chi-square measure*. Master's thesis, Indian Institute of Technology, Kanpur.

Bejerano, G., Friedman, N., & Tishby, N. (2004). Efficient exact p-value computation for small sample, sparse and surprisingly categorical data. *Journal of Computational Biology*, *11*(5), 867–886.

Denise, A., Regnier, M., & Vandenbogaert, M. (2001). Accessing the statistical significance of overrepresented oligonucleotides. In *Workshop on Algorithms in Bioinformatics (WABI)*, pages 85-97.

Dutta, S., & Bhattacharya, A. (2010). Most significant substring mining based on chi-square measure. In *Proc. of 14th Pacific-Asia Conference on Knowledge Discovery and Data Mining*, (pp. 319-327).

Hotelling, H. (1947). Multivariate quality control. *Techniques of Statistical Analysis, 54*, 111–184.

Keogh, E., Lonardi, S., & Chiu, B. (2002). Finding surprising patterns in a time series database in linear time and space. In *Proc. of 8th ACM SIGKDD Int. Conf. on Knowledge Discovery and Data Mining*, (pp. 550-556).

Rahmann, S. (2003). Dynamic programming algorithms for two statistical problems in computational biology. In D. Tsur (Ed.), *Workshop on Algorithms in Bioinformatics (WABI), LNCS 2812* (pp. 151-164).

Read, T., & Cressie, N. (1988). *Goodness-of-fit statistics for discrete multivariate data*. Springer.

Read, T., & Cressie, N. (1989). Pearson's X^2 and the likelihood ratio statistic G^2: A comparative review. *International Statistical Review, 57*(1), 19–43. doi:10.2307/1403582

Regnier, M., & Vandenbogaert, M. (2006). Comparison of statistical significance criteria. *Journal of Bioinformatics and Computational Biology, 4*(2), 537–551. doi:10.1142/S0219720006002028

Ye, N., & Chen, Q. (2001). An anomaly detection technique based on chi-square statistics for detecting intrusions into information systems. *Quality and Reliability Engineering International, 17*(2), 105–112. doi:10.1002/qre.392

Chapter 5
Unbalanced Sequential Data Classification Using Extreme Outlier Elimination and Sampling Techniques

T. Maruthi Padmaja
University of Hyderabad (UoH), India

Raju S. Bapi
University of Hyderabad (UoH), India

P. Radha Krishna
Infosys Lab, Infosys Limited, India

ABSTRACT

Predicting minority class sequence patterns from the noisy and unbalanced sequential datasets is a challenging task. To solve this problem, we proposed a new approach called extreme outlier elimination and hybrid sampling technique. We use k Reverse Nearest Neighbors (kRNNs) concept as a data cleaning method for eliminating extreme outliers in minority regions. Hybrid sampling technique, a combination of SMOTE to oversample the minority class sequences and random undersampling to undersample the majority class sequences is used for improving minority class prediction. This method was evaluated in terms of minority class precision, recall and f-measure on syntactically simulated, highly overlapped sequential dataset named Hill-Valley. We conducted the experiments with k-Nearest Neighbour classifier and compared the performance of our approach against simple hybrid sampling technique. Results indicate that our approach does not sacrifice one class in favor of the other, but produces high predictions for both fraud and non-fraud classes.

DOI: 10.4018/978-1-61350-056-9.ch005

INTRODUCTION

Unbalanced data classification is an important issue in today's datamining community. There are several real world domains like intrusion detection; fraud detection and medical diagnosis (Visa & Ralescu, 2005) are unbalanced in nature. But some of these datasets like promoter recognition (Rani & Bapi, 2008), intrusion detection (Pradeep, Rao, Krishna, Bapi & Laha, 2005; Sanjay, Gulati & Pujari, 2004), and protein sequence prediction (Sikic, Tomic, & Vlahovicek, 2009; Zhao, Li, Chen, & Aihara, 2008) are sequential in nature, where each instance is the ordered list of discrete items. Unbalanced data classification problem is beatitude in those datasets when one class of data (majority class) severely outnumbers the other class (minority class) of data.

We can solve imbalance problem that occur in sequence classification by using data mining techniques. If the imbalance problem is ignored and conventional classification methods are employed with the usual criterion of minimal overall error, then the model estimated will often ignore any contribution from the minority class samples. As such the model learned will only represent predominantly the majority class samples. These classification methods also assume that there is equal cost derived from all classes, which is not true in real world scenarios.

Consider intrusion detection system, (Pradeep, Rao, Krishna, Bapi & Laha 2005; Sanjay, Gulati, & Pujari, 2004) compared to non-intruder system call transactions, the occurrence of intruder transactions is infrequent. So it is extremely difficult to extract the intruder patterns in this scenario. In this work, we consider sequence classification as an unbalanced data classification problem where the majority samples outnumber the minority samples. Usually, the classification algorithms exhibit poor performance while dealing with unbalanced datasets and results are biased towards the majority class. Hence, an appropriate model is needed to classify unbalanced sequential data.

For these types of problems, we cannot rely upon the accuracy of the classifier because the cost associated with fraud sample being predicted as a non-fraud sample is very high. The performance measures that can be used here are cost based metrics, ROC analysis and minority class F-measure.

In this work we considered sequence classification as a binary classification problem and proposed a hybrid sampling approach called extreme outlier elimination with SMOTE and random undersampling. Here *k Reverse Nearest Neighbors (kRNNs)* concept is used as a data cleaning method for eliminating extreme outliers in minority regions before generating extra samples using SMOTE. Synthetic Minority Oversampling Technique (SMOTE) synthetically incorporates new samples in the distribution whereas random undersampling randomly deletes majority class samples from current distribution. Proposed approach is evaluated on a discrete sequential data set named Hill-Valley dataset. We identified optimal classifier based on its *precision*, *recall* and *F-measure* rates. Compared with other models constructed based on one-class classification techniques and other sampling techniques proposed approach yielded better performance.

The remainder of this chapter is organized as follows. In BACKGROUND section, we present the background of the proposed approach. The work related to proposed approach is discussed from two perspectives in Related Work section. Proposed approach and experimental setup is discussed in Solutions and recommendations section. Finally conclusions from the current work and future research directions are provided at the end of the chapter.

BACKGROUND

This section describes the background of the methods used for proposing extreme outlier elimination and Hybrid sampling approach.

Hybrid of Synthetic Minority Oversampling Technique and RUS

Hybrid sampling of SMOTE and random undersampling is a prominent solution for unbalanced data classification problem (Sun et al., 2009; Taft et al., 2009; & Cieslak 2006), here SMOTE+RUS was employed to alleviate from the bias caused non-fraudulent samples. Synthetic Minority Oversampling technique (SMOTE) was introduced by Chawla et al, in which the minority class samples are over-sampled by creating synthetic (or artificial) samples rather than replicating random minority class sample. SMOTE algorithm generates synthetic minority samples between the line segment joining from each minority class sample to its k minority class' nearest neighbors. This approach effectively forces the decision region of the minority class to become more general. The following psudocode describes the SMOTE algorithm.

Latter combined approach of SMOTE and random undersampling (RUS) was devised by the authors of SMOTE to further improve the performance of the classifier towards unbalanced distributions. Science SMOTE projects new samples between minority class geometrical nearest neighbours, minority class outliers (mislabeled points) play a major role and sometimes the newly generated synthetic samples go beyond the actual minority class boundaries. Thus hampers the classifiers generalization ability.

Outlier Selection and Filtering by RNN

Several outlier detection and filtering methods are devised to filter mislabeled training instances for classification problem. Generally they are of distance based (Muhlenbach, Lallich & Zighed, 2004) or classification algorithm based (Brodley and Friedl 1999). In this chapter k- reverse nearest neigbbour ($kRNN$) (Soujanya, Satyanarayana & Kamalakar, 2006) based outlier detection and elimination was employed for mining Hill-Valley sequences. The advantage of ($kRNN$) over other

Algorithm 1. psudocode for SMOTE Algorithm

```
Input:
N=Number of minority class samples
T=SMOTE factor.
k=Number of nearest neighbours
Output:
T * N synthetic samples
Begin
for each sample i in N do
compute k nearest neighbours.
while T ≠  0 do
                choose randomly one neighbour nn from k.
compute the difference dif between i and nn.
Generate a random number gap between 0 and 1.
compute new synthetic point as synth = i + dif * gap.
end while
end for
end
```

distance based outlier methods is the parameter independency. By using (*kRNN*) concept, the neighbourhood density around a point p increases with the increase of the number of neighbours (k value). Following are the notations used in this chapter for describing the reverse nearest neigbbour concept.

X: d-dimensional dataset:

kNN(p): Set of k-nearest neighbors of p.

kRNN(p): Set of k-reverse nearest neighbors of p. A point q belongs to *kRNN(p)*

iff $p \in kNN(q)$.

k nearestneighborset: $kNN(x_p)$ is defined as $\{x_q | d_{pq} < k^{th}$ nearest distance of $x_p\}$.

For given point x_p, the kth smallest distance after sorting all the distances from x_p to the remaining points is the kth nearest distance of x_p.

k reversenearestneighborset: $kRNN(x_q)$ is defined as $\{x_q | x_p \in kNN(x_q)\}$.

k reverse neighbours (*kRNN*) defines influence around a point in terms of neighborhood density. Note that, in case of *kNN*s, for a given k value, each point in the dataset will have at least k nearest neighbors ($> k$ in case of ties) but the *kRNN* set of a point could have zero or more elements. The *kRNN* set of point p gives set of points that consider p as their k-nearest neighbour, for a given value of k. If a point p has higher number of *kRNN*s than another point q, then we can say that p has a denser neighborhood than q. Lesser the number of *kRNN*s, the farther apart are the points in the dataset to q, i.e. the neighborhood is sparse.

According to *kRNN* concept (Soujanya, Satyanarayana & Kamalakar 2006), outlier point is defined as follows: An outlier point is a point that has less than k number of *kRNN*s. That is the cardinality of *kRNN* set is less than k, ($|kRNNs| < k$). Lesser the number of kRNNs, the more distant it is from its neighbors.

Science considered Hill-Valley dataset is highly overlapped and unbalanced, the minority points extremely far from minority class sample subgroups are prone to be mislabeled and degrades the classifier performance while SMOTEing. So here we define the concept called extreme outlier and eliminate them as part of data preprocessing step.

RELATED WORK

The related work for the proposed approach to counter unbalanced sequential classification problem has been approached from two directions. The techniques that are available to handle the unbalanced data sets are reviewed first and corresponding applications in sequence classification are reviewed later.

There have been several approaches for coping with unbalanced datasets. Kubat and Matwin (Kubat & Matwin, 1997), did selective undersampling of majority class by keeping minority classes fixed. They categorized the minority samples into some noise overlapping, the positive class decision region, borderline samples, redundant samples and safe samples. By using Tomek links concept, which is a type of data cleaning procedure used for undersampling, they deleted the borderline majority samples. Ling and Li (Ling & Li, 1998) combined oversampling of the minority class with undersampling of the majority class. They used lift analysis instead of accuracy to measure a classifier's performance. They proposed that the test samples be ranked by a confidence measure and then lift be used as the evaluation criteria. A lift curve is similar to an ROC curve, but is more tailored for the marketing analysis problem. In one experiment, they undersampled the majority class and noted that the best lift index is obtained when the classes are equally represented. In another experiment, they oversampled the minority samples with replacement to match the number of majority samples to the number of minority samples. The oversampling and undersampling combination did not provide significant improvement in the lift index. Study of "whether oversampling is more effective than undersampling" and "which oversampling or undersampling rate should be used" was done by Estabrooks *et al* (Estabrooks, Jo & Japkowicz, 2004), which concluded that combining different expressions of the resampling approach is an effective solution. Batista *et al* (Batista, Prati & Monard, 2004) proposed two hybrid sampling techniques for overlapping datasets namely SMOTE+TOMEK Links and SMOTE+ENN for better-defined class clusters among majority and minority classes. Apart from sampling solutions, some studies (Raskutti & Kowalczyk, 2004) are indicating that one-class classification technique like one-class SVMs (Tax, 2001), one-class neural networks (Japkowicz, Hanson & Gluck, 2000) are also efficient in solving unbalanced data classification problem on some specific applications like anomaly detection.

Concern with unbalanced sequential classification, (Sikic, Tomic & Vlahovicek, 2009) applied a combined approach of sliding window and random forest on the sequence and structure parameters as well as on sole sequence parameters to identify protein- protein interaction sites in sequences and 3D structures. Their study indicated that the combined approach with sequences alone was result with high accuracy. A probability based mechanism was proposed in (Yu, Chou & Darby, 2010) to convert sequences into feature vectors. Latter these feature used to identify protein-protein interactions in an unbalanced data using primary structure. A new algorithm with committee of classifiers is discussed in (Zhao, Li, Chen & Aihara, 2008) for unbalanced protein classification problem.

For the promoter recognition problems SMOTE and ADABOOST algorithms were applied (Rani & Bapi, 2008) on minority majority concepts and this study indicated that a simple ADABOOST improved the promoter recognition rate than SMOTE algorithm. Further a synthetic protein sequence oversampling method (SPSO) (Beigi & Zell, 2007) was proposed using Hidden Markov Model profile (HMM profile) for the prediction of protein sequences and remote homology detection.

Finally to identify intrusions in a database of UNIX system calls different scheme with the combination of one-class k-nearest neighbour classifier and text processing techniques were proposed by (Pradeep, Rao, Krishna, Bapi & Laha, 2005; Sanjay, Gulati & Pujari, 2004). Along with this new scheme for identifying intrusions the authors also proposed different sequence similarity measures using text processing metrics.

This chapter proposes a new hybrid approach of outlier elimination and hybrid sampling for handling noisy sequential unbalanced datasets.

MAIN FOCUS OF THE CHAPTER

Here our basic motivation is to balance the training data distribution so that minority class predicts well. For this, we are generating the required number of artificial minority class samples using SMOTE which generates new samples by interpolation. If we use SMOTE on the entire minority class samples, minority class sub regions may not be emphasized well if the data is very much sparsely distributed. So there is a great need of picking the points that are in denser regions and use only those points for generating artificial fraud class samples using SMOTE. For this, we have to eliminate the points that are far from the minority samples; we call them as *extreme outliers*. The application of existing outlier detection techniques on highly overlapped and unbalanced datasets, half of the minority samples are predicted as outliers. Eliminating half of the minority samples is not feasible as their presence is very less compared with the majority class.

Solutions and Recommendations

The *k* Reverse Nearest Neighbors concept is an efficient solution for this problem. By using the *cardinality* of *kRNN* set, of a point *p*, we can say that the point is in denser region or sparser region. If the point *p* yields the cardinality of *kRNN*set more than *k*, then *p* falls in denser region or else if *p's cardinality* on *kRNN*set yields less than *k* or zero then *p* falls in sparse region. Based on *cardinality* of *kRNN*s the minority points are ranked and least ranked points are eliminated. We proposed extreme outlier concept as a data preprocessing method for minority samples and hybrid sampling approach for balancing the data distribution. An extreme outlier point is a point that has number of *kRNN*s far less than *k,* when *k* values are increased. For example, we can define a point as extreme outlier if its *kRNN*s are less than *k*/10 over systematically increased *k* values.

After elimination of extreme outliers, we applied hybrid sampling approach on Hill-Valley data set. This is a combination of random under-sampling and oversampling. It mainly works based on determining how much percentage of minority class samples (original samples + artificial samples) and majority class samples to add to the training set such that a classifier can achieve best *recall* and *precision* values for minority class. Here, *recall* represents TPrate (the number of minority class samples that are correctly classified) of the minority class. The tradeoff between minority class TPrate and TNrate (the number of majority class samples correctly classified) is being represented by *precision.*. After eliminating minority class extreme outlier, the majority class samples are randomly under-sampled and the minority class samples are over-sampled using SMOTE to emphasize the minority class data regions, which uses euclidian distance metric.

Figure 1 shows the process of generating samples for training the classifier. Initially, minority class and majority class sequences are separated from the dataset and latter *extreme outliers* are eliminated in the minority class sequences using the method described above. Then SMOTE was applied on minority class sequences for the given level of SMOTE factor. For example, if we specify SMOTE factor as 5 and input minority samples are x, then artificial minority samples generated after

Figure 1. Proposed hybrid of kRNN+ hybrid sampling

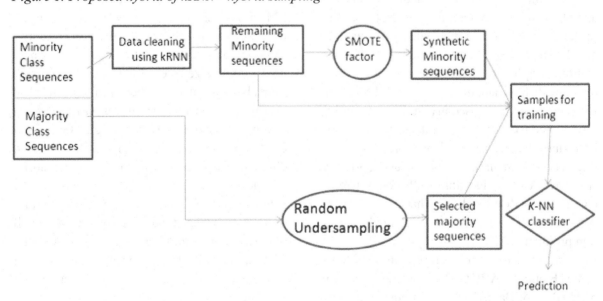

SMOTE are 5x. Generally the choice of optimal SMOTE factor is data dependent. For the dataset under consideration, the class distribution of minority and majority class samples is 10:90 (MI: MJ). So for experiments we considered SMOTE factors of 1, 3, 5, 7 and 9.

Experimental Evaluation

This section depicts the datasets, evaluation metric for estimating classifier performance and comparative study with other methods for approximating the performance of the proposed approach, in terms of experimental results and discussion.

Evaluation Metric

The classifier outcomes, which are required to evaluate the performance, can be represented in the form of a confusion matrix (Table 1).

Table 1 derives the following measures (base lines) to estimate the classifier performance.

True positive Rate (TP rate) is the percentage of correctly classified positive samples.
True negative rate (TN rate) is the percentage of correctly classified negative samples.
False negative (FN rate) is the percentage of incorrectly classified positive samples.
False positive (FP rate) is the percentage of negative examples predicted as positives.

The goal of any ideal classifier is to maximize TP and TN rates. The following are normally applied measures for evaluating classification performance:

Table 1. Confusion matrix

	Predicted Negative	Predicted Positive
Actual Negative	TN	FP
Actual Positive	FN	TP

$$Accuracy = (TP+TN)/(TP+FP+TN+FN) \qquad (1)$$

$$\textbf{TPR}ate = Recall = TP/(TP+FN) \qquad (2)$$

$$Precision = TP/(TP+FP) \qquad (3)$$

$$F\_measure = \frac{2 * \text{Re}\,call * \Pr ecision}{\text{Re}\,call + \Pr ecision}$$
$$(4)$$

For unbalanced data classification point of view accuracy is not an appropriate measure for evaluating the classifier performance. Considering there are only 6% of samples from minority class and 94% of the samples are from majority class, If a classifier miss predicts all minority class samples as majority class samples then the accuracy becomes 94% with the contribution of majority class samples only.

Proposed approach is evaluated using minority class *recall* (Equation 2), *precision* (Equation 3) and *F-measure* (Equation 4). Minority class *F-measure* depicts the performance of the target class in terms of tradeoff between precision and recall, where as recall is simply the TP rate of the target class and precision gives the trade-off between TP and FP rates. If both *precision* and *recall* are high, then F-measure is also high. For unbalanced datasets the precision and recall goals are conflicting, increasing *recall* rates without disturbing the *precision* of the minority class (target class) is a challenging issue.

Dataset

Experiments are conducted on Hill-Valley dataset (http://archive.ics.uci.edu/ml) which is sequential in nature. Each record in this dataset represents 100 points in a two dimension graph. These points in y axis can create either a Hill or Valley. Since the noisy Hill-Valley dataset accurately represents the underlined domain, it is considered for evaluating proposed hybrid approach. Actually this dataset is balanced in nature with 307 records from valley class, 299 records from hill class in the training set and the test set also contains the similar distribution as like training set. For the experimental purpose the Hill-Valley dataset distribution was synthetically unbalanced by keeping only 10% Valley class distribution as it is and making rest of the Valley distribution as Hill class distribution. The training set considered for the experiments was the combination of both training and testing set that is provided in UCI repository (http://archive.ics.uci.edu/ml/). We implemented the *extreme outlier* detection using kRNNs and SMOTE in MATLAB7.0 and used Weka3-4 toolkit for experimenting with the classifiers. Weka (Witten & Frank, 2000) is Java-based knowledge learning and analysis environment developed at the University of Waikato in New Zealand.

Initially we eliminated the *extreme outliers* found from the minority samples using the method described in (Main focus of the chapter). We found that 24 points qualify as *extreme outliers* and eliminated them from the dataset. Proposed approach is validated using *k*-nearest neighbour classifier and compared with hybrid sampling of SMOTE and RUS. Since the dataset considered for the experiments is sequential in nature, validating the proposed approach using global classifiers like decision tree, neural networks can leads to performance degradation because

of loss of sequential information (Pradeep, Rao, Krishna, Bapi, & Laha, 2005). For the dataset under consideration, total number of minority class sequences is 121 and 1091 majority class sequences. Since the unbalanced class distribution ratio for the considered Hill-Valley dataset is 10:90 and we varied the SMOTE factor from 1%, 2%., 5%, 7%...9% in order to make balanced training set distributions. For the k-nearest neighbour classifier the *k* value is set to 3 for all experiments with varied SMOTE factor.

Our observations from the experiments conducted using the proposed *extreme outlier* elimination with *kRNN*s combined with hybrid sampling approach on *k*-NN classifier is as follows: from Table 2 as the SMOTE factor increases from 1% to 5% the minority class *recall* increases from 0.825 to 0.945, *precision* is increases from 0.615 to 0.717 and the *F-measure* increases from 0.705 to 0.815. Our observations from hybrid sampling are as follows from Table 2 as the SMOTE factor increases from 1% to 5% the minority class *recall* increases from 0.843 to 0.944, *precision* is increases from 0.632 to 0.698 and the *F-measure* increases from 0.705 to 0.798. The highest performance was highlighted.

Comparing *kRNN+Hybrid* with normal Hybrid sampling approach the *k*-NN classifier with kRNN+Hybrid yielded superior performance in

Tabel 2. Comparison across Hybrid kRNN+Hybrid over k-NN classifier

SMOTE factor%	Method	Precision	Recall	F-measure
1%	*Hybrid*	0.632	0.843	*0.722*
	kRNN+Hybrid	0.615	0.825	0.705
3%	*Hybrid*	0.688	0.944	0.796
	kRNN+Hybrid	0.716	0.945	***0.815***
5%	*Hybrid*	0.698	0.931	0.798
	kRNN+Hybrid	0.717	0.932	*0.811*
7%	*Hybrid*	0.686	0.931	0.79
	kRNN+Hybrid	0.693	0.939	*0.797*
9%	*Hybrid*	0.694	0.924	*0.793*
	kRNN+Hybrid	0.688	0.926	0.789

terms of minority class prediction with 0.716 *precision*, *0.945 recall* and with 0.815 *F-measure* at 3% SMOTE factor itself. Whereas Hybrid sampling technique alone attained the minority class prediction with 0.698 *precision*, *0.931 recall* and with 0.798 *F-measure* at 5% SMOTE factor. From the both methods *kRNN+Hybrid* yielded superior performance of 0.815 in terms minority class *F-measure* than the simple hybrid sampling even in early rounds of SMOTE factor. From the experiments we also observed that once the maximum performance is achieved at n% SMOTE factor the performance of the classifier deteriorates from (n+1)% SMOTE factor onwards.

Thus intelligent use of *kRNN*s for *extreme outlier* elimination of minority class sequences and SMOTE for generating artificial minority sequences resulted in improving the performance of the unbalanced sequential datasets. Proposed *kRNN+Hybrid* improved the minority class sequence prediction efficiently at early rounds of SMOTE factor without sacrificing the majority class prediction as well than the simple hybrid sampling which generally applied to improve the classifier performance in the case of unbalanced datasets. This method can be further explored to other unbalanced sequential classification domains like bioinformatics and cheminformatics.

Future Research Directions

The unbalanced data classification problem can be solved at data level and classification algorithm level. Concern with unbalanced sequence classification most of the research is carried out at data level with the combination sequence data handling methods. Further the unbalanced sequence classification should be explored at classification algorithm level along with cost of each minority sequence in consideration.

CONCLUSION

This chapter introduced a new approach for eliminating outliers from the noisy and highly unbalanced sequential datasets. In this work we defined the concept called *extreme outlier* and used kRNNs to find them. Results show that, the *extreme outlier* elimination combined with hybrid sampling can improve the accuracy of the classifier for minority class. Here we used SMOTE to artificially create minority class sequences and emphasize the minority class regions after *extreme outlier*s in the minority class sequences are eliminated. Experiments are conducted on highly overlapped sequential dataset named Hill-Valley for *k*-nearest neighbour classifier. The results obtained indicate that, the proposed approach is efficient for minority sequence detection from the unbalanced sequential dataset (Table 2). Though our approach is implemented for discrete real sequence domain like Hill-Valley, it can be applied to other unbalanced sequential domains like bioinformatics and cheminformatics as well.

REFERENCES

Batista, G., Prati, M., & Monard, M. (2004). A study of the behavior of several methods for balancing machine learning training data. *ACM SIGKDD Explorations: Special Issue on Imbalanced Data Sets*, *6*(1), 20–29.

Beigi, M., & Zell, A. (2007). Synthetic protein sequence oversampling method for classification and remote homology detection in imbalanced protein data. In *Proceedings of 1st International Conference on Bioinformatics Research and Development*, (pp. 263-277). Berlin, Germany.

Brodley, C. E., & Friedl, M. A. (1999). Identifying mislabeled training data. *Journal of Artificial Intelligence Research*, *11*, 131–167.

Chawla, N. V., Bowyer, K. W., Hall, L. O., & Kegelmeyer, W. P. (2004). SMOTE: Synthetic minority over-sampling technique. *Journal of Artificial Intelligence Research, 16*, 324–357.

Cieslak, D. A., Chawla, N. V., & Striegel, A. (2006). Combating imbalance in network intrusion datasets. In *Proceedings of IEEE International Conference on Granular Computing,* (pp. 732-737). Athens, Georgia.

Estabrooks, A., Jo, T., & Japkowicz, N. (2004). A multiple resampling method for learning from imbalanced data sets. *Computational Intelligence, 20*(1), 18–36. doi:10.1111/j.0824-7935.2004. t01-1-00228.x

Japkowicz, N., Hanson, S. J., & Gluck, M. A. (2000). Nonlinear autoassociation is not equivalent to PCA. *Neural Computation, 12*(3), 531–545. doi:10.1162/089976600300015691

Kubat, M., & Matwin, S. (1997). Addressing the curse of imbalanced training sets: one sided selection. *Proceedings of the Fourteenth International Conference on Machine Learning,* (pp. 179-186), Nashville, TN: Morgan Kaufmann.

Ling, C., & Li, C. (1998). Data mining for direct marketing problems and solutions. In *Proceedings of the Fourth International Conference on Knowledge Discovery and Data Mining,* (pp. 73-79). New York, NY: AAAI Press.

Muhlenbach, F., Lallich, S., & Zighed, D. A. (2004). Identifying and handling mislabelled instances. *Journal of Intelligent Information Systems, 22*(1), 89–109. doi:10.1023/A:1025832930864

Pradeep, K. M., Venkateswara, R., Radha, K. P., Bapi, R. S., & Laha, A. (2005). Intrusion detection system using sequence and set preserving metric. In *Proceedings of Intelligence and Security Informatics,* (pp. 498-504). Atlanta, USA.

Rani, T. S., & Bapi, R. S. (2008). *Cascaded multi-level promoter recognition of E. coli using dinucleotide features.* In International Conference on Information Technology (pp. 83–88). Bhubaneswar.

Raskutti, B., & Kowalczyk, A. (2004). Extreme re-balancing for SVMs: A case study. *SIGKDD Explorations Newsletter, 6*(1), 60–69. doi:10.1145/1007730.1007739

Sanjay, R., Gulati, V. P., & Pujari, A. K. (2004). Frequency- and ordering-based similarity measure for host-based intrusion detection. *Information Management & Computer Security, 12*(5), 411–421. doi:10.1108/09685220410563397

Sikic, M., Tomic, S., & Vlahovicek, K. (2009). Prediction of protein–protein interaction sites in sequences and 3D structures by random forests. *PLoS Computational Biology, 5*(1), e1000278. doi:10.1371/journal.pcbi.1000278

Soujanya, V., Satyanarayana, R. V., & Kamalakar, K. (2006). *A simple yet effective data clustering algorithm.* In Sixth International Conference on Data Mining, (pp. 1108-1112).

Sun, Y., Castellano, C. G., Mark, R., Adams, R., Alistair, G. R., & Neil, D. (2009). Using pre and post-processing methods to improve binding site predictions. *Pattern Recognition, 42*(9), 1949–1958. doi:10.1016/j.patcog.2009.01.027

Taft, L. M., Evans, R. S., Shyu, C. R., Egger, M. J., & Chawla, N., V., Joyce, A. M., … Michael, W. V. (2009). Countering imbalanced datasets to improve adverse drug event predictive models in labor and delivery. [JBI]. *Journal of Biomedical Informatics, 42*(2), 356–364. doi:10.1016/j. jbi.2008.09.001

Tax, D. (2001). *One-class classification.* PhD thesis, Delft University of Technology.

UCI. (n.d.). *Machine learning repository.* Retrieved from http://archive.ics.uci.edu/ml/

Visa, S., & Ralescu, A. (2005). Issues in mining imbalanced data sets - A review paper. In *Proceedings of the Sixteen Midwest Artificial Intelligence and Cognitive Science Conference*, (pp. 67-73).

Witten, I., & Frank, E. (2000). *Data mining: Practical machine learning tools and techniques with Java implementations*. Morgan Kaufmann Publishers.

Yu, C. Y., Chou, L. C., & Darby, C. (2010). Predicting protein-protein interactions in unbalanced data using the primary structure of proteins. *BMC Bioinformatics, 11*(1), 167..doi:10.1186/1471-2105-11-167

Zhao, X. M., Li, X., Chen, L., & Aihara, K. (2008). Protein classification with imbalanced data. *Proteins: Structure, Function, and Bioinformatics, 70*(4), 1125–1132. doi:10.1002/prot.21870

Chapter 6
Quantization Based Sequence Generation and Subsequence Pruning for Data Mining Applications

T. Ravindra Babu
Infosys Limited, India

M. Narasimha Murty
Indian Institute of Science Bangalore, India

S. V. Subrahmanya
Infosys Limited, India

ABSTRACT

Data Mining deals with efficient algorithms for dealing with large data. When such algorithms are combined with data compaction, they would lead to superior performance. Approaches to deal with large data include working with representatives of data instead of entire data. The representatives should preferably be generated with minimal data scans. In the current chapter we discuss working with methods of lossy and non-lossy data compression methods combined with clustering and classification of large datasets. We demonstrate the working of such schemes on two large data sets.

INTRODUCTION

With increasing number of transactions, reducing cost of storage devices, and the need for generating abstractions for business intelligence, it has become important to search for efficient methods for dealing with large, sequential and time series data. Data mining (Agrawal, et al, 1993; Fayyad,

et al, 1996; Han & Kamber, 1996) focuses on development of scalable and efficient generation of valid, general and novel abstraction from a large dataset.

A transactional dataset consists of records that have transaction-id and the items that make up the transaction. A temporal dataset stores relational data that included time-related attri-

DOI: 10.4018/978-1-61350-056-9.ch006

butes. A sequence dataset contains sequences of ordered events, with or without time information. A time-series dataset contains sequences of values or events obtained over repeat measurements of time periodically like those of spacecraft health data, data from stock exchange, etc. Data Mining is inter-disciplinary subject that encompasses a number of disciplines like Machine Learning, large data clustering and classification, statistics, algorithms, etc.

In the current chapter, we present schemes for non-lossy and lossy compression of data using sequence generation, run-length computation, subsequence pruning leading to efficient clustering and classification of large data. The schemes are efficient, scale up well and provide high classification accuracy.

The proposed scheme integrates the following.

A.   Vector Quantization
B.   Sequence Generation
C.   Item Support and Frequent subsequences (Agrawal et al., 1993; Han et al., 2000)
D.   Subsequence Pruning (Ravindra, Murty, & Agrawal, 2004)
E.   Run length encoding
F.   Support Vector Machines
G.   Classification

The chapter is organized into sections. We discuss motivation for the work in the following section. It is followed by discussion on related work, background terminology and concepts along with illustrations. It is followed by a description of datasets on which we deomstrate working of the proposed schemes. The description includes summary of preliminary analysis of the datasets. Then the following section contains a discussion on proposed scheme, experimentation and results followed by a section on discussion on future research directions. Finally the work is summarized in the last section.

Motivation

When data is large, operating on every pattern to generate an abstraction is expensive both in terms of space and time. In addition, as the data size increases, multiple scans of database would become prohibitive. Hence, generation of abstraction should happen in a small number of scans, ideally a single scan.

Some approaches to deal with large and high dimensional data make use of optimal representative patterns or optimal feature set to represent each pattern. Alternatively, it is interesting to explore whether it is possible to deal with data by compressing the data and work in the compressed domain without having to decompress.

Compression would lead to reduction in space requirements. Further it is also interesting to explore, while compressing the data, whether we can work only on subset of features based on some criterion. This would lead to working in lossy compression domain. However care should be exercised in ensuring that the necessary information is not lost in the process.

We propose two such schemes and examine whether such schemes work efficiently on large datasets in terms of pattern classification.

BACKGROUND

Related Literature

Large data clustering schemes (Jain, Murty & Flynn, 1999) provide ways to deal with large data. Some of the successful methods in this direction have been optimal prototype selection schemes (Ravindra & Murty, 2001; Susheela, 2010), multi-agent systems for large data clustering (Ravindra, Murty & Subrahmanya, 2010; Ravindra, Murty & Subrahmanya, 2009), optimal feature selection (Kim, Street & Mericzer, 2003) and simultaneous selection of prototype and features (Ravindra, Murty & Agrawal, 2005).

Alternate approaches include compressing the data in either lossy form (Ravindra, Murty & Agrawal, 2007) or non-lossy form (Ravindra et al., 2004) and operate on the compressed data directly. This significantly improves space and computation requirements.

Data compression focuses on changing original data representation to an efficient representation by reducing redundancy (Salomon, 2000). Compression is termed lossy when we cannot reproduce the original form. With the objective of dealing with large data efficiently, non-lossy compression is useful as long as classification accuracy of patterns is unaffected or improved. Reduction in number of patterns reduces VC Dimension (Vapnik, 1999) provided Nearest Neighbour Classifier (NNC) accuracy is not affected (Karacah & Krim, 2002).

In the current chapter we discuss ways to deal with large data in terms of lossy and non-lossy compression of data.

Discussion on Related Terms

In the current section, we provide some definitions on which our application of non-lossy compression algorithm (Ravindra et al, 2004) and lossy-compressions schemes are based. We provide a brief description of handwritten digit dataset and intrusion detection data which are considered for demonstrating the proposed schemes.

Consider a data set of 'p' patterns. The data is divided into three parts, p_r, p_v and p_t corresponding to training, validation and test patterns respectively. Let 'q' represent number of binary valued features per pattern. Equivalently, each pattern can be seen as a transaction and features as items. The set of items form *itemset*. In the current chapter, we use patterns and transactions to mean the same. Similarly features and items are used interchangeably.

- **Support** (Agrawal et al., 1993; Han & Kamber, 1996)**:** In the current work, num-

ber of occurrences of an item is referred to support of an item, ω. It should, however, be noted that conventionally, probability/percentage of number of occurrences of an item to total number of transactions represents support. *For example, 11101, 01101, 10010, 10100, 10000 are examples of transactions with binary valued features representing presence (1) or absence (0) of an item.*

- **Frequent Itemset:** The set of items whose support is more than minimum chosen support, ω are referred to as frequent items. *In the above example, with minimum support of 3, item-1 is frequent.*

- **Sequence and subsequence of items** (Goldberg, 1978)**:** Consider two sets of positive integers, viz., I and J. A sequence of integer numbers S:$\{a_1, a_2,...\}$ is a function from I to J. If T is subsequence of positive integers, S o T is called subsequence of S.

- **Length of subsequence:** Number of elements of a subsequence is referred to length of subsequence, 's'.

- **Minimum Frequency for Subsequence Pruning:** It is defined as number of times a subsequence should occur for it to be considered for further processing, η. It helps in compressing or pruning the subsequences. It is defined as a separate parameter to differentiate from minimum support.

- **Block:** Finite number of items forms a block. Number of items in the block is called block length, l.

- **Value of Block:** Decimal equivalent value of a block with binary valued features is referred to as value of the block.

- **Dissimilarity Threshold:** The dissimilarity threshold, ε, in identifying nearest subsequence when original subsequences are pruned using η.

Table 1. Parameters used in lossy data compression scheme

Parameter	Description
p	No. of patterns or transaction
q	No. of features
l	Block length, no. of binary features per block
n	No. of blocks per pattern
ω	Support
s	Length of subsequence
η	Minimum frequency for pruning a subsequence
ε	Dissimilarity threshold for identifying nearest neighbor of subsequence

The symbols used in the current chapter are provided in Table 1. Following examples illustrate above definitions.

Example 4.1. Consider a pattern with binary features as '011000111000'. Sequence is represented by '011000111000'. '011000111' represents subsequence of length, $s= 9$. '011', '000', '111' form blocks of length, $l= 3$ each with corresponding quantized block values of 3,0 and 7.

Example 4.2. Consider 7 patterns or equivalently transactions with 6 features or items each counted from 1 to 6 viz., (110011), (011010), (100010), (101110), (101010), (010101), and (001111). Here, 1 represents of presence and 0 represent absence of an item in the transaction. Support of each of the items is counted by counting number of respective non-zero values. The item-wise supports are (4, 3, 4,3,6,3). Frequent itemsets corresponding to different minimum support or support thresholds of 2,3,4 5,6, and7 respectively are (1,2,3,4,5,6), (1,2,3,4,5,6), (1,3,5), (5), (5) and Null.

Example 4.3. Consider same data as in Example 4.2. We identify blocks of length 2, sequentially from each of the considered transactions, viz., {(1,1), (0,0), (1,1)}, {(0,1), (1,0), (1,0)}, {(1,0),(0,0),(1,0)}, {(1,0),(1,1,),(1,0)}, {(1,0), (1,0), (1,0)}, {(0,1),(0,1),(0,1)}, and {(0,0), (1,1), (1,1)}. Compute block-values and

form subsequences of length-3, each as, (3,0,3), (1,2,2),(2,0,2),(2,3,2),(2,2,2),(1,1,1), and (0,3,3). It should be noted that all the above subsequences have items that have minimum support of $\omega \geq 3$. Here all the subsequences are non-repeating and hence distinct. By considering only frequent items with, say, $\omega \geq 4$, the transactions with frequent features (items) are (100010),(001010),(100010), (101010), (101010),(000000), (001010). Here again, by considering blocks of length 2, the set of subsequences are (2,0,2), (0,2,2), (2,0,2), (2,2,2), (2,2,2), (0,0,0), and (0,2,2). The set of distinct subsequences is (2,0,2), (0,2,2), (2,2,2), and (0,0,0). Observe the reduction in number of distinct subsequences with increasing support, ω.

Run, Run length: In an ordered sequence of elements of two types, maximal subsequence of same type is called a run. Number of elements in a subsequence of same type of elements is referred to as run length.

Example 4.4. For example, a sequence 00011 has subsequences of 000 and 11 of types 0 and 1 respectively. The corresponding run lengths are 3 and 2.

Run-sequence: Sequence of runs of sequence of elements is referred to run-sequence. It forms compressed representation of given sequence of elements.

Example 4.5. Run-sequence of 0001100001 is 3241.

Table 2 contains illustration of concept of non-lossy compression through run-length encoded data along few additional terms. The terms are used further while explaining the proposed schemes.

- **Support Vector Machine (Burges, 1998; Duda, Hart & Stork, 2002):** The focus of the method is to classify given set of patterns by non-linearly mapping them into a sufficiently high dimension such that the two categories are separated by hyperplane (Duda et al., 2002). Training a SVM aims at finding a hyperplane with largest margin which is the distance from the decision hy-

Table 2. Illustration of parameters used in non-lossy compression scheme

Sl. No.	Sequence or Pattern	Run Sequence	Length of Original Sequence	No. of runs	Maximum run-length
1	0101010101	1111111111	10	10	1
2	0000111000	432	10	3	4
3	1000000001	181	10	3	8
4	0001111111	37	10	2	7

perplane. With the help of support vectors which are part of training patterns and are close to decision hyperplane, we classify the unseen patterns.

- **Knowledge-Based Decision Tree (Ravindra et al., 2009):** Knowledge-Based Decision Tree or KBTree exploits domain knowledge on handwritten digit data. Based preliminary analysis, it is observed that classes (0,3,5,6,8) and (1,2,4,7,9) share similar sample statistics. Further statistical analysis showed earlier that the classes (0,6), (3,5,8), (3,5), (4,9), (1,2,7) and (1,7) can be grouped together. Based on this analysis a tree is devised (Ravindra, et al; 2009) that classifies 10-class HW digit data with a decision tree of depth just 4. We make use of the concept in the current work.

- **Leader clustering algorithm (Spath, 1980):** Given a set of patterns, leader algorithm consists of considering any arbitrary pattern as first leader. Every other pattern is sequentially compared with the leader to examine whether it lies within a pre-chosen threshold. When it falls within the threshold, the pattern under consideration belongs to the pattern represented by the leader. When it deviates from the leader with reference to the threshold, the pattern forms new leader. All subsequent patterns are compared with existing set of leaders to decide whether they belong to existing leaders representing corresponding clusters or a new leaders need to be identified.

The leaders form prototypes of the given dataset. Advantage of leader algorithm is that it generates an abstraction of the data with singe database scan. Also, it should be noted that as the threshold value increases number of prototypes would reduce. The value of threshold is trade-off between representability and computation cost.

Handwritten Digit Dataset

Handwritten digit dataset under consideration consists of 10003 labeled patterns. Each pattern is represented as 16X12 matrix. Thus each pattern is characterized by 192 binary valued features. Value of '1' represents the presence and '0', the absence of feature. The dataset is divided into 6670 training, 3333 test patterns. A subset of training data is set out as validation dataset. Equivalently, the dataset can be seen as 10003 transactions with 192 items each with feature value representing presence or absence of the item. Figure 1 represents a set of sample digits.

Figure 1. Sample handwritten digits

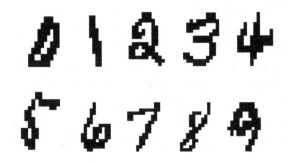

Intrusion Detection Dataset

Intrusion Detection dataset (10% data) that was used during KDDCup99 contest is considered for the study. The data relates to access of computer network by authorized as well as unauthorized users. The access by unauthorized users is termed as intrusion. Different costs of misclassification are attached in assigning a pattern belonging to a class to any other class. The challenge lies in detecting intrusion belonging to different classes accurately minimizing the cost of misclassification. The current data set assumes floating point values.

The training data consists of 41 features. Three of the features are attributes and remaining are floating point numerical values. For effective use of these attributes along with other numerical features, the attributes need to be assigned proper weights based on the domain knowledge. Arbitrary weightages could adversely affect classification results. In view of this, only 38 features are considered for the study. On further analysis it is observed that values of two of the 38 features in the considered 10%-dataset are always zero, effectively suggesting exclusion of these two features (features numbered 16 and 17, by counting first feature as 0). The training data consists of 311029 patterns and the test data consists of 494020 patterns. A closer observation reveals that not all features are frequent. We make use of this fact during the experiments.

The training data consists of 23 attack types that form 4-broad classes, viz., 'dos', 'normal', 'u2r', 'r2l', and 'probe'. As noted earlier test data contains 19 more classes than those in the training data. Since the classification of test data depends on learning from training data, the unknown attack types(or classes) in the test data have to be assigned one of a priori known classes of training data. This is carried out in two ways, viz., (a) assigning unknown attack types with one of the known types by nearest neighbour assignment within Test Data, or (b) assigning with the help of domain knowledge. Independent exercises are carried out to assign unknown classes by both the methods. The results obtained by both these methods differ significantly. In view of this, assignments based on domain knowledge are considered and test data is formed accordingly.

In classifying the data, each wrong pattern assignment is assigned a cost. The cost matrix is provided in Table 3. Observe from the table that cost of assigning a pattern to a wrong class is not uniform. For example, cost of assigning a pattern belonging to class 'u2r' to 'normal' is 3. Its cost is more than that of assigning a pattern from 'u2r' to 'dos', say.

Further, dissimilarity measure plays an important role. The range of values for any feature within a class or across the classes is large. Also the values assumed by different features within a pattern are also largely variable. This scenario suggests use of Euclidean as well as Mahalanobis distance measures. Both the methods are used in carrying out exercises on random samples drawn from the original data. Based on the study on the random samples, it is observed that Euclidean distance measure provided better classification of unseen patterns. Thus, Euclidean measure alone is used further.

With the full data of the given dataset, NNC provides a classification accuracy of 92.11 with a cost of 0.254086}. This result can be made use while analyzing the results reported in the rest of the chapter.

Table 3. Cost matrix

Class Type	'normal'	'u2r'	'dos'	'r2l'	'probe'
'normal'	0	2	2	2	1
'u2r'	3	0	2	2	2
'dos'	2	2	0	2	1
'r2l'	4	2	2	0	2
'probe'	1	2	2	2	0

Table 4. Accuracy of winner and runner up of KDDCUP'99

Description	Winner	Runner-up
Class name:'dos'	99.5%	99.4%
Class name: 'normal'	97.1%	97.5%
Class name: 'r2l'	8.4%	7.3%
Class name: 'u2r'	13.2%	11.8%
Class name: 'probe'	83.3%	84.5%
Cost	0.233	0.2356

Results reported during KDDCUP'99 are provided in Table 4.

Proposed System

In the current section, we present proposed schemes that efficiently handle large data. Initially we discuss need aspect of such schemes, and follow it with an overview of proposed schemes. Subsequently we describe each of the proposed schemes along with previous work carried out in the direction and the present extensions. Results of preliminary data analysis leads to final implementation of the scheme is discussed in the same sub-section. The experimental results are presented in the section titled, "Experimentation and Results".

NEED ASPECT

When we deal with large datasets, one important aspect is to study whether entire data is necessary to generate an abstraction. And whether it is possible to extract a representative subset based on which we generate an abstraction which is as valid as it is generated from entire dataset.

In addition to above, it is interesting to explore whether we can generate a non-lossy compaction or compression of the dataset and operate in the compressed domain without having to decompress

to generate an abstraction (Ravindra et al., 2007). Another view is resort to lossy compression of data (Ravindra et al., 2004) and still be able to generate an abstraction which is at least as good as the one generated by full data. In either case, the schemes would lead to space and time advantage due to compression and less number of operations respectively.

Such schemes are found to be quite useful for data mining applications. We provide outline of methods with the help of discussion on background provided in background section.

OVERVIEW OF COMPRESSION SCHEMES

In the current subsection we discuss previous work done in this direction. This forms the basis for the proposed scheme.

Lossless Compression

The scheme consists of following steps.

A. Consider transaction-type dataset which contains patterns with binary valued features. Some examples of such datasets are sales transaction data, and handwritten digit data with binary valued features.
B. Encode the data as run lengths
C. Use dissimilarity computation scheme (Ravindra et al., 2007) to compute dissimilarity in the compressed domain without having to decompress
D. In order to validate non-lossy nature of compression, decompress the run length encoded data to original form and compare. However the same was theoretically proven earlier (Ravindra et al., 2007)
E. Encode training, validation and test datasets
F. Using kNNC, classification of test data can be done in compressed domain with the help of dissimilarity computation scheme

as mentioned in (d) above, which leads to savings in terms of time and space.

Following are some of the important observations in the implementation of above scheme.

Unequal number of runs: The features of the patterns are binary valued. Since each transaction/pattern is different, the run length and number of runs per pattern are different for different patterns. Thus they lead to unequal number of runs for different patterns, because of intra-class and inter-class variations.

Application of dissimilarity measures: Because of unequal number of runs, it is difficult to apply conventional dissimilarity measures to the data.

Some further exploration possibilities of the above scheme is to examine whether we can generate similarities among the compressed data directly, or is it possible to further compress the data by extraction of some additional features so that we can obtain similarities among the data.

We present an extension of the above scheme as part of discussion on proposed scheme.

Lossy Compression

In brief, the scheme consists of observing that not all items/features contribute to discrimination. Because of this, if by some means, if some of the non-zero features could be eliminated, it would lead to further compaction. Equivalently in terms of runs it would lead to less number of runs per pattern. However, it needs to be validated that such elimination does not affect the overall accuracy of abstraction.

The scheme consists of the following steps. We describe each of the steps.

- Compression by Minimum support
- Data Encoding
- Compression by Subsequence Generation and Pruning
- Encoding Training Dataset

- Dissimilarity Computation of Encoded data
- Encoding Test Dataset
- Classification of Test Patterns

Compression by Minimum Support

The input data often contains noise and contain features that not frequent. The set of active features differs from one pattern to another even within class. In order to obtain proper abstraction, it is necessary remove the noise. Consider the training data. Each pattern is characterized by 'q' items. Compute support for each of the items. Consider a minimum support, 'ω', which is data domain dependent. In order to compute 'ω', we carry out preliminary analysis of data under study. After computing minimum support, we consider only those items of each of the transactions which exceed 'ω'. Thus number of effective items reduces. However, it should be noted here that notwithstanding the reduction in the number of effective items, total number of items 'q' per pattern is left unchanged.

Data Encoding

Subsequent to reduction in number of effective features, subsequence generation is carried out for encoded data. For encoding, consider 'l' number of items as a block and compute decimal equivalent of each block. Value of 'l' is chosen based on preliminary data analysis such that 'q' is integral multiple of 'l'. Thus it provides sequence of decimal values for each pattern.

Subsequence Generation

Sequence of decimals values is further compacted by considering subsequences of decimal values. The length of subsequence 's' is data dependent. Large data representing a scenario is likely to have similarity among different patterns. The value of 's' is essentially a trade-off between achievable compactness and pattern representativeness. At the extremes, *s* takes the value of 1 as minimum and q/l as maximum value. At minimum, number of subsequences equals to q/l subsequences. At maximum entire pattern gets represented as single subsequence.

After the subsequences are computed, we look for distinct subsequences. Least number of distinct subsequences indicates maximum compactness. The number of distinct subsequences is a function of 'ω'.

Subsequence Pruning

Second level of compaction is achieved by pruning distinct subsequences. Distinct subsequences which occur once or less number of times, do not add to discrimination. After generating the distinct subsequences, frequency of each distinct subsequence across entire training data is counted. Consider a data dependent minimum frequency threshold for a distinct subsequence, 'η'. Replace all those distinct subsequences that occur less than 'η' by their nearest neighbours (NN). In order to obtain Generalization, 'η' is chosen to be last possible value above 1.

Encoding Training Dataset

Each of 'p' training patterns is considered. Based on 'ω', the number of items across all the 'p' patterns is minimized. Subsequently, with a block length of 'l' the data is encoded to block values. The subsequences of length 's' are considered. Distinct subsequences across entire training data are identified as k, say. With minimum frequency value of 'η', least frequent distinct subsequences are replaced by their nearest neighbours. At this stage entire training dataset is represented by k_1 distinct subsequence, where $k_1 < k$.

Dissimilarity Computation Between Distinct Subsequences

The number of distinct subsequences k_1 is numbered from 1 to k_1. The combination of distinct subsequences for each pattern is are likely to be different. When patterns contain binary valued features, Hamming distance and Euclidean distance provide equivalent information for discrimination. We consider Hamming distance for computing distance between two encoded values. Dissimilarity between two patterns is computed as sum of dissimilarities between corresponding decimal codes. For example for 4-bit blocks, the range of decimal codes is 0 to 15. To compute distance between blocks, it is sufficient to store $16*17/2=136$ values. In summary distance computation between two training patterns is simplified as given below.

A. With 'l' bit encoding, pattern of 'q' features is reduced to q/l blocks.
B. By considering frequent subsequences, number of distinct subsequences further reduces.
C. Dissimilarity between two patterns is carried out by table look-up.

Encoding Test Dataset

Encoding Test data involves approximation. As discussed earlier, distinct subsequences are computed based on the training data. The distinct subsequences are pruned further. Test dataset is independent of Training data. The pruning parameters are not applicable to test data. Thus test data can always contain subsequences that would have got pruned in the training data. Thus for finding distance between training and test patterns, when a matching subsequence in test pattern is not available in the training data, it is assigned a nearest distance subsequence identified earlier during training in the process of lossy compression. Once assigned, the dissimilarity computation would be same as explained in the previous Subsection.

The scheme is directly applicable to binary valued features. We explore here to see how the scheme can be extended to patterns with real valued feature values. We present a proposed scheme and implementation of the same on network intrusion data of KDDCup 99.

PROPOSED METHODS

The current sub-section contains discussion on proposed methods. We provide two extensions of the work described in Sub-section of proposed system.

Scheme 1

Consider the case of lossless compression of binary feature valued patterns. Runs are computed of the given training and test data. The test data is classified in the compressed domain directly without having to uncompress using a novel scheme. It was shown earlier (Ravindra et al., 2007) that such a scheme is non-lossy and provided a *space advantage of 3 times and CPU time advantage of about 5 times* with handwritten digit data. The same data set is used for exercises in the current Chapter too. The scheme is an extension of the previously reported scheme (Ravindra, et al, 2007).

The scheme consists of additional steps in leading to further compaction and summarization. The steps can be enlisted as below. Figure 2 contains corresponding Schematic.

A.   Given patterns with binary valued features, encode the data as run lengths. We illustrate the concepts considering handwritten digit data. The data covers both training and test patterns.

B.   Compute runs in both horizontal and vertical directions.

C.   Compute maximum number of runs and run of maximum length in both horizontal and vertical directions. It forms 4-dimensional vector.

D.   Use Leader clustering algorithm to cluster patterns class-wise

E.   Consider cluster representatives or leaders and classify the test data both in *run-length encode form* using Support Vector Machines

It should be noted here that the scheme leader enormous compression of given data. We demonstrate the same through some illustrations.

Scheme 2

Consider lossy compression of data. Earlier work in this direction (Ravindra et al., 2004) consisted of two levels of lossy compression. Initially out of original elements only those elements that are frequent with a chosen support are considered for further treatment. This forms *first level of lossy*

Figure 2. Proposed scheme 1

Given Training and Test Data of rectangular patterns, runlength-encode data in horizontal and vertical directions

⇩

Compute 4-dimensional vector containing number of runs and maximum run length in horizontal and vertical directions

⇩

Indentify prototypes with the help of 4-dimensional vector using Leader Clustering Algorithm

⇩

Classify run-compressed test data directly using Support Vector Machines and Prototypes *compression.* Subsequently based on preliminary analysis length of fixed block is derived. Consider fixed blocks of binary valued features and compute decimal equivalents through quantization step. We consider subsequences of fixed length and compute frequency of such subsequences. Subsequences of frequency less than a chosen threshold are eliminated. This forms *second level of compression.* However, test data could still contain some of the eliminated features and subsequences. Hence nearest derived subsequence from the training data is assigned to an hitherto unseen subsequence found in a test pattern. Based on the classification method, a label is assigned to the test pattern. It was shown earlier (Ravindra et al., 2004), that it provided accuracy better than original uncompressed data set.

The scheme proposed earlier worked efficiently with binary valued features, since the application of the scheme is direct in both the levels of lossy compression. However, it needs to be explored whether it could work with floating valued features. We examine the same in our proposed scheme.

The scheme can be summarized through following steps. Figure 3 contains the proposed scheme.

A. Given floating point values of features of a pattern, carry out preliminary statistical analysis on the sample data to find out range of each of feature values.
B. Quantize the range through number of bits and the resolution. This forms equivalent binary representation of floating point values. Together with all the features of the pattern, it forms a pattern with binary valued features.
C. Compute frequent features and eliminate the features that lie below pre-chosen support threshold. It forms *first level compression.*
D. Form blocks of constant length and subsequences of quantized features. Eliminate subsequences of frequency lower that given threshold. It forms *second level compression.*

Figure 3. Proposed scheme 2

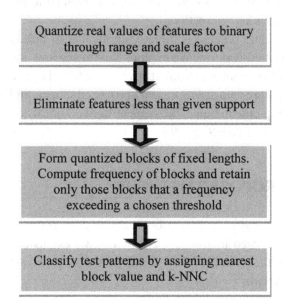

E. Classify test patterns as discussed above.

EXPERIMENTATION AND RESULTS

We carry out brief experimentation in order to demonstrate the working of the schemes. Scheme-1 is demonstrated using handwritten digit dataset and Scheme-2 is demonstrated using KDDCUP99 dataset (KDDCup99 data, 2009). The datasets are described in Subsections of background section.

Scheme-1

We consider handwritten digit data containing 10 classes with labels 0 to 9. Each class has 667 training patterns. The data is considered at the first stage as two sets containing (0,3,5,6,8) and (1,2,4,7,9) based on their shape and similarity based on sample statistics. Total number of training patterns is 6670. They are equally divided into above two sets. The classification scheme is based on Knowledge Based Decision Tree (Ravindra et al., 2009). We demonstrate working of the scheme based on these two datasets.

We compute runs corresponding to each pattern both in horizontal and vertical directions. Each pattern consists of 192 binary features and each pattern is recognizable digit when arranged in 16X12 matrix. Horizontal runs correspond to computation of runs in row-direction and vertical runs correspond to column-direction. Figure 4 contains plot of these runs with reference to patterns. First set of two figures in horizontal direction correspond to pattern wise horizontal and vertical runs respectively of the first set consisting of classes (0,3,5,6,8). Second set of two figures in horizontal direction are horizontal and vertical runs of second set containing training patterns belong to classes (1,2,4,7,9). Following observations can be made from the figures.

- No. of runs in horizontal direction are higher than those in vertical direction. This is due to existence of longer sequence of zero features in vertical directions by the nature of pattern.
- The plots provide range for value of runs for different patterns. For example, in case of class-0 the runs approximately range from about 42 to 58 in horizontal direction and 10 to 32 in vertical direction
- Class-wise runs could possibly be characterized as number of runs and maximum run length. It is further explored to whether the information is good enough for grouping similar patterns.

The patterns are clustered using 4-dimensional vector consisting of the following

1. Number of runs in horizontal direction of the pattern,
2. Maximum run length of the runs within pattern,
3. Number of runs in vertical direction of the pattern
4. Maximum run length of the runs within pattern

We cluster patterns within each class based on these features. Interestingly they successfully group the patterns. The leaders thus computed are considered as prototypes. The corresponding compressed run-length encoded data is extracted. Using these prototypes classification of unseen patterns numbering 3333 is carried out using support vector machines using the package, *svm*^*light* (Chang & Lin, 2001). The classification accuracy obtained using linear kernel is **93.91%**. Further class-wise labeling as we pass through Knowledge Based Decision tree is carried out in similar manner.

Scheme-2

In this case, we consider intrusion detection data of KDDCup 99. Description of the data is provided in background section. Table 5 provides quantization effort corresponding to some features among the 38 features of the data. Feature wise statistics of training data are computed. The table contains a number of interesting statistics. They can be summarized below.

- Ranges of mean values of different features are different.
- Standard deviation which is a measure of dispersion is different for different feature values
- Minimum value of each feature is 0.0
- Maximum values of different features are different ranging from 1.0 to 693375616
- Feature-wise support is different for different features. The support is defined here as number of times a feature assumed nonzero value in the training data.
- If the real values are to be mapped to integers, number of bits required along with corresponding resolution is different for different features.

With support value of 5%, the number of features reduces to 22 and with support value of 10%

Figure 4. Run lengths for set-1 and set-2

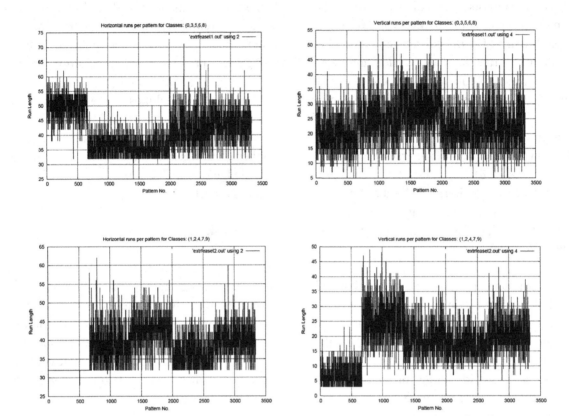

Top two figures represent horizontal and vertical run lengths of Set-1 and bottom two figures represent horizontal and vertical run lengths for Set-2.

the number of features reduces to 17. Experiments are conducted varying threshold for subsequence elimination.

We consider support value of 10%. Further in order to further reduce the dataset size, we subject to clustering as well. We classify the test data using NNC. Table 6 contains the results. The results are presented for subsequence threshold of value '0'. It can be observed from the table that with increasing distance threshold of leader clustering algorithm, number of prototypes reduces. Best classification accuracy obtained and best cost obtained is highlighted. It should be noted that the cost obtained is better that reported values of winner and runner up in KDDCup 99 contest.

FUTURE RESEARCH DIRECTIONS

With reducing costs of storage devices and increasing need for business intelligence, demand for efficient algorithms is continuously on the increase. The work opens up a number of directions for compressed data handling with and without the use of prototype selection as well as feature selection. Some of the future research directions are the following.

- Compress the data in lossy manner and use extracted information of the compressed data for generating prototypes alone. For example, we demonstrated the use of number of runs and maximum run

Table 5. Quantization statistics for few features of intrusion detection data (KDDCup 99,1999)

Feature No.	Mean Value	Std. Deviation	Min.	Max	Bits (VQ)	Resolution	Support
1	47.979302	707.745756	0	58329	16	1.4e-5	12350
2	3025.609608	988217.066787	0	693375616	30	6.0e-10	378679
3	868.529016	33039.967815	0	5155468	23	7.32e-8	85762
4	0.000045	0.006673	0	1	4	0.06	22
5	0.006433	0.134805	0	3.0	4	0.06	22
6	0.000014	0.05510	0	3.0	4	0.06	1238
30	188.666186	106.040032	0	255.0	8	3.9e-3	494019
38	0.0547512	0.230140	0	1.0	4	0.06	341260

length in horizontal and vertical directions to successfully clustering compressed patterns. We can use additional statistics for more effective clustering of the patterns. Clustering can however be validated using classification of unseen patterns.

- Starting with patterns with equal number of features, run length encoding leads to uneven number of extracted features per pattern. Research work towards making the number of extracted features equal would enable application of conventional dissimilarity measures
- Classification of compressed data using SVMs is successful. Multi-kernal SVMs is one important direction of further exploration.
- The direction of lossy compression combined with prototype selection is significantly promising area. Choice of block length is domain dependent. Theoretical extensions can be taken up in this direction.
- Extension of the work in both lossy and non-lossy data compaction for text processing is a promising research direction.

CONCLUSION

Data Mining conventionally focuses efficient and effective algorithms that deal with large data. In the current Chapter we discuss possibility of generating a compaction of data and working in such compressed domain without having to decompress to generate abstraction. We discussed previous work done in these directions. And proposed extensions in terms of using information extracted out of run-length compressed data leading to further compaction. Also, we extended previous work on lossy compression on binary valued feature data to real valued data.

We provided discussion on background terminology, previous work in this direction and proposed two schemes. We described each of the schemes. We carried out experiments demonstrating their working on large data sets of handwritten digit data and intrusion detection data. We briefly discussed possible future directions of the current work.

Table 6. Results on original data having support of 10%

Distance Threshold	No. of Leaders	CA	Cost
5.0	17508	91.83%	0.1588
10.0	15749	**91.85%**	0.1586
20.0	15023	91.83%	**0.1585**
50.0	9669	84.60%	0.2990
100.0	3479	82.97%	0.3300

REFERENCES

Agarwal, R., Imielenski, T., & Swami, A. (1993). Mining association rules between sets of items in large databases. In *Proc. 1993 ACM-SIGMOD Int. Conf. Management of Data (SIGMOD'93)*, (pp. 266-271).

Burges, C. J. C. (1998). A tutorial on support vector machines for pattern recognition. *Data Mining and Knowledge Discovery, 2*(2), 1–47. doi:10.1023/A:1009715923555

Chang, C. C., & Lin, C. J. (2001). *LIBSVM – A library for support vector machines*. Retrieved from http://www.cse.ntu.edu.tw/~cjlin/libsvm/

Duda, R. O., Hart, P. E., & Stork, D. G. (2002). *Pattern classification*. New York, NY: John Wiley and Sons.

Fayyad, U. M., Piatetsky-Shapiro, G., Smyth, P., & Uthurusamy, R. (Eds.). (1996). *Advances in knowledge discovery and data mining*. AAAI/ MIT Press.

Goldberg, R. R. (1978). *Methods of real analysis* (1st ed.). New Delhi, India: Oxford & IBH Publishing Company.

Han, J., & Kamber, M. (1996). *Data mining – Concepts and techniques*. Elesevier Inc.

Han, J., Pei, J., & Yin, Y. (2000). Mining frequent patterns without candidate generations. In *Proc. Of ACM SIGMOD Intl. Conf. of Management of Data (SIGMOD 00)*, (pp. 1-12).

Jain, A. K., Murty, M. N., & Flynn, P. P. (1999). Data clustering: A review. *ACM Computing Review*.

Karacah, B., & Krim, H. (2002). Fast minimization of structural risk by nearest neighbor rule. *IEEE Transactions on Neural Networks, 14*(1), 127–137. doi:10.1109/TNN.2002.804315

KDDCup99. (1999). *Data*. Retrieved from http://kdd.ics.uci.edu/databases/kddcup99/kddcup99.html

Kim, Y. S., Stree, W. N., & Menczer, F. (2003). Feature selection in data mining. In Wang, J. (Ed.), *Data mining: Opportunities and challenges* (pp. 80–105). Hershey, PA: IGI Global. doi:10.4018/9781591400516.ch004

Piatetsky-Shapiro, G., & Frawley, W. J. (1991). *Knowledge discovery in databases*. AAAI/MIT, 1991.

Ravindra Babu, T., Murty, M. N., & Agrawal, V. K. (2007). Classification of run-length encoded binary data. *Pattern Recognition, 40*, 321–323. doi:10.1016/j.patcog.2006.05.002

Ravindra Babu, T., Murty, M. N., & Subrahmanya, S. V. (2009). Multiagent systems for large data clustering. In Cao, L. (Ed.), *Data mining and multi-agent interaction, part 3* (pp. 219–238). doi:10.1007/978-1-4419-0522-2_15

Ravindra Babu, T., Murty, M. N., & Subrahmanya, S. V. (2010). *Multiagent based large data clustering scheme for data mining applications*. Intl. Conf. on Active Media Technology, (pp. 116-127).

Ravindra Babu, T., & Narasimha Murty, M. (2001). Comparison of genetic algorithm based prototype selection schemes. *Pattern Recognition, 34*(2), 523–525. doi:10.1016/S0031-3203(00)00094-7

Ravindra Babu, T., Narasimha Murty, M., & Agrawal, V. K. (2004). Hybrid learning scheme for data mining applications. In *the Proc. Fourth International Conference on Hybrid Intelligent Systems*, (pp. 266-271). Los Alamitos, CA: IEEE Computer Society.

Ravindra Babu, T., Narasimha Murty, M., & Agrawal, V. K. (2005). On simultaneous selection of prototypes and features on large data. In the *Proceedings of PReMI*, (pp. 595-600).

Salomon, D. (2000). *Data compression – The complete reference*. CA: Springer-Verlag.

Spath, H. (1980). *Cluster analysis – Algorithms for data reduction and classification of objects*. West Sussex, UK: Ellis Horwood Limited.

Susheela Devi, V. (2010). *Optimal prototype selection for efficient pattern classification*. VDM Verlag.

Vapnik, V. (1999). *Statistical learning theory* (2nd ed.). New York, NY: John Wiley & Sons.

ADDITIONAL READING

Buccafurri, F., Rosaci, D., Sarne, G. M. L., & Ursino, D. (2002). An agent-based hierarchical clustering approach for e-commerce environments. *In Proceedings of E-Commerce and Web Technologies, 3rd International Conference (EC-Web 2002), France. Lecture Notes in Computer Science, Vol.2455. Springer,* 109–118.

Bulbidge, R., & Buxton, B. (2001). An introduction to support vector machines for data mining. In *Proc. 12ᵗʰ Conf. Young Operational Research (YOR12), 3-15.*

Cao, L., Yu, P. S., Zhang, C., Zhao, Y., & Williams, G. (2007). Domain Driven Data Mining. *SIGKDD Explorations, 9*(Issue 2), 84–86. doi:10.1145/1345448.1345467

Cao, L., & Zhang, C. (2007). F-Trade: An agent-mining symbiont for financial services. [Hawaii, USA.]. *AAMAS, 07*(May), 14–18.

Covert, T., & Hart, P. (1967). Nearest Neighbour pattern Classification. *IEEE Transactions on Information Theory, 13,* 21–27. doi:10.1109/TIT.1967.1053964

Han, J., Pei, J., & Yin, Y. (2000). Mining frequent patterns without candidate generation, *Proc. of ACM SIGMOD International Conference of Management of Data(SIGMOD 00), 1–12.*

Hand, D. J., Mannila, H., & Smyth, P. (2001). *Principles of Data Mining*. MIT Press.

Kaufmann, L., & Rousseeuw, P. J. (1990). *Finding groups in data: An introduction to cluster analysis*. John Wiley & Sons.

Lelewer, D. A., & Hirshberg, D. S. (1987). Data Compression. In ACM Computing Suveys, Vol. 9, 261-296.

Liu, H., & Motoda, H. (Eds.). (2008). *Computational Methods in Feature Selection, Chapman & Hall*. FL: CRC.

Makinen, V., Navarro, G., & Ukkinen, E. (2003). Approximate matching of run-length compressed strings. *Algorithmica, 35*(4), 347–369. doi:10.1007/s00453-002-1005-2

Mitra, P., Murthy, C. A., & Pal, S. K. (2000). Data condensation in large databases by incremental learning with support vector machines. In *Proc. 15ᵗʰ International Conf. on Pattern Recognition, (ICPR'00), Vol. 2, 27*08.

Mitra, P., & Pal, S. K. (2002). Density based multiscale data condensation. *IEEE Transactions on Pattern Analysis and Machine Intelligence, 24*(6), 734–747. doi:10.1109/TPAMI.2002.1008381

Ogston, E., Overreinder, R., van Steen, M., & Brazier, F. (2003). Group formation among peer-to-peer agents: Learning group characteristics. *In 2nd International Workshop, on Agents and Peer-to-peer computing. Lecture Notes in Computer Science, Vol.2872, Springer,* 59–70.

Pal, S. K., & Ghosh, A. (2004). Soft computing data mining. *Information Sciences, 163*(1–3), 1–3. doi:10.1016/j.ins.2003.03.012

Pal, S. K., & Mitra, P. (2004). *Pattern Recognition Algorithms for Data Mining*. Chapman & Hall/CRC.

Park, J., & Oh, K. (2006). Multi-Agent Systems for Intelligent Clustering (2006). *Proc. of World Academy of Science. Engineering and Technology, 11*(February), 97–102.

Piraveenan, M., Prokopenko, M., Wang, P., & Zeman, A. (2008). Decentralized multi-agent clustering in scale-free sensor networks. *Studies in Computational Intelligence, 115*, 485–515. doi:10.1007/978-3-540-78293-3_12

Sayood, K. (2000). *Introduction to Data Compression* (1st ed.). Morgan Kaufmann Publishers.

Scholkopf, B., & Smola, A. J. (2002). *Learning with Kernels, MIT Press*. Cambridge: Massaschussets.

Valiant, L. G. (1984). A theory of the learnable. *Communications of the ACM, 27*(11), 1134–1142. doi:10.1145/1968.1972

Weiss, G. (Ed.). (2000). *Multiagent Systems - A modern approach to Distributed Artificial Intelligence*. The MIT Press.

Wooldridge, M., & Jennings, N. R. Towards a theory of cooperative problem solving. In proc. of the Workshop of Distributed Software Agents and Applications, Denmark, 40–53.

Chapter 7
Classification of Biological Sequences

Pratibha Rani
International Institute of Information Technology Hyderabad, India

Vikram Pudi
International Institute of Information Technology Hyderabad, India

ABSTRACT

The rapid progress of computational biology, biotechnology, and bioinformatics in the last two decades has led to the accumulation of tremendous amounts of biological data that demands in-depth analysis. Data mining methods have been applied successfully for analyzing this data. An important problem in biological data analysis is to classify a newly discovered sequence like a protein or DNA sequence based on their important features and functions, using the collection of available sequences. In this chapter, we study this problem and present two Bayesian classifiers RBNBC (Rani & Pudi, 2008a) and REBMEC (Rani & Pudi, 2008c). The algorithms used in these classifiers incorporate repeated occurrences of subsequences within each sequence (Rani, 2008). Specifically, Repeat Based Naive Bayes Classifier (RBNBC) uses a novel formulation of Naive Bayes, and the second classifier, Repeat Based Maximum Entropy Classifier (REBMEC) uses a novel framework based on the classical Generalized Iterative Scaling (GIS) algorithm.

INTRODUCTION

With the development of biology, biotechnology, bioinformatics and biomedical research, more and more biological data is getting collected and is available for analysis (Wang et al., 2005). Data mining methods have been applied successfully for analyzing this data and many sophisticated mining tools such as *GeneSpring*, *Spot Fire* and *VectorNTI* have also been developed (Wang et al., 2005). The trend of developing data mining based solutions for biological data analysis is rapidly evolving. Details can be found in (Wang et al., 2005, chapter 2).

DOI: 10.4018/978-1-61350-056-9.ch007

A critical problem in biological data analysis is to classify biological sequences based on their important features and functions. This problem is important due to the exponential growth of newly generated sequence data during recent years, which demands for automatic methods for sequence classification. The advantage of automatic sequence classifier is that, prediction of class of an unclassified sequence reduces the time and cost required for performing experiments on the new sequence in laboratory to find its functions and properties. Since the sequences belonging to the same class have similar characteristics, the predicted class will give idea about the function and properties of the new sequence. For example, (1) a protein's structure and functions depend on its amino acid sequence, so if we can predict the class of a new protein sequence on the basis of its amino acid sequence, then we can predict its structure and functions; (2) frequently, it is unknown for which proteins a new DNA sequence codes or if it codes for any protein at all. If we can predict the class of a new coding sequence on the basis of known coding sequences then there is a high probability to predict the proteins it will code for; and (3) prediction of the type of disease can be done by predicting the class of a sample sequence using a set of known sample sequences divided in different classes according to the type of diseases.

The known state-of-the-art solutions for classification problem are mainly based on Sequence Alignment (Altschul et al., 1990, 1997; Pearson & Lipman, 1988), Hidden Markov Model (HMM) (Krogh et al., 1994; Durbin et al., 1998; Eddy, 1998), Probabilistic Suffix Trees (PST) (Bejerano & Yona, 1999; Eskin et al., 2003) and Support Vector Machines (SVM) (Leslie et al., 2002; Ben-Hur & Brutlag, 2003a, 2003b; Weston et al., 2005). Recent approaches (Melvin et al., 2007; Marsolo & Parthasarathy, 2006a, 2006b) have been trying to improve SVM by incorporating domain knowledge, using complex features based on structures and combining it with other classifiers.

In this chapter we discuss two totally data mining based, simple but effective *Bayesian* classifiers for the biological sequences. These classifiers are called Repeat Based Naive Bayes Classifier (RBNBC) and Repeat Based Maximum Entropy Classifier (REBMEC). These classifiers use generic domain independent feature extraction method which requires comparatively less memory and time with the advantage of no need of domain expertise. Also these classifiers incorporate repeated occurrences of subsequences within each sequence known as *repeats* of the subsequences. Note that the existing domain based feature extraction methods are highly memory intensive and time consuming and they need extensive domain knowledge (Ferreira & Azevedo, 2005b, 2006; Lesh et al., 1999, 2000; Huang & Brutlag, 2001).

Naive Bayes is well known as a surprisingly successful classification method that has outperformed much more complicated methods in many application domains (Domingos & Pazzani, 1996; Kotsiantis & Pintelas, 2004; Zhang, 2004). However a direct implementation of *Naïve Bayes* does not work well for biological sequences. In RBNBC it is adapted to work for biological sequences.

On the other hand REBMEC uses a novel framework based on the classical *Generalized Iterative Scaling* (GIS) (Darroch & Ratcliff, 1972) algorithm to find the maximum entropy model for the given collection of biological sequences. The maximum entropy principle has been widely used for various tasks including discretization of numeric values of features (Kotsiantis & Pintelas, 2004), feature selection (Li et al., 2003; Tatti, 2007; Ratnaparkhi, 1998), and various text related tasks like translation (Berger et al., 1996), document classification (Nigam et al., 1999), and part-of-speech tagging (Ratnaparkhi, 1998). REBMEC's approach is inspired by these works because comparison between biological sequence data and natural languages are commonplace (Buehler & Ungar, 2001). Unlike other *Bayesian* classifiers like *Naive Bayes*, maximum entropy based classifiers do not assume independence among features. These classifiers build the model of the dataset using an iterative approach to find the parameter values that satisfy the constraints generated by the features and the training data (Thonangi & Pudi, 2005; Ratnaparkhi, 1997; Buehler & Ungar, 2001). Maximum entropy based classifiers are known to be slow, have high accuracy and serve as a useful benchmark to compare other classifiers.

INTRODUCTION TO BIOLOGICAL SEQUENCES AND DATABASES

In this section, we discuss the various types of biological sequences and the databases which store them. There are three types of biological sequences available for analysis. Following paragraphs briefly explains them.

1. Deoxyribonucleic acid (DNA) acts like a biological computer program that spells out the instructions for making proteins. DNA is a double-stranded nucleic acid molecule twisted into a helix (think of a spiral staircase). Each spiraling strand, comprised of a sugar-phosphate backbone and attached nucleotide bases, is connected to a complementary strand by non-covalent hydrogen bonding between paired nucleotide bases. The nucleotide bases are adenine (A), thymine (T), cytosine (C) and guanine (G). A and T form a base pair connected by two hydrogen bonds while G and C are connected by three hydrogen bonds. Usually one of the two strands is sequenced. Each character in the sequence is a base pair, the other character being present in the sequence of the complementary strand. So a base pair is the unit in which the length of a DNA sequence is measured.

2. Like DNA, Ribonucleic acid (RNA) is a type of nucleic acid but is usually single stranded, except when it folds back on itself. It differs chemically from DNA because it contains Ribose sugar instead of Deoxyribose and a uracil (U) base instead of thymine (T) base. Thus, the four nucleotide bases in RNA are A, C, G and U.

3. A protein is a linear polymer composed of chains of amino acids in a specific order determined by the base sequences of nucleotides in the DNA coding for the protein. A sequence of amino acids is coded for by the sequences of nucleotide bases in a DNA molecule—three bases form a triplet code. Each triplet code codes for one amino acid. A protein is a sequence of amino acids, and can be as long as several thousands of amino acids. There are twenty distinct amino acids, each represented by a letter: alanine (A), cysteine (C), aspartic acid (D), glutamic acid (E), phenylalanine (F), glycine (G), histidine (H), iosleucine (I), lysine (K), leucine (L), methionine (M), asparagines (N), proline (P), glutamine (Q), arginine (R), seine (S), threonine (T), valine (V), tryptophan (W), and tyrosine (Y). The length of a protein sequence is measured in terms of the number of amino acids present in the sequence. The length of a protein sequence can go up to several thousands of amino acids.

Figure 1 shows the amino acid sequence of a protein with primary accession number P91638 taken from SWISS-PROT (Bairoch & Boeckmann, 2003) database. The name of the protein is *Smallminded* protein and is obtained from fruit fly. Its length is 943. The format of the presented information is called FASTA format in which the first line starting with symbol ">" is the header line showing protein ID, name and other information and from next line onwards the amino acid symbols are shown in groups of up to 80 characters.

There are a lot of different databases where biological information such as DNA and protein sequence data are stored, including, general biological data banks such as GenBank (Benson et

Figure 1. Protein sequence from SWISS-PROT database in FASTA format. The header line shows Protein ID and name. From next line onwards amino acid symbols are shown in groups of 60 characters per line.

```
>P91638|P91638 DROME Smallminded protein - Drosophila melanogaster (Fruit fly).
MKKAKPLLHDHLITIRVKKYLEEHIGETYLDVKQMTRELMQKYPEYSRRKFGPFRQLVHQ
AFSIISESYNLDKVSSSEEDCVSEDSEPPPTNSVMNNMMNSLYSQPRKPLAPKPISEPID
ISSGDENEDDSNTKTTNGDGVAAAAAPPPPTPAVQGSALKRLMEEVPEIAVAAKKAKPNT
IHVSSSEAIQKLHQVVGNRAKNLSEDAVPRSKDHRNVPGLYQQLHQNQSRDRLRKFKRDL
EVQHPTESFRDIGGMDSTLKELCEMLIHIKSPEFYFQLGLLPSRGLLLHGPPGCGKTFLA
RAISGQLKMPLMEIPATELIGGISGESEERIREVFDQAIGYSPCVLFIDEIDAIGGNRQW
ASKDMERRIVSQLISSLDNLKANEFGQSVVVIAATTRPDVLDPGLRRIGRFDHEIAIHIP
SRKERREILRIQCEGLSVDPKLNYDKIAELTPGYVGADLMALVSRAASVAVKRRSMKKFR
ELHAASEKNMTTVTLDDDEPSEDAGETPVPDSKGEETAKDAEAEQKVDGDKETSAKDKSE
GDSPNIETPKKATNGNSSIKSPQKTPKKSAEKPTDAAMDVDNVAPEEPKKAVEQEVDSSS
SNDEYYEPTLAELTNFLDNPPEEFADPNFCLTLIDFVDAIKVMQPSAKREGFITVPDTTW
DDIGALEKIREELKLAVLAPVKYPEMLERLGLTAPSGVLLCGPPGCGKTLLAKAIANEAG
INFISVKGPELMNMYVGESERAVRACFQRARNSAPCVIFFDEFDSLCPKRSDGGDGNNSG
TRIVNQLLTEMDGVEERKGVYILAATNRPDIIDPAILRPGRLDTILYVGFPEQSERTEIL
KATTKNGKRPVLADDVDLDEIAAQTEGYTGADLAGLVKQASMFSLRQSLNNGDTNLDDLC
VRSQHFQEALQQLRPSVNEQDRKIYDKLRLKYAAPRVPTLNDK
```

al., 2008), SWISS-PROT (Bairoch & Boeckmann, 2003), and Protein Data Bank (PDB) (Westbrook & M. Berman, 2000). Specifically, GenBank is an annotated collection of all publicly available DNA sequences. The GenBank database comprises the DNA DataBank (DDBJ) (Sugawara et al., 2008) of Japan, the nucleotide sequence database EMBL (Akhtar & Cochrane, 2008) of European Bioinformatics Institute and GenBank at National Center for Biotechnology Information (NCBI). SWISS-PROT is an annotated protein sequence database maintained by the Swiss Institute of Bioinformatics and European Bioinformatics Institute. PDB contains all publicly available solved protein structures. These databases contain large amounts of raw sequence data.

There are a number of derived or structured databases which integrate information from multiple primary sources, and may include relational / cross-referenced data with respect to sequence, structure, function, and evolution. A derived database generally contains added descriptive materials on top of the primary data or provides novel structuring of the data based on certain defined relationships. Derived / structured databases typically structure the protein sequence data into usable sets of data (tables), grouping the protein sequences by family or by homology domains. A protein family is a group of sequences that are functionally or structurally similar. Examples of the derived databases are:

1. PIRSF (Nikolskaya & H. Wu, 2004), Pfam (Finn & Bateman, 2008), PROSITE (Sigrist & Hulo, 2004) and ProDom (Bru & Servant, 2002) are databases of protein families and domains classified automatically on the basis of sequence similarity using sequence alignment based methods.
2. GPCRDB (Horn et al., 2003) and KinBase (Manning et al., 2002) are databases of protein families classified manually on the basis of function of proteins.

Problem Definition

Let $\sum = \{s_1, s_2, ..., s_m\}$ be the set of all possible symbols. A *sequence* is an ordered list of symbols

Table 1. General and derived biological databases

Database Name	Database Type	Website
GenBank	General	http://www.ncbi.nlm.nih.gov/Genbank
SWISS-PROT	General	http://ca.expasy.org/sprot
PDB	General	http://www.rcsb.org/pdb/home/home.do
DDBJ	General	http://www.ddbj.nig.ac.jp
EMBL	General	http://www.ebi.ac.uk/embl
PIRSF	Derived	http://pir.georgetown.edu/pirsf
Pfam	Derived	http://pfam.sanger.ac.uk
PROSITE	Derived	http://ca.expasy.org/prosite
ProDom	Derived	http://prodom.prabi.fr
GPCRDB	Derived	http://www.gpcr.org/7tm
KinBase	Derived	http://kinase.com/kinbase

in $\sum$. The number of symbols in a sequence is referred to as *length* of the sequence. Note that each symbol of a sequence is at a specific position and symbols at different positions can not be interchanged. The given training dataset $\mathbf{D} = \{\mathbf{F_1}, \mathbf{F_2}, ..., \mathbf{F_n}\}$ is a set of $\mathbf{n}$ families, where each *family* (the terms "family" and "class" are used interchangeably in this chapter) is a collection of sequences. The sequences of a family are of different lengths and total number of sequences in each family is different. The goal of the sequence classifier is to label a query sequence S with family F_i for which the posterior probability $\mathbf{P(F_i|S)}$ is maximum. *Bayes formula* allows us to compute this probability from the prior probability $\mathbf{P(F_i)}$, evidence $\mathbf{P(S)}$ and the class-conditional probability $\mathbf{P(S|F_i)}$ as follows:

$$\mathbf{P(F_i|S)=P(S|F_i)P(F_i)/P(S)} \qquad (1)$$

where $\mathbf{P(S)}= \sum_{i=1}^{n} P(S|F_i)P(F_i)$

Since the evidence $\mathbf{P(S)}$ is same for all families, it is ignored. So Equation 1 reduces to

$$\mathbf{P(F_i|S)} \propto P(S|F_i)\,P(F_i) \qquad (2)$$

The prior probability $\mathbf{P(F_i)}$ is computed as the relative frequency of family $\mathbf{F_i}$ in $\mathbf{D}$, i.e., $\mathbf{P(F_i)} = \mathbf{N_i/N}$, where $\mathbf{N_i}$ is the number of sequences in family $\mathbf{F_i}$ and $\mathbf{N}$ is the total number of sequences in the dataset.

Hence the classification problem reduces to the correct estimation of $\mathbf{P(S|F_i)}$, *given the training dataset* $\mathbf{D}$.

Biological Sequence Classifiers

This section gives overview of various biological sequence classifiers categorizing them according to the classification method.

Examples of *Naive Bayesian Sequence Classifiers* can be found in (Andorf et al., 2004; Ferreira & Azevedo, 2005a; Kang et al., 2005, 2006). Andorf et al. (2004) proposes that the Naive Bayes (NB) classifier can be used for protein classification by representing protein sequences as class conditional probability distribution of *k-grams* (short subsequences of amino acids of length k). They present two NB classifier models: (1) NB k-grams, that ignores the statistical dependencies between overlapping k-grams and (2) NB(k), that uses an undirected probabilistic graphical model to capture the relevant dependencies. The relevant probabilities required for specifying these models are estimated using standard techniques for estimation of probabilities using Laplace estimators. The length of *k-grams* used in the classifiers is a user supplied parameter and the performance of the classifiers is very sensitive towards this parameter. The approach used in (Ferreira & Azevedo, 2005a) is to use the unlabeled sequence to find rigid gap frequent subsequences of a certain minimum length and use them to obtain two features: (1) number of relevant patterns and (2) average length of patterns. Then these features are combined in an NB classifier. This classification approach uses a computationally expensive *query driven* subsequence extraction method (Ferreira & Azevedo, 2006) which is guided by many user supplied parameters. This method defers the feature extraction process until classification time and for extracting the subsequences it compares the query sequence with all the sequences of the database. Due to this the computational cost and time complexity of the classification phase increases rapidly with only a small increase in the dataset size, which makes it unsuitable for large datasets.

Kang et al. (2006) introduces a novel word taxonomy based NB learner (WTNBL-ML) for the text and biological sequences. WTNBL-ML is a generalization of NB learner for multinomial event model. For building a word taxonomy *Word Taxonomy Learner* (WTL) is used which uses a hierarchical agglomerative clustering to cluster words based on the distribution of class labels that co-occur with the words. This classifier requires a similarity measure for words to build the word taxonomy which limits its use for biological sequences. Kang et al. (2005) tries to improve the NB classifier for sequences by relaxing the assumption that the instances in each class can be described by a single generative model. They present a recursive NB classifier RNBL–MN, which constructs a tree of Naive Bayes classifiers for sequence classification, where each individual NB classifier in the tree is based on a multinomial event model (one for each class at each node in

the tree). The classifiers presented in (Kang et al., 2005, 2006) build a binary classifier for each class of the dataset which becomes computationally very expensive when the number of classes increases.

Maximum Entropy based Sequence Classifiers are presented in (Pavlov, 2003; Buehler & Ungar, 2001). For modeling a sequence, both (Pavlov, 2003) and (Buehler & Ungar, 2001) use the history of symbols to predict the next symbol of a sequence. Buehler and Ungar (2001) use maximum entropy for modeling protein sequences using *unigram*, *bigram*, *unigram cache* and class based *self triggers* as features. After making simplifying assumptions about the probability distributions, such as assuming length of each sequence to be same and using a user supplied value for this length, they use GIS to find the parameters of the sequence model. Pavlov (2003) presents a sequence modeling method for text and biological sequences using mixtures of conditional maximum entropy distributions. This method generalizes the mixture of first order Markov models by including the long term dependencies, known as *triggers*, in the model components. The presented method uses generalized EM algorithm to learn the mixture of conditional maxent models from the available data.

HMM based Sequence Classifiers (Durbin et al., 1998; Eddy, 1998; Krogh et al., 1994) use Hidden Markov Model (HMM) to build a model for each protein family based on multiple alignments of sequences. A model for a family is one that assigns high probability to the sequences of that family and this model is used to classify an unlabeled sequence. HMM models suffer from known *learnability hardness results* (Abe & Warmuth, 1992), exponential growth in number of states and in practice, require a high quality multiple alignment of the input sequences to obtain a reliable model. These HMM based classifiers use algorithms which are very complex to implement and the models they generate tend to be space inefficient and require large memory.

Similarity based Sequence Classifiers (Altschul et al., 1990, 1997; Pearson & Lipman, 1988) compare an unlabeled sequence with all the sequences of the database and assess sequence similarity using sequence alignment methods like FASTA (Pearson & Lipman, 1988), BLAST (Altschul et al., 1990) or PSI-BLAST (Altschul et al., 1997) and then use the *K*-Nearest Neighbor approach to classify the new sequence based on the class label of the *k* most similar sequences. But as the number of sequences in biological databases is increasing exponentially, this method is infeasible due to the increased time required to align the new sequence with the whole database.

Probabilistic Suffix Tree (PST) based Sequence Classifiers (Bejerano & Yona, 1999; Eskin et al., 2003) predict the next symbol in a sequence based on the previous symbols. Basically a PST (Bejerano & Yona, 1999) is a variable length Markov Model, where the probability of a symbol in a sequence depends on the previous symbols. The number of previous symbols considered is variable and context dependent. The prediction of an input sequence is done symbol by symbol. The probability of a symbol is obtained by finding the longest subsequence that appears in the tree and ends just before the symbol. These probabilities are then combined to determine the overall probability of the sequence with respect to sequences of a database. The conditional probabilities of the symbols used in PSTs rely on exact subsequence matches, which becomes a limitation, since substitutions of symbols by equivalent ones is often very frequent in biological sequences. The proposed classifier of (Eskin et al., 2003) tries to overcome this limitation by generalizing PSTs to SMTs with wild-card support, which is a symbol that denotes a gap of size one and matches any symbol on the alphabet. An experimental evaluation in (Bejerano & Yona, 1999) shows that PSTs perform much better than a typical PSI-BLAST search and as well as HMM. Eskin et al. (2003) shows that SMTs outperform PSTs. This analysis is very interesting since PSTs and SMTs are totally

automated methods without prior knowledge of multiple alignments and score matrices or any human intervention while other methods use extensive prior knowledge. As biological sequence databases are becoming larger and larger, data driven learning algorithms for PSTs or SMTs will require vast amounts of memory.

SVM based Sequence Classifiers (Ben-Hur & Brutlag, 2003a, 2003b; Leslie et al., 2002; Marsolo & Parthasarathy, 2006a, 2006b; Weston et al., 2005; Melvin et al., 2007) either use a set of features of sequence families to train an SVM or use *string kernel* based SVMs, alone or with some standard similarity measure like BLAST or PSI-BLAST or with some structural information. The classifiers of (Ben-Hur & Brutlag, 2003a, 2003b) use a set of *Motifs*—short conserved regions of proteins as features of protein families and train the SVM on this feature set. For extracting *Motifs*, they use a multiple sequence alignment based method called *eMOTIF* (Huang & Brutlag, 2001). The classifier of (Leslie et al., 2002) represents protein sequences as vectors in high-dimensional feature space via a string-based *feature map* and trains an SVM on the feature vectors without calculating the feature vectors explicitly, instead computing their pairwise inner products using a *mismatch string kernel*. Weston et al. (2005) use standard similarity measures like BLAST or PSI-BLAST along with *mismatch string kernel* to improve the performance of the SVM classifier. The classifier of (Marsolo & Parthasarathy, 2006b) uses the frequency scores returned by PSI-BLAST to create a wavelet based summary which is used as the feature vector for the SVM. The classifier of (Marsolo & Parthasarathy, 2006a) uses structure related information along with wavelet based summary as features for the SVM. Melvin et al. (2007) uses *profile-based string kernel* SVMs (Kuang et al., 2004) as base binary classifiers. They use PSI-BLAST to generate the sequence profiles and to define an additional set of base classifiers for extended components of the output vector. This output vector is fed into the *ranking perceptron* to get the final output. The SVM based classifiers require a lot of data transformation but report the best accuracies among existing biological sequence classifiers. Since SVM is basically a binary classifier, to handle a large number of classes, it uses the *one against the rest* method, which becomes computationally very expensive as the number of classes increases.

ESTIMATING FEATURE PROBABILITIES FROM FAMILY OF BIO-SEQUENCES

This section presents the important definitions and terminologies used in this chapter. It also describes one simple domain independent method for finding feature probabilities in a biological sequence dataset when subsequences are used as features.

Preliminaries and Definitions

This section presents the necessary details of terminology and important definitions used in this chapter.

- **Sequence:** Let $\sum = \{A_1, A_2,...,A_m\}$ be the set of all possible symbols. For example, in the case of protein sequences, $\sum$ consists of the 20 amino acid alphabets and for the DNA sequences it consists of the 4 nucleotide alphabets. A *sequence* is a *linear ordered list of symbols* in $\sum$. Examples of this type of sequences are protein or DNA sequences or website navigation paths. The term *linear* is used to make the distinction from the transactional sequences that consist of sequences of itemsets. The number of symbols in a sequence is referred to as *length* of the sequence. Note that each symbol of a sequence is at a specific position and symbols at different positions can not be interchanged. A sequence **S** of length **L** can be represented as concatenation of

L symbols as: $\mathbf{S} = <\mathbf{s_1 s_2 ... s_L}>$, where $\mathbf{s_i} \in \sum$ and $\mathbf{i} = \mathbf{1}$ to **L**. A sample protein sequence is shown in Figure 1.

- **Subsequence:** A *continuous segment of a sequence* is called a *subsequence*. Formally, sequence $\mathbf{S_A} = <\mathbf{a_1 a_2 ... a_u}>$ is a subsequence of sequence $\mathbf{S_B} = <\mathbf{b_1 b_2 ... b_v}>$, if there exists **u** contiguous integers $1 \leq \mathbf{i} < \mathbf{i} + 1 < ... < \mathbf{i} + \mathbf{u} - 1 \leq \mathbf{v}$ such that $\mathbf{a_1} = \mathbf{b_i}$, $\mathbf{a_2} = \mathbf{b_{i+1}},..., \mathbf{a_u} = \mathbf{b_{i+u-1}}$. In other words, subsequence $\mathbf{S_A}$ is fully contained in sequence $\mathbf{S_B}$. Sequence $\mathbf{S_B}$ is called *supersequence* of $\mathbf{S_A}$. Obviously, we have *length* of $\mathbf{S_A} \leq$ **length** of $\mathbf{S_B}$. For example,

$\mathbf{S_1}$ = **KNLSEDAVPRSKDHR** and $\mathbf{S_2}$ = **LYQQLHQ** are subsequences of $\mathbf{S_3}$=**QKLHQVV GNRAKNLSEDAVPRSKDHRNVPGLYQQ LHQNQSRDRLRKFKRDL**.

- **Repeat:** The *multiple occurrence of a subsequence* **S'** *in sequence* **S** is called repeat of **S'** in **S**. For example, subsequence **LHQ** is repeated 2 times in the sequence $\mathbf{S_3}$.
- **Family:** A **family** F = {$\mathbf{S_1}, \mathbf{S_2},..., \mathbf{S_N}$} is a *collection of* **N** *sequences* of variable lengths.
- **Training Data:** The training data **D** = {$\mathbf{F_1}, \mathbf{F_2},..., \mathbf{F_n}$} is a *collection of* n *families*. The number of sequences in each family $\mathbf{F_i} \in \mathbf{D}$ is different.
- **Largest Family:** The family $\mathbf{F_i} \in \mathbf{D}$ with maximum number of sequences.
- **Smallest Family:** The family $\mathbf{F_i} \in \mathbf{D}$ with least number of sequences.

Definition 1. *The* SequenceCount *of a subsequence* X_j *in family* F_i *is the number of sequences of family* F_i *in which subsequence* X_j *is present at least once.*

Definition 2. *The* RepeatCount *of a subsequence* X_j *in family* F_i *is the sum of the number of occurrences of that subsequence in each sequence of the family.*

So, *RepeatCount* of a subsequence sums up all the occurrences of that subsequence from all the sequences of a family.

Definition 3. *A subsequence X_j is frequent in family F_i iff SequenceCount of X_j in F_i $\geq$ σ where σ is the* MinsupCount *for family F_i, and is calculated using the user given support threshold minsup and N_i (total number of sequences in family F_i) as $\sigma = N_i \times minsup$.*

Definition 4. *Let $\mathbf{Z} = \{X_1, X_2, ..., X_{|z|}\}$ be the set of all frequent subsequences extracted from family F_i. Subsequence $X_j \in \mathbf{Z}$ is maximal frequent in family F_i iff not exists $X_k \in \mathbf{Z}$ such that X_k is supersequence of X_j.*

Hence for a maximal frequent subsequence $\mathbf{X_j}$, there are no other frequent subsequences in the family which contain $\mathbf{X_j}$.

Feature Probability Estimation

This section describes how feature probabilities can be estimated from the training data when subsequences are used as features. The discussed classifiers RBNBC and REBMEC use *maximal frequent subsequences* as features.

Either *SequenceCount* or *RepeatCount* may be used to estimate the probability $\mathbf{P(X_j |F_i)}$ of a feature $\mathbf{X_j}$ in a family $\mathbf{F_i}$. Note that since *RepeatCount* is obtained by summing all the occurrences of a feature in all the sequences of a family, it gives more information about the presence of that feature in the family than SequenceCount which only gives information about fraction of sequences in the family containing that feature.

Using *SequenceCount* is simple: [(***SequenceCount*** of $\mathbf{X_j}$)$/\mathbf{N_i}$] is a good estimate of $\mathbf{P(X_j |F_i)}$, where $\mathbf{N_i}$ is the number of sequences in $\mathbf{F_i}$. Though this is simple and efficient, it does not account for multiple occurrences of $\mathbf{X_j}$ in a sequence. The alternative is to use *RepeatCount*. In our study we found that *RepeatCount* results in better accuracy as it uses all the occurrences of a feature in the family.

Use of multiple occurrences of a feature is similar to the multinomial event models (McCallum & Nigam, 1998) used in text classification but RBNBC and REBMEC follow a very different approach to find the feature probabilities which are used to build the model. McCallum and Nigam (1998) study multinomial models for document classification, which capture the word frequency information in each document, and show that these models perform better than the multi-variate *Bernoulli* model. Basically, the multinomial models represent each training sample as a bag of words and use the multinomial distribution method to find the class conditional probability. In contrast, REBMEC and RBNBC model the samples as sequences and find feature probabilities using *RepeatCounts*.

Following method finds $\mathbf{P(X_j |F_i)}$ using *RepeatCount*:

1. Find the number of *slots* available for $\mathbf{X_j}$ in family $\mathbf{F_i}$.

If we consider that the features may overlap:

$$slots_{ij} = \sum_{k=1}^{N_i} [\text{ length of } \mathbf{S_k} - \text{length of } \mathbf{X_j} + 1]$$

(3)

If we consider non overlapping features:

$$slots_{ij} = \sum_{k=1}^{N_i} floor (\text{length of } S_k / \text{length of } X_j)$$

(4)

Where $\mathbf{N_i}$ is the total number of sequences in family $\mathbf{F_i}$ and *floor* function returns the largest integer value.

Find the probability of feature $\mathbf{X_j}$ in family $\mathbf{F_i}$ as:

$$\mathbf{P(X_j |F_i)} = (RepeatCount \text{ of } \mathbf{X_j} \text{ in } \mathbf{F_i}) / slots_{ij}$$

(5)

Equations 3 and 4 find the number of slots available for feature X_j in family F_i, i.e., the total number of times X_j can, in principle, occur in F_i. This is done by summing the available slots in each sequence S_k of the family F_i. Next, Equation 5 estimates the feature probability as the fraction of times X_j actually occurs over the slots. Equation 3 finds the number of slots for overlapping features, i.e., when boundaries of slots for a feature can overlap. Equation 4 finds the number of slots for non overlapping features, i.e., when boundaries of slots for a feature do not overlap.

Handling Problems of Bayesian Classifiers

This section discusses the existing problems of the *Bayesian* classifiers and presents the proposed solutions. It is known that *Bayesian* classifiers like *Naive Bayes* (NB) represent the query sequence as a feature vector and use the feature probabilities to estimate the class-conditional probability. The class-conditional probability is then used to compute the posterior probability of each family. This approach can give rise to following problems:

Problem 1: Features Not Represented in the Training Data: Since calculation of $P(X_j | F_i)$ is based on the presence of X_j in the training data of class F_i, a problem can arise if X_j is completely absent in the training data of class F_i. This problem is called "the problem of zero probabilities". The absence of X_j is quite common because training data is typically too small to be comprehensive, and not because $P(X_j | F_i)$ is really zero. This problem is compounded by the resulting zero probability for any query sequence S that contains X_j. Evidence based on other subsequences of S may point to a significant presence of S in F_i. Due to this problem, the existing Bayesian formulation cannot be applied directly on biological sequences when frequent subsequences are used as features. Known solutions to this problem are:

1. Use a nonuniform feature set, i.e., use different feature set of query sequence S for each class which includes only those features of S which are present in that class. Then set $P(S| F_i) = 0$ only if none of the features of S is present in class F_i.

    a. This solution has a drawback: classes with more matching features of S could be computed as having less posterior probability due to the multiplication of more feature probabilities whose values are always less than one. This results in wrong classification and is illustrated in Example 1.

2. Incorporate a small sample-correction into all probabilities, such as *Laplace correction* (Domingos & Pazzani, 1997; Kotsiantis & Pintelas, 2004), which is frequently used in text classifiers (Bakus & Kamel, 2002). The *Laplace correction* factor requires changing all the probability values, so it is not feasible for datasets with a large feature set like biological datasets.

3. If a feature value does not occur in a given class, then set its probability to $(1/N)$, where N is the number of examples in the training set (Kotsiantis & Pintelas, 2004).

Example 1. Suppose C_1 and C_2 are two classes with **10** samples each, so that the prior probabilities of the classes are $P(C_1) = P(C_2) = 1/2$.

A query sample **S** with features $\{X_1, X_2, X_3, X_4\}$ has two matching features in class C_1 with probabilities

$$P(X_1| C_1) = 1/10 \text{ and } P(X_3| C_1) = 3/10$$

and four matching features in class C_2 with probabilities

$$P(X_1| C_2) = 1/10, P(X_2| C_2) = 2/10, P(X_3| C_2) = 3/10 \text{ and } P(X_4| C_2) = 2/10.$$

Using Equation 1, the posterior probabilities of the classes are obtained as

$P(C_1|S) = 3/200$ and $P(C_2|S) = 6/10000$.

Since $P(C_1|S) > P(C_2|S)$, the query sample gets classified into class C_1, although intuitively we know that class C_2 is more suitable because it contains more matching features than class C_1.

The standard Simple Naive Bayes (Simple NB) classifier uses *SequenceCount* with solution (I) to obtain the model of the dataset. RBNBC and REBMEC uses another solution described below.

Proposed Solution: To handle the problem of zero probabilities the classifiers use a very simple assumption. They assume that the probability of any feature to be present in any family is never zero. So for the features of other families which are not present in a given family, they use a correction probability $\in$, which is the *minimum possible feature probability computed using* RepeatCount. It is obtained as:

$\in$ = 1 / Sum of the lengths of sequences of the largest family (6)

For handling the problem arising from the use of a nonuniform feature set, RBNBC and REBMEC use a query-sequence-based uniform feature set, which is the set of features present in the query sequence *S*, collected from all families. The classifiers then use ϵ as the probability value of features not present in a family. We have experimented with two models of the NB classifier for biological sequences–model A, which is the Simple NB classifier, using solution (I) and model B using our solution with *SequenceCount*–and found that model B performed better than model A. For classifiers like model B, which use *Sequence-Count*, the correction probability ϵ is obtained as:

$\in$ = 1 / Number of sequences of the largest family (7)

Problem 2: Out of Range Probability Values: Probability values obtained using equations such as Equations 5 and 6 are very small. When these very small values are multiplied to obtain the class-conditional probability to be used in Bayesian equation 1, the product can go below the available minimum number range of the computer processor. This is a problem with all *Bayesian* classifiers which work with large feature sets and assume independence among the features and hence directly multiply the feature probabilities to get the class-conditional probabilities.

An appropriate scaling factor, which depends on the dataset, or log scaled formulation is used to avoid this problem. When scaling factor is used then all the feature probability values are multiplied with this scaling factor before they are used to find the class conditional probabilities. We experimented with different scaling factors and found a generic scaling factor (1 / *Avgminprob)*, which can be used for any dataset.

Avgminprob is defined as the *average of minimum possible probability values for features in the dataset*:

Avgminprob = $\alpha + \beta / 2$

where

α = Minimum value of possible Minimum probability in the dataset
β = Maximum value of possible Minimum probability in the dataset

For RBNBC, it is obtained using $\alpha = \epsilon$ defined in Equation 6 and

β = 1 / Sum of the length of sequences of the smallest family (8)

For other NB classifiers like models A and B working with *SequenceCount,* it can be obtained using following values

α = 1 / Number of sequences of the largest family

β = 1 / Number of sequences of the smallest family

We also experimented with the following log scaled formulation of *Bayes* equation and found that both scaling factor and Equation 9 give the same results:

$$LP(F_i|S) = LP(S|F_i) + LP(F_i) \qquad (9)$$

where

$LP(F_i|S) = \log[P(F_i|S)]$
$LP(S|F_i) = \log[P(S|F_i)]$
$LP(F_i) = \log[P(F_i)]$

Since using log scaled formulation is simple, Equation 9 is readily used to find posterior probabilities for all the classifiers. Note that the discussed REBMEC classifier implicitly uses a log scaled approach for finding class-conditional probabilities. In contrast, RBNBC and other Naive Bayes classifiers like Simple NB models A and B have to explicitly use log scaled formulation to find class conditional probabilities.

RBNBC AND REBMEC CLASSIFIERS

This section describes the design of two *Bayesian* sequence classifiers called Repeat Based Naive Bayes Classifier (RBNBC) and Repeat Based Maximum Entropy Classifier (REBMEC). This section discusses the feature extraction process, feature selection phase and classification methods used by the two classifiers.

The RBNBC and REBMEC classifiers run in three phases:

1. **Feature Extraction:** This is the training phase in which first maximal frequent subsequences are extracted as features from each family and stored with their *RepeatCount*

and *SequenceCount*. Then for each family, the counts for maximal features from other families, which are not maximal in this family, are also stored. This is to ensure that all families share the same feature set.

2. **Feature Selection:** The extracted feature set is pruned in this phase using an entropy based selection criterion. The result is a smaller set of features remaining after pruning and their counts within each family. This phase, which performs feature selection, is an optional phase and the classifier can execute the final phase without going through this phase. The feature extraction and selection phases are executed only once to train the classifier. After this the original dataset is no longer required and the classifier works with the reduced feature set left after pruning.

3. **Classification:** This phase is executed for labeling a query sequence with the family having the maximum posterior probability. The classifier first separates all the features belonging to the query sequence from the available feature set from the previous phase. It then uses these features to find the posterior probability of each family and outputs the one with the maximum probability. The methods used in the first two phases are same for both the classifiers, but they use different classification methods for the third phase. While RBNBC uses a Naïve Bayes approach, REBMEC uses a maximum entropy based approach. In the following sections, we discuss the three phases of the classifiers in detail.

Feature Extraction

The first phase for any classifier is the training phase in which it is trained using features extracted from a training dataset. Since classifiers require discriminative features (Han & Kamber, 2001; Lesh et al., 1999) to distinguish between different classes, the first challenge in "classification of biological sequences" is to extract good features from the available sequences. The task of "feature extraction from biological sequences" itself is an open research problem. Some sophisticated feature mining algorithms (Ferreira & Azevedo, 2005b, 2006; Lesh et al., 1999, 2000; Huang & Brutlag, 2001) have been developed for this purpose which uses complex data transformations and domain knowledge. Ben-Hur and Brutlag (2003a, 2003b) propose that *Motifs*–short conserved regions of sequences–are highly predictive features for the biological sequences.

In this chapter, we focus on the classification part of the problem instead of the domain specific feature extraction part. The discussed classifiers use maximal frequent subsequences as features. Use of these very simple features avoids the need for complex data transformations and domain knowledge in the feature extraction process. Based on the observations made by Ben-Hur and Brutlag (2003a, 2003b), we believe that frequent subsequences capture everything that is significant in a collection of sequences. This assumption has borne out well in the experimental results. Since the number of extracted frequent features increases exponentially as *minsup* decreases, to reduce the feature set we opt to use maximal frequent subsequences as features. The careful examinations of extracted features of all families reveal that extracted maximal frequent subsequences of a family are similar to *Motifs* of that family. So, maximal frequent subsequences are able to extract predictive features for the biological sequences. There may be some loss in information by using maximal frequent subsequences as features, however, they have the advantage that they satisfy the following criteria set by Lesh et al. (1999), which are necessary for features of any classifier:

1. **Significant Features:** this is ensured by considering only frequent features, i.e., *SequenceCount ≥ MinsupCount*.

2. **Non-redundant Features:** this is ensured by using maximal frequent subsequences.

3. **Discriminative Features:** For ensuring this, entropy based selection criteria described later in this chapter is used, after extraction of features.

Various methods are available for mining maximal frequent patterns. Examples of such methods can be found in (Roberto J. Bayardo, 1998; Zaki et al., 1997, Gouda & Zaki, 2005; Guan et al., 2004). Most of these methods focus on mining maximal frequent itemsets. Since we need to obtain the *RepeatCount* of the subsequences along with the *SequenceCount*, we use our own *Apriori* (Agrawal & Srikant, 1994) like method called *ExtractMaxSubseq* shown in Figure 2 for extracting maximal frequent subsequences and optimize it using a novel bit-vector based frequent subsequence extraction method shown in Figure 3. Also, to extract all possible features, we set *maxlen*–maximum length of the features to be extracted–as the length of the largest sequence of the training set. Note that using *ExtractMaxSubseq* we extract overlapping features, where boundaries of features can overlap.

As discussed in Preliminary section, all the subsequences **X** satisfying the following criteria

SequenceCount of X ≥ *MinsupCount*

are frequent in family F_i (containing N_i sequences) where ***MinsupCount*** = $N_i \times$ ***minsup*** and among these frequent subsequences, X_j is maximal frequent if there are no other frequent subsequences in the family which contain X_j.

In *ExtractMaxSubseq* algorithm, we use the same user given minimum support threshold *minsup* for all the families for extracting features from each family. In each iteration, the algorithm first initializes *FreqList* (the list containing frequent subsequences of length l) to empty set and then populates this list with extracted frequent subsequences of length l while storing the *SequenceCount* and *RepeatCount*. Then it removes those subsequences from *MaxList* (the list of

Figure 2. The ExtractMaxSubseq algorithm for extracting maximal frequent subsequences as features for each family of the dataset

---

ExtractMaxSubseq Algorithm:

---

for each family F_i :
    Initialize *MaxList* = Φ *# List of features for family F_i*
    for l = 1 to *maxlen* :   *# length of subsequences to consider*
        Initialize *FreqList* = Φ
        Extract all frequent subsequences of length l and add them to *FreqList*
        Store *SequenceCount* and *RepeatCount* of the frequent subsequences
        for each feature $X \in$ *MaxList* :
            if $\exists Y \in$ *FreqList* such that X is subsequence of Y :
                Remove X from *MaxList*
            Add all $Y \in$ *FreqList* to *MaxList*
    Return *MaxList*

Figure 3. Bit-Vector based optimization of frequent subsequence extraction

---

Bit-Vector based Frequent Subsequence Extraction Algorithm:

---

for each sequence S of the family :
    Initialize a bit-vector B_S of '1's of length equal to that of S
for l = 1 to *maxlen*:   *# length of subsequences to consider*
    for each sequence S of the family :
        for each position p in B_S:
            if p = 1:
                extract subsequence X of length l starting from position **p**
                increment counters measuring occurrences of X
                set **p = 0**
        for each extracted subsequence X of length l:
            if *SequenceCount* of X $\geq$ *MinsupCount* :
                for each sequence S containing X :
                    for each occurrence q of X in S :
                        set **p = 1** in B_S corresponding to the position of **q**

---

maximal frequent subsequences) which have a supersequence in *FreqList*. Finally it adds all the frequent subsequences of *FreqList* to *MaxList*, which is to be checked in the next iteration. After the last iteration, *MaxList* contains all the maximal

frequent subsequences which are features of the family F_i.

After extracting features from all the families using *ExtractMaxSubseq* algorithm, one more pass is made over the sequences of each family to find the *SequenceCount* and *RepeatCount* of features of other families which are not maximal frequent in that family. This extra step is performed to make the feature set uniform for all the families, i.e., all families share the same feature set and to ensure that correct probabilities of all the features are available for use in the classification phase. If a feature is not at all present in a family then a small correction probability is used as the probability of that feature.

Optimization of Frequent Subsequence Extraction Using Bit Vectors

The biological sequence datasets contain large number of very long sequences. Due to this, frequent subsequence extraction from a biological sequence dataset is a time consuming and memory intensive process. This process can be optimized by avoiding extraction of infrequent subsequences by storing information of their location in a bit-vector. This optimization has proved to be very effective and reduced the feature extraction time from days to hours. The optimization method is shown in Figure 3 and explained below.

The procedure initializes a bit-vector of '1's for each sequence in a family. The bit-vector of a sequence is of the same length as the sequence. The procedure starts extracting frequent subsequences of length one and iteratively proceeds to longer subsequences. The presence of a '1' in a bit-vector indicates that a frequent subsequence of length l can be extracted from the corresponding position in the sequence. The presence of a '0' indicates that the subsequence of length l at the corresponding position in the sequence is infrequent. It follows that subsequences longer than l from this position will also be infrequent. Hence the bit will remain '0'. In the first phase of each iteration, candidate subsequences of length l are counted.

In the second phase, the bit positions corresponding to frequent subsequences of length l are set to '1', to be considered in the next iteration.

Entropy Based Selection of Discriminating Features

As is typical of frequent pattern mining, the feature extraction phase produces too many Features and creates the problem of curse of dimensionality. This problem increases as the *minsup* decreases, since the number of extracted features increases exponentially as *minsup* decreases. To alleviate this problem we can apply a feature selection phase that selects only discriminating features (Lesh et al., 1999) for each class.

Our feature selection criterion is based on entropy. Entropy based criteria like information gain and gain ratio have been widely used to select features for classifiers (Kotsiantis & Pintelas, 2004). Since our aim is to find discriminating features for each family, we use low values of $H(D|X_j = present)$, i.e., entropy of the dataset in the presence of a feature as the selection criterion :

$$H(D|X_j = present) = \sum_{i=1}^{N} [P(F_i|X_j = present) \log[P(F_i|X_j = present)]]$$

Where $P(F_i|X_j = present) = (SequenceCount$ of X_j in $F_i)/\sum_k (SequenceCount$ of X_j in $F_k)$

Analysis of this criterion gives us the following observations:

1. $H(D|X_j = present) = 0$ when a feature X_j is present in one and only one family.
2. $H(D|X_j = present)$ is higher when a feature X_j is present in all families.

This criteria is opposite of the information gain criteria as it selects features with low entropy values thereby selecting discriminating features. For selecting features we use a user-given threshold H_{th} to compare with the calculated value of $H(D|X_j = present)$, and select all the features satisfying the criteria given below while pruning the others:

$H(D|X_j = present) \leq H_{th}$

Experimentally we found that for very low *minsup* values, using threshold $H_{th} = 0$ gives good results in the classification phase. But for other *minsup* values good results are obtained by setting H_{th} as $1/2H(D)$ or $1/3H(D)$, where $H(D)$ is the total entropy of the dataset which is defined as:

$$H(D) = -\sum_i P(F_i) \log[P(F_i)]$$

This happens because with $H_{th} = 0$, many important features get pruned. In our experiments, the above entropy based selection not only found discriminating features for all families, but also reduced the number of features by 36% for low *minsup* values (for details refer to Rani & Pudi (2008c)).

Classification Phase

As discussed earlier, RBNBC and REBMEC use a very simple assumption to handle the problem of zero probabilities and the problem arising from the use of a nonuniform feature set. The classifiers assume that the probability of any feature to be present in any family *is* never zero and use a query-sequence-based uniform feature set for finding class conditional probabilities. This uniform feature set is the set of features present in the query sequence, collected from all families. So for the features of other families which are not present in a given family, they use a correction probability ϵ, which is the minimum possible feature probability computed using *RepeatCount*. It is obtained as (Equation 6 reproduced here):

$\epsilon = $ **1/Sum of the lengths of sequences of the largest family**

The classifiers use *RepeatCount* of the features in a family to find the probabilities of features present in that family using the method discussed

earlier in this chapter. This method first finds the total number of slots available for feature X_j in family F_i using either Equation 3 or 4 and then finds the feature probability as the fraction of times X_j actually occurs over the slots using Equation 5. Since we are using overlapping features, the classifiers use Equation 3, which finds slots for overlapping features, to find the slots.

Also to tackle the problem of out of range probability values RBNBC explicitly uses a log scaled formulation to find class conditional probabilities and then uses Equation 9 to find the posterior probabilities. REBMEC implicitly uses a log scaled approach for finding class-conditional probabilities that can handle small values and hence easily deals with this problem.

Classification Phase of RBNBC

For classifying a query sequence S, RBNBC finds the query-sequence-based uniform feature set $Z = \{X_1, X_2, ..., X_m\}$, which is the set of features present in S, collected from all families. For computing the posterior probabilities, it uses the same feature set Z for all families. After finding Z, it uses Equation 5 for finding probabilities of features present in a family and uses ϵ as the probability for features not present in that family. It uses these probabilities to compute class conditional probabilities using following equation:

$$LP(S|F_i) = \sum_{j=1}^{m} \log[P(X_j|F_i)] \qquad (10)$$

It then uses these class conditional probabilities to compute the posterior probability of all families using Equation 9 and classifies the query sequence into the family with the largest posterior probability. The pseudo-code for the method discussed above is shown in Figure 4. Steps 2(a), 2(b) and 2(c) of the classification algorithm of RBNBC can be merged together to be executed in **O(1)** time.

Figure 4. Classification by RBNBC

Classification Algorithm of RBNBC:

---

1. Find features from all families which are present in the query sequence S and make uniform feature set $Z = \{\mathbf{X_1,X_2,\ldots,X_m}\}$

2. **for each** family $\mathbf{F_i}$ do

   (a) **for each** feature $\mathbf{X_j} \in \mathbf{Z}$ do

       if $(\mathbf{X_j} \in \mathbf{F_i})$: Compute $\mathbf{P(X_j |F_i)}$ = (*RepeatCount* of $\mathbf{X_j}$ in $\mathbf{F_i}$) / *slots*$_{ij}$

       else: Set $\mathbf{P(X_j |F_i)} = \epsilon$

   (b) Use Equation 10 to compute $\mathbf{LP(S|F_i)}$

   (c) Compute $\mathbf{LP(F_i|S) = LP(S| F_i) + LP(F_i)}$

3. Find family $\mathbf{F_k}$ having the largest value of $\mathbf{LP(F_i|S)}$

4. Classify $\mathbf{S}$ into $\mathbf{F_k}$

The time complexity of the algorithm is $\mathbf{O(n)}$, where n is the number of families.

Classification Phase of REBMEC

For classifying a query sequence S, REBMEC, like RBNBC, finds the query-sequence-based uniform feature set $\mathbf{Z}$, which is the set of features present in $\mathbf{S}$, collected from all families. For computing the posterior probabilities, it uses the same feature set $\mathbf{Z}$ for all families. It uses Equation 5 for finding probabilities of features present in a family and uses ϵ as the probability for features not present in that family.

Using the features in set $\mathbf{Z}$, it makes the constraint set $\mathbf{CS_i}$ for each family. Each feature $\mathbf{X_j} \in \mathbf{Z}$ with its probability $\mathbf{P(X_j |F_i)}$ in family $\mathbf{F_i}$ forms a *constraint* that needs to be satisfied by the statistical model for that particular family. To satisfy the conditions required by GIS based methods, a "correction" feature $\mathbf{f_l}$ is added to the constraint set. For a sample $\mathbf{x}$, a normal feature $\mathbf{f_i}$ gives value of constraint function $\mathbf{f_i(x)}$ as "0" or "1", which denotes presence or absence of that feature in the sample $\mathbf{x}$. But for the correction feature, the value of constraint function $\mathbf{f_l(x)}$ is obtained using following equation:

$$\mathbf{f_l(x) = C} - \sum_{j=1}^{|Z|} \mathbf{f_j(x)} \tag{11}$$

So, unlike the existing features, $\mathbf{f_l(x)}$ ranges from $\mathbf{0}$ to $\mathbf{C}$. This correction feature is assumed to be present in all the samples. The value of $\mathbf{C}$ is taken as the total number of features extracted from the training set. Thus, for each family $\mathbf{F_i}$, there is a constraint set $\mathbf{CS_i} = \{\{(\mathbf{X_j}, \mathbf{P(X_j |F_i)} \mid \mathbf{X_j} \in \mathbf{Z}\} \cup \{f_l, E(f_l)\}\}$, where $\mathbf{E(f_l)}$ is the expectation of $\mathbf{f_l}$ in family $\mathbf{F_i}$. Since there could be multiple models satisfying these constraints, the proposed algorithm *ComputeProb*, like GIS, selects the one with maximum entropy and finds the parameters of that model. In doing so, it finds the class-conditional probability $\mathbf{LP(S|F_i)}$ of that family.

REBMEC then finds the posterior probability of all families using Equation 9. Finally, it classifies the query sequence into the family with the

Figure 5. Classification by REBMEC

Classification Algorithm of REBMEC:

1. Find features from all families which are present in the query sequence **S** and make uniform feature set $Z = \{X_1, X_2, \ldots, X_m\}$

2. **for each** family F_i do
   (a) **for each** feature $X_j \in Z$ do
       if $(X_j \in F_i)$: Compute $P(X_j | F_i) = (RepeatCount$ of X_j in $F_i) / slots_{ij}$
       else: Set $P(X_j | F_i) = \epsilon$

3. Run *ComputeProb* to obtain $LP(S|F_i)$ for all F_i

4. **for each** family F_i do
   Compute $LP(F_i|S) = LP(S| F_i) + LP(F_i)$

5. Find family F_k having the largest value of $LP(F_i|S)$

6. Classify **S** into F_k

---

largest posterior probability. The pseudo-code for the method discussed above is shown in Figure 5.

Dividing the Feature set into Small Sets: To make the large feature set manageable, REBMEC divides the feature set **Z** into small sets of similar features using Hamming Distance based similarity measure *Hamdis*. This similarity measure is a simple modification of the Hamming Distance to take into account features of different length and is defined as:

Hamdis (X_1, X_2) = No. of positions differing in symbols + $|length(X_1) - length(X_2)|$

For dividing the feature set into small sets of highly dependent features, the *ComputeProb* algorithm selects one feature from Z and calculates *Hamdis* for all other features with respect to the selected feature. Then it groups k features with least *Hamdis*, together with the selected feature to make the small feature set Z_f. This process is repeated till there are less than **k** features left in

Z, which are grouped together along with the correction feature.

ComputeProb **Algorithm:** This is a **GIS** based method which, unlike **GIS**, computes the class-conditional probabilities instead of storing the parameter values of each constraint. It builds an approximate maximum entropy model of each family by dividing the feature set into small sets and combining the results assuming independence among the sets. Figure 6 shows pseudo-code of the algorithm and is described below.

It uses bit-vectors T_k to represent the presence/absence of $| Z_f |$ features of the set Z_f. So for a set of **n** features, T_0 to $T_{(2^n)-1}$ represents all the possible samples of the event space. *ComputeProb* iterates over this event space to obtain a probability model which is as close to the real distribution as possible. The iteration stops when the expectation of each feature calculated from the model is almost equal to the expectation obtained from the training data. At this point all the parameter values converge and further iterations do not make any change. Note that during implementation T_ks

Figure 6. The ComputeProb algorithm

ComputeProb Algorithm:

1. Using *Hamdis* divide the feature set **Z** into small sets as **Z'** = {**Z₁**, **Z₂**, . . .,**Z**$_M$},
   such that $\bigcup_i$ **Z**$_i$ = **Z** and **Z**$_i$ ∩ **Z**$_j$ = **Φ**
2. **for each** family **F**$_i$:
3.   Initialize **LP(S|F**$_i$**) = 0**   *# Class conditional Probability*
4.   **for each** small feature set **Z**$_f$ ∈ **Z'** :
5.   Set **last** = (**2**$^{|Z_f|}$)**− 1**
6.   **for k = 0** to *last* :
7.   Initialize **LP(T**$_k$**) = log[1/(***last***+1)]**
8.   **for each** feature **X**$_j$ ∈ **Z**$_f$:
9.   Initialize **μ**$_j$ **= 0**
10.   **while** all constraints are not satisfied
11.   {
12.   **for each** feature **X**$_j$ ∈ **Z**$_f$:
13.   Initialize *Sum*$_j$ **= 0**
14.   **for k = 0** to *last* :
15.   **if T**$_k$ contains **X**$_j$:
16.   Update *Sum*$_j$ = *Sum*$_j$ + **exp(LP(T**$_k$**))**
17.   Set **LP(X**$_j$ **|F**$_i$**) = log(P(X**$_j$ **|F**$_i$**))**
18.   Update **μ**$_j$ = **μ**$_j$ + **LP(X**$_j$ **|F**$_i$**)** − **log(***Sum*$_j$)
19.   **for k = 0** to *last* :
20.   **for** each feature **X**$_j$ ∈ **Z**$_f$:
21.   **if T**$_k$ contains **X**$_j$:
22.   Update **LP(T**$_k$**) = LP(T**$_k$**) + μ**$_j$
23.   Initialize *normSum* **= 0**
24.   **for k = 0** to *last* :
25.   Update *normSum* = *normSum* + **exp(LP(T**$_k$**))**
26.   Set **μ₀ = 1/***normSum*   *#Normalization factor*
27.   **for k = 0** to *last* :
28.   Update **LP(T**$_k$**) = LP(T**$_k$**) + log(μ₀)**
29.   }
30.   Update **LP(S|F**$_i$**) = LP(S|F**$_i$**) + LP(T**$_{last}$**)**
31.   Return **LP(S|F**$_i$**)**

---

need not be stored but can be computed on the fly.

In the first step, it uses *Hamdis* to group the highly dependent features in small sets. And then for computing the class-conditional probability of a family, it computes **LP(S|F**$_i$**)** for each small set of features and later combines them by assuming independence among the sets. For each small feature set **Z**$_f$ ∈ **Z'**, in steps 6 to 9, it initializes the parameters **μ**$_j$ and probabilities **LP(T**$_k$**)**. In steps 12 to 22, it updates the **μ**$_j$ and **LP(T**$_k$**)** values using the probabilities of features obtained from the training data. In steps 23 to 28, it finds the normalization constant **μ₀** and applies it to the **LP(T**$_k$**)** values. Finally, in step 30, it updates the **LP(S|F**$_i$**)** value using the obtained value of **LP(T**$_{last}$**)** for that feature set, where the bit-vector **T**$_{last}$ represents that all the features of the set **Z**$_f$ are present in the query sequence. Note that the **LP(S|F**$_i$**)** values returned by this algorithm are in log scale.

Discussion of Additional Issues: Like other *Bayesian* methods, *GIS* based methods also use very small parameter and probability values, so they also need to tackle "out of range" parameter values discussed in earlier section. In case of GIS based methods, this problem becomes even more serious due to the iterative nature of these methods. To deal with it, *ComputeProb* is designed using log scale.

In our experiments we observed that when the constant **C**, having a large value, is used for finding the increment values of the parameters, the iteration process overshoots the convergence point. So to make the increment value smaller, unlike GIS, we have not used the constant **C** in the calculation of increment value (in step 18). As discussed in (Ratnaparkhi, 1997, 1998), the number of iterations required for the model to converge can be hard-coded and the algorithm can be made to stop once it reaches those many iterations, so the while loop of *ComputeProb* can be iterated for a fixed number of times. In our experiments we observed that all the parameter values converge within 50 iterations only. The calculation of expectation of a feature f_j from the samples of training data **D** is done using following equation (Ratnaparkhi, 1997, 1998):

$$E_{p/}(f_j) = \sum_{x \in D} p/(x)f_j(x)$$

Since the constraint function $f_j(x)$ of a normal feature is a binary function denoting the presence/ absence of that feature in a sample sequence **x**, the expectation of a normal feature in a family F_i is just the probability of that feature in family F_i. For the correction feature f_l, using Equation 11, the above equation transforms to

$$E_{p/}(f_j) = \sum_{x \in D} p/(x) [C - \sum_{j=1}^{|Z|} f_l(x)]$$

where **Z** is the *uniform* features set of the query sequence. According to this equation, calculation of the expectation of f_l in a family F_i requires scanning all the sample sequences of that family.

The probability of a sample sequence **x** in a family F_i (containing N_i sample sequences) can be obtained as $1/N_i$, hence we can make following observations after analyzing the above equation:

1. The minimum value of expectation of f_l calculated using above equation will be (**C** − |**Z**|), when all the features of the feature set **Z** are present in all the sequences of that family.

2. The maximum value of expectation of f_l calculated using above equation will be **C**, when none of the features of the feature set **Z** are present in any sequence of that family.

Based on these observations we use the minimum expectation value (**C** − |**Z**|) as the approximate expectation value of correction feature f_l in each family. This approximation removes the need for scanning all the sequences of a family in the classification phase for calculating the expectation of f_l. In practice we found this approximation to be good. In our experiments we observed that if the correction feature f_l is not added to the constraint set with proper expectation value, then the algorithm is not able to compute correct class conditional probabilities; so using the correction feature properly is a very important part of the algorithm.

We also observed that either the correction feature can be added to each small group of features Z_f with approximate expectation value (|**Z**| − | Z_f |) or only to the last group with value (**C** − |**Z**|). Both the methods give exactly the same result which means that both methods produce the same effect on the parameter values. Since adding the correction feature to each group of features increases the overall running time, it is better to add it to only one group with appropriate expectation value.

Time Complexity: The running time of *ComputeProb* is dominated by the steps which iterate over all possible samples of the event space (steps 14-16 and steps 19-22). For each small feature set Z_f if the algorithm requires *maxiter* number of iterations to converge and there are **M** such small feature sets then the time complexity of the algorithm is **O(***maxiter* *** 2**$^{|Z_f|}$ ***** $|Z_f|$ *** M)**. If each small feature set Z_f contains equal number of features then $|Z_f|$*** M** gives the total number of features in the uniform feature set **Z**, i.e., $|Z_f|$ = $|Z_f|$ *** M**. So the time complexity of *ComputeProb* can be given as

$$O(maxiter * 2^{|Z_f|} * |Z|)$$

Since $|Z_f| << |Z|$, *ComputeProb* improves the time complexity of **GIS** which has the running time complexity **O(***maxiter* *** 2**$^{|Z|}$ *** **$|Z|$**)** (Thonangi and Pudi, 2005). Under practical circumstances, the number of iterations *maxiter* is hard coded and the algorithm is made to stop after those many iterations. Also, to keep the number of possible event space $2^{|Z_f|}$ tractable, at the time of dividing the feature set **Z**, the number of features in the feature set Z_f is kept less than or equal to 10.

Experimental Results and Performance Study

For evaluating the performance of the discussed classifiers two collections of protein families (1) March-2005 Release 9.0 of GPCRDB (Horn et al., 2003) (http://www.gpcr.org/7tm) and (2) Feb-2008 Release 55.0 of SWISSPROT (Bairoch & Boeckmann, 2003) using the list of SWISSPROT protein IDs obtained from Pfam (Finn & Bateman, 2008) version 22.0 were used. It was found that RBNBC algorithm drastically improves the accuracy from 32% (for the direct *Naive Bayes*) to 98% on GPCRDB dataset. Both of the classifiers gave around 90% average accuracy on both the datasets and outperformed the Simple NB classifiers with a margin of more than 30%. For details of results and comparisons with other Bayesian sequence classifiers refer to (Rani & Pudi, 2008a, 2008b, 2008c) and (Rani, 2008).

CONCLUSION

An important problem in biological data analysis is to predict the family of a newly discovered sequence like a protein or DNA sequence, using the collection of available sequences. This problem comes under the classification paradigm. In this chapter, we studied the problem of classification of biological sequences which requires dealing with two separate problems (1) *feature extraction*: extracting differentiating information as features from the available sequences and (2) *classification*: using this feature information to classify a new sequence, i.e., to build a classification model. We focused on the classification part of the problem which involves building a classification model of the collection of biological sequences arranged in different families. A domain independent method for estimating feature probabilities in a sequence dataset when subsequences are used as features was also discussed. We discussed the existing problems of *Bayesian* classifiers and proposed some simple solutions. We also described two *Bayesian* classifiers for the biological sequences which do not use any domain knowledge, REBMEC classifier uses maximum entropy method while RBNBC uses Naive Bayes method. The classification methods proposed in this chapter are generic in nature and can be applied to any domain where the data is represented as collection of sequences.

REFERENCES

Abe, N., & Warmuth, M. K. (1992). On the computational complexity of approximating distributions by probabilistic automata. *Machine Learning, 9,* 205–260. doi:10.1007/BF00992677

Agrawal, R., & Srikant, R. (1994). Fast algorithms for mining association rules in large databases. In *VLDB '94: Proceedings of 20th International Conference on Very Large Data Bases,* (pp. 487–499).

Akhtar, R., & Cochrane, G. (2008). Priorities for nucleotide trace, sequence and annotation data capture at the Ensembl Trace Archive and the EMBL Nucleotide sequence database. *Nucleic Acids Research, 36*, 5–12.

Altschul, S. F., Gish, W., Miller, W., Myers, E. W., & Lipman, D. J. (1990). Basic local alignment search tool. *Journal of Molecular Biology, 215*(3), 403–410.

Altschul, S. F., Madden, T. L., Schaffer, A. A., Zhang, J., Zhang, Z., Miller, W., & Lipman, D. J. (1997). Gapped BLAST and PSI-BLAST: A new generation of protein database search programs. *Nucleic Acids Research, 25*, 3389–3402. doi:10.1093/nar/25.17.3389

Andorf, C., Silvescu, A., Dobbs, D., & Honavar, V. (2004). Learning classifiers for assigning protein sequences to gene ontology functional families. In *Proceedings of the Fifth International Conference on Knowledge Based Computer Systems*, (pp. 256–265).

Bairoch, A., & Boeckmann, B. (2003). The SWISS-PROT protein knowledgebase and its supplement TrEMBL in 2003. *Nucleic Acids Research, 31*(1), 365–370. doi:10.1093/nar/gkg095

Bakus, J., & Kamel, M. S. (2002). Document classification using phrases. In *Proceedings of the Joint IAPR International Workshop on Structural, Syntactic, and Statistical Pattern Recognition*, (pp. 557–565). SpringerVerlag.

Bejerano, G., & Yona, G. (1999). Modeling protein families using probabilistic suffix trees. In *Proceedings of RECOMB*, (pp. 15–24).

Ben-Hur, A., & Brutlag, D. (2003a). Remote homology detection: A motif based approach. *Bioinformatics (Oxford, England), 19*(1), 26–33. doi:10.1093/bioinformatics/btg1002

Ben-Hur, A., & Brutlag, D. (2003b). Sequence motifs: Highly predictive features of protein function. In *Proceedings of Workshop on Feature Selection, Neural Information Processing Systems*.

Benson, D. A., Karsch-Mizrachi, I., Lipman, D. J., Ostell, J., & Wheeler, D. L. (2008). GenBank. *Nucleic Acids Research, 36*, 25–30. doi:10.1093/nar/gkm929

Berger, A. L., Pietra, S. D., & Pietra, V. J. D. (1996). A maximum entropy approach to natural language processing. *Computational Linguistics, 22*(1), 39–71.

Bru, C., & Servant, F. (2002). ProDom: Automated clustering of homologous domains. *Briefings in Bioinformatics, 3*(3), 246–251. doi:10.1093/bib/3.3.246

Buehler, E. C., & Ungar, L. H. (2001). Maximum entropy methods for biological sequence modeling. In *Proceedings of BIOKDD*, (pp. 60–64).

Darroch, J. N., & Ratcliff, D. (1972). Generalized iterative scaling for log-linear models. *Annals of Mathematical Statistics, 43*, 1470–1480. doi:10.1214/aoms/1177692379

Domingos, P., & Pazzani, M. J. (1996). Beyond independence: Conditions for the optimality of the simple Bayesian classifier. In *Proceedings of ICML*, (pp. 105–112).

Domingos, P., & Pazzani, M. J. (1997). On the optimality of the simple Bayesian classifier under zero-one loss. *Machine Learning, 29*(2-3), 103–130. doi:10.1023/A:1007413511361

Durbin, R., Eddy, S., Krogh, A., & Mitchison, G. (1998). *Biological sequence analysis: Probabilistic models of proteins and nucleic acids*. Cambridge University Press. doi:10.1017/CBO9780511790492

Eddy, S. R. (1998). HMMER: Profile hidden Markov modelling. *Bioinformatics (Oxford, England)*, *14*(9), 755–763. doi:10.1093/bioinformatics/14.9.755

Eskin, E., Noble, W. S., & Singer, Y. (2003). Protein family classification using sparse Markov transducers. *Journal of Computational Biology*, *10*(2), 187–214. doi:10.1089/106652703321825964

Ferreira, P. G., & Azevedo, P. J. (2005a). Protein sequence classification through relevant sequence mining and Bayes classifiers. In *Proceedings of EPIA*, (pp. 236–247).

Ferreira, P. G., & Azevedo, P. J. (2005b). Protein sequence pattern mining with constraints. In *Proceedings of PKDD*, (pp. 96–107).

Ferreira, P. G., & Azevedo, P. J. (2006). Query driven sequence pattern mining. In *Proceedings of SBBD*, (pp. 1–15).

Finn, R. D., & Bateman, A. (2008). The Pfam protein families database. *Nucleic Acids Research*, 281–288.

Gouda, K., & Zaki, M. J. (2005). Genmax: An efficient algorithm for mining maximal frequent itemsets. *Data Mining and Knowledge Discovery*, *11*(3), 223–242. doi:10.1007/s10618-005-0002-x

Guan, J. W., Bell, D. A., & Liu, D. (2004). Discovering maximal frequent patterns in sequence groups. In *Proceedings of Rough Sets and Current Trends in Computing*, (pp. 602–609).

Han, J., & Kamber, M. (2001). *Data mining: Concepts and techniques*. Morgan Kaufmann.

Horn, F., Bettler, E., Oliveira, L., Campagne, F., Cohen, F. E., & Vriend, G. (2003). GPCRDB information system for G protein-coupled receptors. *Nucleic Acids Research*, *31*(1), 294–297. doi:10.1093/nar/gkg103

Huang, J. Y., & Brutlag, D. L. (2001). The EMOTIF database. *Nucleic Acids Research*, *29*(1), 202–204. doi:10.1093/nar/29.1.202

Kang, D., Silvescu, A., & Honavar, V. (2006). RNBL-MN: A recursive naive Bayes learner for sequence classification. In *Proceedings of PAKDD*, (pp. 45–54).

Kang, D., Zhang, J., Silvescu, A., & Honavar, V. (2005). Multinomial event model based abstraction for sequence and text classification. In *Proceedings of SARA*, (pp. 134–148).

Kotsiantis, S. B., & Pintelas, P. E. (2004). Increasing the classification accuracy of simple Bayesian classifier. In *Proceedings of AIMSA*, (pp. 198–207).

Krogh, A., Brown, M., Mian, I. S., Sojlander, K., & Haussler, D. (1994). Hidden Markov models in computational biology: Applications to protein modeling. *Journal of Molecular Biology*, *235*, 1501–1531. doi:10.1006/jmbi.1994.1104

Kuang, R., Ie, E., Wang, K., Wang, K., Siddiqi, M., Freund, Y., & Leslie, C. (2004). Profile-based string kernels for remote homology detection and motif extraction. *Journal of Bioinformatics and Computational Systems*, *3*(3), 152–160.

Lesh, N., Zaki, M. J., & Ogihara, M. (1999). Mining features for sequence classification. In *KDD '99: Proceedings of the Fifth ACM SIGKDD International Conference on Knowledge Discovery and Data Mining*, (pp. 342–346).

Lesh, N., Zaki, M. J., & Ogihara, M. (2000). Scalable feature mining for sequential data. *IEEE Intelligent Systems*, *15*(2), 48–56. doi:10.1109/5254.850827

Leslie, C., Eskin, E., & Noble, W. (2002). Mismatch string kernels for SVM protein classification. In *Proceedings of Neural Information Processing Systems*, (pp. 1417–1424).

Li, J., Liu, H., & Wong, L. (2003). Mean-entropy discretized features are effective for classifying high-dimensional bio-medical data. In *Proceedings of BIOKDD*, (pp. 17–24).

Manning, G., Whyte, D. B., Martinez, R., Hunter, T., & Sudarsanam, S. (2002). The protein kinase complement of the human genome. *Science*, *298*(5600), 1912–1934. doi:10.1126/science.1075762

Marsolo, K., & Parthasarathy, S. (2006a). On the use of structure and sequence-based features for protein classification and retrieval. In *Proceedings of ICDM*, (pp. 394-403).

Marsolo, K., & Parthasarathy, S. (2006b). Protein classification using summaries of profile-based frequency matrices. In *Proceedings of BIOKDD06: 6th Workshop on Data Mining in Bioinformatics (with SIGKDD Conference)*, (pp. 51–58).

McCallum, A., & Nigam, K. (1998). A comparison of event models for naive Bayes text classification. In *Proceedings of AAAI-98 Workshop on Learning for Text Categorization*, (pp. 41–48).

Melvin, I., Ie, E., Weston, J., Noble, W. S., & Leslie, C. (2007). Multi-class protein classification using adaptive codes. *Journal of Machine Learning Research*, *8*, 1557–1581.

Nigam, K., Lafferty, J., & McCallum, A. (1999). Using maximum entropy for text classification. In *Proceedings of IJCAI-99 Workshop on Machine Learning for Information Filtering*, (pp. 61–67).

Nikolskaya, A. N., & Wu, C. H. (2004). PIRSF: Family classification system at the protein information resource. *Nucleic Acids Research*, *32*, 112–114. doi:10.1093/nar/gkh097

Pavlov, D. (2003). Sequence modeling with mixtures of conditional maximum entropy distributions. In *Proceedings of ICDM*, (pp. 251–258).

Pearson, W. R., & Lipman, D. J. (1988). Improved tools for biological sequence comparison. *Proceedings of the National Academy of Sciences of the United States of America*, *85*(8), 2444–2448. doi:10.1073/pnas.85.8.2444

Rani, P. (2008). *Novel Bayesian sequence classifiers applied on biological sequence*s. Masters thesis. IIIT Hyderabad, India.

Rani, P., & Pudi, V. (2008a). Repeat based naïve Bayes classifier for biological sequences. In *ICDM* (pp. 989–994). RBNBC.

Rani, P., & Pudi, V. (2008b). *RBNBC: Repeat based naïve Bayes classifier for biological sequences. (Technical report, IIIT/TR/2008/126)*. India: IIIT Hyderabad.

Rani, P., & Pudi, V. (2008c). Repeat based maximum entropy classifier for biological sequences. In *COMAD* (pp. 71–82). REBMEC.

Ratnaparkhi, A. (1997). *A simple introduction to maximum entropy models for natural language processing*. (Technical report, IRCS Report 97-98), Institute for Research in Cognitive Science, University of Pennsylvania.

Ratnaparkhi, A. (1998). *Maximum entropy models for natural language ambiguity resolution*. PhD thesis, University of Pennsylvania.

Roberto, J., & Bayardo, J. (1998). Efficiently mining long patterns from databases. In *SIGMOD '98: Proceedings of the 1998 ACM SIGMOD International Conference on Management of Data*, (pp. 85–93).

Sigrist, C. J. A., & Hulo, N. (2004). Recent improvements to the PROSITE database. *Nucleic Acids Research*, *32*, 134–137. doi:10.1093/nar/gkh044

Sugawara, H., Ogasawara, O., Okubo, K., Gojobori, T., & Tateno, Y. (2008). DDBJ with new system and face. *Nucleic Acids Research*, *36*, 22–24. doi:10.1093/nar/gkm889

Tatti, N. (2007). Maximum entropy based significance of itemsets. In *Proceedings of ICDM*, (pp. 312–321).

Thonangi, R., & Pudi, V. (2005). ACME: An associative classifier based on maximum entropy principle. In *Proceedings of ALT*, (pp. 122–134).

Wang, J. T. L., Zaki, M. J., Toivonen, H., & Shasha, D. (Eds.). (2005). *Data mining in bioinformatics*. Springer.

Westbrook, J. D., & Berman, H. M. (2000). The protein data bank. *Nucleic Acids Research*, *28*(1), 235–242. doi:10.1093/nar/28.1.235

Weston, J., Leslie, C., Ie, E., Zhou, D., Elisseeff, A., & Noble, W. S. (2005). Semisupervised protein classification using cluster kernels. *Bioinformatics (Oxford, England)*, *21*(15), 3241–3247. doi:10.1093/bioinformatics/bti497

Zaki, M. J., Parthasarathy, S., Ogihara, M., & Li, W. (1997). New algorithms for fast discovery of association rules. In *Proceedings of KDD*, (pp. 283–286).

Zhang, H. (2004). The optimality of naive Bayes. In *Proceedings of FLAIRS Conference*.

Section 3
Applications

Chapter 8
Approaches for Pattern Discovery Using Sequential Data Mining

Manish Gupta
University of Illinois at Urbana-Champaign, USA

Jiawei Han
University of Illinois at Urbana-Champaign, USA

ABSTRACT

In this chapter we first introduce sequence data. We then discuss different approaches for mining of patterns from sequence data, studied in literature. Apriori based methods and the pattern growth methods are the earliest and the most influential methods for sequential pattern mining. There is also a vertical format based method which works on a dual representation of the sequence database. Work has also been done for mining patterns with constraints, mining closed patterns, mining patterns from multi-dimensional databases, mining closed repetitive gapped subsequences, and other forms of sequential pattern mining. Some works also focus on mining incremental patterns and mining from stream data. We present at least one method of each of these types and discuss their advantages and disadvantages. We conclude with a summary of the work.

INTRODUCTION

What is Sequence Data?

Sequence data is omnipresent. Customer shopping sequences, medical treatment data, and data related to natural disasters, science and engineering processes data, stocks and markets data, telephone calling patterns, weblog click streams, program execution sequences, DNA sequences and gene expression and structures data are some examples of sequence data.

DOI: 10.4018/978-1-61350-056-9.ch008

Notations and Terminology

Let I = {$i_1, i_2, i_3 \ldots i_n$} be a set of items. An item-set X is a subset of items i.e. X ⊆ I. A sequence is an ordered list of item-sets (also called elements or events). Items within an element are unordered and we would list them alphabetically. An item can occur at most once in an element of a sequence, but can occur multiple times in different elements of a sequence. The number of instances of items in a sequence is called the length of the sequence. A sequence with length l is called an l-sequence. E.g., s=<a(ce)(bd)(bcde)f(dg)> is a sequence which consists of 7 distinct items and 6 elements. Length of the sequence is 12.

A group of sequences stored with their identifiers is called a sequence database. We say that a sequence s is a subsequence of t, if s is a "projection" of t, derived by deleting elements and/or items from t. E.g. <a(c)(bd)f> is a subsequence of s. Further, sequence s is a δ-distance subsequence of t if there exist integers $j_1 < j_2 < \ldots < j_n$ such that $s_1 \subseteq t_{j1}, s_2 \subseteq t_{j2} \ldots s_n \subseteq t_{jn}$ and $j_k - j_{k-1} \leq \delta$ for each k = 2, 3... n. That is, occurrences of adjacent elements of s within t are not separated by more than δ elements.

What is Sequential Pattern Mining?

Given a pattern p, support of the sequence pattern p is the number of sequences in the database containing the pattern p. A pattern with support greater than the support threshold min_sup is called a frequent pattern or a frequent sequential pattern. A sequential pattern of length l is called an l-pattern. Sequential pattern mining is the task of finding the complete set of frequent subsequences given a set of sequences. A huge number of possible sequential patterns are hidden in databases.

A sequential pattern mining algorithm should:

A.   find the complete set of patterns, when possible, satisfying the minimum support (frequency) threshold,

B.   be highly efficient, scalable, involving only a small number of database scans

C.   be able to incorporate various kinds of user-specific constraints.

APPROACHES FOR SEQUENTIAL PATTERN MINING

Apriori-Based Method (GSP: Generalized Sequential Patterns) (Srikant & Agrawal, 1996)

The Apriori property of sequences states that, if a sequence S is not frequent, then none of the super-sequences of S can be frequent. E.g, <hb> is infrequent implies that its super-sequences like <hab> and <(ah)b> would be infrequent too.

The GSP algorithm finds all the length-1 candidates (using one database scan) and orders them with respect to their support ignoring ones for which support < min_sup. Then for each level (i.e., sequences of length-k), the algorithm scans database to collect support count for each candidate sequence and generates candidate length-(k+1) sequences from length-k frequent sequences using Apriori. This is repeated until no frequent sequence or no candidate can be found.

Consider the database as shown in Figure 1. Our problem is to find all frequent sequences, given min_sup=2.

Figure 1. Database

Database		Length-1 Patterns	
Seq Id	**Sequence**	**Cand**	**Seq**
10	<(bd)cb(ac)>	<a>	3
20	<(bf)(ce)b(fg)>	<b>	5
30	<(ah)(bf)abf>	<c>	4
40	<(be)(ce)d>	<d>	3
50	<a(bd)bcb(ade)>	<e>	3
		<f>	2
		~~<g>~~	~~1~~
		~~<h>~~	~~1~~

As shown in Figure 2, using Apriori one needs to generate just 51 length-2 candidates, while without Apriori property, 8*8+8*7/2=92 candidates would need to be generated. For this example, Apriori would perform 5 database scans, pruning away candidates with support less than min_sup. Candidates that cannot pass support threshold are pruned.

1st scan: 8 candidates. 6 length-1 sequence patterns.

2nd scan: 51 candidates. 19 length-2 sequence patterns. 10 candidates not in DB at all

3rd scan: 46 candidates. 19 length-3 sequence patterns. 20 candidates not in DB at all

4th scan: 8 candidates. 6 length-4 sequence patterns.

5th scan: 1 candidate. 1 length-5 sequence patterns.

Some drawbacks of GSP are: a huge set of candidate sequences are generated, multiple scans of database are needed and it is inefficient for mining long sequential patterns (as it needs to generate a large number of small candidates).

Apart from finding simple frequent patterns, GSP generalizes the problem by

A. Allowing a user to specify time constraints (minimum and/or maximum time period between adjacent elements in a pattern)

B. Relaxing the restriction that the items in an element of a sequential pattern must come from the same transaction, instead allowing the items to be present in a set of transactions whose transaction-times are within a user-specified time window.

C. Given a user-defined taxonomy (is-a hierarchy) on items, allowing sequential patterns to include items across all levels of the taxonomy.

Vertical Format-Based Method (SPADE: Sequential Pattern Discovery using Equivalent Class) (Zaki, 2001)

This is a vertical format sequential pattern mining method. SPADE first maps the sequence database to a vertical id-list database format which is a large set of items <SID (Sequence ID), EID (Event ID)>. Sequential pattern mining is performed by growing the subsequences (patterns) one item at a time by Apriori candidate generation.

As shown in Figure 3, all frequent sequences can be enumerated via simple temporal joins (or intersections) on id-lists. They use a lattice-theoretic approach to decompose the original search space (lattice) into smaller pieces (sub-lattices) which can be processed independently in main-memory.

Their approach usually requires three database scans, or only a single scan with some pre-processed information, thus minimizing the I/O costs. SPADE decouples the problem decomposition from the pattern search. Pattern search could be done in a BFS (breadth first search) or a DFS

Figure 2. Length-2 candidates

	<a>	<b>	<c>	<d>	<e>	<f>		<a>	<b>	<c>	<d>	<e>	<f>
<a>	<aa>	<ab>	<ac>	<ad>	<ae>	<af>	**<a>**		<(ab)>	<(ac)>	<(ad)>	<(ae)>	<(af)>
<b>	<ba>	<bb>	<bc>	<bd>	<be>	<bf>	**<b>**			<(bc)>	<(bd)>	<(be)>	<(bf)>
<c>	<ca>	<cb>	<cc>	<cd>	<ce>	<cf>	**<c>**				<(cd)>	<(ce)>	<(cf)>
<d>	<da>	<db>	<dc>	<dd>	<de>	<df>	**<d>**					<(de)>	<(df)>
<e>	<ea>	<eb>	<ec>	<ed>	<ee>	<ef>	**<e>**						<(ef)>
<f>	<fa>	<fb>	<fc>	<fd>	<fe>	<ff>	**<f>**						

Figure 3. Frequent sequences

SID	EID	Items
1	1	a
1	2	abc
1	3	ac
1	4	d
1	5	cf
2	1	ad
2	2	c
2	3	bc
2	4	ae
3	1	ef
3	2	ab
3	3	df
3	4	c
3	5	b

a		b		...
SID	EID	SID	EID	...
1	1	1	2	
1	2	2	3	
1	3	3	2	
2	1			
3	2			

ab			ba			...
SID	EID(a)	EID(b)	SID	EID(b)	EID(a)	...
1	1	2	1	2	3	
2	1	3				

aba			
SID	EID(a)	EID(b)	EID(a)
1	1	2	3

(depth first search) manner. The vertical id-list based approach is also insensitive to data-skew. It also has linear scalability with respect to the number of input-sequences, and a number of other database parameters.

Pattern Growth Based Methods

These methods help in avoiding the drawbacks of the Apriori based methods.

FreeSpan (Frequent pattern projected Sequential pattern mining)(Han, Pei, Asl, Chen, Dayal, & Hsu, 2000) & *PrefixSpan (Pei, et al., 2001)* uses frequent items to recursively project sequence databases into a set of smaller projected databases and grows subsequence fragments in each projected database. This process partitions both the data and the set of frequent patterns to be tested, and confines each test being conducted to the corresponding smaller projected database.

FreeSpan first scans the database, collects the support for each item, and finds the set of frequent items. Frequent items are listed in support descending order (in the form of item:support) E.g., flist=a:4, b:4, c:4, d:3, e:3, f:3.

According to flist, the complete set of sequential patterns in S can be divided into 6 disjoint subsets: (1) the ones containing only item 'a', (2) the ones containing item 'b', but containing no items after 'b' in flist, (3) the ones containing item 'c', but no items after 'c', in flist, and so on, and finally, (6) ones containing item 'f'.

The subsets of sequential patterns can be mined by constructing projected databases. Infrequent items, such as 'g' in this example, are removed from construction of projected databases.

Note that {b}, {c}, {d}, {e}, {f}-projected databases are constructed simultaneously during one scan of the original sequence database. All sequential patterns containing only item 'a' are also found in this pass. This process is performed recursively on projected databases. Since FreeSpan projects a large sequence database recursively into a set of small projected sequence databases based on the currently mined frequent sets, the subsequent mining is confined to each projected database relevant to a smaller set of candidates.

The major cost of FreeSpan is to deal with projected databases. If a pattern appears in each sequence of a database, its projected database

Figure 4. PrefixSpan

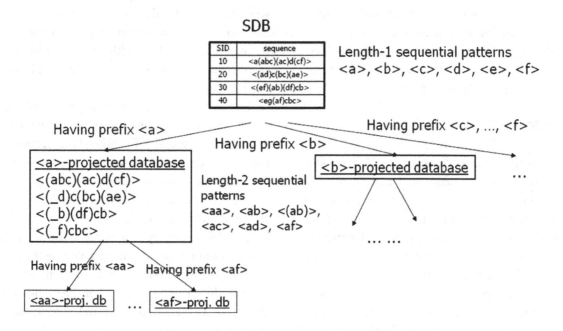

does not shrink (except for the removal of some infrequent items). Moreover, since a length-k subsequence may grow at any position, the search for length-(k+1) candidate sequence will need to check every possible combination, which is costly.

PrefixSpan (Prefix-projected Sequential pattern mining) works similar to FreeSpan except that the partitioning is done using prefixes of sequences. E.g., for a sequence <(abc)(ac)d(cf)>, <ab> is a prefix which has <(_c)(ac)d(cf)> as the corresponding suffix (projection) as shown in Figure 4.

Its general idea is to examine only the frequent prefix subsequences and project only their corresponding postfix subsequences into projected databases because any frequent subsequence can always be found by growing a frequent prefix. Thus the search space for our example will be partitioned into the following six subsets according to the six prefixes: (1) the ones having prefix <a>... and (6) the ones having prefix <f>. In each projected database, sequential patterns are grown by exploring only local frequent patterns. The subsets of sequential patterns can be mined by

constructing corresponding projected databases and mining each recursively.

PrefixSpan first finds sequential patterns having prefix <a>. Recursively, all sequential having patterns prefix <a> can be partitioned into 6 subsets: (1) those having prefix <aa> (2) those having prefix <ab>... and finally, (6) those having prefix <af>. These subsets can be mined by constructing respective projected databases (only if the prefix is frequent) and mining each recursively. Similarly, we can find sequential patterns having prefix <b>, <c>, <d>, <e> and <f> respectively, by constructing <b>-, <c>-, <d>-, <e>- and <f>-projected databases and mining them respectively.

No candidate sequence needs to be generated by PrefixSpan. Projected databases keep shrinking. The major cost of PrefixSpan is the construction of projected databases. To further improve mining efficiency, two kinds of database projections are explored: level-by-level projection and bi-level projection. Moreover, a main-memory-based pseudo-projection (using pointers rather than physically copying postfix sequences) technique is developed for saving the cost of projection and speeding up processing when the projected (sub)-database and its associated pseudo-projection processing structure can fit in main memory. PrefixSpan mines complete set of patterns much faster than both GSP and FreeSpan.

Constraint Based Methods

Conventionally, users can specify only min_sup as a parameter to a sequential pattern mining algorithm. There are two major difficulties in sequential pattern mining: (1) effectiveness: the mining may return a huge number of patterns, many of which could be uninteresting to users, and (2) efficiency: it often takes substantial computational time and space for mining the complete set of sequential patterns in a large sequence database. To prevent these problems, users can use constraint based sequential pattern mining for focused mining of desired patterns. Constraints could be anti-monotone, monotone, succinct, convertible or inconvertible. Anti-monotonicity means "if an item-set does not satisfy the rule constraint, then none of its supersets satisfy". Monotonicity means "if an item-set satisfies the rule constraint, then all of its supersets satisfy". Succinctness means "All and only those patterns guaranteed to satisfy the rule can be enumerated". Convertible constraints are those which are not any of anti-monotonic, monotonic, succinct but can be made anti-monotonic or monotonic constraints by changing order of elements in the set. Inconvertible constraints are the ones which are not convertible.

In the context of constraint-based sequential pattern mining, (Srikant & Agrawal, 1996) generalized the scope of the Apriori-based sequential pattern mining to include time constraints, sliding time windows, and user-defined taxonomy. Mining frequent episodes in a sequence of events studied by (Mannila, Toivonen, & Verkamo, 1997) can also be viewed as a constrained mining problem, since episodes are essentially constraints on events

in the form of acyclic graphs. The classical framework on frequent and sequential pattern mining is based on the anti-monotonic Apriori property of frequent patterns. A breadth-first, level-by-level search can be conducted to find the complete set of patterns.

Performance of conventional constraint-based sequential pattern mining algorithms dramatically degrades in the case of mining long sequential patterns in dense databases or when using low minimum supports. In addition, the algorithms may reduce the number of patterns but unimportant patterns are still found in the result patterns. (Yun, 2008) uses weight constraints to reduce the number of unimportant patterns. During the mining process, they consider not only supports but also weights of patterns. Based on the framework, they present a weighted sequential pattern mining algorithm (WSpan).

(Chen, Cao, Li, & Qian, 2008) incorporate user-defined tough aggregate constraints so that the discovered knowledge better meets user needs. They propose a novel algorithm called PTAC (sequential frequent Patterns mining with Tough Aggregate Constraints) to reduce the cost of using tough aggregate constraints by incorporating two effective strategies. One avoids checking data items one by one by utilizing the features of "promising-ness" exhibited by some other items and validity of the corresponding prefix. The other avoids constructing an unnecessary projected database by effectively pruning those unpromising new patterns that may, otherwise, serve as new prefixes.

(Masseglia, Poncelet, & Teisseire, 2003) propose an approach called GTC (Graph for Time Constraints) for mining time constraint based patterns (as defined in GSP algorithm) in very large databases. It is based on the idea that handling time constraints in the earlier stage of the data mining process can be highly beneficial. One of the most significant new features of their approach is that handling of time constraints can be easily taken into account in traditional level-wise approaches since it is carried out prior to and separately from the counting step of a data sequence.

(Wang, Chirn, Marr, Shapiro, Shasha, & Zhang, 1994) looked at the problem of discovering approximate structural patterns from a genetic sequences database. Besides the minimum support threshold, their solution allows the users to specify: (1) the desired form of patterns as sequences of consecutive symbols separated by variable length don't cares; (2) a lower bound on the length of the discovered patterns; and (3) an upper bound on the edit distance allowed between a mined pattern and the data sequence that contains it. Their algorithm uses a random sample of the input sequences to build a main memory data structure, termed generalized suffix tree, that is used to obtain an initial set of candidate pattern segments and screen out candidates that are unlikely to be frequent based on their occurrence counts in the sample. The entire database is then scanned and filtered to verify that the remaining candidates are indeed frequent answers to the user query.

(Garofalakis, Rastogi, & Shim, 2002) propose regular expressions as constraints for sequential pattern mining and developed a family of SPIRIT (Sequential pattern mining with regular expression constraints) algorithms. Members in the family achieve various degrees of constraint enforcement. The algorithms use relaxed constraints with nice properties (like anti-monotonicity) to filter out some unpromising patterns/candidates in their early stage. A SPIRIT algorithm first identifies C' as a constraint weaker than C. Then it obtains F_1=frequent items in D that satisfy C'. Further, it iteratively generates candidates C_k using F and C', prunes candidates in C_k that contain subsequences that satisfy C' but are not in F, identifies F_k as the frequent sequences in C_k by scanning the database to count support and updates F to $F \cup F_k$. Finally, sequences in F that satisfy the original condition C are output.

General SPIRIT constrained mining framework can be specified as:

```
PROCEDURE SPIRIT(D,C)
Begin
    1. Let C'=a constraint weaker
(i.e., less restrictive) than C.
    2. F=F₁=frequent items in D
that satisfy C'
    3. K=2
    4. Repeat {
        a. //candidate generation
        b. Using C' and F generate
Cₖ={potentially frequent k-sequences
that satify C'}
        c. //candidate pruning
        d. Let P={s∈Cₖ: s has a sub-
sequence t that satisfies C' and t∉F}
        e. Cₖ=Cₖ-P
        f. //candidate counting
        g. Scan D counting the sup-
port for candidate k-sequences in Cₖ
        h. Fₖ-frequent sequences in
Cₖ
        i. F=F∪Fₖ
        j. K=K+1
    5.          }until
TerminatingCondition(F < C') holds
    6. //enforce the original
(stronger) constraint C
    7. Output sequences in F that
satisfy C
    8. End
```

Given a user specified RE constraint C, the first SPIRIT algorithm SPIRIT(N) ("N" for "Naive") only prunes candidate sequences containing elements that do not appear in C. The second one, SPIRIT(L) ("L" for "Legal"), requires every candidate sequence to be legal with respect to some state of automata A(C). The third, SPIRIT(V) ("V" for "Valid"), filters out candidate sequences that are not valid with respect to any state of A(C). The fourth, SPIRIT(R) ("R" for "Regular"), pushes C all the way inside the mining process by counting support only for valid candidate sequences.

The above interesting studies handle a few scattered classes of constraints. However, two problems remain. First, many practical constraints have not been covered. Also there is a need for a systematic method to push various constraints into the mining process. Unfortunately, some commonly encountered sequence-based constraints, such as regular expression constraints, are neither monotonic, nor anti-monotonic, nor succinct. (Pei, Han, & Wang, 2007) mention seven categories of constraints:

1. **Item constraint:** An item constraint specifies subset of items that should or should not be present in the patterns.
2. **Length constraint:** A length constraint specifies the requirement on the length of the patterns, where the length can be either the number of occurrences of items or the number of transactions.
3. **Super-pattern constraint:** Super-patterns are ones that contain at least one of a particular set of patterns as sub-patterns.
4. **Aggregate constraint:** An aggregate constraint is the constraint on an aggregate of items in a pattern, where the aggregate function can be sum, avg, max, min, standard deviation, etc.
5. **Regular expression constraint:** A regular expression constraint CRE is a constraint specified as a regular expression over the set of items using the established set of regular expression operators, such as disjunction and Kleene closure.
6. **Duration constraint:** A duration constraint is defined only in sequence databases where each transaction in every sequence has a time-stamp. It requires that the sequential patterns in the sequence database must have the property such that the time-stamp difference between the first and the last transactions in a sequential pattern must be longer or shorter than a given period.

7. **Gap constraint:** A gap constraint set is defined only in sequence databases where each transaction in every sequence has a timestamp. It requires that the sequential patterns in the sequence database must have the property such that the timestamp difference between every two adjacent transactions must be longer or shorter than a given gap.

A constraint C_{pa} is called prefix anti-monotonic if for each sequence 'a' satisfying the constraint, so does every prefix of 'a'. A constraint C_{pm} is called prefix monotonic if for each sequence 'a' satisfying the constraint, so does every sequence having 'a' as a prefix. A constraint is called prefix-monotone if it is prefix anti-monotonic or prefix monotonic.

The authors describe a pattern-growth (PG) method for Constraint-based sequential pattern mining which is based on a prefix-monotone property. They show that all the monotonic and anti-monotonic constraints, as well as regular expression constraints, are prefix-monotone, and can be pushed deep into a PG-based mining. Moreover, some tough aggregate constraints, such as those involving average or general sum, can also be pushed deep into a slightly revised PG mining process. In the recursive FP growth framework, the authors first compute all the length-1 frequent prefixes. Then they compute the corresponding projected databases. Each of the frequent prefixes of length (l+1) are further processed recursively only if they satisfy the constraint C.

Closed Sequential Pattern Mining

CloSpan (Yan, Han, & Afshar, 2003) is an algorithm for the mining of closed repetitive gapped subsequences (Figure 5). A closed sequential pattern s is a sequence such that there exists no super-pattern s', s' ⊃ s, and s' and s have the same support. E.g., given <abc>: 20, <abcd>:20, <abcde>: 15, we know that <abcd> is closed. If the database contains 1 long sequence with 100 elements and min support is 1, this sequence will generate 2^{100} frequent subsequences, though there is only one of these which is closed. Mining of closed sequences reduces the number of (redundant) patterns but attains the same expressive power. Note that if s' ⊃ s, s is closed iff two projected DBs have the same size. CloSpan uses backward sub-pattern and backward super-pattern pruning to prune redundant search space thereby preventing unnecessary computations.

CloSpan is basically similar to PrefixSpan with sub-pattern and super-pattern checks which involve checking and matching of the size of the databases. The authors show that CloSpan performs better than PrefixSpan in terms of execution time.

Sequential Pattern Mining in Data Streams: SS-BE and SS-MB (Mendes, Ding, & Han, 2008)

Data stream is an unbounded sequence in which new elements are generated continuously. Memory usage is limited and an algorithm is allowed to perform only a single scan over the database. Two effective methods for stream-based sequential pattern mining are SS-BE (Stream Sequence miner using Bounded Error) and SS-MB (Stream Sequence miner using Memory Bounds).

SS-BE Method can be outlined as follows:

A. Break the stream into fixed-sized batches.
B. For each arriving batch, apply PrefixSpan. Insert each frequent sequence found into a tree.
C. Periodically prune the tree (the number of batches seen is a multiple of the pruning period).
D. Output all sequences corresponding to nodes having count >= $(\sigma-\epsilon)N$.

This method outputs no false negatives and true support of false positives is at least $(\sigma-\epsilon)$.

E.g., suppose $\sigma = 0.75$, $\epsilon = 0.5$ and data stream D: <a,b,c>, <a,c>, <a,b>, <b,c>, <a,b,c,d>, <c,a,b>, <d,a,b>, <a,e,b>. Let the first batch B_1 contain the first four sequences and the second batch B_2 contain the next four. The algorithm first applies PrefixSpan to B_1 with min_sup as 0.5. The frequent sequences found are: <a>:3, <b>:3, <c>:3, <a,b>:2, <a,c>:2, and <b,c>:2. A frequent pattern tree is created. Let the pruning period be two batches. So algorithm proceeds to batch B_2. The frequent sequences found are: <a>:4, <b>:4, <c>:2, <d>:2, and <a,b>:4. The frequent pattern tree would look as shown in the figure below. Now SS-BE would prune the tree by identifying and removing all nodes guaranteed to have true support below $\epsilon = 0.5$ during the time they were kept in the tree. Thus <d>:2, <ac>:2 and <bc>:2 are pruned away.

Figure 5. CloSpan

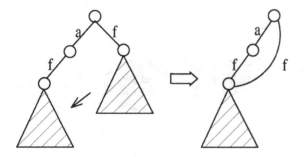

Backward super-pattern pruning

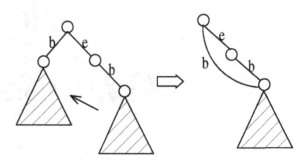

Backward sub-pattern pruning

Finally SS-BE outputs all sequences having count at least $(\sigma-\epsilon)N = (0.75 - 0.5)*8 = 2$.

Thus output is <a>: 7, <b>: 7, <c>: 5, <a, b>:6. Note that there are no false negatives and only one false positive: <c>.

SS-MB method is similar to SS-BE except that in step 3, rather than pruning the tree after a time period, the tree size is limited to 'm' nodes. Due to this, SS-MB can only guarantee no false negatives after execution. E.g. in the above example, assume that 'm' is 7. Then after batch B_2 is processed, the tree contains 8 nodes and hence the node with minimum support <b,c> is removed (Figure 3). Because of the specific 'm', SS-MB can control amount of memory used explicitly.

The authors show that the two methods are effective solutions to the stream sequential pattern mining problem: running time scales linearly, maximum memory usage is limited and a very small number of false positives are generated.

Mining Incremental Patterns: IncSpan (Incremental Mining of Sequential Patterns) (Cheng, Yan, & Han, 2004)

Many real life sequence databases, such as customer shopping sequences, medical treatment sequences, etc., grow incrementally. It is undesirable to mine sequential patterns from scratch each time when a small set of sequences grow, or when some new sequences are added into the database. Incremental algorithm should be developed for sequential pattern mining so that mining can be adapted to frequent and incremental database updates, including both insertions and deletions. However, it is nontrivial to mine sequential patterns incrementally, especially when the existing sequences grow incrementally because such growth may lead to the generation of many new patterns due to the interactions of the growing subsequences with the original ones. There are two kinds of database updates in applications: (1) inserting new sequences (INSERT) and (2) appending new item-sets/items to the existing sequences (APPEND). Let DB be the old database, Δdb be the change and DB' be the new database. Thus, DB' = DB $\cup \Delta db$.

It is easier to handle the first case: INSERT. An important property of INSERT is that a frequent sequence in DB' = DB $\cup \Delta db$ must be frequent in either DB or Δdb (or both). If a sequence is infrequent in both DB and Δdb, it cannot be frequent in DB'. Thus, only those patterns that are frequent in Δdb but infrequent in DB need to be searched in DB to find their occurrence count.

Figure 6. SS-BE pruning tree

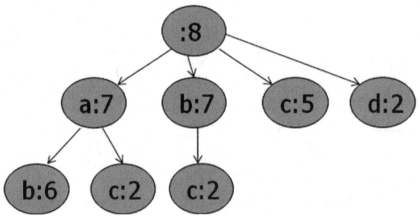

(Zhang, Kao, Cheung, & Yip, 2002) propose another algorithm of incremental mining to handle the case of INSERT in sequential pattern mining.

For the second case, consider that new items only get appended. Suppose |DB|=1000 and |Δdb|=20, min_sup=10%. Suppose a sequence 's' is infrequent in DB with 99 occurrences (sup = 9:9%). In addition, it is also infrequent in Δdb with only 1 occurrence (sup = 5%). Although 's' is infrequent in both DB and Δdb, it becomes frequent in DB' with 100 occurrences.

This problem complicates the incremental mining since one cannot ignore the infrequent sequences in Δdb, but there are an exponential number of infrequent sequences even in a small Δdb and checking them against the set of infrequent sequences in DB will be very costly. (Parthasarathy, Zaki, Ogihara, & Dwarkadas, 1999) proposed an incremental mining algorithm, called ISM, based on SPADE by exploiting a concept called negative border. However, maintaining negative border is memory consuming and not well adapted for large databases. (Masseglia, Poncelet, & Teisseire, Efficient mining of sequential patterns with time constraints: Reducing the combinations, 2009) developed another incremental mining algorithm using candidate generate-and-test approach, which is costly, especially when the sequences are long because it requires multiple scans of the whole database.

For the third case, where the database is updated with both INSERT and APPEND, the problem becomes even more complicated. There are two approaches: (1) handling them separately by first performing APPEND then INSERT; (2) treat the inserted sequences as appending to empty sequences in DB: a special case of APPEND. Then this problem is reduced to APPEND.

Given a minimum support threshold, min_sup, a sequence is frequent if its support >=min_sup; given a factor $\mu <= 1$, a sequence is semi-frequent if its support<min_sup but >μ*min_sup; a sequence is infrequent if its support<μ*min_sup. Let FS be the set of all frequent sequential patterns and SFS be the set of semi-frequent sequential patterns.

Given a sequence database DB, min_sup, the set of frequent subsequences FS in DB, and an appended sequence database DB' of D, the problem of incremental sequential pattern mining is to mine the set of frequent subsequences FS' in DB' based on FS instead of mining on DB' from scratch. A simple algorithm, SimpleSpan, exploits the FS in the original database and incrementally mines new patterns. SimpleSpan updates the support of every frequent sequence in FS, adds it to FS' and uses it as a prefix to project database. In addition, SimpleSpan scans the new database DB' to discover new frequent single items and uses them as prefix to project database using PrefixSpan. One problem of SimpleSpan is that it makes a large number of database projections, which is costly. The drawback of SimpleSpan is that it has no information about infrequent sequences in the original database DB. But such information can enable us to reduce search space and find new frequent sequences efficiently.

IncSpan uses the technique of buffering semi-frequent patterns by maintaining a set SFS in the original database DB. Since the sequences in SFS are "almost frequent", most of the frequent subsequences in the appended database will either come from SFS or they are already frequent in the original database. With a minor update to the original database, it is expected that only a small fraction of subsequences which were infrequent previously would become frequent. This is based on the assumption that updates to the original database have a uniform probability distribution on items. It is expected that most of the frequent subsequences introduced by the updated part of the database would come from the SFS. The SFS forms a kind of boundary (or "buffer zone") between the frequent subsequences and infrequent subsequences.

IncSpan algorithm can be outlined as follows.

A. Scan Δdb for single items. If a new item or an infrequent item becomes frequent or semi-frequent, add it to FS' or SFS'. For every item in FS', use it as prefix to construct projected database and discover frequent sequences recursively.

B. Check every pattern in FS and SFS in Δdb to adjust the support of those patterns.

1. If a pattern becomes frequent, add it to FS'. Then check whether it meets the projection condition. If so, use it as prefix to project database. Discover frequent or semi-frequent patterns in the projected database. To improve the performance, shared projection can be used in this step.

2. If a pattern is semi-frequent, add it to SFS'.

The authors also mention two optimization techniques, reverse pattern matching and shared projection to improve the performance.

Multidimensional Sequential Pattern Mining: UNISEQ (Pinto, Han, Pei, Wang, Chen, & Dayal, 2001)

Consider pattern P1= {try a 100 hour free internet access package⇒subscribe to 15 hours/ month package⇒upgrade to 30 hours per month package⇒upgrade to unlimited package}. This pattern may hold for all customers below age of 35 (75% customers). But for other customers, pattern P2= {try a 100 hour free internet access package⇒ upgrade to 30 hours per month package} may hold. Clearly, if sequential pattern mining can be associated with customer category or other multi-dimensional information, it will be more effective since the classified patterns are often more useful. (Pinto, Han, Pei, Wang, Chen, & Dayal, 2001) propose two categories of methods: a. integration of efficient sequential pattern mining and multi-dimensional analysis methods (Seq-Dim and Dim-Seq). b. embedding

multi-dimensional information into sequences and mine the whole set using a uniform sequential pattern mining method (Uni-Seq).

A multi-dimensional sequence database has the schema (RID, A_1, A_2 ... A_m, S) where RID is the record identifier, A_1 ... A_m are the attributes and S is the sequence. A multi-dimensional pattern 'p' would match a tuple 't' in the database, if the attribute values match (or the attribute value is *) and 's' is a subsequence of the sequence stored in 't'. e.g. t=(10, business, Boston, middle, <(bd)cba>)

UniSeq (Uniform Sequential): Multi-dimensional information in a tuple 't' in multi-dimensional DB can be embedded in the sequence by introducing a special element. E.g. 't' can be rewritten as (10, <(business Boston middle)(bd) cba>). Let the database containing such modified tuples be called MD-extension DB and denoted as SDB-MD. Now the problem is: Given, SDB-MD and min_sup, output the complete set of multi-dimensional sequential patterns. UniSeq mines sequential patterns in SDB-MD using PrefixSpan. For each sequential pattern 'p' in SDB-MD, it outputs the corresponding multi-dimensional sequential pattern in SDB. As an alternative, instead of embedding the multi-dimensional information into the first element of each sequence, it can be attached as the last element. Both the alternatives have almost identical performance results. Thus, UniSeq reduces the problem to mining one extended sequence database and is therefore easy to implement. But, all dimension values are treated as sequential items. Hence, it cannot take advantage of efficient mining algorithms for multi-dimensional non-sequential computational methods. Hence, cost of computing becomes high when data has large number of dimensions.

A SDB-MD can be partitioned into two parts: dimensional information and sequence. So, we can first mine patterns about dimensional information (called multi-dimensional patterns or MD-patterns) and then find sequential patterns from projected sub-database (tuples containing the MD-pattern) or vice versa. Dim-Seq first finds

MD-patterns and then for each MD-pattern, it forms MD-projected database and mines sequential patterns in projected databases. Seq-Dim first mines the sequential patterns. For each sequential pattern, it forms projected MD-database and then finds MD-patterns within projected databases. Seq-Dim is more efficient and scalable in general compared to Dim-Seq.

Mining Closed Repetitive Gapped Subsequences (Ding, Lo, Han, & Khoo, 2009)

Patterns often repeat multiple times in a sequence e.g., in program execution traces, sequences of words (text data), credit card usage histories. Given two sequences like S_1 =AABCDABB, S_2 = ABCD, is pattern AB more frequent then CD? To answer this question, one needs to define a notion of repetitive support, sup(P) as max{|INS|: INS is a set of non-overlapping instances of P}. The aim is to maximize the size of the non-overlapping instance set. Note that if P' is a super-pattern of P, then sup(P') ≤ sup(P).

To solve this problem, the authors propose a greedy instance-growth algorithm. The intuition is to extend each instance to the nearest possible event. Consider a database of two sequences as shown in Figure 7.

The algorithm uses a procedure INSgrow(P, INS, e) which does the following. Given a leftmost support set INS of P, with |INS| = sup(P), and event e, it extends each instance in INS to the nearest possible event e and returns a support set INS⁺ of pattern P∘e (P concatenated with e). Thus, using this method, one can find all the frequent patterns by doing DFS in the pattern space.

Further, they define pattern extension as set of patterns with one more event. E.g., if $P = e_1 e_2 \ldots e_m$, PExtension(P, e) = $\{ee_1 e_2 \ldots e_m, e_1 e e_2 \ldots e_m, \ldots, e_1 e_2 \ldots e_m e\}$. Pattern P is not closed iff sup(P) = sup(Q) for some Q ∈ Extension(P, e). Also note that it is possible that AB is not closed but ABAC is closed. To prune the search space, they propose the following instance-border checking principle. Pattern P is prunable if there exists Q ∈ Extension(P, e) for some e such that sup(P) = sup(Q) (P is not closed) and for each (i, $<k_1, k_2, \ldots, k_{|P|}>$) ∈ INS^P and (i, $<k_1', k_2', \ldots, k_{|Q|}'>$) ∈ INS^Q: $k_{|Q|}' \le k_{|P|}$ where INS^P and INS^Q are (leftmost) support sets of P and Q respectively.

OTHER SEQUENTIAL PATTERN MINING METHODS

(Kum, Chang, & Wang, Sequential Pattern Mining in Multi-Databases via Multiple Alignment, 2006) proposed a new sequential pattern mining method based on multiple alignment (rather than the usual support-based approach) for mining multiple databases. Multiple databases are mined and summarized at the local level, and only the summarized patterns are used in the global mining process. For summarization, they propose the theme of approximate sequential pattern

Figure 7. Database of two sequences

	1	2	3	4	5	6	7	8	9
S1	A	B	C	A	C	B	D	D	B
S2	A	C	D	B	A	C	A	D	D

Support set I^A	Support set I^AC	Support set I^ACB
(1,<1>)	(1,<1,3>)	(1,<1,3,6>)
(1,<4>)	(1,<4,5>)	(1,<4,5,9>)
(2,<1>)	(2,<1,2>)	(2,<1,2,4>)
(2,<5>)	(2,<5,6>)	
(2,<7>)		
sup(A)=5	sup(AC)=4	sup(ACB)=3

mining roughly defined as identifying patterns approximately shared by many sequences. They propose an algorithm, ApproxMAP, to mine approximate sequential patterns, called consensus patterns, from large sequence databases in two steps. First, sequences are clustered by similarity. Then, consensus patterns are mined directly from each cluster through multiple alignment.

Further, (Kum, Chang, & Wang, Benchmarking the effectiveness of sequential pattern mining methods, 2007) benchmarked the effectiveness of sequential pattern mining methods by comparing a support-based sequential pattern model with an approximate pattern model based on sequence alignment using a metric that evaluates how well a mining method finds known common patterns in synthetic data. Their comparison study suggests that the alignment model will give a good summary of the sequential data in the form of a set of common patterns in the data. In contrast, the support model generates massive amounts of frequent patterns with much redundancy. This suggests that the results of the support model require more post processing before it can be of actual use in real applications.

(Laur, Symphor, Nock, & Poncelet, 2007) introduced statistical supports to maximize mining precision and improve the computational efficiency of the incremental mining process. As only a part of the stream can be stored, mining data streams for sequential patterns and updating previously found frequent patterns need to cope with uncertainty. They introduce a new statistical approach which biases the initial support for sequential patterns. This approach holds the advantage to maximize either the precision or the recall, as chosen by the user, and limit the degradation of the other criterion. Moreover, these statistical supports help building statistical borders which are the relevant sets of frequent patterns to use into an incremental mining process.

(Lin, Chen, Hao, Chueh, & Chang, 2008) introduced the notion of positive and negative sequential patterns, where positive patterns include the presence of an item-set of a pattern, and negative patterns are the ones with the absence of an item-set.

Items sold in a store can usually be organized into a concept hierarchy according to some taxonomy. Based on the hierarchy, sequential patterns can be found not only at the leaf nodes (individual items) of the hierarchy, but also at higher levels of the hierarchy; this is called multiple-level sequential pattern mining. In previous research, taxonomies had crisp relationships between the categories in one level and the categories in another level. In real life, however, crisp taxonomies cannot handle the uncertainties and fuzziness inherent in the relationships among items and categories. For example, the book Alice's Adventures in Wonderland can be classified into the Children's Literature category, but can also be related to the Action & Adventure category. To deal with the fuzzy nature of taxonomy, (Chen & Huang, A novel knowledge discovering model for mining fuzzy multi-level sequential patterns in sequence databases, 2008) apply fuzzy set techniques to concept taxonomies so that the relationships from one level to another can be represented by a value between 0 and 1. They propose a fuzzy multiple-level mining algorithm (FMSM) to extract fuzzy multiple-level sequential patterns from databases. In addition, another algorithm, named the CROSS-FMSM algorithm, is developed to discover fuzzy cross-level sequential patterns.

(Kuo, Chao, & Liu, 2009) use K-means algorithm to achieve better computational efficiency for fuzzy sequential pattern mining.

Many methods only focus on the concept of frequency because of the assumption that sequences' behaviors do not change over time. The environment from which the data is generated is often dynamic; the sequences' behaviors may change over time. To adapt the discovered patterns to these changes, (Chen & Hu, Constraint-based sequential pattern mining: the consideration of recency and compactness, 2006) introduce two new concepts, recency and compactness and incorporate them into traditional sequential pattern mining. The concept of recency causes patterns to quickly adapt to the latest behaviors in sequence databases, while the concept of compactness ensures reasonable time spans for the discovered patterns. An efficient method is presented to find CFR-patterns (compactness, frequency, and recency).

CONCLUSION

We discussed basics of sequential pattern mining. We presented an exhaustive survey of different sequential pattern mining methods proposed in the literature. Sequential pattern mining methods have been used to analyze this data and identify patterns. Such patterns have been used to implement efficient systems that can recommend based on previously observed patterns, help in making predictions, improve usability of systems, detect events and in general help in making strategic product decisions. We envision that the power of sequential mining methods has not yet been fully exploited. We hope to see many more strong applications of these methods in a variety of domains in the years to come. Apart from this, new sequential pattern mining methods may also be developed to handle special scenarios of colossal patterns, approximate sequential patterns and other kinds of sequential patterns specific to the applications.

REFERENCES

Chen, E., Cao, H., Li, Q., & Qian, T. (2008). Efficient strategies for tough aggregate constraint-based sequential pattern mining. *Inf. Sci.*, *178*(6), 1498–1518. doi:10.1016/j.ins.2007.10.014

Chen, Y.-L., & Hu, Y.-H. (2006). Constraint-based sequential pattern mining: The consideration of recency and compactness. *Decision Support Systems*, *42*(2), 1203–1215. doi:10.1016/j.dss.2005.10.006

Chen, Y.-L., & Huang, T. C.-K. (2008). A novel knowledge discovering model for mining fuzzy multi-level sequential patterns in sequence databases. *Data & Knowledge Engineering*, *66*(3), 349–367. doi:10.1016/j.datak.2008.04.005

Cheng, H., Yan, X., & Han, J. (2004). IncSpan: Incremental mining of sequential patterns in large database. *KDD '04: Proceedings of the Tenth ACM SIGKDD International Conference on Knowledge Discovery and Data Mining*, (pp. 527-532).

Ding, B., Lo, D., Han, J., & Khoo, S.-C. (2009). *Efficient mining of closed repetitive gapped subsequences from a sequence database*. ICDE 09.

Exarchos, T. P., Tsipouras, M. G., Papaloukas, C., & Fotiadis, D. I. (2008). A two-stage methodology for sequence classification based on sequential pattern mining and optimization. *Data & Knowledge Engineering*, *66*(3), 467–487. doi:10.1016/j.datak.2008.05.007

Garofalakis, M., Rastogi, R., & Shim, K. (2002). Mining sequential patterns with regular expression constraints. *IEEE Transactions on Knowledge and Data Engineering*, *14*(3), 530–552. doi:10.1109/TKDE.2002.1000341

Han, J., Pei, J., Asl, B. M., Chen, Q., Dayal, U., & Hsu, M. C. (2000). FreeSpan: Frequent pattern-projected sequential pattern mining. *KDD '00: Proceedings of the Sixth ACM SIGKDD International Conference on Knowledge Discovery and Data Mining* (pp. 355-359). Boston, MA: ACM.

Kum, H.-C., Chang, J. H., & Wang, W. (2006). Sequential pattern mining in multi-databases via multiple alignment. *Data Mining and Knowledge Discovery*, *12*(2-3), 151–180. doi:10.1007/s10618-005-0017-3

Kum, H.-C., Chang, J. H., & Wang, W. (2007). Benchmarking the effectiveness of sequential pattern mining methods. *Data & Knowledge Engineering*, *60*(1), 30–50. doi:10.1016/j.datak.2006.01.004

Kuo, R. J., Chao, C. M., & Liu, C. Y. (2009). Integration of K-means algorithm and AprioriSome algorithm for fuzzy sequential pattern mining. *Applied Soft Computing*, *9*(1), 85–93. doi:10.1016/j.asoc.2008.03.010

Laur, P.-A., Symphor, J.-E., Nock, R., & Poncelet, P. (2007). Statistical supports for mining sequential patterns and improving the incremental update process on data streams. *Intelligent Data Analysis*, *11*(1), 29–47.

Lin, N. P., Chen, H.-J., Hao, W.-H., Chueh, H.-E., & Chang, C.-I. (2008). Mining strong positive and negative sequential patterns. *W. Trans. on Comp.*, *7*(3), 119–124.

Mannila, H., Toivonen, H., & Verkamo, I. (1997). Discovery of frequent episodes in event sequences. *Data Mining and Knowledge Discovery*, *1*(3), 259–289. doi:10.1023/A:1009748302351

Masseglia, F., Poncelet, P., & Teisseire, M. (2003). Incremental mining of sequential patterns in large databases. *Data & Knowledge Engineering*, *46*(1), 97–121. doi:10.1016/S0169-023X(02)00209-4

Masseglia, F., Poncelet, P., & Teisseire, M. (2009). Efficient mining of sequential patterns with time constraints: Reducing the combinations. *Expert Systems with Applications*, *36*(3), 2677–2690. doi:10.1016/j.eswa.2008.01.021

Mendes, L. F., Ding, B., & Han, J. (2008). Stream sequential pattern mining with precise error bounds. *Proc. 2008 Int. Conf. on Data Mining (ICDM'08)*, Pisa, Italy, Dec. 2008.

Parthasarathy, S., Zaki, M., Ogihara, M., & Dwarkadas, S. (1999). Incremental and interactive sequence mining. *In Proc. of the 8th Int. Conf. on Information and Knowledge Management (CIKM'99)*.

Pei, J., Han, J., Asl, M. B., Pinto, H., Chen, Q., Dayal, U., et al. (2001). PrefixSpan mining sequential patterns efficiently by prefix projected pattern growth. *Proc.17th Int'l Conf. on Data Eng.*, (pp. 215-226).

Pei, J., Han, J., & Wang, W. (2007). Constraint-based sequential pattern mining: The pattern-growth methods. *Journal of Intelligent Information Systems*, *28*(2), 133–160. doi:10.1007/s10844-006-0006-z

Pinto, H., Han, J., Pei, J., Wang, K., Chen, Q., & Dayal, U. (2001). Multi-dimensional sequential pattern mining. *CIKM '01: Proceedings of the Tenth International Conference on Information and Knowledge Management* (pp. 81-88). New York, NY: ACM.

Seno, M., & Karypis, G. (2002). SLPMiner: An algorithm for finding frequent sequential patterns using length-decreasing support constraint. *In Proceedings of the 2nd IEEE International Conference on Data Mining (ICDM)*, (pp. 418-425).

Srikant, R., & Agrawal, R. (1996). *Advances in database technology EDBT '96.*, (pp. 3-17).

Wang, J. L., Chirn, G., Marr, T., Shapiro, B., Shasha, D., & Zhang, K. (1994). Combinatorial pattern discovery for scientific data: Some preliminary results. *Proc. ACM SIGMOD Int'l Conf. Management of Data*, (pp. 115-125).

Xing, Z., Pei, J., & Keogh, E. (2010). A brief survey on sequence classification. *SIGKDD Explorations Newsletter*, *12*(1), 40–48. doi:10.1145/1882471.1882478

Yan, X., Han, J., & Afshar, R. (2003). CloSpan: Mining closed sequential patterns in large datasets. *Proceedings of SDM*, (pp. 166-177).

Yun, U. (2008). A new framework for detecting weighted sequential patterns in large sequence databases. *Knowledge-Based Systems*, *21*(2), 110–122. doi:10.1016/j.knosys.2007.04.002

Zaki, M. J. (2000). Sequence mining in categorical domains: Incorporating constraints. *CIKM '00: Proceedings of the Ninth International Conference on Information and Knowledge Management* (pp. 422-429). New York, NY: ACM.

Zaki, M. J. (2001). SPADE: An efficient algorithm for mining frequent sequences. *Machine Learning*, *42*(1-2), 31–60. doi:10.1023/A:1007652502315

Zhang, M., Kao, B., Cheung, D., & Yip, C. (2002). Efficient algorithms for incremental updates of frequent sequences., In *Proc. of the 6th Pacific-Asia Conference on Knowledge Discovery and Data Mining* (PAKDD'02).

ADDITIONAL READING

Adamo, J.-M. (2001). *Data Mining for Association Rules and Sequential Patterns: Sequential and Parallel Algorithms*. Secaucus, NJ, USA: Springer-Verlag New York, Inc. doi:10.1007/978-1-4613-0085-4

Alves, R., & Rodriguez-Baena, D. S., Aguilar-Ruiz, & S., J. (2009). Gene association analysis: a survey of frequent pattern mining from gene expression data. *Briefings in Bioinformatics*, 210–224.

Fradkin, D., & Moerchen, F. (2010). Margin-closed frequent sequential pattern mining. *UP '10: Proceedings of the ACM SIGKDD Workshop on Useful Patterns* (pp. 45-54). New York, NY, USA: ACM.

Garofalakis, M., Rastogi, R., & Shim, K. (2002). Mining Sequential Patterns with Regular Expression Constraints. *IEEE Transactions on Knowledge and Data Engineering*, 530–552. doi:10.1109/TKDE.2002.1000341

Han, J., & Kamber, M. (2006). *Data Mining: Concepts and Techniques* (2nd ed.). Morgan Kaufmann Publishers.

Joshi, M. V., Karypis, G., & Kumar, V. (2000). Parallel Algorithms for Mining Sequential Associations: Issues and Challenges (2000).

Li, T.-R., Xu, Y., Ruan, D., & Pan, W.-m. Sequential pattern mining. In R. Da, G. Chen, E. E. Kerre, & G. Wets, *Intelligent data mining: techniques and applications* (pp. 103-122). Springer.

Lin, M.-Y., Hsueh, S.-C., & Chan, C.-C. (2009). Incremental Discovery of Sequential Patterns Using a Backward Mining Approach. *Proceedings of the 2009 International Conference on Computational Science and Engineering* (pp. 64-70). Washington, DC, USA: IEEE Computer Society.

Lu, J., Adjei, O., Chen, W., Hussain, F., & Enach-escu, C. (n.d.). *Sequential Patterns Mining*.

Masseglia, F., Cathala, F., & Poncelet, P. *The PSP approach for mining sequential patterns*. Springer.

Shintani, T., & Kitsuregawa, M. (1998). Mining Algorithms for Sequential Patterns in Parallel: Hash Based Approach. *Proceedings of the Second Pacific–Asia Conference on Knowledge Discovery and Data mining*, (pp. 283-294).

Srinivasa, R. N. (2005). Data mining in e-commerce: A survey. *Sadhana*, 275–289. doi:10.1007/BF02706248

Teisseire, M., Poncelet, P., Scientifique, P., Besse, G., Masseglia, F., & Masseglia, F. (2005). *Sequential pattern mining: A survey on issues and approaches. Encyclopedia of Data Warehousing and Mining, nformation Science Publishing* (pp. 3–29). Oxford University Press.

Tzvetkov, P., Yan, X., & Han, J. (2005). TSP: Mining top-k closed sequential patterns. *Knowledge and Information Systems*, 438–457. doi:10.1007/s10115-004-0175-4

Wang, W., & Yang, J. (2005). *Mining Sequential Patterns from Large Data Sets (Advances in Database Systems)*. Secaucus, NJ, USA: Springer-Verlag New York, Inc.

Yang, L. (2003). Visualizing frequent itemsets, association rules, and sequential patterns in parallel coordinates. *ICCSA '03: Proceedings of the 2003 international conference on Computational science and its applications* (pp. 21-30). Montreal, Canada: Springer-Verlag.

Zhao, Q., & Bhowmick, S. S. (2003). Sequential Pattern Matching: A Survey.

Chapter 9
Analysis of Kinase Inhibitors and Druggability of Kinase–Targets Using Machine Learning Techniques

S. Prasanthi
University of Hyderabad, India

S. Durga Bhavani
University of Hyderabad, India

T. Sobha Rani
University of Hyderabad, India

Raju S. Bapi
University of Hyderabad, India

ABSTRACT

Vast majority of successful drugs or inhibitors achieve their activity by binding to, and modifying the activity of a protein leading to the concept of druggability. A target protein is druggable if it has the potential to bind the drug-like molecules. Hence kinase inhibitors need to be studied to understand the specificity of a kinase inhibitor in choosing a particular kinase target. In this paper we focus on human kinase drug target sequences since kinases are known to be potential drug targets. Also we do a preliminary analysis of kinase inhibitors in order to study the problem in the protein-ligand space in future. The identification of druggable kinases is treated as a classification problem in which druggable kinases are taken as positive data set and non-druggable kinases are chosen as negative data set. The classification problem is addressed using machine learning techniques like support vector machine (SVM) and decision tree (DT) and using sequence-specific features. One of the challenges of this classification problem is due to the unbalanced data with only 48 druggable kinases available against 509 non-drugggable kinases present at Uniprot. The accuracy of the decision tree classifier obtained is 57.65 which is not satisfactory. learning approaches has not been reported in literature.

DOI: 10.4018/978-1-61350-056-9.ch009

A two-tier architecture of decision trees is carefully designed such that recognition on the non-druggable dataset also gets improved. Thus the overall model is shown to achieve a final performance accuracy of 88.37. To the best of our knowledge, kinase druggability prediction using machine

PATTERN DISCOVERY IN KINASES

Human genome contains about 518 protein kinase genes, which constitute about 2% of all human genes (Vulpetti & Bosotti, 2004). Protein kinases regulate almost all biochemical pathways. They play a critical role in signal transduction, physiological responses, and in the functioning of nervous and immune systems. They also control many other cellular processes like metabolism, transcription, cell cycle progression, cyto-skeletal rearrangement and cell movement, apoptosis, and differentiation (Bakheet & Doig, 2009).

Kinases are enzymes which help in phosphorylation of substrates facilitating the transfer of phosphate group from ATP. They may phosphorylate up to 30% of the proteome (Manning et al., 2002), (Manning, 2005). Since kinases participate in signal transduction pathways of cell cycle and cell differentiation they are known to be targets for diseases. Abnormal phosphorylation of the protein kinases is a cause of disease and hence needs to be inhibited by small drug-like molecules called kinase inhibitors. Some of the well-known inhibitors are Serine/Threonine kinase inhibitors and Tyrosine kinase inhibitors which are named on the basis of the amino acid whose phosphorylation is inhibited. Kinase inhibitors are developed in the treatment of diseases like cancers, inflammatory disorders, neurological disorders, diabetes mellitus, heart disease etc. Some of the available kinase inhibitor drugs are Imatinib, Nilotinib and Gefitinib.

In this study we present two perspectives of drug discovery: one from the view point of kinase target and the other from kinase inhibitor. Even though kinases are known to be targets for diseases, not all kinases are druggable. Hence it is important to distinguish druggable kinase tar-

gets from non-druggable kinases. Further kinase inhibitors need to be studied to understand the specificity of a kinase inhibitor in choosing a particular kinase target. The ultimate goal, in some sense, is to predict the matching between a target and its corresponding inhibitor(s) with the help of target and ligand properties individually and together with protein-ligand interaction features. In this paper we restrict ourselves to addressing the problem of druggability of kinases and conduct a feature analysis of kinase inhibitors. The problem of matching will be taken up in future. In the next section we present a study of significant properties of kinase inhibitors.

BACKGROUND

Vieth et al., (2004) conduct a study of kinase targets and inhibitors in order to identify medicinally relevant kinase space. Using both sequence based information and the small molecule selectivity information, they presented the first dendogram of kinases based on small molecule data. This study concludes that the structural basis of kinase inhibitor selectivity will require knowledge of complexes of one ligand with multiple targets. Classification of kinase inhibitors with a bayesian model was studied by Xia et al., (2004). Using Bayesian statistics, a model for general and specific kinase inhibitors was proposed. They have considered serine/ threonine and tyrosine kinase inhibitors (Amgen compounds) from CORP data set. Kinase model was generated using properties like number of hydrogen bond donors, halogens, aromatic residues, value of AlogP and molecular weight. The general kinase model described was trained on tyrosine kinase inhibitors achieving prediction accuracy of 80%.

In order to initiate the study of kinase inhibitors we need both kinase target and inhibitor features that are available in various databases.

Databases of Chemical Compounds

A drug molecule is required to satisfy the well-known properties known as Lipinski's rules (Lipinski et al., 1997). Drug Bank (http://www.drugbank.ca) is a popular data base housing FDA approved drugs and the corresponding targets. We consider features of drug molecules that are available also in other data bases like Protein Data Bank (*http://*www.rcsb.org), ZINC (http://www.zinc.docking.org) and Protein Ligand Interaction Database (PLID) (Reddy et al., 2008). We present here a study of kinase inhibitors and differentiate kinase from non-kinase inhibitors at the feature level.

Protein Data Bank (PDB) is a central repository for all the structures of proteins, nucleic acids and other bio-macromolecules. PDB has been the main source of all protein structures identi-fied either as complex with bound ligand or in uncomplexed form. A few structures of kinase inhibitors are shown in Figure 1. It is computationally hard to extract features from a 3D structure and hence it is represented as a two dimensional structure. Further, the 2D-structure is represented in a one-dimensional string format. SMILES is a popular string format that is used to express the 2-dimensional representation of protein structure. Many databases like ZINC and Drug Bank provide SMILES notation specification for chemical compounds.

For example, the formula of the kinase inhibitor IC261 is C18H17NO4 and the SMILES notation is COC1=CC(OC)=C(C=C2C(=O) NC3=CC=CC=C23)C(OC)=C1. Extraction of relevant features using string algorithms is very fast and hence efficient.

The DrugBank database is a unique bioinformatics and cheminformatics resource that contains detailed drug and the corresponding target data with the sequence, structure, and pathway information. The database contains nearly 4800

Figure 1. 2-dimensional representations of a few kinase inhibitors are shown

SU5416   **GW5074**   **IC261**

Indirubin-3-oxime   **SU4312**

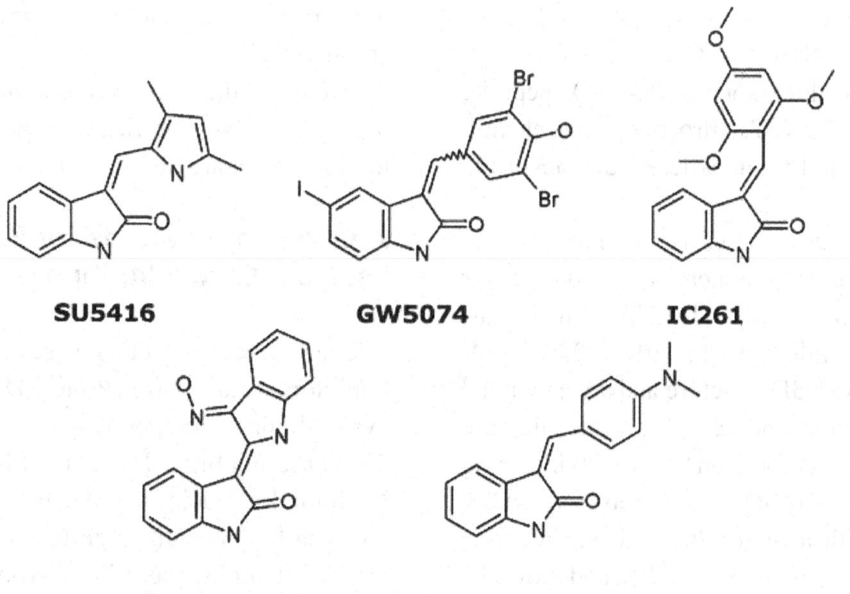

drug entries including nearly one third of which are FDA-approved drugs. Further, protein drug target sequences which are linked to these FDA approved drug entries are present in the data base. Each drug contains more than 100 descriptors half of which correspond to drug descriptors and the other half being linked to target data.

Some of the features computed from SMILES notation in Drug Bank that are being used for the study are listed:

1. Number of atoms (Carbon, Oxygen, Nitrogen)
2. Number of non-metals (Phosphorous, Sulphur)
3. Number of halogens (Chlorine, Bromine, Fluorine)
4. Number of metal atoms (Gold, Silver, Iron, Selenium)
5. Number of cyclic groups present (acyclic, bicyclic, tricyclic, tetracyclic, >5 cycles)
6. Functional Groups

The functional groups that are extracted from Drug Bank are as follows: -N-H-R, Alkylamine, -N-R, dialkylamine, -COOH, Carboxylic acid, -COOR Ester, -COOCl, Acid chloride, -R-C-O=N, -CN, Cyano -N=C=O isocyanate, -C=C ethylene, -C#C acetylene, -N#N Azo, -CHO aldehyde, -C=O, Ketone, -C=S, thioketone, -NH-C=O, peptide, -O-N=O Nitroso, -NO2, Nitro, thiophene, phenol, pyrolidini, phenyl furan, where # denotes triple bond.

ZINC Database (ZINC) is a free database of commercially available chemical compounds for virtual screening including drug-like compounds. ZINC contains a library of nearly 750,000 molecules, each with 3D structure and are annotated with molecular properties. The molecules are available in several common file formats including SMILES, mol2, 3D SDF etc. A Web-based query tool along with a molecular drawing interface enables the database to be searched and browsed. Currently ZINC provides 9 calculated properties

- molecular weight, logP, De_apolar, De_polar, number of HBA, number of HBD, tPSA, charge and NRB for each molecule.

Kinase inhibitors can be characterized by the whole compound features as well as protein-ligand binding site. The binding site details are collected from Protein Ligand Database (PLID).

Protein Ligand Interaction Database (PLID) was built by Reddy et al., (2008) developed from PDB. PLID contains binding area residues for all the complexed proteins in the PDB. Additionally, it consists of physico-chemical, thermal and quantum chemical properties of the ligands and the active site. The modules of Ligand Extractor and *BERF* ((Binding Environment Residue Finder) are developed to build the data base. Apart from identifying binding residues, *BERF* also calculates two important properties such as fraction of contact (f) and average tightness (g) which quantify the interaction between the protein and ligand as described in PLID. $f = Na/N$ and $g = Np/Na$ where Na = total number of ligand atoms in the binding environment, Np = total number of protein atoms in the binding environment and N = total number of ligand atoms. To summarize, the features extracted with regard to a protein ligand binding site are number of binding pockets, tightness, fraction of contact and amino acid frequency at binding sites.

We begin the study by extracting and analyzing some of the significant properties of kinase inhibitors that are discussed above.

Analysis of Features for Kinase vs. Non-Kinase Inhibitors

The structures for both kinase and non-kinase inhibitors are taken from Protein Data Bank. 1492 available drug compounds were separated into 47 kinase inhibitor drugs and 1445 non-kinase inhibitor drugs. Kinase and non-kinase inhibitors are seen to vary quite significantly in the binding site feature space. All the properties of these

Table 1. Summary of the features computed from various chemical databases.

Feature (Normalized)	Kinase	Non-kinase
Molecular weight range (g/mol)	0.147-3096.4	0.0186-29.49
Predicted logP range	-0.117-0.212	-0.00913-0.0064
Cyclic	0-0.83	0-0.95
Acyclic	0-0.08	0-0.18
Chiral	0-0.39	0-0.65
Heterocyclic	0-0.80	0-0.85
Monocyclic	0-0.20	0-0.16
Bicyclic	0-0.22	0-0.17
Tricyclic	0-0.20	0-0.18
Tetracyclic	0-0.05	0-0.2
>5 cycles	0-0.13	0-0.30
Fraction of Contact	0-0.01	0-0.000143
Fraction of Tightness	0-0.00238	0-0.0436
Number of Binding pockets	1-16	1-210

drugs are extracted from PLID and Drug bank and tabulated in Table 1 (Priya, 2010).

Additionally, several specific functional groups like -COOR, N-R and peptide, amide and peptide were found to be significant for kinases whereas -COOR and ketone, -C#C-, Thioketone,-NHR and amide, -NHR and NR and amide and ketone and peptide etc are found to be abundant in non-kinases, where # denotes triple bond.

It is clear from Table 1 that especially features that are extracted from PLID like fractions of contact and tightness as well as number of binding pockets are potentially useful for discrimination of kinase and non-kinase inhibitors. This classification problem needs to be investigated further. In the next section, the problem of kinase druggability is now viewed from the kinase target perspective.

A target protein is druggable if it has the potential to bind the drug-like molecules. Rest of the paper is devoted to address the binary classification problem of predicting a given kinase sequence as druggable or not.

DRUGGABILITY

Vast majority of successful drugs or inhibitors achieve their activity by binding to, and modifying the activity of a protein leading to the concept of druggability which was introduced by Hopkins and Groom (2002). Proteins that can bind drug-like compounds with binding affinity below 10 μM are considered druggable proteins.

Related Work

Hopkins and Groom describe a druggable genome as the genome which expresses the proteins that are able to bind the drug-like molecules. Approximately 10% of the human genome is involved in disease onset or progression (i.e ~3000 potential targets). The genes which are common to both druggable genome and involved in diseases are in between 600-1500. Russ and Lampel (2005) gave an update on the druggable genome and suggest that the count of the druggable genes is in between 2000 and 3000, coinciding with the previous estimates (~3000).

Hajduk, Huth and Tse (2005) predict druggability by analyzing the 3D structures of the proteins. As a first step, they find true ligand-binding sites on the protein surface using geometry-based or energy-based algorithms. In the next step, in order to find the small drug- molecules which bind with high affinity and specificity, they used NMR-based screening. They also derive druggable indices from the analysis of NMR data and the characteristics of known ligand-binding sites. Druggability indices can be used for computational assessment of proteins with known structure. Further, they indicate that about 44% of protein kinases contain a druggable pocket. They show high variability in conformations, several loop regions which suggest the use of multiple crystal structures and the conformational dynamics in druggability assessment.

Availability of experimental 3D-structures for the proteins is limited (Hajduk, Huth & Tse, 2005).

So, we need to depend on the homology models for the druggability assessment. But the results are uncertain since there is no closely related protein with 3D structure that is available (Hillisch, Pineda & Hilgnefeld, 2004). For predicting the novel proteins that have no or low homology to known targets, Han et al. (2007) use machine learning method such as support vector machines. A protein sequence is classified as druggable or non-druggable. They obtain an average overall prediction accuracy of 83.6%, lower than the prediction by BLAST search (http://blast.ncbi.nlm.nih.gov) which was 96.3%. This may be due to the prediction of non-similar proteins as druggable. SVMs perform well for the proteins of less than 20% sequence identity also. By selecting optimal set of descriptors using feature selection methods the performance of SVM is further improved.

More recently, Bakheet and Doig (2009) while analyzing human protein drug and non-drug targets list some properties as desirable in a human drug targets, namely: high hydrophobicity, high length, low pI etc and its participation in a crucial biological pathway. They also identified some proteins in the non-target set that have target like properties.

In this paper we do not consider all human protein drug targets but focus on human kinase drug target sequences since kinases are known to be potential drug targets. The identification of druggable kinases is treated as a classification problem in which druggable kinases are taken as positive data set and non-druggable kinases are chosen as negative data set. The classification problem is addressed using machine learning techniques like support vector machine (Cortes & Vapnik, 1995) and decision tree (Mitchell, 1997). Firstly, feature extraction of the kinases and its analysis is carried out.

Data Set

Kinase sequences which are drug targets as well as kinase non-drug target sequences need to be collected. Drug Bank provides data for drug targets and Uniprot (http://www.uniprot.org) is utilized to extract non-drug target kinase sequences. Approved 1610 drug target protein sequences which are readily available in Drug Bank are taken. On redundancy removal of up to 95% similarity using PISCES software, drug target set count reduced to 1556 sequences. 52 human kinase drug targets were found in this data set. As EC classification number is required eventually, the proteins which contain the EC class information are only taken which were of 48 in number. Finally 48 human kinase drug target sequences are considered for positive data set. As for the negative data set, Uniprot contains more than 5 million protein sequences. Among these human kinase sequences are 707 in number of which upon redundancy removal 702 have remained. On removal of the identified human kinase drug target sequences, 650 kinase sequences can be considered as non-drug target sequences. Further 509 sequences are found to contain EC classification information. Thus 509 human kinase non-drug target set was prepared. An analysis of amino acid composition is carried out on these data sets.

Amino Acid Feature Profile

Amino acid (AA) composition among druggable and non-druggable kinases is estimated and plotted in Figure 2. It can be seen that AA profile is not significantly differentiating druggable from non-druggable kinases. On the other hand, as clearly shown in Figure 3 the variance of AA composition seems to distinguish druggable from non-druggable kinases. Alanine is found to be most varying followed by proline. Isoleucine is found to be least varying.

Conventional physico-chemical features regarding proteins considered in the literature are length of the protein sequence, average residue weight, charge, hydrophobicity, isoelectric point and EC class (Vulpetti & Bosotti, 2004, Sharma et al., 2004, Raja, Sobha Rani & Durga Bhavani, 2004).

Figure 2. Amino acid frequency profile of druggable and non-druggable kinases

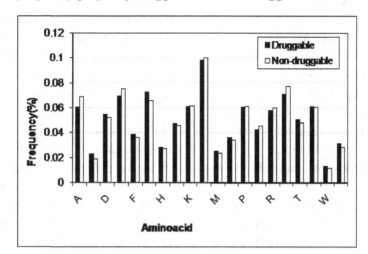

Figure 3. Variance of amino acid frequency distribution between druggable and non-druggable kinases

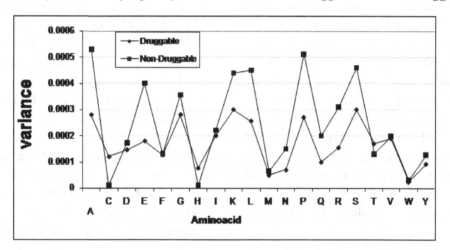

We investigate druggability of kinases experimenting extensively with various features derived from physico-chemical properties of amino acid residues and amino acid composition. The physico-chemical properties include hydrobhobicity which is calculated using the table given by Kyte and Doolittle (1982). The difference in average feature values of other features like charge, hydrophobicity etc are found to be small in magnitude whereas the average length of druggable kinases is found to be significantly smaller than that of non-druggable kinases. The values are noted in the Table 2.

Table 2. Average feature values for druggable kinases and non-druggable kinases.

Feature	Average feature value for druggable kinases	Average feature value for non-druggable kinases
Charge	6.7	6.2
Hydrophobicity	-0.38	-0.4
Isoelectric point	7.21	7.34
Length (AA)	620	740

Classification Results

One of the challenges of this classification problem is due to the unbalanced data with only 48 druggable kinases available against 509 non-drugggable kinases present at Uniprot. Therefore there is a need for carefully designing the experiments such that the non-druggable dataset does not dominate the classification task.

Identification of druggable kinases from non-druggable kinases is carried out using decision tree classifiers. Though support vector machines are quite popular among bioinformatics community, the interpretation of the classification is non transparent. On the other hand, a decision tree classifier is based on deductive logic and rules can be derived from the decision tree. Performance of the classification results is discussed in this section.

Decision tree models the training data set by choosing an attribute that maximally discriminates positive from negative data set and applies this procedure recursively. The decision tree thus constructed is used to classify the instances of the test data set. Each path from the root to a leaf node corresponds to a decision rule. Efficient implementations of these classifiers are available in Weka (http://www.cs.waikato.ac.nz/~ml), an open source software developed by University of Waikato.

The druggable kinase data set considered as positive data set is small with 48 sequences and the non-druggable kinases as negative data set which is of size 500. We would like to choose 2/3rd of the positive data set for training and the remaining for testing purposes. Since there is an imbalance in the data set sizes, different subsets of size 32 from the total negative set are chosen to train and test the classifier along with 32 sequences from the positive data set. These data sets thus built are denoted as Set1, Set2,..., Set6. During preliminary investigation, it was found that the physico-chemcial properties are not significantly contributing to the performance results. Hence the features that are considered for final experimenta-

tion are the 20 amino acid composition features together along with protein sequence length. We have constructed decision tree models for each of the data sets Set1, Set2,..., Set6. Average performance accuracy of the six data sets for all feature sets is given in the Table 3.

It is clear from the experiments that unavailability of enough positive data against a large negative data set is impacting the results negatively. In order to tackle this issue, firstly we collect all the negative 'difficult' sequences those which are not correctly classified by a majority of the classifiers. Then we refine the classifier models by training them with difficult negative sequences and retaining the positive sets as in earlier experiments. In this second level of experimentation, we build again six models and using voting strategy, each test sequence is classified as positive or negative as per the number of votes for that decision is greater than or equal to 3. The results of the second level of experimentation are given in Table 4. Table 5 gives the overall accuracies after the two-tier level of classification.

In this section we propose a general strategy on how to improve performance of a classifier. It is seen for this problem that the negative set is being poorly identified and many of its sequences occur as false positives during classification.

Table 3. Druggable kinase prediction accuracies of decision tree classifier for different models constructed choosing different subsets from the negative data set.

Model	True Positives(%)	True Negatives (%)
1	75	50.7
2	25	51.7
3	56	52.36
4	68.75	48.26
5	25	47.63
6	62.5	46
After Voting	68.75	57.1

Table 4. The models re-trained with difficult negative sequences classify these sequences with a better accuracy of 60%.

Model	True Positives (%)	True Negatives (%)
1	43.8	45.9
2	50	37.7
3	37.5	62.3
4	37.5	52.5
5	75	36.1
6	56.3	37.7
After Voting	62.5	60.65

Table 5. Overall accuracy of test data set after the second level classification.

Overall Accuracy	TP	TN	Precision
	62.5	90.08	88.37

Hence we build a second level of classifiers to which only the sequences which are classified as positives in the first level are given as the test set. Therefore if the classifier is well-trained, we expect that the false positives of the first level would be recognized as negative which is their true identity. Thus the overall model of classification is a two-tier model whose final performance accuracy has risen to 88.37 from the earlier precision of 57.65.

DISCUSSION AND CONCLUSION

Vulpetti and Bosotti (2004) define the ATP binding pocket of protein kinases as a set of 38 residues that can interact with inhibitors through side chain interactions. ATP binding pocket can be divided into adenine, sugar, phosphate and buried regions. The survey presented by Vulpetti and Bosotti (2004) supports the existence of *aromatic* C-H...O hydrogen bonds in kinase protein–ligand interac-

tions. The buried region on the other hand consists of *hydrophobic* amino acids. It is interesting that the decision tree classifier picks up hydrophobic amino acid residues like Metheonine, Histidine, Glycine and Leucine for high discrimination between druggable and non-druggable kinases. It is to be corroborated by the biologists of the specific role that these features and the length of a protein sequence play in the phosphorylation process.

From the drug perspective, the measures of fraction of contact and tightness seem to be important and have to be investigated further. Existing work in literature concentrates on a higher level classification problem of discriminating druggable protein from a non-druggable protein (Han et al., 2007). They obtain classification accuracies for druggable proteins in the range 64-71% and for non-druggable proteins it is of the order of 85-85.8%. In this work we obtained an accuracy of nearly 62.5% for druggable kinases and 90.08% for non-druggable kinase prediction. To the best of our knowledge kinase druggability prediction is not reported in literature.

Of course the model built is limited to the available data set and the kinase data set is quite small having only 40 sequences. Hence the robustness of the model needs to be validated through other methods. The bigger problem would be to predict the matching between a target and its corresponding inhibitor(s) with the help of target as well as ligand properties. Hence kinase inhibitors and targets need to be studied to understand the specificity of a kinase inhibitor in choosing a particular kinase target which will be taken up in the future.

ACKNOWLEDGMENT

The authors would like to thank Dr G.Narahari Sastry, Indian Institute of Chemical Technology (IICT), Hyderabad, India for suggesting the problem and for the continuous interactions in the project. The authors would like to acknowledge

Ms Preethi Badrinarayan, Research student, IICT for clarifying biological aspects of the problem and Ms Sowjanya, M.Tech Bioinformatics student for re-validating some of the experimental work.

REFERENCES

Bakheet, T. M., & Doig, A. J. (2009). Properties and identification of human protein drug targets. *Bioinformatics (Oxford, England)*, *25*(4), 451–457. doi:10.1093/bioinformatics/btp002

Berman, H. M., Westbrook, J., Feng, Z., Gilliland, G., Bhat, T. N., Weissig, H., et al. (2000). *The Protein Data Bank, Nucleic Acids Research*, *28*, 235-242. Retrived on January 11, 2011 from *http://*www.rcsb.org

Cortes, C., & Vapnik, V. (1995). Support-Vector Networks. *Machine Learning*, *20*, 273–297. doi:10.1007/BF00994018

Hajduk, P. J., Huth, J. R., & Tse, C. (2005). Predicting protein druggability. *Drug Discovery Today*, *10*, 1675–1682. doi:10.1016/S1359-6446(05)03624-X

Han, L. Y., Zheng, C. J., Xie, B., Jia, J., Ma, X. H., & Zhu, F. (2007). Support vector approach for predicting druggable proteins: recent progress in its exploration and investigation of its usefulness. *Drug Discovery Today*, *12*, 304–313. doi:10.1016/j.drudis.2007.02.015

Hillisch, A., Pineda, L. F., & Hilgenfeld, R. (2004). Utility of homology models in drug discovery process. *Drug Discovery Today*, *9*, 659–669. doi:10.1016/S1359-6446(04)03196-4

Hopkins, A. L., & Groom, C. R. (2002). The druggable genome. *Nature Reviews. Drug Discovery*, *1*, 727–730. doi:10.1038/nrd892

Irwin, J. J., & Shoichet, B. K. (2005). ZINC - A Free Database of Commercially Available Compounds for Virtual Screening. *J. Chem. Inf. Model.*, *45*(1), 177-82. Retrieved on January 11, 2011 from http://www.zinc.docking.org

Johnson, M., Zaretskaya, I., Raytselis, Y., Merezhuk, Y., McGinnis, S., & Madden, T. L. (2008). *Nucleic Acids Res. 36 (Web Server issue)*, W5–W9. Retrieved on January 11, 2011 from http://blast.ncbi.nlm.nih.gov

Kyte, J., & Doolittle, R. F. (1982). A simple method for displaying hydropathic character of a protein. *Journal of Molecular Biology*, *157*, 105–132. doi:10.1016/0022-2836(82)90515-0

Lipinski, C. A., Lombardo, F., Dominy, B. W., & Feeney, P. J. (1997). Experimental and computational approaches to estimate solubility and permeability in drug discovery and development settings. *Advanced Drug Delivery Reviews*, *23*, 3–25. doi:10.1016/S0169-409X(96)00423-1

Manning, G. (2005). Genomic overview of the kinases. In I. Greenwald (Ed.), *WormBook*, The *C. elegans Research Community (pp.* 1-19).

Manning, G., Whyte, D. B., Martinez, R., Hunter, T., & Sudarsanam, S. (2002). The protein kinase complement of the human genome. *Science*, *298*, 1912–1934. doi:10.1126/science.1075762

Mitchell, T. M. (1997). *Machine Learning*. New York: McGraw-Hill Series in CompSci.

Priya Lakshmanan. 2010. Establishing signature for kinase inhibitors. Unpublished M.Tech dissertation, University of Hyderabad, India.

Raja, G., Sobha Rani, T., & Durga Bhavani, S. (2004). Global feature extraction techniques for identification of secondary structures of a protein sequence. In International Conference on Information Technology (pp.101-108). India: Universities Press.

Reddy, A. S., Amarnath, H. S. D., Bapi, R. S., Sastry, G. M., & Sastry, G. N. (2008). Protein ligand interaction database (PLID). *Comp. Biol. and Chem., 32*, 387-390. Retrieved on January 11, 2011 from http://203.199.182.73/gnsmmg/databases/plid/

Russ, A. P., & Lampel, S. (2005). The druggable genome:an update. *Drug Discovery Today, 10*, 1607–1610. doi:10.1016/S1359-6446(05)03666-4

Sharma, S., Kumar, V., & Sobha Rani, T. Durga Bhavani, & S., Bapi Raju, S. (2004). Application of neural networks for protein sequence classification. In *Intelligent Sensing and Information Processing* (pp.325-328). India: IEEE Press.

Uniprot: http://www.uniprot.org

Vieth, M., Higgs, R. E., & Roberston, D. H. (2004). Kinomics- structural biology and chemogenomics of kinase inhibitors and targets. *Biochimica et Biophysica Acta, 1697*(1-2), 243–257.

Vulpetti, A., & Bosotti, R. (2004). Sequence and structural analysis of kinase ATP pocket residues. *IL Farmaco, 59*, 759–765. doi:10.1016/j.farmac.2004.05.010

Weka. *http://www.cs.waikato.ac.nz/~ml/*

Wishart, D. S., Knox, C., Guo, A. C., Cheng, D., Shrivastava, S., Tzur, D., et al. (2008). DrugBank: a knowledgebase for drugs, drug actions and drug targets. *Nucleic Acids Res., 36 (Database issue)*, D901-6. Retrieved on January 11, 2011 from http://www.drugbank.ca

Xia, X., Maliski, E. G., Gallant, P., & Rogers, D. (2004). Classification of kinase inhibitors using bayesian model. *Journal of Medicinal Chemistry, 47*, 4463–4470. doi:10.1021/jm0303195

KEY TERMS AND DEFINITIONS

Druggability: The ability of a portion of a genome to be targeted by a drug.

Drug-Target: The genome sequence that has the potential to bind the drug-like molecules.

Inhibitor: Any substance that interferes with a chemical reaction, biologic activity or that reduces the catalytic activity of an enzyme.

Kinase: An enzyme that catalyzes the transfer of a phosphate group or another high-energy molecular group to an acceptor molecule.

Ligand: A ligand is a substance that is able to bind to and form a complex with a biomolecule to serve a biological purpose.

Machine Learning: Machine learning is a discipline of artificial intelligence that focuses on automatically learning to recognize complex patterns and make intelligent decisions based on data.

Chapter 10
Identification of Genomic Islands by Pattern Discovery

Nita Parekh
International Institute of Information Technology Hyderabad, India

ABSTRACT

Pattern discovery is at the heart of bioinformatics, and algorithms from computer science have been widely used for identifying biological patterns. The assumption behind pattern discovery approaches is that a pattern that occurs often enough in biological sequences/structures or is conserved across organisms is expected to play a role in defining the respective sequence's or structure's functional behavior and/or evolutionary relationships. The pattern recognition problem addressed here is at the genomic level and involves identifying horizontally transferred regions, called genomic islands. A horizontally transferred event is defined as the movement of genetic material between phylogenetically unrelated organisms by mechanisms other than parent to progeny inheritance. Increasing evidence suggests the importance of horizontal transfer events in the evolution of bacteria, influencing traits such as antibiotic resistance, symbiosis and fitness, virulence, and adaptation in general. In the genomic era, with the availability of large number of bacterial genomes, the identification of genomic islands also form the first step in the annotation of the newly sequenced genomes and in identifying the differences between virulent and non-virulent strains of a species. Considerable effort is being made in their identification and analysis and in this chapter a brief summary of various approaches used in the identification and validation of horizontally acquired regions is discussed.

INTRODUCTION

Numerous biological events are responsible for the gradual change in the genetic information of an organism over the course of time such as gene conversions, rearrangements (e.g., inversion or translocation), large-scale deletions and insertions of foreign DNA (e.g., plasmid integration, transposition) apart from point mutations. Horizontal Gene Transfer (HGT) is a major event responsible to cause significant alterations in the genome composition. It is defined as the transfer of DNA between diverse organisms by mechanisms other

DOI: 10.4018/978-1-61350-056-9.ch010

than direct descent (vertical inheritance). The clusters of genes acquired as a single unit by horizontal transfer are called "Genomic Islands (GIs)" and are typically 10 - 200 Kb in size. These horizontally acquired regions are responsible in causing significant alterations in the genome composition and may provide the organism to carry out new functions resulting in adaptation to a changing environment. Any biological advantage provided to the recipient organism by the transferred DNA creates selective pressure for its retention in the host genome and several pathways of horizontal transfer have been established influencing traits such as antibiotic resistance, symbiosis and fitness, virulence and adaptation in general (Koonin *et al*, 2001; Lawrence & Ochman, 2002; Andersson, 2005; Gogarten & Townsend, 2005). For example, HGT has been demonstrated in many pathogenic strains of bacteria and shown to be responsible for its virulence. Thus, depending on their acquired functions these genomic islands are further classified as pathogenicity islands, metabolic islands, secretion islands, resistance islands and symbiosis islands (Lio & Vannucci, 2000).

General Characteristics of Genomic Islands (GIs)

The genomic islands are found to contain some characteristic features shown in Figure 1 which have been exploited for their identification (Dobrindt *et al*, 2004; Juhas *et al*, 2009). They typically contain in their vicinity intact (or residual) mobile genetic elements, such as genes coding for integrases (Int) or transposases that are required for chromosomal integration and excision, are generally found to be flanked by direct repeats (DR) and are sometimes inserted in the vicinity of tRNAs and tmRNAs, commonly referred to as tRNA genes. Typically GIs also carry multiple functional and fragmented insertion sequence (IS) elements for carrying out the transposition event (Dobrindt *et al*, 2004). The identification of these elements basically involves searching various databases of these elements, *viz.*, RepBase Update, tRNA database, etc. by pattern matching.

Apart from the structural features observed in the vicinity of a genomic island, these regions also exhibit bias in the nucleotide compositions. In any genome, ancestral (vertically transmitted) genes experience a particular set of directional mutation pressures mediated by the specific features of the replication machinery of the cell, such as the balance of the dNTP pools, mutational biases of the DNA polymerases, efficiency of mismatch repair systems and so on (Lawrence, 1999). As a result each genome exhibits its own unique signatures such as distinct variations in the GC content, dinucleotide relative abundance, variations in the usage of *k*-mer words, codon usage and amino acid usage. Thus, 'foreign' genes acquired through lateral transfer retain the characteristics of the donor genome which may significantly differ from that of the host genome (Lio & Vannucci, 2000, Lawrence & Ochman 1998). Thus variations in the occurrences of patterns of dinucleotides and oligonucleotides along the length of the genome, which capture the biases

Figure 1. General characteristics of genomic islands (adapted from Dobrindt et al., 2004).

in the nucleotide compositions are useful for the identification of genomic islands and are referred to as parametric methods.

The possibility of horizontal gene transfer usually emerges when a gene/protein sequence from a particular organism shows the strongest similarity to a homolog from a distant taxon. For example, in a phylogenetic tree construction, if a bacterial protein groups with its eukaryotic homologs (of a particular eukaryotic lineage) compared to homologs from other bacteria, one can conclude the presence of a horizontal gene transfer event. Approaches based on comparative genomics and phylogenetic analysis are used to identify patterns of conserved genes between closely-related and distantly-related taxa.

Thus presence of mobile elements, repeats, tRNA genes, genes that form part of prophages, pathogenicity islands, transposases, integrases and recombinases are useful in the identification of GIs. Atypical sequence characteristics of acquired genes and restricted phylogenetic distribution in specific lineages are other features useful in their identification. Based on these characteristic features, various methods for identifying potential foreign genes can be categorized as follows:

- **Parametric Methods:** based on nucleotide compositions,
- **Signal-Based Methods:** for analysis of the flanking regions of the GIs for tRNA genes, mobile elements, repeats, etc.
- **Alignment-Based Methods:** comparative genomics approach, and
- **Clustering-Based Approach:** phylogenetic analysis

However, no single method can reliably identify a genomic island and hence it would be advantageous to use number of measures exploiting the characteristic features of genomic islands. A brief description of each of these approaches is discussed below.

APPROACHES FOR IDENTIFYING GENOMIC ISLANDS

Parametric Methods: Anomalous Nucleotide Composition

Measures based on anomalous nucleotide composition, called *parametric methods*, are the most widely used approaches for identifying recent horizontal transfers. The underlying assumption of this approach is that biased mutation pressures, called A-T/G-C pressure, within bacterial genomes impart distinctive biases to the composition of long-term residents of the genome, such that recently acquired genes will appear deviant by comparison if they have evolved in a genome with different mutational biases (Muto and S. Osawa, 1987; Lawrence & Ochman, 1997). The bias in the nucleotide base composition of a genome results in variations in dinucleotide and higher oligonucleotide frequencies and biases in the usage of codons and amino acids within the genes. Various approaches have been proposed to identify a 'typical' gene based on nucleotide composition (Garcia-Vallve *et al*, 2000; Karlin, 2001), dinucleotide frequencies (Jenks, 1998), codon usage biases (Garcia-Vallve *et al*, 2003; Karlin & Ladunga, 1994) or patterns inferred by Markov chain analysis (Campbell *et al*, 1999). An advantage of these parametric approaches is that putative transferred genes can be identified without relying on comparisons with other organisms, thus providing an independent means of assessing the impact of gene transfer across lineages (Hsiao *et al*, 2003). Some other characteristic measures include: dinucleotide relative abundance (genomic signature), amino acid usage, high AT content, *k*-mer (word) distribution and GC skew. The general approach involves computing these measures in a sliding window and comparing with the corresponding genomic average, whenever the complete genome sequences are available. The regions that deviate from the average genome values by a certain threshold may have a different origin and are predicted as genomic islands. These measures can be classified into two major classes based on the analysis required at genome-level or at the gene-level and are briefly described below.

Measures Involving Analysis at the Genome Level

These approaches rely only on the availability of the complete genomic sequence and attempt to capture compositional deviation from the genome backbone. These measures are computed over the whole genome of the organism. These measures are based on word count of *k*-mers (words of size *k*), *viz.*, di-nucleotides, tri-nucleotides, tetra-nucleotides, etc. across the genome. The major advantage of these measures is that these do not require pre-existing annotation of the genome or the comparison of homologous sequences, and can, therefore, be applied directly to newly sequenced genomes. Some of the commonly used genome-based measures are briefly described below.

GC content anomalies: Many evolutionary mechanisms have been proposed to explain GC content diversity among bacteria, and it is believed that a species's genomic GC content is set by a balance between selective constraints at the level of codons and amino acids and directional mutational pressure at the nucleotide level (Yoon *et al*, 2005). Thus the GC content can be used as a signature of an organism. It is one of the simplest and most extensively used approaches for identifying genomic islands. It is computed as a ratio of the G+C content (i.e., frequency of G and C nucleotides) in non-overlapping sliding windows along the length of the genome by the overall GC content of the whole genome. If there is significant difference in the GC content of any window with the genomic average, the region is considered to be possibly horizontally transferred. However, this method fails to identify a horizontally transferred region if the donor and host genome both have similar GC content.

Genomic signature: It has been shown that the set of dinucleotide relative abundance values constitutes a "genomic signature" of an organism that may reflect the influence of factors such as DNA replication and repair machinery, context-dependent mutation rates, DNA modifications, and base-step conformational tendencies that impose limits on the compositional and structural patterns of a genomic sequence (Karlin, 1998). The dinucleotide biases assess differences between the observed dinucleotide frequencies and those expected from random associations of the component mononucleotide frequencies (Karlin, 2001). To identify genomic island, the average absolute abundance difference is computed which is defined as a measure of genomic signature difference between the sliding window (f_w) and the whole genome value (*g*):

$$\delta^*(f_w, g) = 1/16 \sum | \rho^*_{xy}(f_w) - \rho^*_{xy}(g) |$$

where $\delta^*(f_w, g)$ is the di-nucleotide bias of window f_w with respect to the whole genome *g*, $\rho^*_{xy} = f^*_{xy} / f^*_x f^*_y$ where f^*_x denotes the frequency of the mononucleotide *X* and f^*_{xy} that of the di-nucleotide *XY*, both computed from the sequence concatenated with its inverted complement (Karlin & Marzek, 1997). A major advantage of genome signature analyses is in their ability to identify anomalous DNA regions containing large stretches of non-coding DNA or small putative genes.

k-mer Distribution: It has been proposed by Karlin that most horizontally acquired genomic regions have distinct word (*k*-mer) compositions. For *k*-mers of size *k* (*k* = 2 - 9), a total of 4^k different possible *k*-mers are computed, both for the whole genome and for each non-overlapping sliding window. The average *k*-mer difference is then defined as

$$\delta^*_k(w, g) = \frac{1}{n} \sum_{i=1}^{n} \left| f^w_i - f^g_i \right|$$

where $n = 4^k$, is the number of distinct k-words (words of length k), f_i^w is the frequency of the ith k-mer pattern in the window and f_i^g the corresponding value for the whole genome (Nag *et al*, 2006; Jain *et al*, 2008). Windows exhibiting significant deviation from the genomic average are identified as probable GIs. This measure is also useful to identify genomic islands devoid of genes. Utilizing higher order motifs is more likely to capture deviation from the genome background compositional distribution, as long as there is enough data to produce reliable probability estimates. However, for $k > 6$, this measure becomes computationally very expensive.

Recently another method based on k-mer distribution, called the *centroid* method proposed by Rajan *et al* (2007). In this method, the genome is first partitioned into non-overlapping bins of equal size and frequencies of all possible words for a given word size are listed corresponding to each bin, considering words in both the DNA strands. This list represents the word frequency vector for the bin. The average frequency of each word across all bins is computed and is called the centroid. The distance from the centroid is used as the criterion for determining the outliers corresponding to the compositionally distinct bins.

The above measures are typically carried out in non-overlapping windows of a fixed size. If the window is too large, then the resolution of the output is low. If the window is too small, then the output is noisy and difficult to interpret. In either case, one is likely to miss regions where there is an abrupt change in the nucleotide composition. Also, in general, a window of a fixed size will not completely cover the whole genomic island; typically neighbouring windows may partially cover the horizontally acquired regions. This also poses the problem of identifying the true boundaries of the genomic islands. This problem can be addressed by considering overlapping sliding windows. The extent of overlap is then an important parameter as it will increase the computational effort required. An alternative approach would be to identify probable genomic islands by signal-based methods and analyze the regions between, say two transpoases, by the above measures; this would allow for variable length windows of genomic regions.

The measures at the genome level described above identify large genomic regions ($\sim$ 50KB) which may contain a number of genes. To identify the boundaries of the horizontally transferred regions and further confirm their foreign origin, one may explicitly perform analyses on the genes in this putative GI and its flanking regions. These measures, which involve analysis of only gene sequences or their translations, are also useful when the whole genome sequence of an organism is not available, but only a limited set of genes from the organism are available. Most commonly used measures at the gene level are discussed below.

Measures Involving Analysis at the Gene Level

Codon Usage Bias: Codon usage variation, i.e., unequal usage of synonymous codons, is a very well known phenomenon and has been studied in a wide diversity of organisms. Virtually every codon has been shown to be preferentially used in some organisms and rarely used in others. The causes of codon usage variation are many-fold. Mutational bias (the tendency displayed by some organisms to have unbalanced base composition) is frequently a contributing factor. Some organisms have extremes of base composition and this can influence the selection of codons. Prokaryotes and also eukaryotes show preference for certain synonymous codons over others, despite all of them coding for the same amino acid. This unequal usage of synonymous codons is referred to as codon bias. There exists a correlation between taxonomic divergence and similarity of codon usage and hence it is now accepted as a signature of a particular taxonomic group. At the gene level, bias in codon usage is the most widely used measure for the identification of horizontally transferred genes.

Codon frequencies for a set of genes lying within a particular window, F, is computed and its standard deviation from the complete gene set of the organism (or a second representative gene set), G, is obtained. The codon usage difference of the set of genes F relative to the genome (or second set of genes) G is given by

$$B(F \mid G) = \sum_a p_a(F) [\sum_{(x,y,z)=a} |f(x,y,z) - g(x,y,z)|]$$

where $p_a(F)$ are the normalized amino acid frequencies of the gene family F and $f(x,y,z)$ are normalized average codon frequencies such that:

$$\sum_{(x,y,z)=a} f(x,y,z) = 1$$

where the sum extends over all synonymous codons, i.e., coding for the same amino acid a (Karlin *et al*, 1998). If a gene's codon usage difference relative to the average gene in the genome exceeds a threshold and if its codon usage also differs from highly expressed genes such as ribosomal protein genes, chaperone genes and protein synthesis genes, then it is likely to be a horizontally transferred gene (Karlin, 2001).

Amino Acid Bias: This bias refers to the deviation in the frequency of usage of individual amino acids over the average usage of all 20 amino acids. Similar to species-specific codon preference, preference of the usage of amino acids across the organisms has been observed. The amino acid bias between a set of genes F and the genome (or second set of genes) G is given by:

$$A(F \mid G) = (1/20) \sum_{i=1}^{20} | a_i(F) - a_i(G) |$$

where $a_i(F)$ is average amino acid frequency of a_i in F (Karlin, 2001).

GC Content at Codon Positions: The compositional biases at the first and third positions have been reported to be positively correlated to expressivity and genomic G+C content, respectively (Gutierrez *et al*, 1996). Hence the computation of GC content at each codon position is highly specific for each organism and acts as a unique signature to the organism (Yoon *et al*, 2005). This involves computing the frequency of occurrence of G and C at the three codon positions, GC_1, GC_2 and GC_3 respectively. The mean GC-content at the three codon positions for the set of genes belonging to a sliding window are compared with the corresponding values for the complete gene set (or a second gene set) of the organism. If this difference in the GC content at the first and third codon positions for any window and the genomic average (or second gene set) is larger than a certain threshold, the genes in that window are most likely horizontally transferred genes. Highly expressed genes such as ribosomal genes, chaperones, etc. also have their GC content different from the genomic average and need to be cross-checked to avoid false predictions. Thus, to confirm if the genes in a particular window are horizontally transferred, one need to compare these measures with a set of highly expressed genes and with a representative gene set of the organism. If the gene(s) under investigation deviates from both these sets, then it is likely to have a foreign origin.

Apart from only the horizontally transferred genes, many other genes in a genome may exhibit biases in their usage of codons and amino acids and also variations in the GC content at the codon positions. For example, the highly expressed genes in most prokaryotic genomes, *viz.*, ribosomal protein genes, translation and transcription processing factors, and chaperone and degradation protein complexes exhibit properties deviating from the average gene. Hence, the horizontally transferred genes predicted by the above measures should also be compared with highly expressed genes, in order to reduce the error in predictions. The major limitation of measures involving gene analysis is thus the requirement of a well-annotated genome.

The different methods may often give different results; therefore a combination of parametric methods should be used to obtain a consensus for the detection of potential HGT. Providing a number of these approaches on a single integrated platform is desirous as this would improve the confidence of prediction. With this aim we have developed a web-based tool, an Integrated Genomic Island Identification Tool (IGIPT) where various measures discussed above have been implemented on a single platform (Jain *et al*, 2008). The major advantage of the tool is that it allows filtering of GIs by a user-defined threshold value and also allows extraction of the flanking regions of the predicted GIs for further analysis, such as presence of transposable elements, direct repeats, tRNA and tmRNA genes, etc. These extracted contigs can be fed back to the tool for identifying true boundaries, thereby reducing the effort of scanning the genome in multiple overlapping windows.

The parametric methods based on anomalous nucleotide composition are limited by the amelioration of foreign genes (Garcia-Vallve *et al*, 2000); that is, newly acquired genes will experience the same mutational biases as long-term residents of the genome and will eventually fail to be recognized as anomalous. These methods, thus, reliably detect only recently acquired genes. However, a significant fraction of prokaryotic genomes, up to 15%–20% of the genes, belong to this class of recent horizontal acquisitions, suggesting their importance. Another problem associated with these methods is that genes arriving from donor genomes experiencing similar mutational biases will not be detected, because the acquired sequence will not appear unusual in the recipient genome. For e.g., the average GC content of *E. coli*, *Shigella* and *Salmonella* lineages is approximately 50%, 51% and 52%, respectively, while for the Gram-positive *Staphylococcus* and *Streptococcus* lineages the average GC content is 33% and

38%, respectively. The parametric methods will fail to identify transfer of genetic material from one to another genome in the above groups. Also, genes might appear atypical owing to stochastic factors (especially if they are short) or as a result of various mutational and selection variations and hence may be misinterpreted as HGT regions. This suggests need for more sensitive measures of sequence composition for better prediction of HGT events. The highly expressed genes also exhibit codon usage and GC content deviating substantially from the average gene. Hence, putative alien genes identified by the parametric approaches need to be compared against these highly expressed genes of the acceptor (host) genome, to remove false predictions. It has been observed that these methods can predict very different classes of genes as HGT, hence using of a single method could give biased results (Ragan *et al*, 2006). The other limitation of the parametric approach is that the likely source of these alien genes cannot be identified since these measures do not rely on comparing genes between organisms. Even with these limitations, the parametric approaches are popular because of their ease of implementation.

Signal-Based Methods for Analysis of Flanking Regions of Putative Genomic Islands

In Figure 1 the structural features of a typical genomic island is shown. Thus apart from an analysis of genes in a putative genomic island, regions in the vicinity of these regions can be searched for relics of sequences that might have helped in their integration, such as remnants of translocation elements, attachment sites of phage integrases, transfer origins of plasmids, presence of transposable elements, tRNA and tmRNA genes and direct repeats. Using tRNAscan-SE (Lowe & Eddy, 1997) in the vicinity or within the putative horizontally transferred region or searching for direct repeats and transposable elements against the RepBase Update (Jurka *et al*, 2005) can help in improving the confidence of prediction. Looking for at least one mobility genes in the vicinity of the putative GI provides more accuracy to the GI prediction than by parametric methods alone. Mobility genes can be identified by conducting an HMMer search of each predicted gene against PFAM mobility gene profiles and by searching the genome annotation for terms that are commonly used to describe mobility genes (Langille *et al*, 2010). This requires the genome annotation to be complete and accurate. Thus, accuracy of the prediction of GIS can be increased by coupling the anomalous nucleotide composition analysis with the identification of these structural features. To facilitate such an analysis of the flanking regions, we have provided the option to download the predicted GI and its flanking regions in our tool, IGIPT (Jain *et al*, 2008).

Although genomic islands have these conserved structures, they need not have all of these characteristics to be defined as genomic islands, making their identification a difficult task. Hence one needs to check for all these characteristic features and if more than of these elements are found in the vicinity of a probable GI, one could be more certain of the HGT event.

An alternative approach to detect GIs could be to divide the genome according to the presence of transposable elements: the stretch of a chromosome from the start of a transposon sequence to the start of the next transposon sequence. One may then use the parametric methods discussed above on this fragment to look for horizontally transferred genes (Nag *et al*, 2006).

Alignment-Based Methods: Comparative Genomics Approach

With the advent of large-scale genome sequencing projects, this approach is soon becoming the most useful approach for identification of an HGT event. It is an alternative approach to sequence-composition based methods and involves comparison of multiple genome sequences, say, within a *species* or *genus* to look for clear phyletic patterns of non-vertical inheritance. Thus, by comparison of genomes of two strains of bacteria, if one can identify clusters of genes in one strain not present in other closely related genomes, but found in very distantly related species (as judged by their degree divergence in 16S rRNAs or other orthologs), then a horizontally transferred event can be confirmed. In the case of comparison of virulent and non-virulent strinas, these genes may be responsible for the virulence of the organism and their identification is important for drug targeting. Whole-genome alignment methods such as Mauve (Darling *et al*, 2004) or MUMmer (Delcher *et al*, 2002) can be used for identification of GIs by comparative genomics approach.

The major limitation of this approach is the non-availability of genomic sequences of closely related species or strains. The other limitation of this approach is the selection of both the query and the comparative genomes, which may result in inconsistent selection criteria due to the unfamiliarity of different phylogenetic distances within genera (Langille *et al*, 2008). If the genomes being compared are very closely related, this approach will not be able to detect GIs acquired before speciation. On the other hand, if the genomes being compared include distantly related species, one may be lead to false-predictions as a result of rearrangements. IslandPick is a method that automatically selects genomes for comparison that are within a proper evolutionary distance and identifies regions that are unique to only a single genome (Langille *et al*, 2008).

The above discussed approaches can only indicate the presence of a horizontally transferred event, but cannot identify the source or origin. Phylogeny-based approach discussed below is the only approach which helps in validating the presence of a GI and may also identify the likely source of its origin.

Clustering-Based Approach: Phylogenetic Analysis

The horizontally transferred genes exhibit an unusually high degree of similarity between the donor and the recipient strains. Furthermore, because each transfer event introduces a specific set of genes into a single lineage, the acquired trait will be limited to the descendents of the recipient strain and absent from closely related taxa, thereby producing a scattered phylogenetic distribution for genes with foreign origin (Ochman *et al*, 2000). Thus, in some cases, it may be possible to establish the evolutionary history of a gene by analyzing its distribution among various lineages. If a gene is confined to one taxon or species, it is more likely to have been acquired through gene transfer than to have been lost independently from multiple lineages. This is the only method which can help in identifying the likely source of the alien genes. However, one cannot rule out the possibility that a particular phenotypic trait such as resistance to certain antibiotics have evolved independently in diverse lineages through point mutations in existing genes (Ochman *et al* 2000). Hence, it may not always be possible to distinguish between convergent evolution and horizontal transfer on the basis of phylogenetic analyses alone. In both comparative genome analyses and phylogenetic analyses, the requirement of multiple genomes whose complete sequences are available, usually limits their application. An excellent review of detecting GIs by this approach is given by Koonin *et al*, 2001 and is summarized below. The presence of a HGT can be confirmed when one observes:

- **Unexpected Ranking of Sequence Similarity Among Homologs:** A gene sequence (or a protein sequence) from a particular organism shows the strongest similarity to a homolog from a distant taxon.
- **Unexpected Phylogenetic Tree Topology:** In a well-supported tree, a bacterial protein groups with its eukaryotic homologs rather than homologs from other bacteria and shows a reliable affinity with a particular eukaryotic lineage.
- **Unusual Phyletic Patterns:** A phyletic pattern is basically the pattern of species present or missing in the given cluster of orthologs (COGs). This distribution of COGs by the number of represented species suggests major roles of lineage-specific gene loss and horizontal gene transfer in evolution.
- **Conservation of Gene Order between Distant Taxa--Horizontal Transfer of operons:** The evolution of bacterial and archaeal genomes involves extensive gene shuffling, and there is little conservation of gene order between distantly related genomes. Thus, the presence of three or more genes in the same order in distant genomes is extremely unlikely unless these genes form an operon. Also, it has been shown that each operon typically emerges only once during evolution and is maintained by selection ever after. Therefore, when a (predicted) operon is present in only a few distantly related genomes, horizontal gene transfer seems to be the most likely scenario. If such cases can be confirmed by phylogenetic tree analysis for multiple genes comprising the operon, they provide the strongest indications of horizontal transfer.

The major limitation of this approach is having a reference species tree which has been constructed using genes that have never been horizontally transferred. However, identifying such a gene(s) is not an easy task. AMPHORA (a pipeline for AutoMated PHylogenOmic inference) is a method that tries to construct a large genome tree, using a selected list of genes that are shared across most genomes (Wu & Eisen, 2008). It has an automated pipeline developed that uses 31 'marker' genes, a hidden Markov model (HMM)-based multiple alignment program, and maximum likelihood to construct an organism tree for 578 species. The phylogenetic based HGT prediction methods cannot usually detect transfers between sister branches in a tree (very closely related species) and sparsely distributed genes may not be detected if the gene tree is consistent (or inconclusive) with the species tree. Future research may minimize these limitations either through increased species sampling or by combining the power of phylogenetic and sequence composition based approaches.

WEB-BASED TOOLS AND DATABASES

A large number of tools and databases exist which use different properties of genomic islands for their identification. A few are based on the compositional bias measures, others involve stochastic and probabilistic measures, while few others use comparative genomics approach. A recent review on the various web-based resources for GI identification and their performance is given by Langille *et al* (2010).

PAI-IDA: (http://compbio.sibsnet.org/projects/pai-ida/) The method uses iterative discriminant analysis that combines three compositional criteria to distinguish PAIs/GIs from the rest of the genome: G+C content, dinucleotide frequency and codon usage (Tu and Ding, 2003). A small set of known PAIs from a few genomes were used as the initial training data to generate the parameters used in the linear functions to discriminate anomalous regions from the rest of the genome. Then, through iteration, the discriminant function is improved by taking additional predicted anomalous regions into account. The program can be used for searching virulence-related factors in newly sequenced bacterial genomes and is freely available for download.

GC-Profile: (http://tubic.tju.edu.cn/GC-Profile/) It is an interactive web-based tool for visualizing and analyzing the variation of GC content in genomic sequences. It implements a segmentation algorithm based on the quadratic divergence, and integrates a windowless method for the $G + C$ content computation, known as the cumulative GC profile which partitions a given genome or DNA sequence into compositionally distinct domains (Gao & Zhang, 2006; Zhang *et al*, 2005). The precise boundary coordinates given by the segmentation algorithm and the associated cumulative GC profile for analyzing the variation of GC content along the length of the genome or chromosome makes it a very useful tool.

SIGI-HMM: (www.tcs.informatik.uni-goettingen.de/colombo-sigihmm) The program SIGI-HMM predicts GIs and the putative donor of each individual alien gene and is publicly available for download along with the program Artemis for visualizing its output (Waack *et al*, 2006). The algorithm exploits taxon specific differences in codon usage for the identification of putative alien genes and the prediction of their putative origin. Codon usage of each gene is compared against a carefully selected set of Codon Usage tables representing microbial donors or highly expressed genes. The product of the codon usage frequency for each gene is calculated using the host codon frequency table and all the frequency tables that are available for other organisms (donor tables). Based on certain cut-offs, it decides if each gene resembles another species (that is, a putative donor species) more closely than the host species and, if so, the gene is labelled as a putative foreign gene. An inhomogeneous hidden Markov model (HMM) is implemented on a gene level to distinguish between normal background variations in codon usage and variations that are due to genuine HGT events, and which incorporates the removal of highly expressed genes.

SWORDS: (http://www.isical.ac.in/~probal/main.htm) The authors have proposed an unsupervised statistical identification of genomic islands (Nag *et al*, 2006). SWORDS is a statistical tool for analyzing short oligonucleotide frequencies. As transposons are known to be involved in horizontal acquirement into the genome, they divide the genome according to the presence of transposable elements, from the start of a transposon sequence to the start of the next transposon sequence considered as a fragment. The frequencies of the k-words are computed for each fragment using SWORDS and standard hierarchical average linkage cluster analysis carried out among the chosen segments of a specific chromosome. The fragments having very different word usage compared to the other fragments of the same chromosome branch out and shows up as genomic island fragments in the dendrogram tree.

IslandPick: (http://www.pathogenomics.sfu. ca/islandviewer/) IslandPick uses a comparative genomics approach to detect GIs by automatically identifying suitable genomes for comparison for a given query genome as input. This selection process allows GI predictions to be pre-computed for any genome without any bias from manual genome selection. Once the comparison genomes are selected, whole-genome alignments are constructed using Mauve, and BLAST is used as a secondary filter to ensure that the region is not a recent duplication that is not aligned by Mauve. IslandPick predictions are automatically updated monthly for all currently available genomes using default criteria, and unpublished genomes can be submitted privately for analysis (Langille *et al*, 2008). Since IslandPick requires several phylogentically related genomes to be sequenced to be able to make a prediction; therefore, predictions are not be available for many genomes. IslandViewer is available from the same site for visualization and download of the pre-computed GIs for all published sequenced genomes.

MobilomeFINDER: (http://mml.sjtu.edu. cn/MobilomeFINDER) It as a comprehensive, comparative-genomics-based "mobile genome" (mobilome) discovery platform in bacterial strains allowing high-throughput genomic island discovery by using microarray-derived comparative genomic hybridization data and comparative analysis of the contents and contexts of tRNA sites (tRNAcc) and/or other integration hotspots

in closely related bacteria. It integrates ArrayOme and tRNAcc software packages for the discovery pipeline (Ou *et al*, 2007).

PredictBias: (http://www.davvbiotech.res.in/ PredictBias/) It is a web application for the identification of genomic and pathogenicity islands in prokaryotes based on composition bias (%GC, dincucleotide and codon bias), presence of insertion elements (Transposase, Integrase, tRNA), presence of genes encoding proteins similar to known virulence factors (*viz.*, adhesins, invasin, toxin & others) by searching against Virulence Factor Profile database (VFPD) and absence from closely related non-pathogenic species by using the 'compare genome feature' of the tool (Pundhir *et al*, 2008). An important feature of this tool is that it provides comparative analysis of an island in related non-pathogenic species which aids in validating the results and defining the boundaries of PAIs.

IGIPT: (http://ccnsb.iiit.ac.in/nita/IGIPT/srk/ index.php): Integrated Genomic Island Prediction Tool (IGIPT) is a web-based tool for identifying genomic islands (GI) in prokaryotic genomes (Jain *et al*, 2008). It provides six different measures which capture variations in the nucleotide composition of a region compared to that of the genomic average. Measures for analysis at the genome level include computing GC content, genomic signature based on dinucleotide biases and k-mer biases ($k = 2 - 6$) based on word biases, in sliding windows and comparing with the genomic average. These measures can be used in the absence of any annotation of the genomes. At the gene level, the three measures incorporated involve computing biases in codon and amino acid usages and GC content at the three codon positions. These measures can also be applicable when the complete genome of an organism is not available, but only few genes are available. The tool provides output in excel format, giving values of various measures in each window making it suitable for plotting purposes. The tool also provides option to screen the anomalous windows based on user-defined cut-off based on standard deviation. On the web-server, provision to extract the predicted GIs and its flanking region for further investigations facilitates screening of transposable elements, repeats, tRNA and mobility genes in the proximity of GIs.

A large number of pre-computed databases of Genomic Islands (GIs) and Pathogenecity Islands (PAI) are available on the web which can be used for further analysis. A few of these are summarized below.

IslandPath: (http://www.pathogenomics.sfu. ca/islandpath/) It is a network service incorporating multiple DNA signals and genome annotation features into a graphical display of a bacterial or archaeal genome to aid the detection of genomic islands. It provides a list of bacterial genomes in which GIs have been identified based on G+C content in predicted ORFs (instead of sliding window), dinucleotide bias for gene clusters, the location of known or probable mobility genes, the location of tRNAs and with annotation features retrieved from public resources. It provides a whole-genome graphical web interface for convenient visualization and analysis of genomic islands highlighting features associated with GI (Hsiao *et al*, 2003).

HGT-DB: (http://genomes.urv.cat/HGT-DB) Under the hypothesis that genes from distantly related species have different nucleotide compositions, the Horizontal Gene Transfer DataBase (HGT-DB) includes statistical parameters such as G+C content, codon and amino acid usages, for identifying genes that deviate in these parameters for prokaryotic complete genomes. For each genome, the database provides statistical parameters for all the genes, as well as averages and standard deviations of G+C content, codon usage, relative synonymous codon usage and amino acid content, as well as lists of putative horizontally transferred genes, correspondence analyses of the codon usage and lists of extraneous groups of genes in terms of G+C content. For each gene, the database lists several statistical parameters, including total and positional G+C content, and determines whether the gene deviates from the mean values of its own genome (Garcia-Vallve *et al*, 2003).

PAIDB: (http://www.gem.re.kr/paidb) Pathogenicity Island Database (PAIDB) is a relational database of all reported PAIs and potential PAIs regions predicted by a method that combines feature based and similarity based analyses. Due to the difficulty in assigning virulence features to a gene, a gene is considered a virulence gene in the database only if it was experimentally validated or reported in literature. Apart from the sequence exhibiting compositional bias, PAIDB provides GI information for these regions if they are found to be homologous to previously described PAIs. Using the PAI Finder search application, a multi-sequence query can be analyzed for the presence of potential PAIs and the PAIs can be browsed by species, text searched or searched with BLAST (Yoon *et al*, 2007).

NMPDR: (www.nmpdr.org/) The National Microbial Pathogen Database Resource (NMPDR) contains the complete genomes of ~ 50 strains of pathogenic bacteria, and > 400 other genomes that provide a broad context for comparative analysis across the three phylogenetic domains (McNeil *et al*, 2007). The current edition of the NMPDR includes 47 archaeal, 725 bacterial, and 29 eukaryal genomes providing curated annotations for comparative analysis of genomes and biological subsystems, with an emphasis on the food-borne pathogens and STD pathogens.

Islander: (http://kementari.bioinformatics. vt.edu/cgi-bin/islander.cgi) The Islander database is a comprehensive online resource of GIs in completely sequenced bacterial genomes identified using the algorithm by Mantri and Williams (2004). It exploits the feature that islands tend to be preferentially integrated within tRNA and tmRNA genes and identify the fragmented parts of the RNA genes using BLAST to mark the endpoints of the genomic islands.

FUTURE RESEARCH DIRECTIONS

Since genomic islands contain genes responsible for the virulence, antibiotic resistance, ecological importance and responsible for the adaptability, improved prediction of such regions from primary sequence data is of significant interest. Integration of the various approaches is the need of the hour as it has been observed that various methods discussed above may result in different sets of genes as HGT. With large bacterial genomes now available, new algorithms based on biological insights from the large samples, especially from closely related organisms must be developed for improving the prediction of genomic islands and also understanding the mechanisms of transfer. More accurate bioinformatics tools are needed especially for precise identification of the boundaries of the genomic islands. Sequences from metagenomics projects provide another challenge since in these datasets the organism sources of the sequences are unknown and short sequence reads from next-generation sequencing further complicates the problem.

CONCLUSION

The identification of genomic islands (GIs) is a key task in annotation pipelines, especially in the case of pathogens since it helps in identifying virulent genes which can be potential drug targets. In this chapter we have discussed three main types of approaches used for the identification and validation of genomic islands. The parametric methods, based on anomalous nucleotide compositions are the most widely used method for detecting GIs because of the ease with which these can be used. These methods require only the genome (which may or may not be annotated) or a representative set of genes of an organism for detecting the GIs. Searching in the neighbourhood of the predicted GIs by any signal-based methods for the presence of tRNA or tmRNA genes, direct repeats,

mobility genes, etc. can help in reducing the false predictions. Filtering of highly expressed genes such as ribosomal protein genes, and prophages can further improve the prediction accuracy of the parametric methods. The different methods may sometimes give different results; therefore a combination of parametric methods should normally be used to obtain a consensus for the detection of potential HGT. It should be noted that only recent horizontal acquisitions can be identified by the parametric methods as a result of the process called amelioration. Thus both parametric and signal-based methods extract the characteristic features within a genomic island for its identification. However, different regions in a genome may exhibit similar compositional biases, for e.g., highly expressed genes. Hence the predicted GIs must be confirmed by other approaches. If the genomes of the closely related species of the genome of interest are available, then these predictions should further be confirmed by comparative genomics approach. The choice of the genomes used for comparison is very crucial in this analysis, since comparison with very closely related genomes may not be able to detect GIs acquired before speciation. On the other hand, comparison with genomes of distantly related species may lead to false-predictions. To validate the GI and identify the source of the horizontal transfer event, phylogenetic analysis of all the genes in the predicted GI is essential. If all the genes in a neighbourhood show similar phylogenetic relationship, different from the average gene of the genome, then a GI can be confirmed. However care should be taken while analyzing the phylogenetic relationship since this approach may not be able to distinguish between convergent evolution and horizontal transfer. In both comparative genomics and phylogenetic analysis approaches, the requirement of multiple genomes from closely and distantly related species is required. If genes in the predicted GIs by parametric or signal-based methods, exhibit either similarity to a homolog from a distant taxon, or unusual phyletic patterns in clusters of orthologs, or presence of a conserved operon in a few distantly related organisms confirm their horizontal acquisitions. Each of the approaches discussed above has its strengths and weaknesses and a combination of methods is often most suitable.

REFERENCES

Andersson, J. O. (2005). Lateral gene transfer in eukaryotes. *Cellular and Molecular Life Sciences, 62*(11), 1182–1197. doi:10.1007/s00018-005-4539-z

Campbell, A. (1999). Genome signature comparisons among prokaryote, plasmid and mitochondrial DNA. *Proceedings of the National Academy of Sciences of the United States of America, 96*(16), 9184–9189. doi:10.1073/pnas.96.16.9184

Darling, A. C. E., Mau, B., Blattner, F. R., & Perna, N. T. (2004). Mauve: Multiple alignment of conserved genomic sequence with rearrangements. *Genome Research, 14*(7), 1394–1403. doi:10.1101/gr.2289704

Delcher, A. L., Phillippy, A., Carlton, J., & Salzberg, S. L. (2002). Fast algorithms for large-scale genome alignment and comparison. *Nucleic Acids Research, 30*(11), 2478–2483. doi:10.1093/nar/30.11.2478

Dobrindt, U., Hochhut, B., Hentschel, U., & Hacker, J. (2004). Genomic islands in pathogenic and environmental microorganisms. *Nature Reviews Microbiology, 2*(5), 414–424. doi:10.1038/nrmicro884

Gao, F., & Zhang, C. T. (2006). GC-Profile: A Web-based tool for visualizing and analyzing the variation of GC content in genomic sequences. *Nucleic Acids Research, 34*, W686–W691. doi:10.1093/nar/gkl040

Garcia-Vallve, S., Guzman, E., Montero, M. A., & Romeu, A. (2003). HGT-DB: A database of putative horizontally transferred genes in prokaryotic complete genomes. *Nucleic Acids Research, 31*(1), 187–189. doi:10.1093/nar/gkg004

Garcia-Vallve, S., Romeu, A., & Palau, J. (2000). Horizontal gene transfer in bacterial and archaeal complete genomes. *Genome Research, 10*, 1719–1725. doi:10.1101/gr.130000

Gogarten, J. P., & Townsend. (2005). Horizontal gene transfer, genome innovation and evolution. *Nature Reviews Microbiology, 3*, 679–687. doi:10.1038/nrmicro1204

Gutierrez, G., Marquez, L., & Marin, A. (1996). Preference for guanosine at first codon position in highly expressed Escherichia coli genes. A relationship with translational efficiency. *Nucleic Acids Research, 24*(13), 2525–2527. doi:10.1093/nar/24.13.2525

Hsiao, W., Wan, I., Jones, S. J., & Brinkman, F. S. L. (2003). IslandPath: Aiding detection of genomic islands in prokaryotes. *Bioinformatics (Oxford, England), 19*(3), 418–420. doi:10.1093/bioinformatics/btg004

Jain, R., Ramineni, S., & Parekh, N. (2008). Integrated genome island prediction tool (IGIPT). In *IEEE Proceedings of International Conference on Information Technology* (ICIT2008), (pp. 131-132). DOI: 10.1109/ICIT.2008.42

Jenks, P. J. (1998). Microbial genome sequencing beyond the double helix. *BMJ (Clinical Research Ed.), 317*(7172), 1568–1571.

Juhas, M., van der Meer, J. R., Gaillard, M., Harding, R. M., Hood, D. W., & Crook, D. W. (2009). Genomic islands: Tools of bacterial horizontal gene transfer and evolution. *FEMS Microbiology Reviews, 33*(2), 376–393. doi:10.1111/j.1574-6976.2008.00136.x

Jurka, J., Kapitonov, V. V., Pavlicek, A., Klonowski, P., Kohany, O., & Walichiewicz, J. (2005). Repbase update, a database of eukaryotic repetitive elements. *Cytogenetic and Genome Research, 110*(1-4), 462–467. doi:10.1159/000084979

Karlin, S. (1998). Global dinucleotide signatures and analysis of genomic heterogeneity. *Current Opinion in Microbiology, 1*(5), 598–610. doi:10.1016/S1369-5274(98)80095-7

Karlin, S. (2001). Detecting anomalous gene clusters and pathogenicity islands in diverse bacterial genomes. *Trends in Microbiology, 9*(7), 335–343. doi:10.1016/S0966-842X(01)02079-0

Karlin, S., & Ladunga, I. (1994). Comparisons of eukaryotic genomic sequences. *Proceedings of the National Academy of Sciences of the United States of America, 91*(26), 12832–12836. doi:10.1073/pnas.91.26.12832

Karlin, S., & Mrazek, J. (1997). Compositional differences within and between eukaryotic genomes. *Proceedings of the National Academy of Sciences of the United States of America, 94*(19), 10227–10232. doi:10.1073/pnas.94.19.10227

Karlin, S., Mrazek, J., & Campbell, A. M. (1998). Codon usages in different gene classes of the E. coli genome. *Molecular Microbiology, 29*(6), 1341–1355. doi:10.1046/j.1365-2958.1998.01008.x

Koonin, E. V., Makarova, K. S., & Aravind, L. (2001). Horizontal gene transfer in prokaryotes: Quantification and classification. *Annual Review of Microbiology, 55*, 709–742. doi:10.1146/annurev.micro.55.1.709

Langille, M. G. I., Hsiao, W. W. L., & Brinkman, F. S. L. (2008). Evaluation of genomic island predictors using a comparative genomics approach. *BMC Bioinformatics, 9*, 329–338. doi:10.1186/1471-2105-9-329

Langille, M. G. I., Hsiao, W. W. L., & Brinkman, F. S. L. (2010). Detecting genomic islands using bioinformatics approaches. *Nature Reviews Microbiology, 8*(5), 373–382. doi:10.1038/nrmicro2350

Lawrence, J. G. (1999). Selfish operons: The evolutionary impact of gene clustering in prokaryotes and eukaryotes. *Current Opinion in Genetics & Development, 9*(6), 642–648. doi:10.1016/S0959-437X(99)00025-8

Lawrence, J. G., & Ochman, H. (1997). Amelioration of bacterial genomes: Rates of change and exchange. *Journal of Molecular Evolution, 44*(4), 383–397. doi:10.1007/PL00006158

Lawrence, J. G., & Ochman, H. (2002). Reconciling the many faces of lateral gene transfer. *Trends in Microbiology, 10*(1), 1–4. doi:10.1016/S0966-842X(01)02282-X

Lio, P., & Vannucci, M. (2000). Finding pathogenicity islands and gene transfer events in genome data. *Bioinformatics (Oxford, England), 16*(10), 932–940. doi:10.1093/bioinformatics/16.10.932

Lowe, T. M., & Eddy, S. R. (1997). tRNAscan-SE: A program for improved detection of transfer RNA genes in genomic sequence. *Nucleic Acids Research, 25*(5), 955–964. doi:10.1093/nar/25.5.955

Mantri, Y., & Williams, K. P. (2004). Islander: A database of integrative islands in prokaryotic genomes, the associated integrases and their DNA site specificities. *Nucleic Acids Research, 32*, D55–D58. doi:10.1093/nar/gkh059

McNeil, L. K., Reich, C., Aziz, R. K., Bartels, D., Cohoon, M., & Disz, T. (2007). The National microbial pathogen database resource (NMPDR): A genomics platform based on subsystem annotation. *Nucleic Acids Research, 35*, D347–D353. doi:10.1093/nar/gkl947

Nag, S., Chatterjee, R., Chaudhuri, K., & Chaudhuri, P. (2006). Unsupervised statistical identification of genomic islands using oligonucleotide distributions with application to vibrio genomes. *Sadhana, 31*(2), 105–115. doi:10.1007/BF02719776

Ochman, H., Lawrence, J. G., & Groisman, E. A. (2000). Lateral gene transfer and the nature of bacterial innovation. *Nature, 405*(6784), 299–304. doi:10.1038/35012500

Ou, H. Y., He, X., Harrison, E. M., Kulasekara, B. R., Thani, A. B., & Kadioglu, A. (2007). MobilomeFINDER: Web-based tools for in silico and experimental discovery of bacterial genomic islands. *Nucleic Acids Research, 35*, W97–W104. doi:10.1093/nar/gkm380

Pundhir, S., Vijayvargiya, H., & Kumar, A. (2008). PredictBias: A server for the identification of genomic and pathogenicity islands in prokaryotes. *In Silico Biology, 8*(3-4), 223–234.

Ragan, M. A., Harlow, T. J., & Beiko, R. G. (2006). Do different surrogate methods detect lateral genetic transfer events of different relative ages? *Trends in Microbiology, 14*(1), 4–8. doi:10.1016/j.tim.2005.11.004

Rajan, I., Aravamuthan, S., & Mande, S. S. (2007). Identification of compositionally distinct regions in genomes using the centroid method. *Bioinformatics (Oxford, England), 23*(20), 2672–2677. doi:10.1093/bioinformatics/btm405

Tu, Q., & Ding, D. (2003). Detecting pathogenicity islands and anomalous gene clusters by iterative discriminant analysis. *FEMS Microbiology Letters, 221*(2), 269–275. doi:10.1016/S0378-1097(03)00204-0

Waack, S., Keller, O., Asper, R., Brodag, T., Damm, C., & Fricke, W. F. (2006). Score-based prediction of genomic islands in prokaryotic genomes using hidden Markov models. *BMC Bioinformatics, 7*, 142–153. doi:10.1186/1471-2105-7-142

Wu, M., & Eisen, J. A. (2008). A simple, fast, and accurate method of phylogenomic inference. *Genome Biology, 9*(10), R151. doi:10.1186/gb-2008-9-10-r151

Yoon, S. H., Hur, C. G., Kang, H. Y., Kim, Y. H., Oh, T. K., & Kim, J. F. (2005). A computational approach for identifying pathogenicity islands in prokaryotic genomes. *BMC Bioinformatics, 6*, 184–194. doi:10.1186/1471-2105-6-184

Yoon, S. H., Park, Y. K., Lee, S., Choi, D., Oh, T. K., Hur, C. G., & Kim, J. F. (2007). Towards pathogenomics: A Web-based resource for pathogenicity islands. *Nucleic Acids Research, 35*, D395–D400. doi:10.1093/nar/gkl790

Zhang, C. T., Gao, F., & Zhang, R. (2005). Segmentation algorithm for DNA sequences. *Physical Review E: Statistical, Nonlinear, and Soft Matter Physics, 72*, 041917. doi:10.1103/PhysRevE.72.041917

KEY TERMS AND DEFINITIONS

Comparative Genomics: Involves comparing whole genomes/chromosomes of two or more organisms.

Genomic Islands (GIs): The movement of genetic material between phylogenetically unrelated organisms by mechanisms other than parent to progeny inheritance.

Horizontal Gene Transfer (HGT): The transfer of genes by mechanisms other than direct descent (vertical inheritance) between diverse organisms.

Laterally Transferred Genes: Same as Horizontally transferred genes.

Pathogenicity Islands (PAIs): The genomic islands containing genes responsible for the virulence of the bacterial strains.

Phylogeny: The evolutionary relationship between taxonomic group of organisms (e.g., specis or population).

Chapter 11
Video Stream Mining for On-Road Traffic Density Analytics

Rudra Narayan Hota
Frankfurt Institute for Advanced Studies, Germany

Kishore Jonna
Infosys Labs, Infosys Technologies Limited, India

P. Radha Krishna
Infosys Labs, Infosys Technologies Limited, India

ABSTRACT

Traffic congestion problem is rising day-by-day due to increasing number of small to heavy weight vehicles on the road, poorly designed infrastructure, and ineffective control systems. This chapter addresses the problem of estimating computer vision based traffic density using video stream mining. We present an efficient approach for traffic density estimation using texture analysis along with Support Vector Machine (SVM) classifier, and describe analyzing traffic density for on-road traffic congestion control with better flow management. This approach facilitates integrated environment for users to derive traffic status by mining the available video streams from multiple cameras. It also facilitates processing video frames received from video cameras installed in traffic posts and classifies the frames according to traffic content at any particular instance. Time series information available from various input streams is combined with traffic video classification results to discover traffic trends.

INTRODUCTION

The speed and precision of natural vision system for living beings (human, animal, birds or insects) is amazing, yet less explored because of complexity involved in the biological phenomena. Every intelligent system (Intelligent robotics, Intelligent Traffic system, Interactive medical applications

and human intension recognition in retail domain etc.) in many industries is attempting to simulate natural vision system. The major hurdles in such process are high computational complexity because of very high dimensional images data and the semantic gap between the image content and the observed concepts from natural images/scenes. Recent progress in computational power

DOI: 10.4018/978-1-61350-056-9.ch011

and understanding of local and global concepts in images opens path for new line of work in dynamic automation. Table 1 summarizes some of the emerging applications in various domains and existing challenges in vision based solutions.

Video cameras are used in various industry segments for security, surveillance and object tracking purposes. Inferences derived from Video analytics systems will be of great importance for taking critical decisions and predictions in varied industry application scenarios. One such application area is traffic and transport management by using video cameras installed at traffic posts in a city. The traffic can be congested in some areas and the vehicular flow towards that area still increases the congestion. To avoid these types of issues, the area under congestion has to be estimated and the vehicular flow has to be directed in other possible routes. Because of the difficulty faced in recent traffic management and suitability of applying vision based approaches, it is of high interest in recent time. In the rest of this

chapter, we focus on traffic density problems, issues and solution approach.

Traffic density and traffic flow are important inputs for an intelligent transport system (ITS) to manage traffic congestion better. Presently, this is obtained through loop detectors (LD), traffic radars and surveillance cameras. However, installing loop detectors and traffic radars tends to be difficult and costly. Currently, more popular way of circumventing this is, to develop some sort of Virtual Loop Detector (VLD) by using video content understanding technology to simulate behavior of a loop detector and to further estimate the traffic flow from a surveillance camera. But difficulties arise when attempting to obtain a reliable and real-time VLD under changing illumination and weather conditions.

In this work, we present an approach to estimate on-road traffic density using texture analysis and Support Vector Machine (SVM) classifier, and analyze traffic density for on-road traffic congestion control and flow management. Our system provides an integrated environment for

Table 1. Vision based application in different domain and issues

Domain	Applications	General functions in computer vision systems	Issues of Computer vision Systems
1. Health Care	Computer-aided diagnosis, surgical applications, Mammography Analysis, Detection of Carcinoma tissue, Retrieval of similar diagnosed images.	i. Image acquisition: (Sensors-light, ultra sonic, tomography, radar) ii. Pre-processing (Re-sampling, Noise reduction, Enhancement, Scale normalization) iii. Feature extraction (Lines, edges, interest points, corners, blobs, color, shape and texture) iv. Detection/Segmentation (region of interest, foreground and background separation, Interest points) v. High-level processing (Object Detection, Recognition, Classification and Tracking)	i. Various types of image and videos (binary, gray, color), different data types (GIF, BMP, JPEG and PNG), and sizes (SQCIF, QCIF, CIF, 4CIF). ii. Camera Sabotage (FOV obstruction, sudden pan, tilt, zoom) and Discontinuity in video streams iii. Illumination (varied intensity and multiple source of lights) iv. Blurring v. Occlusion vi. Different object size vii. Changing Field of View in moving cameras
2. Transport	Small to large vehicle detection, Vehicle count, Traffic density estimation, Incident detection, Traffic rule violation detection, Eye and head tracking for automatic drowsiness detection, Lane/Road detection etc.		
3. Security Surveillance	People detection and tracking, Abnormal behavior recognition, Abandoned Objects, Biometric pattern recognition (Face, Finger prints), Activity monitoring in mines etc		
4. Manufacturing	Camber measurement, Item detection and classification, and Vision-guided robotics etc.		
5. Retail	Cart detection, Vegetable recognition etc.		

users to derive traffic status by mining available video camera signals. Proposed traffic decision support system process the video frames received from video cameras installed in traffic signals and classifies the frames according to traffic content at any particular instance. One of our goals is to classify each given frame into low, medium or high traffic density category with given ROI (Region of Interest). Secondly, we apply analytics on output of density estimator to manage and optimize the traffic flow within the city. Cameras installed at multiple locations of a city provide video sequences as frames to video analytics solution. This solution classifies frames to provide the category information. Time series information available from the inputs sequence is combined with traffic video classification, and used in traffic trend estimation for any specified time interval. Our developed solution demonstrates the working model on various cameras placed at different location of the city.

The rest of the chapter is organized as follows. In the Background Section, we describe the basics of video streaming, video stream mining and SVM Classifier that are related to our work. Next, we briefly discuss existing approaches for estimating traffic density. In the Video Stream Mining for Traffic Density Estimation section, we describe our approach for specific traffic application scenarios followed by the method of texture feature extraction to represent the local image patch and classification task. We also describe the data sets used and present the results obtained followed by discussion. We conclude the chapter with a summary.

BACKGROUND

Video Streaming

Streaming video is defined as continuous transportation of images via internet and displayed at the receiving end which appears as a video. Video streaming is the process where packets of data in continuous form were given as input to display devices. The player takes the responsibility of synchronous processing of video and audio data. The difference between streaming and downloading video is that in downloading video, the video is completely downloaded and we cannot perform any operations on the file while it is being downloaded. The file is stored in the dedicated portion of memory. In streaming technology, the video is buffered and stored in a temporary memory, and once the temporary memory is cleared the file is deleted. Operations can be performed on the file even when the file is not completely downloaded.

The main advantage of video streaming is that there is no need to wait for the whole file to be downloaded and processing video can be started after receiving first packet of data. On the other hand, streaming a high quality video is difficult as the size of high definition video is huge and bandwidth may not be sufficient. Also, the bandwidth has to be good so that there will not be any breaking in the video flow. It can be revealed that for video files of smaller size, downloading technology can be used; and for larger files streaming technology is more suitable. Still there is a space for improvement in streaming technology, by finding an optimized method to stream a high definition video with smaller bandwidth through the selection of key frames for further operations.

Video Stream Mining

Stream mining is a technique to discover useful patterns or patterns of special interest as explicit knowledge from a vast quantity of data. A huge amount of multimedia information including video is becoming prevalent as a result of advances in multimedia computing technologies and high-speed networks. Due to its high information content, extracting video information from continuous data packets is called as video stream mining. Video stream mining can be considered as subfields of data mining, machine learning and knowledge discovery. In mining applications, the goal of a classifier is to predict the value of the class variable for any new input instance provided with adequate knowledge about class values of previous instances. Thus in video stream mining, a classifier is trained using the training data (class values of previous instances). The mining process will be ineffective if samples are not a good representation of class value. To get good results from classifier, the training data should include majority of instance that a class variable can possess.

SVM-Based Classifier

Classifying data is a crucial task in machine learning. When an instance is given as input, the classifier should categorize to which class the input belongs. Classifier should know the boundaries and data points of its classes. In this work, we used SVM classifier for classifying the traffic density.

SVM's (Cristianini & Shawe-Taylor, 2000; Vapnik 1998) are very effective than other conventional non- parametric classifiers (e.g., the RBF Neural Networks, Nearest-Neighbor (NN), and Nearest-Center (NC) classifiers) in terms of classification accuracy, computational time,

and stability to parameter setting. The theory of SVM is to create a hyper-plane which separates the classes with maximum accuracy. There can be many hyper-planes to separate the two categories. The largest separation between the two categories is considered as the best plane.

The hyper-plane is chosen such that the distance between the nearest different class points is maximum. This is called as the "maximum-margin hyper plane". The margin (γ) and hyper-plane (w) for a non-linearly separable class is shown in Figure 1. A hyper-plane, which is denoted by $(w, b) \in R^n \times R$, consists of all x satisfying $\langle w, x \rangle + b = 0$.

The problem thus can be formed as:

$$\text{Minimize } \frac{1}{2}\|w\|^2 \text{ subject to } y_i(\langle w, x_i \rangle + b) \geq 1.$$

$$(1)$$

The solution to this optimization problem of SVM's is given by the saddle point of the Lagrange function. Let C be the upper bound of the Lagrange multipliers α_i, and then equation (1) can be formulated as

Figure 1. Margin and hyper plane classification problem

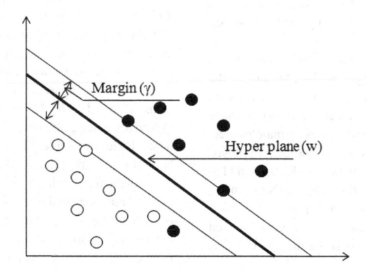

$$L(\alpha) = \sum_i \alpha_i - \frac{1}{2} \sum_i \sum_j \alpha_i \alpha_j y_i y_j \langle x_i, x_j \rangle$$

(2)

with constraints $\sum_i \alpha_i y_i = 0$ and $0 \le \alpha_i \le C$.

TRAFFIC DENSITY ESTIMATION APPROACHES

Heavy traffic congestion of vehicles, mainly during peak hours, creates a big problem in major cities all around the globe. The ever-increasing number of small to heavy weight vehicles on the road, poorly designed infrastructure, and ineffective traffic control systems are major causes for traffic congestion problem. Intelligent Transportation System (ITS) with scientific and modern techniques is a good way to manage the vehicular traffic flows in order to control traffic congestion and for better traffic flow management. For this ITS takes estimated on-road density as input and analyze the flow for better traffic congestion management.

One of the most used technologies for determination of traffic density is the Loop Detector (LD) (Stefano et al., 2000). These loop detectors are placed at the crossing and junctures. Once any vehicle passes over, it generates signals. Signals from all the LDs placed in crossing are combined and analyzed for traffic density and flow estimation. Recently, more popular way of circumventing automated traffic analyzer is by using video content understanding technology to estimate the traffic flow from a set of surveillance cameras (Lozano, et. al., 2009; Li, et. al., 2008). Because of low cost and comparatively easier maintenance, video based system with multiple CCTV (Closed Circuit Television) cameras are also used in ITS, but mostly for monitoring purpose (Nadeem, et. al., 2004). Multiple screen displaying the video streams from different location are displayed at central location to observe the traffic status

(Jerbi, et. al., 2007; Wen, et. al., 2005; Tiwari, et. al., 2007). Presently this monitoring system is a manual task of observing these videos continuously or storing them for lateral use. In this set up it is very difficult to recognize any real time critical happenings (e.g., heavy congestions).

Recent techniques such as Loop detector have major disadvantages of installation and proper maintenance. Computer vision based traffic application is considered as cost effective option. Applying image analysis and analytics for better congestion control and vehicle flow management in real time has multiple hurdles, and most of them are in research stage. Some of the important limitations for computer vision based technology are as follows:

- Difficulty in choosing the appropriate sensor for deployment.
- Trade-off between computational complexity and accuracy.
- Semantic gap between image content and perception poses challenges to analyze the images hence it is difficult to decide which feature extraction techniques to use.
- Finding a reliable and practicable model for estimating density and making global decision.

The major vision based approaches for traffic understanding and analyses are object detection and classification, foreground and back ground separation, and local image patch (within ROI) analysis. Detection and classification of moving objects through supervised classifiers (e.g. Ada-Boost, Boosted SVM, NN etc.) (Li, et. al., 2008; Ozkurt & Camci, 2009) are efficient only when the object is clearly visible. These methods are quite helpful in counting the number of vehicles and tracking them individually, but in traffic scenario due to high overlapping of objects, most of the occluded objects are partially visible and very low object size makes these approaches impracticable. Many researchers have tried to separate foreground from background in video sequence either by temporal difference or optical flow (Ozkurt & Camci, 2009). However, such methods are sensitive to illumination change, multiple sources of light reflections and weather conditions. So, vision based approach for automation has its own advantages over other sensors in terms of cost on maintenance and installment process. Still the practical challenges need high quality research to realize it as solution. Occlusion due to heavy traffic, shadows (Janney & Geers, 2009), varied source of lights and sometimes low visibility (Ozkurt & Camci, 2009) makes it very difficult to predict traffic density and flow estimation.

Given the fact that, low object size, high overlapping between objects and broad field of view in surveillance camera setup, estimation of traffic density by analyzing local patches within given ROI is an appealing solution. Further, levels of congestion constitute a very important source of information for ITS. This is also used for estimation of average traffic speed and average congestion delay for flow management between stations. In this work, we developed a solution to estimate vehicular traffic density and apply analytics to manage traffic flow.

VIDEO STREAM MINING FOR TRAFFIC DENSITY ESTIMATION

In a set up of multiple cameras placed at different location/junctions our target is to extract meaningful insights from video frames grabbed from video streams. This is achieved by estimating traffic density at each of these junctions. Applying analytics on this time series data is useful for trend monitoring and optimal route finding. Since a very specific portion of whole image in the camera field-of-view is of our interest, first we provide an option for users to choose a flexible convex polygon to cover the best location in the camera field view for density estimation. One such example is shown in Figure 2. Here, we

first categorize each frame, from selected camera and its field of view, into different density classes (Low, Medium and High category) according to the traffic present in it by using supervised classification method. These classification results are archived in database for selected video frames. Database also contains time series information for each frame extracted from video sequence. Analyzer component will mine the time series data along with classification data to provide the traffic patterns. User will be given option to visualize the mined results to view average traffic condition in timely basis.

The presented system serves as automation for manual monitoring system by alert generation in critical situations. It can aid in traffic monitoring system and reduces labor-intensive work. Our system can work in real time for multiple cameras (e.g., 100 cameras at the same time). The output of the proposed method is further used for analytics in the traffic flow. Alarms generation for abnormal traffic condition, trend monitoring and route identification are the major use of traffic density estimation. This helps in vehicular flow routing, shorted or less congested path finding (Gibbens & Saacti, 2006).

The basic flow diagram of the proposed methodology is shown in Figure 3. The major modules are: Camera/ROI selection, Classifier, Traffic flow analyzer and Dashboard to show the output. The detail diagram for traffic density estimation is shown in Figure 4 and its components are explained below.

ROI (Region of Interest) Selection

In surveillance camera setup, the camera field-of-view covers a very wide region. But the informative data lies only in small region. So it is better to remove the unnecessary information from image and process only useful information. Moreover, it is also important to select significant region of interest for effective analysis. The user has to select points (coordinates) in the image such that

Figure 2. Region of interest for traffic density estimation

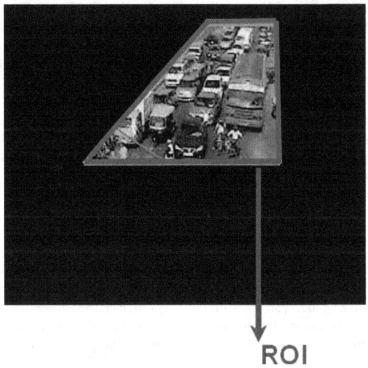

Figure 3. Traffic density solution flow diagram

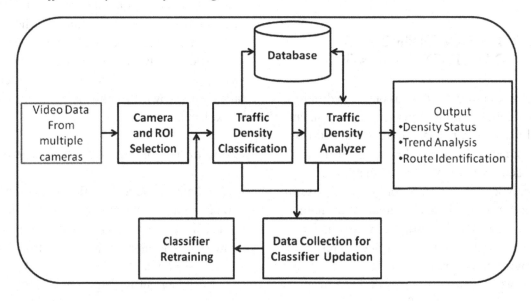

Figure 4. Block diagram of traffic density classification

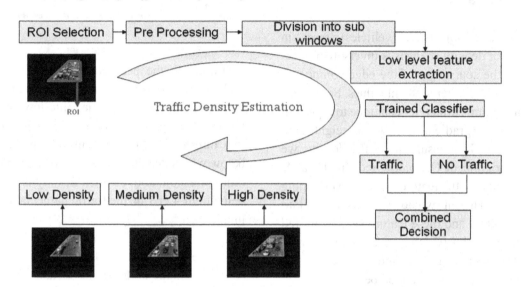

the connection of these points form a closed region (convex polygon) on which the model classifier operates. The ROI can be of any shape but region should cover the view of entire traffic congestion.

Preprocessing

Lighting and illumination are very important factors while collecting clear images. Bad lighting, shadows due to buildings or obstacles and light variation from day to night etc. would hamper the precision of traffic density estimation. For the same density of traffic, the density estimation may vary from day to night because of variation in lighting. So there is a necessity to preprocess the image patches before estimation. This preprocessing includes contrast enhancement which helps in processing the shadowed region adequately. Smoothing is another operation in the preprocessing which cutoffs the major variation in the image. Contrast enhancement as well as smoothing helps in better gradient feature extraction and it has following advantages:

- Robust system for variation of intensity of light source.

- Takes care for low visibility of objects.
- Tackle well in noisy scenarios.

Division into Sub Windows

An inherent problem with global feature extraction and representation approaches is that they are sensitive to local image variations (e.g., pose changes, illumination changes, and partial occlusion). Local feature extraction methods, on the other hand are less sensitive to these effects. Moreover, utilization of geometric information and constraints in the configuration of different local features make them robust (either explicitly or implicitly while constructing target object models). The entire image (within ROI) is not processed at a time as it can be of any shape and size (option given for users to select ROI). The image within the ROI is divided into small windows of size W x W with overlapping of D pixels (These W and D are parameters to find the best size and overlapping of windows) and the sub-windows are given as input to the classifier.

Texture Feature

The number of objects (e.g. vehicles) present in the ROI for density analysis is inversely proportional to the sparseness of the edge component or pixels with higher gradient values. So, we use textural feature extraction technique to represent the variation (gradient) among the neighboring pixel values. To measure the traffic density, we used Histogram of Oriented Gradient (Dalal & Triggs, 2005) as the feature for each overlapping local patch. The sub-windows are converted into feature vectors and these feature vectors are fed to SVM classifier (Cristianini & Shawe-Taylor, 2000) for classifying them into 'Traffic' class or 'No Traffic' class as described below.

Classification

Each of the extracted feature vectors of the sub-windows are classified by a trained classifier. This binary classifier is developed with large number of manually selected image data with and without the presence of traffic objects. The classifier generates classification confidence which can be negative or positive. The positive output denotes the Traffic congestion in image patch and the negative represents no traffic or less traffic condition. The cumulative results from all the sub-windows are calculated as Percentage of Traffic Density. As camera field-of-view covers a wide range in ground (approximately from 2 meter to 100 meter view), the number of objects can be placed in the near field of view is comparatively smaller than the number of object in farther view. So, we considered weights (by linear interpolation) as higher weight for the farther patch decision than that of nearer patch while accumulating the global decision. The decision of classifier is based on weighted confidence which is computed according to distance of the sub-windows from the camera field-of-view. That is, the percentage of global traffic density is obtained as:

$$Traffic\ Density\,(\%) = \frac{No.of\ subwindows\ with\ traffic}{Total\ number\ of\ windows\ within\ ROI} * 100$$

(3)

Based on the percentage of traffic density with respect to the two user defined threshold values, the image is classified into low, medium or high density as follows. Let T1 and T2 be the two thresholds, T1 be the minimum threshold below which density is low and T2 be the maximum threshold above which density is consider being high. Let T be the traffic percentage of the image then,

- The image is 'Low' Density if T <= T1.
- The image is 'Medium' Density if T1 < T <= T2.
- The image is 'High' Density if T >T2.

The step wise algorithm is presented in Table 2.

Retraining the Classifier

The trained classifier may not be perfect and accurate in decision making. To make the classifier robust and accurate, images which are wrongly classified have to be collected and use them to retrain the classifier. To make the trained classifier robust against the changing scenarios, different light sources and camera positioning, we have provided the option of retraining the classifier for better density estimation. Periodically the user can collect data which are wrongly classified and retrain classifier (with cross validation) to get appropriately trained for particular setting (e.g. view angle, distance and height).

Results and Observations

For our experiments and performance comparison of the proposed approach of traffic density estimation, we considered both synthetic as well as real world data sets.

Table 2. Traffic density estimation algorithm

Input	**Image : Extracted Image frame from video stream** **T1 & T2 : Threshold for categorization of Image frame density within ROI** **W : Size of the local window patch** **D : Overlapping Pixel width among the local window**
Output	Categorization of Image into Low, Medium or High traffic density
Steps:	
1	Select a flexible convex polygonal region of interest (ROI), covering the complete expected traffic area.
2	Divide the image patch within the ROI into widows of size WxW with overlapping D pixels.
3	Extract texture feature for each of the image patch.
4	Classify each local window by using the extracted feature vector and trained binary classifier for presence of traffic or not
5	Compute the percentage of traffic density within ROI by using equation 1.
6	Apply threshold T1 and T2 to categorize the frame into low, medium or high.

The synthetic data sets are prepared by placing segmented vehicles on the traffic images with different density patterns. To simulate on-road traffic with different densities (from 0 to 100%), we placed different number of vehicle samples on the empty road images. The manual way of creating synthetic data helps us to control the density amount in discrete state, which we used for performance evaluation.

Different kinds of traffic densities with mixed number of vehicles are shown in Figure 5. We created six different data set with 1, 3, 5, 10 13 and 17 vehicles placed at random positions (within ROI) and each set contains 100 images. We categorized the first two types (images with 1 and 3 vehicles) as low density, images with 5 vehicles as medium density and the last two types as high density.

Figure 5. Synthetic traffic data with different number of vehicles.(a)1, (b)3, (c)5,(d)10, (e)13 and (f)17

Figure 6. Results showing classification of image frames

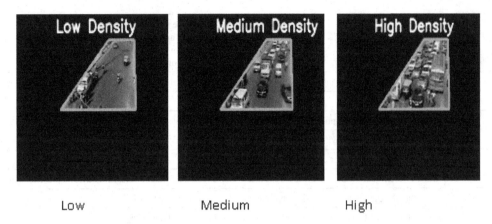

Figure 7. Density estimation performance for (a) synthetic and (b) real world data

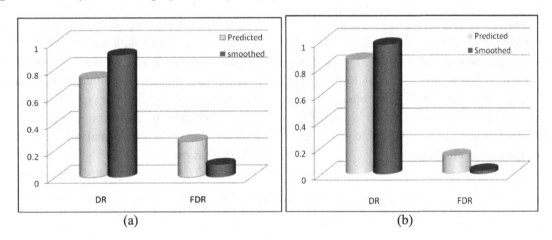

Real data sets are collected from the surveillance cameras placed at the traffic posts. These data sets are collected with time stamp. For experimental purpose, we selected a set of images from the video sequence captured in 24x7 bases and labeled them as low, medium and high traffic density according to their vehicle occupancy. The experiment is done on bmp images of 24 BPP (bits per pixels) data and of 352x288 pixels in size.

Some of the classification results on real data representing three categories are shown in Figure 6. It can be observed that the images with higher vehicle occupancy are classified as high or me-

dium than low density class. The performances of correct classification on both synthetic and real data are shown in Figure 7(a) and 7(b) respectively. The percentages of density prediction are shown in Figure 8. From the annotated data we computed the thresholds for image categorization (threshold are shown in thick and dotted lines). It can be observed from the density curve that after smoothing the predicted density in time window, the abruptness of the density variation reduces and hence accuracy of correct classification increases for both the data sets.

The performance of correct classification in synthetic data is improved from 86.3% to 97.5%

Figure 8. Traffic density flow and classification on (a) synthetic and (b) real data

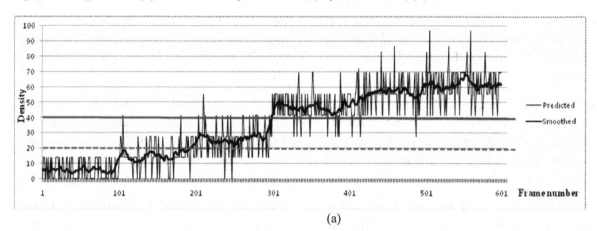

(a)

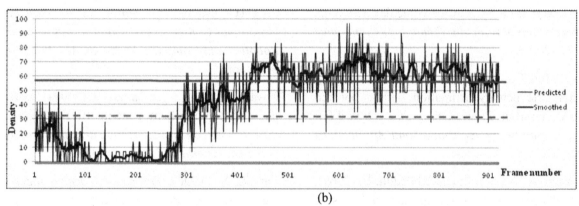

(b)

by smoothening, and in the case of real data set we achieved 90.7% accuracy.

CONCLUSION

In this chapter, we described a computer vision based approach for on-road traffic density estimation and analytics for flow control management. The efficacy of this method is supported with various experiments on synthetic and real world data sets. The performance of traffic analytics are presented for texture feature extraction techniques. With extensive experiments, we show that the gradient features with contrast normalization and smoothing works reasonably well in the real

life data sets. The presented work can be further enhanced by extending with reliable re-trainable model which is adaptive in changing scenarios and weather condition.

REFERENCES

Cristianini, N., & Shawe-Taylor, J. (2000). *Support vector machines and other kernel-based learning methods*. Cambridge University Press.

Dalal, N., & Triggs, B. (2005). Histograms of oriented gradients for human detection. *Proceedings of International Conference on Computer Vision & Pattern Recognition (CVPR '05), 1*, 886—893.

Gibbens, R. J., & Saacti, Y. (2006). *Road traffic analysis using MIDAS data: Journey time prediction. (Technical Report, UCAM-CL-TR-676). Computer Laboratory*. England: University of Cambridge.

Janney, P., & Geers, G. (2009). Framework for illumination invariant vehicular traffic density estimation. *Proceedings of Pacific Rim Symposium on Image and Video Technology (PSIVT 2009)*, Japan.

Jerbi, M., Senouci, S.-M., Rasheed, T., & Ghamri-Doudane, Y. (2007). An infrastructure-free traffic Information System for vehicular networks. *Proceedings of Vehicular Technology Conference (VTC-2007)*.

Li, Z., Tan, T., Chen, J., & Wassantachat, T. (2008). On traffic density estimation with a boosted SVM classifier. Proceeding *of 2008 Digital Image Computing - Techniques and Applications (DICTA2008)*, Australia.

Lozano, A., Manfredi, G., & Nieddu, L. (2009). An algorithm for the recognition of levels of congestion in road traffic problems. *Mathematics and Computers in Simulation, 79*(6), 1926–1934. doi:10.1016/j.matcom.2007.06.008

Nadeem, T., Dashtinezhad, S., Liao, C., & Iftode, L. (2004). TrafficView: A scalable traffic monitoring system. *Proceedings of IEEE International Conference on Mobile Data Management (MDM'04)*.

Ozkurt, C., & Camci, F. (2009). Automatic traffic density estimation and vehicle classification for traffic surveillance systems using neural networks. [MCA]. *Mathematical and Computational Applications An International Journal, 14*(3), 187–196.

Stefano, L. D., Milani, I., & Viarani, E. (2000). Evaluation of inductive-loop emulation algorithms for UTC systems. *Proceedings of the Sixth International Conference on Control, Automation, Robotics and Computer Vision (ICARCV 2000)*, Singapore.

Tiwari, G., Fazio, J., & Baurav, S. (2007). Traffic planning for non-homogeneous traffic. *Sadhna (Special Issue on Transportation Research - Safety and Sustainability), 32*(4), 309-328.

Vapnik, V. (1998). *Statistical learning theory*. New York, NY: Wiley-Interscience.

Wen, Y.-H., Lee, T.-T., & Cho, H.-J. (2005). Missing data treatment and data fusion toward travel time estimation for ATIS. *Journal of the Eastern Asia Society for Transportation Studies, 6*, 2546–2560.

Chapter 12
Discovering Patterns in Order to Detect Weak Signals and Define New Strategies

Anass El Haddadi
University of Toulouse III, France & University of Mohamed V, Morocco

Bernard Dousset
University of Toulouse, France

Ilham Berrada
University of Mohamed V, Morocco

ABSTRACT

Competitive intelligence activities rely on collecting and analyzing data in order to discover patterns from data using sequence data mining. The discovered patterns are used to help decision-makers considering innovation and defining the strategy for their business. In this chapter we present four methods for discovering patterns in the competitive intelligence process: "correspondence analysis," "multiple correspondence analysis," "evolutionary graph," and "multi-term method."

INTRODUCTION

A successful business is often conditioned by its ability to identify, collect, process, and disseminate information for strategic purposes. However, a company can be over-informed, and not be able to search through all this information. Now, to be competitive it must know their environment. The establishment of a competitive intelligence (CI) approach is the inevitable answer to this challenge.

In the last few years, a lot of work has been done in order to ensure CI approaches. Discovering weak signals and define new strategies have been the main motivation for applying them in company contexts. The CI approach can provide the company with detailed information about its environment through internal and external information which it has access to. This environmental scanning is intended to assist decision makers in their choice of strategies.

DOI: 10.4018/978-1-61350-056-9.ch012

In our CI approach, we use techniques for extracting knowledge from textual data to study scalable relational data from the information environment of a company. In this context, we propose our competitive intelligence tools: "TETRALOGIE[1]" and "Xplor" (Web service of TETRALOGIE). These tools extract the weak signals and define new strategies using sequence data mining from a corpus. These patterns are used also in various areas: biology (Qindga and al., 2010; Shuang and Si-Xue, 2010), traffic prediction (Zhou *and al.*, 2009; Zhou *and al.*, 2010), space research (Walicki and Ferreira, 2010; Yun and al., 2008), and so on.

In this chapter, a CI approach based on sequence data mining is detailed. It uses four methods:

- **Correspondence Analysis (CA)**, which aims at detecting the evolution of a research area, authors, company's, keywords, etc… or the temporal sequence, that allows us to have an overview of changes in very specific areas.
- **Multiple Correspondence Analysis (MCA)**, which aims at detecting the time series for decision making.
- **Multi-term Method**, which aims at extracting the weak signals.
- **Evolutionary Graph**, which shows in detail the structural changes of networks over time. For example, we detect the appearance and changes in social networks.

This document is organized as follows. First, we identify in section 1 the knowledge extraction process in order to demonstrate our methodology of analysis, and various measures of information structure. In section 2, we explain extraction of strategic information and the discovery of patterns by correspondence analysis (CA). Section 3 presents the patterns of weak signals, and describes methods to detect a pattern for new

strategies in a company. In Section 4, we explain the methodology to detect "temporal," "pattern" sequences using evolutionary graphs. And finally in section 5, to illustrate the methods presented in the previous sections, a presentation of a complete analysis of emerging field of agronomy in China is performed by our research team.

KNOWLEDGE EXTRACTION PROCESS IN CI

The key step of the CI process is the selection of information, which is to develop a "corpus", depending on the target, which will be later analyzed through methods of text mining. We often use the term "corpus" to describe large sets of semi or fully-structured textual data available electronically.

Following predefined criteria, this step allows us to focus on data defined as "interpretable" and with high informative potential. Data is firstly prepared by selecting it according to objectives fixed using the techniques of information retrieval (Büttcher *et al., 2010*) (Croft *et al.,* 2010). This process (Saltan & McGill, 1984) seeks to match a collection of documents and the user needs (Maniez et Grolier, 1991), translated in the form of a request (Kleinberg, 1999) through an information system. This is composed of an automatic or semi-automatic indexing module, a module of document/request matching and possibly a module of query reformulation.

Different models are used in search engines to match the query with the document, such as the probabilistic model (Sparck-Jones, 2000), the connexionnist and genetic model (Boughanem et al., 2000), the flexible model (Sauvagnat, 2005), the language modeling (Ponte & Croft, 1998), etc.

Monitoring devices are based on two types on information: formal and informal.

CONSTRUCTION OF THE CORPUS OF DATA

In the approach we propose, target data is selected according to the purpose of exploitation (Dkaki *et al.*, 1997). Initially, these methods cut the data into units (words, dates or strings of characters), then they apply mathematical and statistical calculations in order to obtain, in the form of graphs or charts, a representation of units according to relations or proximity that have been calculated.

The corpus is composed of 'notes', i.e documents structured in fields (Dkaki *et al.*, 2000). The word, a unit which is too semantically poor, has been replaced by the notion of 'term' that can be associated to a concept in an ontology Hernandez *et al.*, 2007).

A 'field', the basic unit, is the informational container identified by a tag and a piece of data, for example author, date, address, and organization. An 'item' is the container of the field, i.e the data. It can be (Dousset, 2003):

- **Mono-Valued**: having only one possible value, such as date or language ex. PUBLICATION YEAR=2010 ;
- **Multi-Valued**: having multiple values, such as names of several authors for a co-authored article, delimited by separators;
- **Diversified**: if the field contains several values representing different concepts. For example SOURCE=Lancet, 2010-01, -32p., This field can be decomposed into a magazine, a publication date: 2010-01, which itself is divided into year and month, a reference: 32p. indicating the page number.

PROCESSING OF DATA STRUCTURE

Data processing (El Haddadi *et al.*, 2010) has been used to treat data in its native form. The native format provides several advantages including bet-ter responsiveness, an easier update of the corpus and a preservation of all information. However, to fit almost all structures, it is necessary to use meta-data which are tools of format description whose aim is to:

- find a technique to differentiate between documents (or textual units);
- identify markers of semantic fields in the database and give them a name and standard initials;
- determine their usefulness and their priority;
- determine judicious cutting techniques to extract each type of information.

We also noted that over 90% of cases encountered can be treated without reformatting. Indeed, it is possible to work simultaneously on different formats and different sources by developing correspondence rules between the relevant (or useful) fields using second-level meta-data. These can both orchestrate the synchronization of all formats, and interface with a unique semantic extraction tool. Each source has a specific format, which itself has a specific descriptor (first-level meta-data). A collection of formats is managed by a generic descriptor (second level meta-data: the conductor). For each database, structured or semi-structured, it is advisable to define its own specific format descriptor that allows interfacing with our platform of information processing "TETRALOGIE".

DATA CROSSBREEDING

Once the data corpus is built, information is crossed, either within the same type (associations) or between two different types in order to achieve a first static study of their mutual influences: contingency matrix, frequency matrix, matrix of presence-absence and co-occurrence matrix. It is also possible to explode the obtained tables by the time (by homogeneous period): Cube.

Once the data corpus is built, information is crossed, either within the same type (associations) or between two different types in order to achieve a first static study of their mutual influences: contingency matrix, frequency matrix, matrix of presence-absence and co-occurrence matrix. It is also possible to split the obtained tables using time (organized by homogeneous period) to achieve scalable and prospective analysis which are the only ones to highlight the strategic dimension of a field, and detection of sequential pattern.

After this step, a set of analysis methods is deployed to extract information from these endogenous structures. Now, we can start the reporting for detecting pattern, or temporal sequence.

EXTRACTION OF STRATEGIC INFORMATION AND THE DISCOVERY OF PATTERNS BY THE CORRESPONDENCE ANALYSIS (CA)

CA can be applied to qualitative data: tables of individuals - qualitative modal variables, matrix of presence – absence, matrices of contingencies and correlations. Before the implementation of the CA, data preprocessing is necessary:

- Standardization of rows of the matrix (sum of unitary weight),
- Add at the bottom of the matrix, an identity matrix, to consider the pure variables (columns) as additional individuals.

Below is an example of a factorial map obtained after CA on a co-occurrence matrix Topics - Authors for a large laboratory in research on computers. We can notice groups of authors correlated by the theme of their research, interface themes (between two groups of authors), experts of interfaces, interface themes, sequence variation of themes. After verification, the thematic teams detected correspond exactly to those of the publicity for that laboratory. This is like the discovery of a pattern sequence of a theme, i.e., the variation of a theme continues in a research laboratory. This allows assumptions about the trend of research in a laboratory.

Three observations are possible:

- The concerned laboratory has conducted an objective presentation of its structure,
- It is possible to obtain a perfect knowledge of this structure from the outside,
- Moreover, the qualities and imperfections of this structure are now known.

When we focus on a particular element (Period, author, topic) or group, it is possible to highlight it using rotations, i.e. data mining sequences, choice of axes and zoom on one side of the view. In some cases (too many items to display), we can manipulate only the searched class of items. In the example shown below, we chose to manipulate the outcome of CA conducted on a matrix of co-occurrence between keywords and first authors.

THE PATTERNS OF WEAK SIGNALS

The method of extracting weak signals is based on data mining sequences (evolutionary analysis) and structural semantic fields. This method involves the following tools:

- Matrix of crossing semantic terms with time,
- Extraction of emerging terms (by normalization, then by sorting the last column),
- Matrix of co-occurrence crossing emerging terms with themselves,
- Sort by diagonal blocks of this matrix,
- Extraction of blocks representing the emerging and consistent concepts.

Figure 1. The factorial 4D map of CA topic

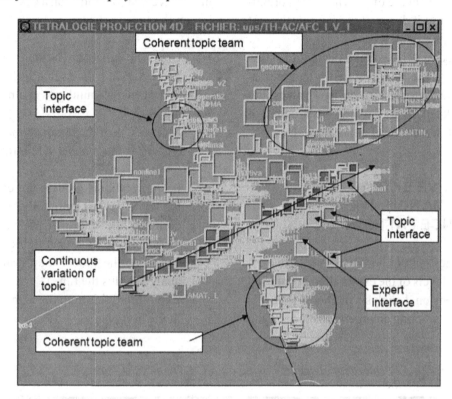

SORT METHOD FOR EXTRACTING WEAK SIGNALS

Sort by Blocks on the Absolute Links

This technique has many applications:

- Search for related classes,
- For each class, an internal block sorting brings directly together the most linked elements (i.e. a pattern of sequence),
- Reorganization of a closely related matrix in diagonal blocks.

Its use in text analysis allows, as shown below, to detect emerging semantic classes which are the most pronounced. We therefore start by creating a crossing matrix of the new terms. This emergent terminology can eventually form groups corresponding to emerging concepts. A single term is not enough because it may be a change in terminology which englobes an old concept, which now has a specific vocabulary (often a single word replaces an expression or a compound word).

Sort by Blocks on Relative Links

This technique is used when the crossed terms have very different frequencies. Indeed, in the texts, much used or common terms in the field are mixed with others that are more precise and target specificities. If we want to find groups that match these emerging semantic or rare issues, we must first go to the relative mode before doing the sorting. Note that for symmetric matrices of co-occurrence crossing exclusive modalities (e.g. authors or keywords), the diagonal elements are in fact the frequencies in the corpus.

We kept two techniques in TETRALOGIE.

- The first serves to normalize the matrix, i.e. to modify this matrix, then to sort it. It has the advantage of the choice of normalization, but it destroys the initial values of the matrix.

- The second is based on a compatible standard with the non symmetric matrices. It sorts the matrix based on new values, but keeps the old ones. So only the structure of the matrix changes, but not the values.

INTERACTIVE EXTRACTION OF INFORMATION: THE EMERGENCE PATTERN

The emergence pattern introduces the time variable at many levels of the exploration in the level of multidimensional analysis methods. Below is a method of extracting emergence patterns using

interactive manipulations on a CA made depending on the time variable:

- Cross the variable to be analyzed with time expressed in periods that have sufficiently homogeneous numbers (in a ratio of 1 to 2 at most),
- Make a CA of the obtained matrix,
- Visualize the map of temporal modalities (columns only),
- Using rotations, process the cloud of data to isolate the last temporal component in a corner of the window (1997 at the top, on the left in the following figure),
- Visualize the global map (variable to be analyzed plus the time),
- Export onto this map the azimuth obtained in the first one,

Figure 2. Extraction of emergent elements basing on a CA Thematic - Time.

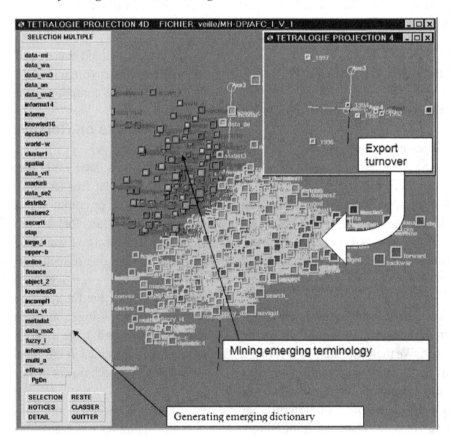

- Extract items that are located beyond or near the icon associated with the last period (in orange on the 4D map),
- Generate the filter containing all the emerging modalities of the analyzed variable.

This filter can then be reused to cross the emergences between themselves and to find the emerging concepts.

We will then extend this type of approach to other strategies for knowledge discovery based mainly on interactivity, detecting the emergence pattern: new semantic network, new innovation...

Detection of Weak Signals

This method is to extract an emerging semantic class that represents what happens repeatedly in a given field. So, we must:

- Start from a Keywords – Dates matrix or even better, from a Terms – Dates matrix,
- Extract the emergent sequence patterns terminology,
- Cross it with itself (square matrix of co-occurrence),
- Sort this matrix by diagonal blocs,
- Extract the more visible classes,
- Ask for details (list of words connected togeher).

The result often exceeds all expectations, because the underlying concepts are completely new. This destabilizes the experts who often declare themselves incompetent in the matter. Of course, new subjects detected by this method must be subject to a more in-depth analysis, which can be obtained by crossing their specific terminology with the actors in the field and other concepts.

Figure 3. Illustration of the method of weak signal extracting

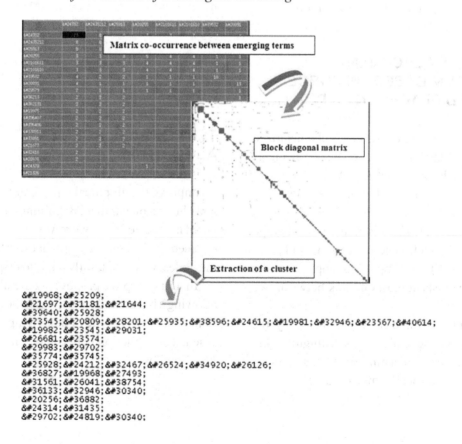

一批
品种和
高效
对光温敏雄性不育小麦
与对照
根尖
生理
设计
效应结果表明
进一步
等方面
败育的
传递
建立
理想的

It is also desirable to re-examine the origin of the information on this new theme (of which the research equation is given to us) to complete its identity and to better understand its potential.

The Evolutionary Graphs and Patterns

The notion of graphical representation includes all the techniques to develop a visualization of data in the plan so as to make reading easier (Loubier & Dousset, 2007; Loubier, 2009). The graph presentation is intended to help explore data, the tasks encountered in information visualization are broadly related to Information Retrieval:

- Rapid exploration of unknown information;
- Demonstration of relationships, structures and sequence pattern in the information;
- Demonstration of paths to relevant information;
- Classifying interactive information.

TEMPORAL PLACEMENT ALGORITHM BASED ON FORCE DIRECTED PLACEMENT (FDP)

The data is represented in a graph G characterized by two sets: a set $V = \{v_1, v_2, ..., v_n\}$ whose elements are called nodes and a set $E = \{e_1, e_2, ..., e_m\}$, derived from a set parts of V, whose elements are called arcs.

We note $G = (V, E)$. G is an undirected graph (there is no distinction between *(u, v)* and *(v, u)* for u and v in V) and simple (no loops *(v, v)* into E and there exists at most one link between two vertices).

The temporal dimension is affected by the consideration of several periods distinguished in the form of co-occurrence matrix. For each period every node has a specific metric value.

Thus the global metric denoted M_g a node s, consisting of the sum of metric m for periods p_1, $p_2, ...p_n$, which will be marked as follows:

$$M_{sg} = m_{sp1} + m_{sp2} + ... + m_{spn}$$

Each node is represented by a histogram where the size of each bar is relative to the value of the metric for the period.

However, it is important to characterize the temporal data to allow a more comprehensive analysis. To do this, for each period, we assimilated a point of reference. For each period, if the node has a metric value greater than zero, then an invisible arc is created to reach the node to mark. We apply the algorithm of association between the nodes S_j and landmarks *mark_i* of periods:

```
For each period i{
        For each node j{
If m_spi>0 then creat_arc(node1=s,
node2=mark_i, weight= m_spi X2);
j++ ;
}
i++ ;
}
```

TEMPORAL PLACEMENT ALGORITHM

To improve the graphical representation of graph and obtain a planar display (minimizing the number of intersected arcs) we rely on the analogy "arc = placement". The system produces forces between the nodes, which naturally leads to displacement.

In a first step we propose a general algorithm allowing a better rendering for graphic representation, whatever the type of data (temporal or not), when: The attraction between two nodes u and v is defined by:

$$f_a(u,v) = \frac{\beta \times d_{uv}^{\alpha_a}}{K}$$

$$f_r(u,v) = \frac{a_r x K^2}{d_{uv}^c}$$

β is a constant. d_{uv} is the distance between u and v. α_a used to increase/decrease the attraction.

α_a used to increase/decrease the attraction and c is a constant.

The K factor is calculated in terms of the area of design window and the number of nodes in the graph. For this, L is the length of the window, l the width and N is the number of the visible nodes in the graph.

The temporal placement algorithm based on the application of the repulsion between all nodes. In a second step, all attractions are taken into account, for any pair of nodes connected.

In this algorithm, the parameters were studied to obtain relevant results:

$$K = \sqrt{\frac{Lxl}{N}}$$

Thus, to calculate the *attraction*: is a constant, initialized to 2;

If the nodes u and v are not connected by an arc then $f_a(u,v) = 0$.

The repulsion between two nodes u and v is defined by:

- $d_{uv}^{\alpha\varepsilon}$ is the distance between u and v, where corresponds to the value of the slider can interact on the ride.

To calculate the *repulsion*:

Box 1.

```
For each node u {if u is visible
            then {
                        Calculating distance d(u,v) ;
                        For each node v {
                                            fr(u,v, d(u,v));
                                if there is an arc between u and v{
                                        fa(u, v);
                                    if (u ou v is a temporal mark)
                            Slider_force_reperes_temporels X f_a(u, v, d(u,v));
                                        }
                }}}
For each node u {
        if (u is not a mark)
                Moving nodes ;
                }
/* *Verification of no-over lapping nodes by comparing position**/
For each node u{
For each node v{
                        if(x_u,y_u) == (x_v, x_y)
                        then change position of v.
                        }}
```

- α_r is the value of the slider, to interact on the repulsion ;
- c is a constant, initialized to 1,5.

In the example (cf. Figure 4), we study specific authors in the field of data mining within four periods: 2003, 2004, 2005, 2006-7. For each period, a mark is assigned, listed in red on the Figure 4 and each node with a metric valuated for a period is then linked to a corresponding reference by an invisible arc. On the first graph of Figure 4, no force of attraction and repulsion has been applied. On the second, they are applied. It is noticeable that every part of the second graph is specific to a time characteristic called "temporal sequence".

The nearer a node is to a landmark, the stronger it is characterized by this period. The peaks located halfway between two markers reveal a part of the two periods. Thus, in the following figure, it is easy to distinguish the peaks specific to 2003 because it is the set of nodes located around the landmark. This reveals the presence of the node during the first period with a characteristic metric value.

Similarly for other periods, the nearer a node is to the center of the figure, the greater the number of periods to which it belongs. Thus, the authors represented in the center of the Figure are the most persistent. Those represented near the landmark 2003 are the oldest and those nearest to 2006-7 are the most newly emerging authors.

Our experiences lead us to recommend a specific data mining sequence for a better visual result, regarding the setting of these three forces.

- Step 1: Apply a very high value of attraction in order to obtain a concentrated grouping of data. Apply the temperature up through the slider to enable rapid and efficient movement of nodes.
- Step 2: Reduce the force of attraction and repulsion increase, to get a readable graph.

Figure 4. An evolving graph (left graph), application of temporal placement, parameterized using the slider «Force temporal» (right graph)(Loubier 2009).

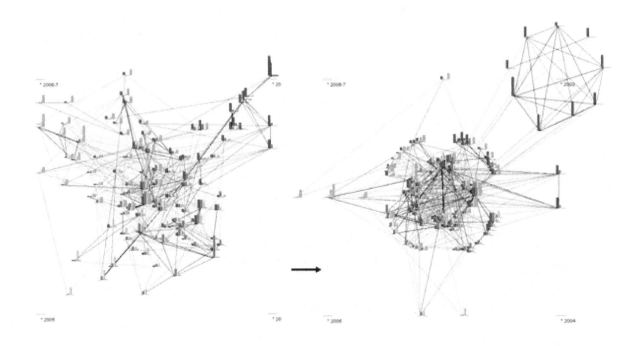

Reduce temperature to avoid too abrupt a movement of vertices.

- Step 3: Adjust the three sliders substantially, lowering the temperature, until a satisfactory result.

Analysis of Temporal Structure and Detection of "Temporal Sequence"

The visualization of temporal data should be able to provide the right information at the right time, for decision making. In this approach, a very important aspect is the dynamic surveillance of system "the temporal sequence, the pattern sequence, performance evolution, the detection of faint signals, changes collaborations, alliances, associations".

From the results emerge a readability of temporal characteristics, simplifying decision-makers' work on evolutionary data. Following the application of these forces, a typology appears significant and nodes neighboring a single landmark are characterized by the unique presence for that period (if the authors occasionally appear). These are located between several specific periods to which they are near. Thus, authors are pioneers in the central area of study, that is to say present for all periods.

The application of this algorithm allows to observe groups of data according the common temporal characteristics, allowing a temporal classification.

Thus, this proposal improves the performance by:

- Reducing cognitive resources mobilized by the user to analyze the temporal information;
- Increasing opportunities for detection of evolutionary structures (changes between

Figure 5. Social network analysis: Extraction of the main teams by authorship

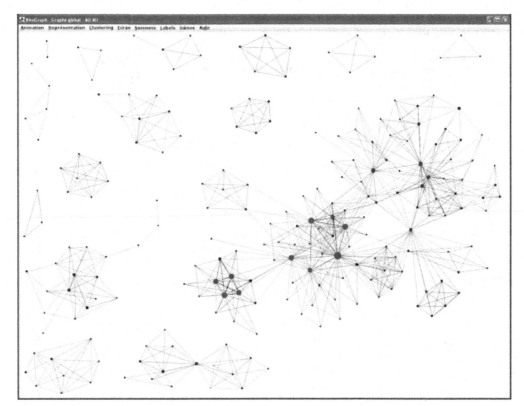

data relationships, significant consolidation, strategic positions, centrality,...);

- Monitoring of events (changes in structure, appearance or movement patterns, clusters,...);

Analysing Emerging Field of Agronomy in China

To illustrate the methods presented in the previous sections, we present the evolution of author relationships and the weak signal of emerging field of agronomy in china, performed in (Dousset, 2009; Guenec, 2009). To do so, we use the scientific digital library (DL)[2].

Social Network

Figure 5 presents the topology of the main teams. We can immediately see that there is very little co-authoring in the Chinese scientific publications we analyzed. A second observation is that

the teams are generally directed by a main author who has control of 2, 3 or 4 distinct sub-teams.

Evolution of Author Relationships

The evolutionary graphs (section 4) and patterns of sequence method consist in using a three dimensional cross referencing table where two dimensions represent the authors (thus co-authoring is represented) and the third dimension corresponds to time. We can then visualize the evolution of the author network on a graph. Figure 6 displays this network. At the bottom left corner, for example, the authors associated with 2006-8 are the only ones to appear.

Figure 6 brings together the sequence pattern of the main Chinese teams in the emerging field of agronomy. Some collaboration continues whereas others can be seen as emergent, moreover there are collaborations that either finish for a period of time or stop altogether. It is easy to locate the leaders of the author groups; indeed the

Figure 6. Networking and sequence pattern of the main teams (co-authoring).

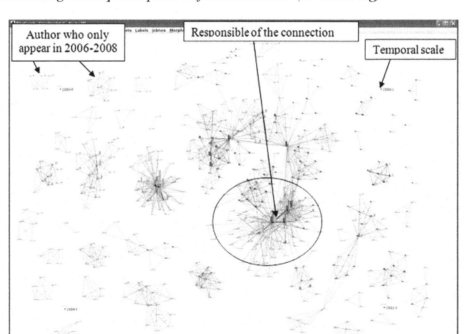

size of each histogram is proportional to the appearances of the author in the collection. It is also easy to extract the authors that appear in the end year only (green) or in the beginning year (red). Finally Figure 6 also shows the main authors who are responsible for the connections between teams, for example, the team represented at the center of Figure 6.

This analysis can be completed using a correspondence analysis based on the same three dimensional cross referencing table. This shows the trajectories of the authors when they collaborate with other authors. In the data we analysed, no such mobility could be extracted.

Detecting Weak Signals

To detect weak signals (section 3), we first extract the keywords and the known terms from the title and abstract. Then we detect the new sequences patterns that exceed a number of occurrences. Afterwards we cross reference these new n-grams with time and we keep only those which occur frequently during the end time period (here 2006-

2008). Finally these terms are cross referenced (co-occurrence) and we sort the subsequent matrix to obtain diagonal blocks. Each block represents an emergent concept identified by a new terminology which does not exist in the keyword field and which only occurs in some documents. Weak signals can then be validated by cross referencing them with all the other fields and in particular the keywords. In Figure 7, part a) we represent the cross referencing matrix; each plot indicates a non-nil value for the cross referencing. Along the diagonal of the matrix, a certain number of clusters consist of new terms and correspond to a semantic group. Each cluster is extracted in a square sub-matrix and can be visualized in the form of a semantic graph (Figure 7b). This information should then be submitted to an expert in the field for validation.

CONCLUSION

Strategic analysis lies at the heart of any competitive organization. There are many ways to perform

Figure 7. Analysis of newly detected terms and their clusters

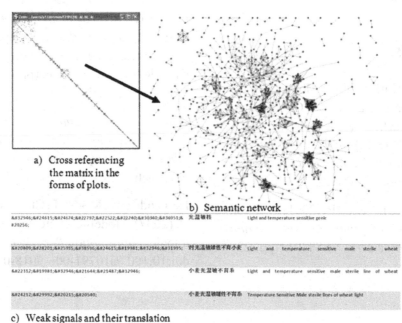

a) Cross referencing the matrix in the forms of plots.

b) Semantic network

c) Weak signals and their translation

an analysis of internal and external factors which bear an influence on the strategy of a company. In this chapter, we have suggested a CI approach based on sequence data mining for discovering weak signals, patterns, emergence patterns and define new strategies.

CI is expressed on the basis of a sequence data mining. Therefore, using the appropriate methods of mining and discovering is essential to decision makers in any business. Discovering weak signals and define new strategies suggests that companies have to use CI approaches. Thus, the companies have adopted this analysis approach of environment for strategy execution in order to achieve better performance. The sequence data mining and procedures described in this chapter provide a framework which companies can use to adopt good practices in competitive intelligence.

With the method presented here, the decision makers are able to clearly discover the company's strategy. Moreover, they have a method for analyzing internal and external information. In addition, sequence patterns of strategy can be identified and monitored to reach the intended goals. Given a CI approach based on sequence data mining, companies can build good practices in strategic analysis.

REFERENCES

Boughanem, M., Chrisment, C., Mothe, J., Soulé-Dupuy, C., & Tamine, L. (2000). Connectionist and genetic approaches to achieve IR. In Crestani, F., & Gabriella, P. (Eds.), *Soft computing in information retrieval techniques and applications* (pp. 173–198). Springer-Verlag.

Boughanem, M., & Dousset, B. (2001). *Relationship between push and optimization subscriptions in documentation centers*. VSST'01, (pp. 239-252). Tome 1.

Büttcher, S., Clarke, C. L. A., & Cormack, G. V. (2010). *Information retrieval: Implementing and evaluating search engines*. MIT Press.

Croft, B., Metzler, D., & Strohman, T. (2011). *Search engines: Information retrieval in practice*. Addison-Wesley.

Dkaki, T., Dousset, B., Egret, D., & Mothe, J. (2000). Information discovery from semi-structured sources – Application to astronomical literature. *Computer Physics Communications*, *127*(2-3), 198–206. doi:10.1016/S0010-4655(99)00509-3

Dkaki, T., Dousset, B., & Mothe, J. (1997). *Mining information in order to extract hidden and strategical information*. 5th International Conference RIAO, (pp. 32-51).

Dousset, B. (2003). *Integration of interactive knowledge discovery for strategic scanning. Habilitation*. Toulouse: Paul Sabatier University. in French

Dousset, B. (2009). *Extracting implicit information by text analysis from websites in unicode*. Nancy: VSST. in French

El haddadi, A., Dousset, B., Berrada, I., & Loubier, E. (2010). *The multi-sources in the context of competitive intelligence*. Paper presented at the Francophone Conference on Mining and Knowledge Management, (pp. A1-125-A1-136). Hamammat, Tunisia.

Guenec, N. (2009). *Chinese scientific information: An essential information source to any business intelligence competitive watch*. Nancy: VSST. in French

Hernandez, N., Mothe, J., Chrisment, C., & Egret, D. (2007). Modeling context through domain ontologies. *Information Retrieval*, *10*(2), 143–172. doi:10.1007/s10791-006-9018-0

Huiyu, Z., Mabu, S., Shimada, K., & Hirasawa, K. (2009). *Generalized time related sequential association rule mining and traffic prediction.* International Conference on Evolutionary Computation, (pp. 2654-2661).

Huiyu, Z., Mabu, S., Xianneng, L., Shimada, K., & Hirasawa, K. (2010). *Generalized rule extraction and traffic prediction in the optimal route search.* International Conference on Evolutionary Computation, (pp. 1-8).

Jolliffe, I. T. (2002). *Principal component analysis* (2nd ed.). Springer.

Kleinberg, J. M. (1999). Authoritative sources in a hyperlinked environment. *Journal of the ACM, 46*(5), 604–632. doi:10.1145/324133.324140

Loubier, E. (2009). *Analysis and visualization of relational data by graph morphing taking temporal dimension into account.* PhD Thesis, in French. Toulouse, France: Paul Sabatier University.

Loubier, E., & Dousset, B. (2007). *Visualisation and analysis of relational data by considering temporal dimension.* International Conference on Enterprise Information Systems, (pp. 550-553). INSTICC Press.

Maniez, J., & Grolier, E. (1991). *A decade of research in classification.*

Mardia, K. V., Kent, J. T., & Bibby, J. M. (1979). *Multivariate analysis.* Academic Press.

Ponte, J. M., & Croft, B. (1998). A language modeling approach to information retrieval. Proceedings of the 21st Annual International ACM SIGIR Conference on Research and Development in Information Retrieval, (pp. 275–281).

Qingda, Z., Qingshan, J., Sheng, L., Xiaobiao, X., & Lida, L. (2010a). *An efficient for protein pattern mining.* International Conference on Computer Science and Education, (pp. 1876-1881).

Salton, G., & Mcgill, M. (1984). *Introduction to modern information retrieval. McGrawHill Int.* Book Co.

Sauvagnat, K. (2005). *Flexible model for information retrieval in the corpus of semi-structured documents.* Unpublished thesis. Toulouse, France: Paul Sabatier University.

Shang, B., & Si-Xue, B. (2009). *The maximal frequent pattern mining of DNA sequence.* IEEE International Conference on Granular Computing (pp. 23-26).

Sparck Jones, K., Walker, S., & Robertson, S. E. (2000). A probabilistic model of information retrieval: Development and comparative experiments. *Information Processing & Management, 36*(6), 779–840. doi:10.1016/S0306-4573(00)00015-7

Walicki, M., & Ferreira, D. R. (2010). *Mining sequences for patterns with non-repeating symbols.* International Conference on Evolutionary Computation (pp. 1-8).

Yun, L., Yunhao, Y., Yan, S., Xin, G., & Ling, C. (2008). *Mining self-adaptive sequence patterns based on the sequence fuzzy concept lattice.* Second International Symposium on Intelligent Information Technology Application (pp. 167-171).

ADDITIONAL READING

Journal Papers

Gay., B. and Dousset., B.(2005). *Innovation and network structural dynamics: Study of the alliance network of a major sector of the biotechnology industry.* Research Policy, Elsevier, http://www.sciencedirect.com/, Vol. 34 N. 10, p. 1457-1475.

Ghalamallah., I., Loubier., E.and Dousset., B. (2008). Business intelligence_a proposal for a tool dedicated to the analysis relational. SciWatch Journal, hexalog, Barcelona - Spain, Vol. 3: http://mtdjournals.wordpress.com/issues/sciwatch-journal/

Karouach, S., & Dousset, B. (2003). Visualisation de relations par des graphes interactifs de grande taille. [Information Sciences for Decision Making]. *Journal of ISDM, 6*(57), 12.

Mothe, J., Chrisment, C., Dkaki, T., Dousset, B., & Karouach, S. (2006).Combining mining and visualization tools to discover the geographic structure of a domain.: Computers, Environment and Urban Systems, Elsevier, Special issue: Geographic Information Retrieval, N. 4, p. 460-484.

Mothe., J., Chrismeent., C., Dousset., B. and Aloux., J.(2003). *DocCube: Multi-Dimensional Visualisation and Exploration of Large Document Sets.* Journal of the American Society for Information Science and Technology, JASIST, Special topic section: web retrieval and mining, Vol. 7 N. 54, p. 650-659

Edited Books

Clark, R. M. (Ed.). (2009). *Intelligence Analysis: A Target-centric Approach.*

Coutenceau, C., Valle, C., Vigouraux, E., Poullain, M., Jacquin, X., & Gillieron, A. (Eds.). (2010). *Guide pratique de l'intelligence économique (French edition)*. Eyrolles.

Jenster, P. V., & Solberg, K. (Ed.). (2009). *Market intelligence, building strategic* insight. Copenhagen business school press.

Miller, F. P. Vandome. A. F. and McBrewster. J. (Ed.). (2009). *Competitive Intelligence: Competitive intelligence, Intelligence (information gathering), Competitor analysis, Society of Competitive Intelligence Professional, ... SWOT analysis, Business intelligence.*

Richards, J. H., & Randolph, H. P. (Eds.). (2010). *Structured Analytic Techniques for Intelligence Analysis.*

Seena, S. (Ed.). (2009). *Competitive Intelligence Advantage: How to Minimize Risk, Avoid Surprises, and Grow Your Business in a changing World*. Wiley.

Waters, T. J. (Ed.). (2010). Hyperformance: Using Competitive Intelligence for Better Strategy and Execution.

Website

Dousset. B., *Tetralogie web site.*http://atlas.irit.fr (French Edition)

KEY TERMS AND DEFINITIONS

Sequence: A sequentially ordered set of related things or ideas.

Temporal Sequence: An arrangement of events in time.

Mining Sequence: Is concerned with finding statistically relevant patterns between data examples where the values are delivered in a sequence. It is usually presumed that the values are discrete, and thus time series mining is closely related, but usually considered a different activity. Sequence mining is a special case of structured data mining.

Competitive Intelligence: Is a systematic and ethical program for gathering, analyzing, and managing external information that can affect your company's plans, decisions, and operations. (Defined by the Society of Competitive Intelligence Professionals (SCIP)).

Weak Signals: Is a factor of change hardly perceptible at present, but which will constitute a strong trend in the future.

Social Network: Is a social structure made up of individuals (or organizations) called "nodes", which are tied (connected) by one or more specific types of interdependency, such as friendship, common interest, financial exchange, etc.

Decision Making: The thought process of select a logical choice from among the available options. When trying to make a good decision, a person must weigh up the positive and negative points of each option, and consider all the alternatives. For effective decision making, a person must be able to forecast the outcome of each option as well, and based on all these items, determine which option is the best for that particular situation. (from BusinessDictionary.com)

Innovation: The act of introducing something new (the american heritage dictionary); A new idea, method or device (Webster online); Change that creates a new dimension of performance (Peter Drucker); The introduction of new goods (...), new methods of production (...), the opening of new markets (...), the conquest of new sources of supply (...) and the carrying out of a new organization of any industry (Joseph Schumpeter); Innovation is a new element introduced in the network which changes, even if momentarily, the costs of transactions between at least two actors, elements or nodes, in the network (Regis Cabral); The three stages in the process of innovation: invention, translation and commercialization (Bruce D. Merrifield); The ability to deliver new value to a customer (Jose Campos); Innovation is the way of transforming the resources of an enterprise through the creativity of people into new resources and wealth (Paul Schumann); Innovation does not relate just to a new product that would come into the marketplace. Innovation can occur in processes and approaches to the marketplace (David Schmittlen); http://atlas.irit.fr; http://www.cqvip.com.

Chapter 13
Discovering Patterns for Architecture Simulation by Using Sequence Mining

Pınar Senkul
Middle East Technical University, Turkey

Nilufer Onder
Michigan Technological University, USA

Soner Onder
Michigan Technological University, USA

Engin Maden
Middle East Technical University, Turkey

Hui Meen Nyew
Michigan Technological University, USA

ABSTRACT

The goal of computer architecture research is to design and build high performance systems that make effective use of resources such as space and power. The design process typically involves a detailed simulation of the proposed architecture followed by corrections and improvements based on the simulation results. Both simulator development and result analysis are very challenging tasks due to the inherent complexity of the underlying systems. The motivation of this work is to apply episode mining algorithms to a new domain, architecture simulation, and to prepare an environment to make predictions about the performance of programs in different architectures. We describe our tool called Episode Mining Tool (EMT), which includes three temporal sequence mining algorithms, a preprocessor, and a visual analyzer. We present empirical analysis of the episode rules that were mined from datasets obtained by running detailed micro-architectural simulations.

DOI: 10.4018/978-1-61350-056-9.ch013

INTRODUCTION

The goal of computer architecture research is to design and build high performance systems that make effective use of resources such as space and power. The design process typically involves a detailed simulation of the proposed architecture followed by corrections and improvements based on the simulation results. Both simulator development and result analysis are very challenging tasks due to the inherent complexity of the underlying systems. In this chapter, we present our work on applying sequence mining algorithms (Mannila et al., 1997; Laxman et al. 2007) to the analysis of computer architecture simulations (Onder, 2008). Sequence mining is an important branch of data mining and was designed for data that can be viewed as a sequence of events with associated time stamps. Using sequence mining to analyze architectural simulations carries significant advantages for three main reasons. First, a time based analysis is essential because events that repeat or certain events that are clustered temporally can affect processor performance. Second, automated and well-defined techniques give more profound insights as compared to manual analysis. In the literature, there are few studies that propose using data mining and machine learning for architecture simulation analysis. In (Hamerly, et. al., 2006), clustering is used as the basic method to find repetitive patterns in a program's execution. In another recent work (Akoglu & Ezekwa, 2009), the use of sequence mining for improving the prefetching techniques is investigated. The existence of a considerable amount of unexplored uses of sequence mining for architecture simulation analysis is the third motivation for our study.

Our research methodology is as follows. We first take a micro-architecture definition developed using a special description language (Zhou & Onder, 2008). The definition includes a specification of the micro-architectural components of a computer system, how these components interact, and how they are controlled. We then simulate the written specification on benchmark programs and record the behavior of the system using a micro-architecture simulator (Onder, 2008). We finally feed the recorded results into the sequence based mining tool we developed. Our tool is called Episode Mining Tool (EMT) and consists of three modules. The first module is the data preprocessor which transforms the raw output data of the architecture simulation into processable data. The second module is the episode miner that takes the inputs along with the user specified options and applies sequence mining algorithms to generate the frequent episodes and rules seen in the data. The episode miner includes implementations of three algorithms, namely window based episode mining algorithm (Mannila et al., 1997), minimal occurrence based episode mining algorithm (Mannila et al., 1997), and non-overlapping occurrence based algorithm (Laxman et al, 2007). The third module of EMT is the visual analyzer, which produces graphical charts depicting the frequent episodes and rules.

In our experiments, the primary functionality of EMT is to generate a variety of patterns that show strong relationships between microprocessor events. In addition to this, relationship between event types and Instructions Per Cycle (IPC) changes can be investigated. Such an analysis provides information on how the particular software being run interacts with the processor and allows us to create concise information about the nature of the benchmark programs. As another analysis, it is possible to compare the patterns generated for two different architectures and to analyze the difference between them. Such a comparison provides helpful information to predict the behavior of new architectures without actually running simulations on them.

This chapter is organized as follows. In the Background Section, we describe the components of computer hardware that are related to this work, how processor performance is improved, and how simulation based techniques are used. In the Representation Section, we show how micro-architectural events are represented as time sequence data. In the Episode Mining Section, we present the algorithms implemented and used. In the Empirical Work Section, we explain the experiments performed and their results. In the Episode Mining Tool Section, we describe the features and usage of our tool. We conclude with a summary, lessons learned, and further potential applications of our findings.

BACKGROUND

The section presents an overview of the research in computer processors. We explain the main factors that contribute to processor performance and the complexities involved in modern systems. We describe the role of micro-architecture simulators in assessing performance and use this to motivate our research. For more detailed information on mis-speculation, interested readers may refer to (Shen & Lipasti, 2005, Osborne, 1980, Hennessy & Patterson, 2007).

Fundamentals of Micro-Architecture Research

The main driving force in computer architecture research is to improve processor performance. In computer architecture literature, the *iron law of processor performance* is given by the following equation (Shen & Lipasti, 2005):

The left hand side of the equation shows that a processor's performance is measured in terms of the time it takes to execute a particular program. The first factor on the right hand side of the equation shows the number of instructions that will be executed. This refers to the dynamic count of instructions as opposed to the static count, where the former may involve many iterations of the instructions in the latter due to the loops. The second factor shows the average number of machine cycles required for each instruction. Similar to the first factor, this number is a feature

of a particular program. The last factor refers to the length of time of each machine cycle and is a hardware feature. Obviously, decreasing one or more of the factors involved in the iron law will reduce execution time, and thus improve performance. In this work, we focus on the second factor, namely, how to reduce the average number of cycles each instruction takes.

The types of instructions that comprise a program are defined by the *instruction set architecture* (ISA) of the machine. Widely known ISAs are IBM 360/370 and Intel IA32. An ISA constitutes a contract between the hardware and the software and consequently is the basis for developing system software such as operating systems and compilers. Computer architecture research usually does not involve changing ISAs because alterations require updating the system software, a process that can easily take in the order of 10 years (Shen & Lipasti, 2005). As a result, much of the research is devoted to developing new micro-architectures. In fact, the main factors that contributed to the significant speed up of computers during the recent decades are the advances in the chip manufacturing technology and the advances in the parallelism internal to the processor (Hennessy & Patterson, 2007).

The average number of machine cycles spent per instruction during the execution of a program is referred to as *cycles per instruction* (CPI). The fundamental technique to increase CPI is to use processor level parallelism through instruction pipelining and multiple instruction execution. *Pipelining* splits an instruction into *stages* each of which can be overlapped with different stages of other instructions. *Multiple instruction execution* means fetching multiple instructions at a time and executing them in parallel.

We illustrate the concept of pipelining in Figure 1. The figure shows five instructions (I1 through I5) running on a pipelined processor. The five vertical bars represent the stages. In this case, there are five stages corresponding to a *pipeline depth* of five. The stages are the instruction fetch stage (IF), instruction decode/register fetch stage (ID), execution/effective address stage (EX), memory access/branch completion stage (MEM), and write-back stage (WB).

$$\frac{1}{Performance} = \frac{time}{program} = \frac{instructions}{program} \times \frac{cycles}{instruction} \times \frac{time}{cycle}$$

A pipeline depth of five allows five instructions to be executed in parallel. In this case, instruction I1 is about to complete and is in the final stage of write-back, instruction I2 is in memory access stage, instruction I3 is in execution stage, instruction I4 is in decoding stage, and instruction I5 is starting at its fetch stage. In general, perfect parallelism cannot be achieved with pipelining because the pipeline might need to stall in order to avoid incorrect execution of dependent instructions. For example, if instruction I2 uses a value that is computed by instruction I1, then these two instructions cannot execute in parallel and instruction I2 must be stalled until I1 writes the value needed by I2 to memory. There is a vast body of research that is devoted to detecting and mitigating pipeline hazards.

While pipelining overlaps different phases of instruction execution, pipelined processors are limited to the completion of at most one instruction per cycle under ideal conditions. In other words, when there are no stalls in the pipeline, a pipelined processor can achieve a cycles per instruction (CPI) value of at most one. Modern processors exceed this limit by employing multiple instruction issue. *Multiple instruction issue* is the basic principle behind *Instruction Level Parallel* processors. Multiple instruction issue is almost always combined with instruction pipelining and allows simultaneous processing of many instructions where instruction execution is overlapped both in terms of distinct instructions as well as their phases such as fetch and decode. Such processors are called *superscalar processors*. For example, a dual issue superscalar pipeline can have at most two instructions at each stage.

Similar to the case with simple pipelining, hazards occur both horizontally (between instructions in different stages) as well as vertically (between instructions in the same stage) in superscalar processors. For example, any two instructions which are simultaneously in the EX phase cannot be data-dependent on each other.

Pipelining of instruction steps and multiple instruction issue requires fetching new instructions into the pipeline at every clock cycle. For sequentially executing instructions, fetching a new instruction every cycle can easily be achieved by incrementing the program counter that is being used to fetch the current instruction so that at the beginning of the next cycle a new instruction can enter the pipeline. However, programs are not ex-

Figure 1. Five pipelined instructions

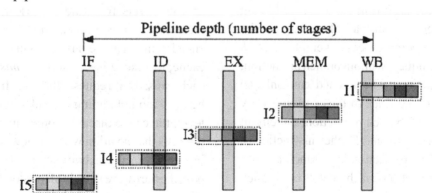

ecuted sequentially because they contain decision instructions which alter the control flow of the program. Such instructions are called *conditional branch instructions*, or, shortly *branch instructions*. These instructions test a value and based on the outcome of the test, change the program counter to either the next sequential instruction (i.e., branch not taken) or to another target instruction (i.e., branch taken). Consider the following simple if-then-else statement:

```
if (x > y) then
  z = x - y     (instruction 1)
else
  z = y - x     (instruction 2)
```

The instructions corresponding to the above statement consist of a branch instruction that jumps to the part containing **instruction 1** if the condition x>y is true. The execution sequentially proceeds to the section containing **instruction 2** if the condition is false. The layout of the machine instructions is as follows.

```
        branch if x>y to label 1
        instruction 2 (a = y - x)
        branch to label 2
label 1:  instruction 1 (a = x - y)
label 2:  the instructions following
the if statement
```

Unfortunately, in a pipelined implementation, the value of the branch condition might not be readily available because it is in the process of being computed. Therefore, instead of waiting for the outcome, contemporary processors employ *branch prediction* techniques. Without branch prediction, the next instruction to be fetched can only be determined after the value of the condition x > y is computed. With branch prediction, the circuit computes a prediction and fetches instruction 1, if the result of the prediction is ``branch taken'', and fetches instruction 2 if the result is ``branch

not taken''. This is called *speculative execution* or *control speculation*.

The prediction is typically computed by observing the past behavior of branch instructions. If the prediction is correct, the new instructions fetched by using the predicted direction and target are correct and the execution can continue unhindered. On the other hand, if the prediction is wrong, the processor must undo the effects of the incorrectly fetched instructions. In computer architecture terminology, an incorrect prediction is called a *mis-prediction*. The cost of mis-prediction is dependent on the micro-architecture of the processor and it is a function of the number of stages between the execute stage of the pipeline and the fetch stage, as well as the mechanism for restoring the state of the processor to the point before the execution of the mispredicted branch instruction. Branch prediction can also be performed statically, although this kind of prediction is currently used only by optimizing compilers, and not by contemporary processors (Hennessy & Patterson, 2007; Shen & Lipasti, 2005).

The processors of today are much faster than the memory. Therefore, most processors include multiple levels of data and instruction caches. A *cache* is a fast memory with a limited size. In this hierarchy, the processor is at the top and the cache it interacts with is called an L1 (level one) cache. Typically, an L1 cache is small and can run at a speed close to the processor's speed. Below this, there can be an L2 caches and even an L3 cache. Each cache in this sequence is slower and bigger as one travels from the processor towards the memory. Each cache keeps most frequently referenced items. If an item is not found in a particular cache, the cache is said to have *missed*. When a cache misses, it requests the item from the level below. Upon obtaining the value from the lower level, the cache discards some unused item, and replaces that position with the new one. Research in memory cache technology involves improving both the hardware speeds of memory units and the algorithms for dealing with cache misses.

The Domain of Micro-Architecture Research and Data Mining

The domain of micro-architecture offers a very rich environment suitable for the application of data mining techniques. Advanced techniques such as control and data speculation, multiple instruction processing and pipelining create an environment where it becomes extremely difficult to detect and understand the interaction of various techniques. In addition to the difficulty brought in by the interaction of these advanced techniques, the picture is further complicated by out-of-order instruction execution.

In order to achieve a high degree of instruction-level parallelism, contemporary processors find and execute instructions in a different order than the program specified order. This way, instructions are executed as early as possible based on the availability of data and resources they need. In many cases, instructions are executed speculatively as in the case of branch prediction before they are known that they should be executed. Furthermore, the order of memory operations might also be changed to facilitate the early execution of those which already have their data.

Such an approach results in a very dynamic environment in which many simultaneous events arise at any given clock cycle and these events interact with and affect each other. For example, the execution of a memory operation may result in a cache miss in a given cycle but modern processors do not wait for the cache miss to complete, but rather put the instruction that encountered the cache miss aside and continue executing other instructions. Note that an instruction that missed in the cache might actually be an instruction that has been executed speculatively and the cache miss event may be followed by a control mis-speculation event. Similarly, a previous cache miss might just complete yielding a mixture of events within a window of execution that originated at different cycles. Furthermore, this behavior is a strong function of the implemented micro-architecture as well as the program executing on this micro-architecture. For example, even if two micro-architectures differ simply in the number of buffered instructions or the number of available cache ports, the events observed during the execution of programs might differ significantly. Events such as a series of cache misses overlapping with a branch mis-prediction might not occur in one of the micro-architectures because the branch instruction may not be within the buffered instructions, or, the maximum number of cache misses has been exceeded in the other.

In addition to the interaction of various events in this dynamic environment, there is great variability in terms of instantaneous performance. Because the branch instructions disrupt the normal fetch flow, a variable number of instructions can be fetched and executed in a given cycle. As a result, the observed IPC value changes from clock cycle to clock cycle and this change is a strong function of the program that is being executed. For example, floating point intensive scientific programs typically offer highly uniform sequential blocks of instructions resulting in less variability in the observed IPC in different parts of the execution of the program. Similarly, delays originating from memory hierarchy such as cache misses significantly affect the amount of available instruction-level parallelism, i.e., the potential overlap of instruction execution, and hence the IPC (Shen & Lipasti, 2005).

Because of the complexity of the interaction of these events, state-of-the-art research techniques rely on many time consuming simulations and trial-and-error techniques. On the other hand, proper data mining driven analysis performed on the observed sequence of events, their interaction, and the effect of their interaction on performance, can present valuable hints to the micro-architect. In the next section, we illustrate how micro-architectural events can be efficiently represented and analyzed by using time sequence data mining.

Representation of Architecture Events as Sequence Data

As previously pointed out, computer architecture studies rely on simulations without exception. These simulators range from simple functional simulators to detailed cycle-accurate simulators. A *functional simulator* typically only simulates the instruction set of a processor and focuses on correct execution of programs so that the compiler, system software and operating system related software development can be carried out. *Cycle-accurate simulators* simulate the behavior of the hardware in sufficient detail so that the number of cycles observed during the simulation of a given program will be exactly the same as the number of cycles when the program is executed on a real processor.

In order to perform data mining, we use the results provided by the Flexible Architecture Simulation Toolkit (FAST) system, which is a cycle-accurate simulator developed by one of the authors (Onder, 2008). The FAST toolkit provides the means to describe and automatically generate cycle-accurate simulators from a processor description. The tool has been in use for about a decade for advanced micro-architecture studies by academia and industry researchers. The specific case we used for this chapter is a dual core superscalar processor that enters the *run-ahead* mode upon encountering a L2 cache miss. In this mode, the instructions are executed but their results are not committed to the processor state. The goal is to execute as far as possible and reference the memory addresses so that the cache requests will be initiated early. The second processor serves as a state-recovery processor and the thread running in that processor updates the processor state to the correct values once the data from the cache is returned. In other words, the simulated architecture involves the interaction of two threads originating from the same program. The *main-thread* is the actual execution of the program. The *recovery-thread* is only responsible

for repairing damaged values during the run-ahead mode. Further details of the micro-architecture are described in Zhou & Onder's article on the use of fine-grained states (2008).

Because several events take place at each cycle, we have designed a simple data set in the form of a sequence of lines where each line is in the following format:

```
<cycle> <event> <inst-PC> <mem-addr>
<block-addr> <replacement-block-addr>
```

In other words, our simulator writes a summary line for each event observed during the simulation. In this data format, only the first two are useful for sequence mining as we are interested in the interaction of various events. The rest of the line has been used to validate, track, and debug the correctness of the collected information. For example, by observing the replacement address field, we can verify the cache accesses are being simulated correctly. The instruction program counter value (inst-PC) allows us to track which instruction has actually caused the event in question. A good example is a cache miss triggered by an instruction must have the same value when the data has been loaded. For sequence mining, we filtered the data and used the format shown below:

```
<Time of occurrence> <Event type>
```

The *time of occurrence* value is simply the cycle number observed by the processor. *Event type* is represented by a number. The numbers denoting the events and the corresponding descriptions are listed in Table 1.

Prior to applying data mining algorithms, we frequently processed the original data sets multiple times for various reasons discussed in the following sections. The most important reason is the huge amount of data that results. For example, a few seconds of actual execution time for a program typically results in billions of cycles and hence gigabytes of data. In the next section, we

Table 1. The events that take place during micro-architecture simulation

Event ID	Event
01	Main-thread branch mis-prediction
02	Main-thread L1-miss
03	Main-thread L2-miss
04	Main-thread load mis-speculation
05	Main-thread rollback due to branch mis-prediction
06	Main-thread rollback due to load mis-speculation
07	Main-thread enters runahead mode
08	Recovery-thread is forked
09	Main-thread is killed due to a branch mis-prediction's rollback in recovery-thread
10	Main-thread is killed due to a load-wrong-value in recovery-thread
11	Main thread enters the blocking mode
12	Recovery-thread catches up the main-thread which is under runahead-mode. Kill the main thread.
13	Recovery-thread catches up the main-thread which is under blocking-mode. Recovery-T is done.
21	Recovery-thread branch mis-prediction
22	Recovery-thread L1-miss
23	Recovery-thread L2-miss
24	Recovery thread load
25	Recovery thread roll back due to branch missprediction
26	Recovery thread roll back due to load missprediction
100	L1 data cache: a block (block-addr) is fetched from L2, a victim (replacement-block-addr) block is kicked out if conflicted.
200	L2 data cache: a bloc k(block-addr) is fetched from memory, a victim (replacement-block-addr) block is kicked out if conflicted.

describe the algorithms we used and the results we obtained.

EPISODE MINING OF EVENT BASED ARCHITECTURE SIMULATION DATA

Computer architecture researchers are interested in identifying both expected and unexpected patterns in simulation data. The retrieval of expected patterns increase the confidence in the methodologies used. The discovery of unexpected patterns reveals previously unknown features of the programs and micro-architectures that are being investigated. Of particular interest to our research are *sequence data mining* techniques that show the relations between groups of events along a time interval. In this context, an *event* is a simple happening that takes a unit amount of time. An *episode* is a partially ordered collection of events.

The data mining tool we developed is called Episode Mining Tool (EMT) and it incorporates three types of temporal data mining algorithms that were used for mining architecture simulation data:

1. Window episode mining algorithms (WINEPI) for parallel and serial episodes developed by Mannila et al. (1997)
2. Minimal occurrence based algorithms (MINEPI) for serial and parallel episodes developed by Mannila et al. (1997)
3. Non-overlapping occurrence counting algorithms for parallel and serial episodes developed by Laxman at al. (2007)

In general, we directly employed the original pseudo code of these algorithms. However at certain points, we have made modifications due to the differences between the structure of our dataset and the reference dataset of these algorithms. A detailed presentation of the tool we developed can be found in the section "Episode Mining Tool (EMT)".

The WINEPI Approach

WINEPI is a window-based approach which counts the number of occurrences of episodes in a given dataset. The dataset is represented as an event sequence consisting of events with associated times of occurrence as shown in Figure 2. In this figure, there are 12 time points representing machine cycles and are labeled from C01 to C12. Five events take place within these 12 cycles, and no events happen during C04 through C08 and during C11 through C12. The figure also depicts sample windows of size four. The first window ends at cycle C01 and the last window begins at the last cycle (C12). A *parallel episode* is defined as a collection of events that are not ordered. For example, in Figure 2, the parallel episode consisting of events 1 and 5 appears at the time interval [C01, C02] and also at [C09, C10]. If the window size is eight or more, another occurrence in reverse order is observed at [C02, C09]. The occurrence at [C02, C09] is in reverse order. A *serial episode* is defined as a collection of events that are totally ordered. For example, [1 => 5] denotes an episode where event 1 is followed by event 5. In the figure, the interval [C02, C09] does not contain an occurrence of episode [1 => 5], whereas intervals [C01, C02] and [C09, C10] do.

The WINEPI algorithm works by generating all the episodes of length 1, keeping only those episodes with a frequency above a user defined threshold, using these to generate the episodes with length 2, and repeating this process as the episode set grows. The set of all length l+1 episodes that can be generated from the set of length l episodes is called a *candidate set*. An episode that meets or exceeds the frequency threshold is called a *frequent episode*. Retaining only the frequent episodes from the candidate set minimizes the number of candidates, reduces the number of passes on the dataset and allows the algorithm to have a time complexity that is independent of the length of the event sequence and is polynomial in the size of the collection of frequent episodes. The candidate generation operations are very similar for parallel and serial episodes.

The *frequency of an episode* is defined as the ratio of the windows containing the episode to the total number of windows. For example, in Figure 2, there are 6 windows that contain the parallel episode consisting of events 1 and 5. Thus, the frequency of this episode is 6/15=0.4. An *episode rule* is defined as an expression $\alpha => \beta$, where β is a super episode of α. The *confidence*

Figure 2. Windows of a time sequence

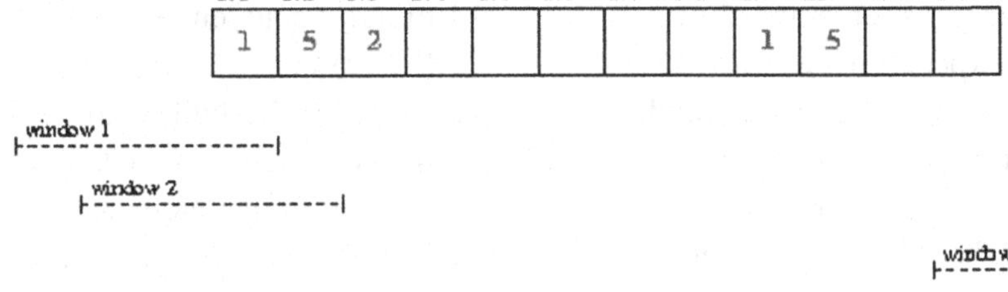

of a rule is computed by dividing the frequency of the consequence (β) with the frequency of the premise (α). For example, if an episode α with a single event 2 (L1 cache miss) has a frequency of 0.02 and an episode β with two events 2,2 has a frequency of 0.01, then the confidence of event 2 being followed by another event 2 is 0.01/0.02=0.5. In other words, the rule [2 => 2, 2] has a confidence of 0.5.

The process for finding the frequent episodes is remarkably different for parallel and serial episodes. Consider two consecutive windows w and w' where w = (t_{start}, t_{start} + win-1) and w' = (t_{start} + 1, t_{start} + win). These two windows share the events between t_{start} + 1 and t_{start} + win - 1. Therefore, after the episodes in w are recognized, the updates are done incrementally in data structures to shift the window w to get w'. In recognizing parallel episodes, a simple counter is sufficient. For each candidate parallel episode α, a counter α.event_count that holds the number of events of α that are present in the window. However, for serial episodes, a state automaton that accepts the candidate episodes needs to be used. There is an automaton for each serial episode denoted by α and there can be several instances of each automaton at the same time, so that the active states reflect the (disjoint) prefixes of α occurring in the window. For further details, the reader may refer to Mannila et al.'s description (1997).

The original algorithm has three input parameters: window width, frequency threshold and confidence threshold. We have added a fourth parameter, maximum length of the episodes to be generated. This addition is due to the fact that it may be necessary to concentrate on episodes much shorter than the window size, and helps constrain the size of the set of candidate episodes.

Although the basics of the algorithm have been followed in this work, we have made two more modifications in addition to the new parameter limiting the maximum length of episodes. The first one is that we have followed a different approach about processing the input dataset and avoided reading the entire data into memory. Reading the input file once into memory has the advantage of reducing the I/O operations. However, the simulator produces huge datasets of size 10GB or more, and it is not possible to read it entirely into main memory. Therefore, we used an iterative technique for processing the input data and kept only one window in main memory. At each iteration, the program slides from one window to the next by dropping the first event and adding the incoming event, as shown in Figure 3.

As the second modification, we changed the process of recognizing the occurrences of serial episodes in the WINEPI approach. The original algorithm keeps a single automaton per episode. In the architecture domain, we need to count all possible occurrences of an episode. Therefore, we designed a straight-forward algorithm for recognizing the occurrences of the serial episodes, which uses the sliding window mechanism. In our approach, we get all the events into the window and check whether each candidate episode

Figure 3. Window in memory

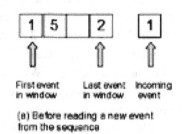

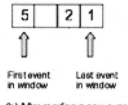

First event in window | Last event in window | Incoming event

(a) Before reading a new event from the sequence

First event in window | Last event in window

(b) After reading a new event from the sequence

occurs in this window or not. The important point is to check all combinations of the events because there may be multiple events in each cycle as shown in Figure 4. In such a situation, to check whether a candidate episode such as "{C,C,A,C}" occurs, we should check the following combinations:

- {A,B,A,A,C}: Episode does not occur
- {B,B,A,A,C}: Episode does not occur
- {C,B,A,A,C}: Episode does not occur
- {A,B,C,A,C}: Episode does not occur
- {B,B,C,A,C}: Episode does not occur
- {C,B,C,A,C}: Episode occurs

The MINEPI Approach

In the WINEPI algorithm, the episode counting is done on a per window basis. The MINEPI approach uses the minimal occurrences of episodes as the basis. The *minimal occurrence of an episode* α is defined as a time interval T such that T contains α and there are no subintervals of T that also contain α. For example, in Figure 2, the minimal occurrences of parallel episode containing events 1 and 5 are the time intervals: [C01, C02], [C02, C09], and [C09, C10]. Rather than looking at the windows and considering whether an episode occurs in a window or not, in this approach, we now look at the exact occurrences of episodes and

Figure 4. Processing multiple events in a single cycle

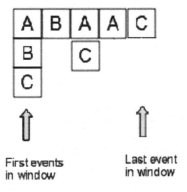

the relationships between those occurrences. One of the advantages of this approach is that focusing on the occurrences of episodes allows us to more easily find rules with two window widths, one for the left-hand side and one for the whole rule, such as "if A and B occur within 15 seconds, then C follows within 30 seconds" (Mannila et al., 1997). Our implementation follows the original algorithm. For each frequent episode, we store information about the locations of its minimal occurrences. In the recognition phase we can then compute the locations of the minimal occurrences of a candidate episode α as a temporal join of the minimal occurrences of two subepisodes of α_1 and α_2 of α. To be more specific, for serial episodes the two subepisodes are selected so that α_1 contains all events except the last one and α_2 in turn contains all except the first one. For parallel episodes, the subepisodes α_1 and α_2 contain all events except one; the omitted events must be different.

The Non-Overlapping Episodes Approach

The WINEPI and MINEPI algorithms allow episodes to overlap and this results in observing more occurrences of a superepisode than the episode itself. To remedy this situation, Laxman et al. (2007) define *non-overlapping episodes* as two episodes that do not share any events and define algorithms that use this concept. Consider the example shown in Figure 5. In the given time sequence, two overlapping occurrences of the serial episode "1 followed by 2" can be observed. These two episodes overlap because they share event 1 at cycle C01. In the same sequence, four overlapping occurrences of the episode "1 followed by 2, which is followed by 3" can be observed. As a result, the super-episode appears more frequently than the episode itself. When overlapping occurrences are disregarded, both episodes appear only once in the same time sequence.

The non-overlapping algorithm has the same worst-case time and space complexities as the

Figure 5. Non-overlapping occurrences

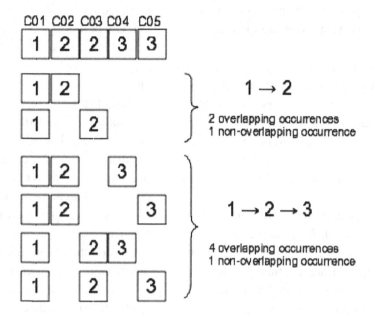

windows-based counting algorithms. However, empirical investigations reveal that the non-overlapped occurrence based algorithm is more efficient in practice. Our implementation follows the basic algorithm (Laxman et al., 2007). In order to count the non-overlapped occurrences of an episode, we need only one automaton. Until the automaton reaches its final state, we do not need a new instance of this automaton after the initialization. The same methods in the WINEPI implementation have been used in order to generate candidate episodes in each iteration and rule generation process.

EXPERIMENTS AND RESULTS

We have conducted a series of experiments, which involve the steps of micro-architecture development, simulation data collection, data mining tool runs, filtering and analysis by the domain experts. During this endeavor, we have collected about 25

gigabytes of data using the Spec 2000 benchmark suite. The benchmarks have been simulated for about 10 million cycles. In all runs, window sizes of 4, 8, 16 and 32 events have been used with very low threshold values ranging from 0.1 to 10^{-9} with the purpose of capturing rare episodes. After analyzing the results of hundreds of runs during the exploration phase, we focused on three sets of experiments. In the first and the second sets we analyzed the episode rules mined from unfiltered and filtered datasets, respectively. In the third set, we used datasets that were generated from program structure rather than micro-architecture event sequences and explored the resulting patterns.

The first set of experiments was conducted using the simulator results on a superscalar microprocessor with dual processors. The original data set contained 12,377,038 cycles corresponding to the execution of the program and had a size of about 25 GB. We applied the WINEPI algorithm with a window size of 4 and used 0.00 for the frequency threshold in order to obtain all the possible rules. We generated both parallel and serial episodes and the interpreted the results in two categories, namely, rules with high confidence and rules with low confidence.

In the high confidence category, we thoroughly scanned the rules with top confidence values and we discovered "expected and present," "coincidental," "expected but not present," and "unexpected" rules. In Table 2, we present a subset of the rules generated by our tool where the rule confidence is equal to 1.0 and the rules are "expected and present".

Some rules appeared to be coincidental, even with a confidence of 1.0. For example rules [1 => 1, 7], [7 => 1, 7], [1 => 1, 8] and [8 => 1, 8] bear no significance from an architectural perspective. Event 1 denotes a branch mis-prediction and does not have a causal relationship to events 7 (entering run-ahead mode) or 8 (forking the recovery thread). Other examples of coincidental rules are [3, 26 => 1, 3, 26], [4, 26 => [1, 4, 26] and [5, 200] => [5, 200, 100]. In the first two, events 3 and 4 refer to events in the main-thread, whereas event 26 is a recovery-thread event. In the last rule, event 5 is main-thread rollback due to branch mis-speculation and events 100 and 200 are related to cache fetches.

Notably missing from the set of expected rules are rules such as [7 => 8, 11, 13] indicating that once the main-thread enters run-ahead mode (7), it should fork the recovery thread (8), the main-thread should enter blocking mode where it is waiting for the recovery thread to finish (11) and the recovery thread catches up the main-thread (13). This rule is not found by the WINEPI algorithm because there are hundreds or thousands of events between the beginning and the ending of such sequences. With the limited window sizes that can practically be used, the sequence never resides in the window completely. We tackle this problem through filtering and discuss the results later in this section.

We observed a number of rules which were not readily obvious to the micro-architect ("unexpected" rules). The rule [3, 26 => 1, 3, 26] is quite interesting because it indicates that whenever the main thread L2 miss (3) coincides with a recovery thread load mis-speculation (26), this always happens when there is a branch mis-prediction (1). This is a consequence of the features of the micro-architecture used in the study. In the micro-architecture implementation, the processor never speculates a load instruction again if the particular load instruction has been misspeculated in the past. For the recovery thread to misspeculate the load, it should not have seen the load instruction before; for the main thread, a branch mis-prediction shows that the main thread is executing a piece of code it should not have been executing. In this case, it is likely that the code contains data references that have not been touched before, which explains the L2 miss. Since the recovery thread is following main-thread's branch predictions, it in turn means the code area is new to the recovery thread as well and this results in a load mis-speculation in the recovery thread. The rule [4, 26 => 1, 4, 26] is the sister rule to [3, 26 => 1, 3, 26], this time the same phenomenon happening in the main-thread only. These rules show that branch mis-predictions, load mis-speculations and cache misses are inherently related with each other. Although this relationship is known to exist, the WINEPI results strongly

Table 2. Sample high-confidence rules out of WINEPI which were expected

Rule	Explanation
[7 => 7, 8]	Run-ahead mode main thread always forks the recovery thread.
[25 => 25, 9]	When the recovery thread gets a branch mis-prediction, the main thread is killed.
[3, 200 => 3, 200, 100]	Main thread L2 miss, L2 data fetch coincides with L1 misses.
[1 => 1, 5]	Branch mis-prediction leads to rollback.

confirm that the relationship is stronger than what is believed in the domain.

The rule [5, 200 => 5, 200, 100] indicates that a roll-back after a branch mis-prediction (5) that coexists with an L2 data fetch event (200) will result in an L1 fetch event (100) as well. This rule indicates that some of the data fetches initiated during a mispredicted branch will arrive after the mis-prediction has been detected. The studied micro-architecture follows the common practice and does not tag data requests to the memory with respect to branch instructions. Further investigation of benefits of such tagging is necessary, nevertheless the observation is quite interesting.

Besides these high confidence rules which were found through the WINEPI experimentation, lower confidence, yet significant observations have also been made. During the program execution in a speculative processor, multiple branch mis-predictions may be observed in rapid succession. One of the main reasons behind this observation is the exploitation of instruction-level parallelism. The processor issues multiple instructions at each cycle and never waits for the resolution of branches as long as pending branch instructions continue to resolve correctly, i.e., predictions continue to be correct. As a result, at any given time there are many branch instructions waiting for resolution. When one of these branch instructions is mis-predicted, several others preceeding this branch might have been mispredicted as well. This fact is supported through a rule [1 => 1, 1]: a branch mis-prediction (1) leads to multiple branch mis-predictions (1, 1).

On a few occasions, similar to the phenomenon discussed above branch mis-predictions (1) may lead to additional cache misses (3). The rule [1 => 1, 3] shows such expected clustering of events.

Rule [4 => 1, 4] indicates that an incorrect load value obtained from a load speculation may trigger branch mis-speculations, obviously unexpectedly. This rule is another example which yields information that is not common knowledge in computer architecture. Although a deeper analysis of the processor behaviour is needed to assess the frequency and the importance of the phenomenon, it clearly is a case which indicates that there is merit in investigating architectural simulation data using data mining techniques.

In order to understand this particular case better, consider the process of load speculation in an ILP processor. Load speculation is the process of executing load instructions out of program order, before preceeding store instructions complete. Consider the following code:

```
I1:         SW  $8, a1
I2:         LW  $4, a2
```

If I2 is executed before I1 and a1 != a2, this will lead to improved performance because the instructions waiting for the value of register 4 can proceed sooner. If a1 = a2, the load instruction will obtain the stale value from the memory and a load mis-speculation will result. We reason that the observed case arises because of the interaction of load mis-speculation with branch prediction and validation. Consider the sequence:

```
I1:         SW  $8, a1
I2:         LW  $4, a2
I3:         Beq $4, $8, L1
```

and assume that I3 has been correctly predicted. However, if the load has been speculatively executed and the speculation is not successful the load will obtain the wrong value. The branch instruction, although correctly predicted, may be considered an incorrect prediction because the processor upon verifying the values of $4 and $8 does not find them to be equal. Note that the processor would correctly conclude that the branch was correctly predicted had the memory operations been executed in program order. As a result, we observe [4 => 1, 4], i.e., a load mis-speculation (4) leads to a branch mis-prediction (1) as well as an additional load mis-speculation (4).

Each set of experiments clearly indicates the need to apply domain specific information and filter the data as necessary. This is a necessity due to several reasons. First of all, the sheer size of the collected event data makes it very difficult to seek relationships among events which are too far away from each other. The required window size and the resulting computational needs are very difficult to meet, even with a well thought-out and efficient implementation of the existing algorithms. Second, some of the architectural events are rare and their observation requires very low settings of threshold values. This in turn results in unacceptably high computational times. It is much more efficient to filter the information from the dataset which is known to be unnecessary or unrelated, based on the domain knowledge. As a result, in our second set of experiments we progressively applied filtering as data mining results showed both known and unknown relationships among the micro-architectural events. In these experiments, we extracted the rules for parallel episodes using 0.0005 for frequency and confidence thresholds, and varying window sizes of 4, 8, 16, and 32.

In order to observe the effects of window size on the results, we have filtered event sequences which have an opening and closing event associated with them. One such example was discussed previously, after going into the run-ahead mode, a certain sequence of events should happen and eventually, the run-ahead mode should terminate. Removing these event sequences from the input file enabled the WINEPI algorithm discover relationships among events separated from each other by long distances. In this respect, one well-known fact in computer architecture research is that cache misses are clustered. In other words, when the processor experiences a cache miss, it is followed by a sequence of additional cache misses. This is because, when there is a cache miss for a particular item that is part of the program's working set, the rest of the working set is also not in the cache. What is not known clearly is how these clusters are related to each other. In the following

experiment, we have collected data and listed those with the highest confidence. Rules [7 => 7, 8] and [8 => 7, 8] had been explained before. Rule [3, 3, 2 => 3, 3, 2, 2] illustrates the clustering effect. Both L1 and L2 cache misses rapidly follow each other. This local cluster is easily seen by even a small window size, but all such rules indicate an interesting behavior. As shown in Table 3 and Figure 6, as the window size is increased, the confidence also increases. Although further analysis would make a better case, it is quite likely that the observed behavior is due to encountering clusters of cache misses which are close to each other. Such inter-cluster formation is difficult to see in smaller window sizes, but as the window size gets bigger, additional cache misses from the following cluster also can be seen and analyzed by the episode miner.

Table 3 indicates the results of filtering in this manner. Each row indicates the confidence values observed at the given window size indicated by the column. Events 5, 6, 9, 10, 11, 12, 13, 25, 26, 100 and 200 have been removed from the data set. These events are closing events for micro-architecture events that have a beginning and ending. The corresponding graph is plotted in Figure 6. Observe that rules such as [7 => 7, 8] have very little variation as a function of window size since their occurrence is in close proximity always, whereas rules which have events separated far from each other demonstrates consistent increase in confidence values as the window size is increased.

Using data mining in the computer architecture domain is not limited to analyzing the relationship among events observed through the micro-architecture studies. In fact, programs and their behavior can also be analyzed using episode mining. In order to illustrate the concept, we have modified our micro-architecture simulator so that upon seeing certain types of instructions, it generates a corresponding event. By representing critical instructions as events, it becomes possible to see how the interaction of various instructions

Table 3. Effect of window size on rule confidence

Rules	4	8	16	32
[7 => 7, 8]	1	1	1	1
[8 => 7, 8]	1	1	1	1
[3, 3, 2 => 3, 3, 2, 2]	0.947425	0.952256	0.953822	0.95738
[3, 23, 23 => 3, 3, 23, 23]	0.938679	0.956189	0.973992	0.97849
[3, 23 => 3, 3, 23]	0.938033	0.953017	0.966461	0.965144
[3, 2, 2 => 3, 3, 2, 2]	0.930421	0.942661	0.950478	0.96378
[2 => 2, 2]	0.925434	0.942002	0.948303	0.95308
[3, 3, 23 => 3, 3, 23, 23]	0.920951	0.951008	0.95706	0.969514
[3, 23 => 3, 23, 23]	0.920318	0.947853	0.94966	0.956289
[3, 2 => 3, 2, 2]	0.913168	0.938552	0.946946	0.954705

relate to observable performance criteria such as IPC. For this purpose, we focus on instructions that change the program's control flow: function calls, function returns, backward and forward branch instructions. Each of these instructions is assigned an event id as given below:

Figure 6. Graph plot for the effect of window size on rule quality

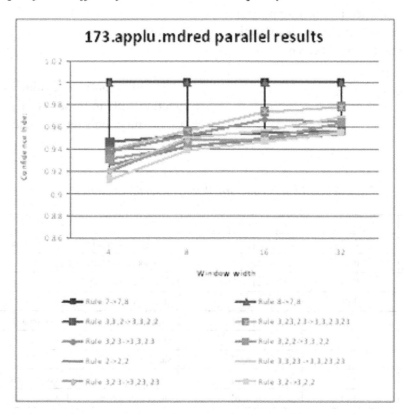

```
Event ID    Instruction
1           backward branch
2           forward branch
3           function return
4           function call
5            load
6            store
```

We have analyzed the resulting data set using our tool with WINEPI for serial episodes. Table 4 shows a summary of the highest confidence rules.

In architectures which use load and store instructions to access memory, every function starts with a series of store instructions to save the contents of the register and they reload the values of the register before returning. It is highly likely that most store clustering (rule 7) occurs because of this phenomenon. Although, this is common knowledge in the domain, data mining results point to new micro-architecture designs can exploit the fact that multiple store instructions would be forth-coming once a function call is detected. A very frequent type of operation in most programs is to test a value, and conditionally load a value, or, modify a storage location's value.

For example:

```
if (a < b)
{
z= 5;
```

```
// this really becomes a store
}
```

is captured by rule 5 and it is quite frequent. Similarly, consider the same piece of code, this time slightly modified:

```
if (a < b)
    {
    z=x; //this may be a load and a
store, or no store, or no load,
        // depending on the avail-
ability of the values in registers.
    }
```

Such code is responsible for rule 5, and possibly 10. One of the most interesting observations is the capture of the program's structure through rule 1:

```
if (foo() < 1)
    {
        // this really is a forward
branch
    }
```

The high confidence value indicates that most function calls in these set of programs actually test the function's return value.

Table 4. Summary of highest confidence rules for WINEPI serial episodes

Rule number	Confidence	Rule	Explanation
1	0.67	[3 => 3, 2]	Function return is followed by a forward branch.
2	0.67	[4 => 4, 6]	Function call is followed by a store.
3	0.63	[5 => 5, 5]	Loads are clustered.
4	0.57	[6 => 6, 6]	Stores are clustered.
5	0.56	[2 => 2, 5]	Forward branches are followed by a store.
6	0.52	[6, 6 => 6, 6, 6]	Stores are clustered.
7	0.50	[4, 6 => 4, 6, 6]	Same as (6)
8	0.50	[5, 4 => 5, 4, 6]	Load, function call is followed by store.
9	0.50	[6, 4 => 6, 4, 6]	Store, function call is followed by store.
10	0.37	[5, 2 => 5, 2, 5]	Load followed by forward branch is followed by further loads.

Our results demonstrate that the application of data mining in the computer architecture and compiler domain enhances the analysis capabilities beyond what is typically achieved through profiling. While profiling can provide exact information about a particular point in the program, data mining provides global knowledge about the structure of the program.

EPISODE MINING TOOL (EMT)

General Properties

Episode Mining Tool (EMT) is a tool developed to investigate the relationships between events in a given event sequence. It was designed to incorporate a variety of sequence mining algorithms for parallel and serial episodes, to provide support in the domain of micro-architecture simulations, and to facilitate ease of use by researchers. The tool was implemented in Java programming language and includes specific features for mining architectural events. However, it is general purpose, provides fundamental functionalities, and can be used for episode mining in other domains. Interested users can access the EMT site through the authors' websites at http://www.cs.mtu.edu and http://ceng.metu.edu.tr.

The main features of EMT are as follows:

- Before processing the input data, the event types can be filtered in order to concentrate on certain event types.
- The tool supports the analysis of input data containing IPC values with the events.
- It is possible to analyze the input data in unconventional formats such as an input file containing several event sequences where each one is written in a separate line. In such a case, these lines are processed as if they are separate input files.
- Users can analyze the event sequences with any of the three episode mining techniques in the tool under window width, minimum support threshold and minimum confidence threshold parameters.
- The patterns generated by episode mining can be visually analyzed with respect to support, confidence and length of the patterns.
- Multiple output files can be analyzed in a single step and they can be grouped with respect to the common rules or episodes.

Components of EMT

There are three main components in EMT:

- ***Data pre-processor:*** This component includes pre-processing operations that can be applied on dataset and generates a new input file with a postfix "_processed". The supported pre-processing operations are as follows:
    - Event types that will not be included in the analysis and thus will be filtered can be specified.
    - If there are IPC values in the input sequence, the pre-processor can compute the changes in the IPC values and produce a new input file containing the "delta-IPC" values.
    - If the input file includes a set of sequences where each one is represented with a line, the pre-processor generates a new input files for each sequence.
- ***Episode miner:*** This component provides the core data mining functionalities of EMT. It provides window based, minimal occurrence based and non-overlapping occurrence based episode mining for serial and parallel episodes. The selected technique generates frequent patterns for the input data (after pre-processing if necessary) under the provided parameters. The generated output file includes frequent episodes with their

frequency values and strong rules with their confidence values.

- *Visual analyzer:* This component is the visualization part of EMT. Extracted frequent episodes and rules can be presented in the form of various types of graphs. In addition, multiple output files can be analyzed together and grouped with respect to support or confidence values in a single step.

Usage

EMT has two usage modes: *command line mode* and *GUI mode*. The command line mode was designed to facilitate automated processing of the results. In this mode, the results are written into a file that becomes an input file for further analysis. The pre-processor and episode miner components, which are actually two separate executable files, can be used in the command line mode. The visual analyzer component, on the other hand, contains the GUI modules and presents the resulting patterns in the form of human friendly charts. Therefore, in the GUI mode, in addition to pre-processor and episode miner components, output analyzer is also available.

- **The GUI Mode:** When EMT starts running in GUI mode, the very first screen presents the operations menu, from which the user can either select pre-processing, episode mining or output analysis as the operation.

If pre-processing operation is selected, the user is firstly asked to specify the file to be worked on through the browser. As the first pre-processing task, the user can specify the event types to be filtered as depicted in Figure 7.

Once this specification is completed, according to the structure of the input file, the type of pre-processing operation is selected and applied. If the dataset contains IPC values, a new input is generated according to the changes in IPC values. If the input dataset contains unique sequences, new input files can be generated for each of the line in dataset. The pre-processing method selection interface is presented in Figure 8.

For investigating the relationships between the rules of unique sequences and IPC changes, we should first provide an input file in an appropriate form. To this aim, another operation called "Process Unique Sequence Lists with IPC changes" is provided. In addition, the user can enter IPC change level. Another operation available

Figure 7. Filtering event types in GUI mode

under the pre-processing component is filtering the results obtained from episode mining operation.

If episode mining operation is selected, user is firstly asked to select the technique to be applied for each type of episodes from the algorithm menu, which includes the following menu items:

- WINEPI Parallel Episodes
- WINEPI Serial Episodes
- Non-overlapping Parallel Episodes
- Non-overlapping Serial Episodes
- MİNEPI Parallel Episodes
- MINEPI Serial Episodes

According to the selected algorithm, the user provides the relevant parameters such as window width, minimum frequency threshold, minimum confidence threshold, maximum episode length and input types of events to be ignored, through the dialog boxes of EMT. Then, the user selects the input file containing the dataset to be processed according to the chosen method. Finally, the user gives the name of the output file where the results

to be written and when the execution is completed, the user is notified.

If the output analyzer operation is selected, the results of episode mining operations can be visualized in different types of charts. As the first step, the user should specify whether the output analysis would be done on single or multiple outputs. The user interface for this selection is shown in Figure 9.

Once this selection is completed, the user is prompted for file selection through the browser. As the next step, the user specifies whether to analyze episodes or rules. Afterwards, in order to limit the number of items to be visualized, user can select the length of rules or episodes. Lastly, the chart type for visualization is selected through the GUI. In Figure 10, a sample visual analysis is shown in which the grouping of rules from multiple outputs are represented as a bar chart with respect to their confidence values.

The command-line mode: In command line, the user gives the necessary parameters to run pre-processor and the results are printed to the

Figure 8. Selecting the pre-processing method in GUI mode

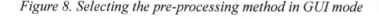
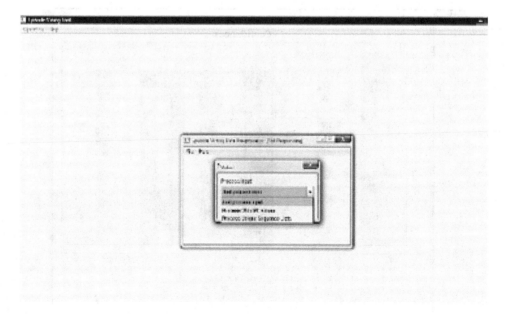

Figure 9. Output analysis on single or multiple outputs

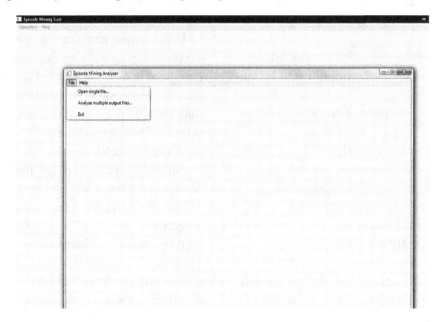

specified output file. Here, the parameters should be given in the following format:

```
DataPreProcessor.jar <input file>
<outputFile> <option>
```

The option can be "--IPC" to process the input containing IPC values, "--unique-sequence" to process the input file containing unique sequences in its each line, "--AnalyseRulesWithIPC" to generate rules obtained from unique sequences and

Figure 10. Resulting chart after grouping the output files in GUI mode

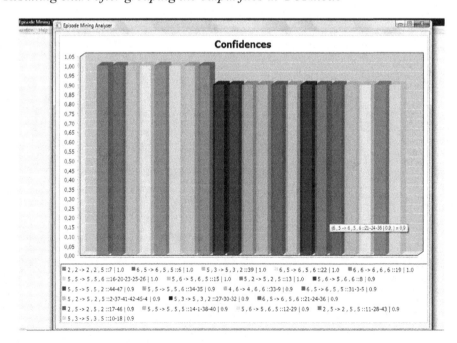

IPC changes in given files and "--filterAnalysis" to filter the rules containing only a rule and an IPC level value. A sample command is given below:

```
D:\>DataPreProcessor.jar input.dat
output.txt --IPC
```

For episode mining, the user supplies the parameters in the following format:

```
EpisodeMiner.jar <input file> <win-
dow width> <min frequency> <max epi-
sode length> <min confidence> <algo-
rithm string> <output file> <window
width-2>
```

Here, the parameter "window width-2" is used only for MINEPI algorithm and the parameter *algorithm string* is an option string containing 6 characters where each of these characters represent an implemented algorithm and must be either 0 or 1. The order of the algorithms to be specified is as follows:

- WINEPI for parallel episodes
- WINEPI for serial episodes
- Non-overlapping counts for parallel episodes
- Non-overlapping counts for serial episodes
- MINEPI for parallel episodes
- MINEPI for serial episodes

Below we show a sample episode miner call. In this example, the command line with the algorithm string as "000001" denotes selecting only "MINEPI for serial episodes".

```
D:\>EpisodeMiner.jar input.dat 3 0.01
4 0.05 000001 output.txt 5
```

CONCLUSION

Data mining is an important tool for data-rich domains. One of the branches of data mining is mining sequence data where the data can be viewed as a sequence of events each having a time of occurrence. Sequence and episode mining techniques and algorithms have been applied to various domains such as medicine or telecommunications. The motivation of this work is to apply episode mining algorithms to a new domain, architecture simulation, and to prepare an environment to make predictions about the performance of programs in different architectures. In micro-architecture research, the behavior of designed architectures are observed through simulations on benchmark programs. These simulations generate outputs consisting of sequence of program execution events occurring at each clock cycle. This provides a very rich environment for applying sequence mining techniques. Extracting patterns about the behavior of the designed architecture can facilitate the process of improving the design in two ways. First, in addition to expected patterns, sequence mining can reveal previously undetected behavior patterns. Second, this automated approach shortens the analysis of simulation results, which is conventionally held manually. Furthermore, it may even be possible to make predictions about behavior without simulation.

Within the scope of this study, we have developed an analysis tool named *Episode Mining Tool (EMT)*, in order to analyze the architecture simulation results. The tool includes the implementation of three different episode mining techniques: window-based episode mining, non-overlapping occurrence based episode mining and minimal occurrences based episode mining. In addition to the episode mining module, EMT includes modules for pre-processing and visualization of the generated patterns. The pre-processing module supports several features that are specific to the domain, such as handling the IPC values in the data set.

We have conducted several analyses on benchmark results by using EMT. As the first analysis task, we have found patterns involving a limited set of events that are accurate for architecture simulation. Therefore, we have accomplished our first goal for finding patterns supporting the expected behaviors and some general rules for the computer architecture by using sequence mining techniques. In order to discover new patterns that can facilitate predicting the behavior of programs, we have further analyzed the program executions and we have observed that the program blocks can be summarized and represented by a set of unique sequences. Therefore, we have analyzed these unique sequences, and generated rules showing the characteristic behavior of the program blocks. In addition, we have analyzed the IPC changes between the executions of blocks in different architectures and extracted relationships between IPC change values and the rules. As a result, these relationships discovered in EMT may help predicting the performance of a program in a given architecture without running or simulating the program.

This work provided invaluable experiences to the collaborators who had very diverse backgrounds:

- Several trials were needed to understand and select the most suitable algorithms and parameters. We ran the experiments many times to understand the effects of window size and frequency thresholds.
- We learned to deal with huge datasets by restricting the event types and number of episodes. This helped keep experiment run times reasonable but most were still in the range of several days.
- The analysis of the mining results required several iterations. Most of the application domains in the literature reviewed are suitable for finding the rules with highest frequencies. In our micro-architecture domain, we are also interested in the patterns

of rule occurrence such as, where are the cache misses are clustered, how do the rule confidences change within different sections of the program, or can any anomalies be observed in the processor's behavior. As a result, we had to set very low values for frequency thresholds and had to deal with a plethora of rules that looked identical.

The work described in this chapter lays the foundation for future work in a number of directions. For example, in this work, instance based events are considered and the duration of the events are not analyzed. In order to extend this approach, continuous events having duration values may be evaluated by using temporal data mining techniques. Therefore, more interesting and hidden relations between sequences and subsequences of events might be discovered. The visualization module can be further improved to facilitate effective communication of the results to the domain experts in micro-architecture or other domains. Especially, the output analyzer component can be considered as a starting point and more visual features such as time series charts containing frequent episodes or confident rules generated from program blocks can be added to aid with the analysis of results. In the future, it will be interesting to relate the performance of the program to its structure through the use of data mining.

REFERENCES

Akleman, L., & Ezekwa, C. U. (2009). *FREQuest: Prefetching in the light of frequent episodes*. Retrieved from http://www.cs.cmu.edu/~lakoglu/classes/arch_paper.pdf

Hamerly, G., Perelman, E., Lau, J., Calder, B., & Sherwood, T. (2006). Using machine learning to guide architecture simulation. *Journal of Machine Learning Research*, 7, 343–378.

Hennessy, J. L., & Patterson, D. A. (2007). *Computer architecture: A quantitative approach* (4th ed.). Amsterdam, Holland: Elsevier.

Laxman, S., Sastry, P. S., & Unnikrishnan, K. P. (2007). A fast algorithm for finding frequent episodes in event streams. In P. Berkhin, R. Caruana, & X. Wu (Eds.), *Proceedings of the Thirteenth ACM SIGKDD International Conference on Knowledge Discovery and Data Mining (KDD-07)* (pp. 410-419).

Mannila, H., Toivonnen, H., & Verkamo, A. I. (1997). Discovery of frequent episodes in event sequences. *Data Mining and Knowledge Discovery, 1*(3), 259–289. doi:10.1023/A:1009748302351

Onder, S. (2008). ADL++: Object-oriented specification of complicated instruction sets and micro-architectures. In P. Mishra and N. Dutt (Eds.), *Processor description languages, volume 1 (systems on Silicon)* (pp. 247-274). Burlington, MA: Morgan Kaufmann (Elsevier) Publishers.

Osborne, A. (1980). *An introduction to microcomputers, vol 1: Basic concepts* (2nd ed.).

Rau, B. R., & Fisher, J. A. (1993). Instruction-level parallel processing: History, overview and perspective. *The Journal of Supercomputing, 7*(1-2), 9–50. doi:10.1007/BF01205181

Shen, J. P., & Lipasti, M. H. (2005). *Modern processor design: Fundamentals of superscalar processors*. New York, NY: McGraw-Hill Companies.

Zhou, P., & Onder, S. (2008). Improving single-thread performance with fine-grain state maintenance. In A. Ramirez, G. Bilardi, & M. Gschwind N (Eds.), *Proceedings of the 5th Conference on Computing Frontiers (CF-08)* (pp. 251-260). New York, NY: ACM.

ADDITIONAL READING

Data Mining Agrawal, R., Imielinski, T., & Swami, A. N. (1993). *Mining Association Rules between Sets of Items in Large Databases* (pp. 207–216). SIGMOD.

Fang, W., Lu, M., Xiao, X., Hel, B., & Luo, Q. (2009). *Frequent Itemset Mining on Graphics Processors, Data Management On New Hardware*, Proceedings of the Fifth International Workshop on Data Management on New Hardware, Session: Exploiting parallel hardware, pages: 34 – 42.

Hand, D., Mannila, H., & Smyth, P. (2001). *Principles of Data Mining*, Massachusetts Institute of Technology, 2001, ISBN 0-262-08290-X.

Jin, R., & Agrawal, G. (2005). *An Algorithm for In-Core Frequent Itemset Mining on Streaming Data*. Fifth IEEE International Conference on Data Mining (ICDM'05), pages:210-217.

Keogh, E., Lonardi, S., & Ratanamahatana, C. A. (2004). Towards Parameter-Free Data Mining. In R. Kohavi, J. Gehrke, & W. DuMouchel (Eds.) *Proceedings of the 10th ACM SIGKDD International Conference on Knowledge Discovery and Data Mining (KDD-04)* (pp. 205-215).

Kotsiantis, S., & Kanellopoulos, D. (2006). Association Rules Mining: A Recent Overview. *International Transactions on Computer Science and Engineering*, vol:32 pages:71-82.

Margahny, M. H. & and Mitwaly, A. A. (2007). Fast Algorithm for Mining Association Rules. *International Journal of computer and software*, vol:2 No:1.

Nanyang, Q. Z. (2003). *Sequential Pattern Mining: A Survey*. Technical Report 2003118, Nanyang Technological University, Singapore.

Ramakrishnan, N. (2009). The pervasiveness of data mining and machine learning. *IEEE Computer, 42*(8), 28–29.

Seifert, J. W. (2004). Analyst in Information Science and Technology Policy Resources, CRS Report RL31798, *Data Mining: An Overview.*

Usama, F., Piatetsky-Shapiro, G, & Smyth, P. (1996). From Data Mining to Knowledge Discovery in Databases, *AI Magazine,* vol:17 pages:37-54.

Wang, J., & Han, J. (2004). *BIDE: Efficient Mining of Frequent Closed Sequences.* ICDE, Proceedings of the 20th International Conference on Data Engineering, page:79, ISBN:0-7695-2065-0.

Wojciechowski, M., & Maciej Zakrzewicz, (2004). *Data Mining Query Scheduling for Apriori Common Counting.* 6th Int'l Baltic Conf. on Databases and Information Systems.

Yun, U., & Leggett, J. J. (2005), *WFIM: Weighted Frequent Itemset Mining with a weight range and a minimum weigh*t, SIAM International Data Mining Conference.

Zaïane, O. R. (1999). *CMPUT690 Principles of Knowledge Discovery in Databases, University of Alberta, Chapter-1.* Introduction to Data Mining.

Zaki, M. J., & Ching-Jui H. (2005). CHARM: An Efficient Algorithm for Closed Itemset Mining. *IEEE Transactions on Knowledge and Data Engineering,* vol:17 issue:4, pages: 462-278.

Agarwal, B. (Fall 2004). *Instruction Fetch Execute Cycle.* CS 518 Montana State University.

Jimenez, D. A. (2003). *Reconsidering Complex Branch Predictors.* In Proceedings of the 9th International Symposium on High-Performance Computer Architecture, page:43.

Johnson, J. D. (1992, December). *Branch Prediction Using Large Self History.* Stanford University, Technical Report No. CSL-TR-92-553.

Laplante, P. A. (2001). *Dictionary of Computer Science, Engineering and Technology.* CRC Press, 2001, ISBN 0849326915.

McKee, S. A. (2004). *Reflections on the memory wall.* Conference On Computing Frontiers, Special session on memory wall, page: 162.

Murdocca, M., & Vincent Heuring, V. (2007). *Computer Architecture and Organization, An Integrated Approach.* Wiley.

Shen, J. P., & Lipasti, M. (2005). *Modern processor design: Fundamentals of Superscalar Processors.* ISBN 0-07-057064-7.

Thisted, R. A. (1998). *Computer Architecture, Encyclopedia of Biostatistics. Wiley* (5th ed.). New York: Kip Irvine, Assembly Language for Intel-Based Computers.

Tullsen, D. M., Eggers, S. J., & Levy, H. M. (1995). *Simultaneous multithreading: maximizing on-chip parallelism.* International Symposium on Computer Architecture, pages: 392-403.

Yeh, T., & Yale, N. Patt, Y. N. (1991). *Two-level adaptive training branch prediction.* International Symposium on Micro-architecture, pages: 51–61.

Chapter 14
Sequence Pattern Mining for Web Logs

Pradeep Kumar
Indian Institute of Management Lucknow, India

Raju S. Bapi
University of Hyderabad, India

P. Radha Krishna
Infosys Labs, Infosys Limited, India

ABSTRACT

Interestingness measures play an important role in finding frequently occurring patterns, regardless of the kind of patterns being mined. In this work, we propose variation to the AprioriALL Algorithm, which is commonly used for the sequence pattern mining. The proposed variation adds up the measure interest during every step of candidate generation to reduce the number of candidates thus resulting in reduced time and space cost. The proposed algorithm derives the patterns which are qualified and more of interest to the user. The algorithm, by using the interest, measure limits the size the candidates set whenever it is produced by giving the user more importance to get the desired patterns.

INTRODUCTION

Finding frequent sequence pattern from large transactional databases is one of the successful data mining endeavors introduced by Agarwal and Srikant (1995). It obtains frequent sequential patterns of items satisfying the condition that the number of their occurrences, called support, in the item sequence, called transaction database, is greater than or equal to a given threshold, called

DOI: 10.4018/978-1-61350-056-9.ch014

minimum support. The obtained frequent patterns could be applied to analysis and decision making in applications like time-series stock trend, web page traversal, customer purchasing behavior, content signature of network applications, etc.

The task of sequence pattern mining is to discover the frequently occurring subsequences from the large sequence database. Regardless of how frequent these sequences occur it is also required to exploit the relationships among the sequences.

One of the challenging problems with sequence generating systems is the large number of sequences being generated. These generated rules may be of no practical value or interest to the analyst. To overcome the problem researchers have started using to measure the usefulness or interestingness of rules. Whenever a interestingness measure is applied, there is clear tradeoff between accuracy and the coverage of knowledge.

Interestingness decreases with coverage for a fixed number of correct responses (remember accuracy equals the number of correct responses divided by the coverage).

In this chapter our focus is to mine sequential patterns from sequence database. For this work we choose web usage mining domain is used to demonstrate our approach. The current approach is highly applicable in any domain where data exhibits sequentiality in nature.

In this chapter we introduce a general framework of mining sequential patterns using interest measure. The sequential patterns obtained due to the modified algorithm are compared to the original sequence pattern mining algorithm, AprioriALL (Agarwal &Agarwal, 1995).

Our research is motivated by following two observations:

- Limited customization, the user has no option to choose the type of pattern catering to his need depending on his interest.
- The patterns derived are not interesting as Support is not a good interestingness measure for either association rules or sequential patterns.

Now we formally define our research problem addressed in this work. The problem of Sequential Pattern Mining in general to web mining can be stated as "Given a set of user sessions,, with each session consisting of a list of elements and each element consisting of a set of items and given user specified minimum interest value, min_support, the problem is to generate all candidates which satisfy the minimum interest value and to find all the sequences whose occurrence frequency in the set of sequences is no less than min_support "

Mining sequential patterns has become an important data mining task with broad applications in business analysis, career analysis, policy analysis, and security. Many papers on sequential pattern mining focus on specific algorithms and evaluating their efficiency (Ayers et al, 2002, Pei et al 2001, Srikant & Agarwal, 1996).

In this work, we focus on the problem of mining sequential patterns. Sequential pattern mining finds interesting patterns in sequence of sets. Mining sequential patterns has become an important data mining task with broad application areas. For example, supermarkets often collect customer purchase records in sequence databases in which a sequential pattern would indicate a customer's buying habit.

Currently after many years of research in the Market basket analysis through Sequence Pattern Mining problem (Agarwal & Agarwal 1995, Pei et al 2001, Srikant & Agarwal, 1996) the trend is shifting to the other areas of application of sequence pattern mining. One such area is web mining. Lot of research has been done to make the process of finding useful information and (Interesting) knowledge from web data more efficient.

The current work is motivated by the candidate set and the test approach used in the basic AprioriAll algorithm (Agarwal & Agarwal, 1995). Similar to AprioriAll algorithm traversal of sequences takes place using the breadth first search technique. All the combinations of candidate set and frequent itemset takes place at the K-Level. As we are concentrated on web user traversals i.e, the user can visit back and froth a sites, the proposed algorithm considers the combinations of back and forth nature ((1,2) and (2,1)).Web data exhibit sequentiality in nature. The interrelationship among the web-pages visit with in a session can be used to predict the navigational behavior of the user.

SEQUENCE PATTERN MINING USING SUPPORT-INTEREST FRAMEWORK

The effectiveness of a set of Web pages depends not only on the content of individual web pages, but also on the structure of the pages and their ease of use. The most common data mining technique used on click-stream-data is that of uncovering traversal patterns. A traversal pattern is a set of pages visited by a user in a session. The knowledge gained from the frequently references of the contiguous pages is useful to predict future references and thus can be used for prefetching and caching purposes. The knowledge acquired from the backward traversals of the set of contiguous pages is used to improve the quality of web personalization by adding new links to shorten web page traversals in future.

In context to web usage mining the sequential pattern is defined as an ordered set of pages that satisfies a given support and is maximal (i.e., it has no subsequence that is also frequent). Support is defined not as the percentage of sessions with the pattern, but rather the percentage of the customers who have the pattern. Since a user may have many sessions, it is possible that a sequential pattern should span a lot of sessions. It also needs not be contiguously accessed pages. A k-sequence is a sequence of length k (i.e., is it has k pages in it).

Support is the basic (monotonic) measure to be used in the sequence pattern mining for pruning and reducing the candidates to be generated. In order to incorporate any new measure in the existing sequence pattern mining framework we need to prune and reduce the candidate generation. This can be done at post processing phase i.e, after the pruning phase using support measure. Thus, any interestingness measure can be used in the existing algorithm framework. Interest measure can be used to prune the candidate set of un-interestingness in nature. The measure can be incorporated in the preprocessing phase in the algorithm. Measure is used in the candidate generation phase to prune

the candidate set. In the modified algorithm we have used the interest measure for pruning the redundant patterns.

The main aim of modifying the AprioriAll algorithm is to reduce the size of the candidate sets at every iteration thus, reducing the time needed for scanning the database. The reduced time needed in scanning the database results in improved efficiency. From the set of candidate set generated not all the candidate set is interesting and useful. There may be two possible reasons for the same. Firstly, the algorithm considers only the time order into account during a candidate generation phase and does not consider the user property and secondly while pruning the candidate set the algorithm generates lot of candidate sets which are not interesting in nature hence, the time and space requirement is high.

In the modified algorithm, in every step to generate a candidate set the candidate set elements of the previous step which satisfies the user specified interest value should be taken over in the next step and the remaining set should be left out. On the other hand, the candidate sets generated at every step is pruned in the light of the property of AprioriALL algorithm and the result is called C'k. Thus, we can reduce the size of candidate set generated sharply at each iteration. This, results in reduced complexity of the time and space. The particular change in the phase of the candidate generation helps us to reduce the time and space requirement as only the required interested candidates are generated and passed on for the candidate test phase to qualify by support. There by giving the user a qualified interestingness pattern as sought or required by the user. Algorithm 1 details the complete modified algorithm.

The algorithm starts with a database D consisting of sequences. Since the current work focuses on web usage mining here sequences refers to web user sessions. Each user session consists of sequence of web pages. The user specified support value is supplied as a input to prune the candidate set. In order to have only the useful and interesting patterns the algorithm takes IT as a input to further prune the candidate set. The algorithm outputs the largest sequence which satisfies both the user specified support and interest measure. The algorithm begins with generating the candidate set using a procedure Apriorimodgen(). The pruning of sequential patterns is done using following definition.

Definition 1

If a sequential pattern S1 contains another pattern S2, and the interestingness value of S2 is not significantly better than S1, then S2 is redundant and are pruned. A sequential pattern <A1A2... Am> contains another sequential pattern <B1B2... Bn> if there exist integers i1 < i2 <... < in such that B1 $\subseteq$ Ai1, B2 $\subseteq$ Ai2,..., Bn $\subseteq$ Ain, where Ai (i = 1,...,m) and Bi (i = 1,...,n) are sets of objects.

Definition 2

If a sequential pattern consists of repeated occurrences of the same set of objects, the pattern is pruned. For example, pattern <AAAAA> contains the same set of objects A and is thus pruned according to this rule.

The algorithm proposed is naïve approach to get the sequence of particular interest to the user. For high min_support value the algorithm performs well as the ranking of the patterns is performed at each iteration. As the number of candidates generated is less hence time and space is also saved.

EXPERIMENTAL RESULTS

We implemented our approach using Java and performed experiments on a 2.4 GHz, 256 MB, and Pentium-IV machine running on Microsoft Windows XP 2002. We collected data from the UCI dataset repository (http://kdd.ics.uci.edu/).

In our experimentation we evaluated the time requirements and the quality of pattern generated due to both the AprioriALL algorithm and the modified algorithm. In the modified algorithm the patterns generated by the qualification from interest measure reduces the number of candidate set generated. Hence the candidate set generated due to the user specified support value is less. Hence, incorporating interest measure in the AprioriALL algorithm resulted in only interesting rules and pruning of uninteresting rules. The modified algorithm uses the concept of extracting subsequence information. Since the support needed in sequence generation is calculated at the subsequence generation it results in saving the time to generate the maximal sequence. In our experimentation we used the minimum support of 10%. Figure 1 shows the sequence length generated for different size of databases. As can be observed from the figure that ApioriALL algorithm generates the subsequences of length 5 where as the modified algorithm generates the subsequences of lengths 3.

In the modified algorithm, the number of patterns generated is more than the patterns generated in candidate generation phase. The modified algorithm finds an edge over any level based algorithm in the way that it keeps track of the subsequences information. We also noted down the time required by the AprioriAll algorithm and modified algorithm. Figure 2 shows the time required by both the algorithms. In Figure 2 the curve represented by Apriori-All shows the time taken(in milliseconds) for deriving the sequences by the original algorithm (Apriori-All) and the other curve depicts the time taken by the modified algorithm to get in the user specified interestingness pattern. We use the condition for interest satisfying join from the candidate generation phase of length three.

As can be noted from the figure 2, initially for both the algorithms (AprioriAll and modified algorithm) time requirements are almost the same. But as the number of customers increases the

Algorithm 1. The Modified Algorithm

```
Input:
D = {t1, t2, t3, …, tn}where t1, t2, …,tn are user sessions.
S = Minimum Support threshold value
IT= Minimum interest value (0 < IT <= 1)
Output:
Sequential Patterns qualified with interestingness measure.
Begin
L1 = large 1-Itemsets;
For (k = 2; Lk-1! = 0; k++) do
  Begin
          Ck= Apriorimodgen(Lk-1,S)
          For each transaction ti ∈ D
                do
                  Ci =subset (Ck, ti);
                  For all candidate c ∈ Ci do
                          c.count++;
                              Lk={c Ck| c.count > S)
      End
Find all maximal reference sequences from L;
End
Procedure Apriorimodgen (Lk-1,  S)
Begin
Ck= null;
      For each Itemset Li  to Lk-1
          For each Itemset Lj to Lk-1
                    If (Interest (Li, Lj) > IT)
                    Begin
                          C = Li join Lj
                          has Infrequent -Subset (c, Lk-1)
                    End
For each Itemset Li  L1 // to give identity sequences of length
                    Li → Li
                    Return Ck;
End
Procedure Apriorimodgen (Lk-1, S) in turn uses the procedure has Infrequent
Subset(c, Lk-1) to prune the candidate set using interest measure.
Procedure has Infrequent-Subset(c,Lk-1)
Begin
For each (k-1) subset s of c
        If s ∈ Lk-1 then
        return false;
 Else true;
End
Procedure Interest(Li, LJ)
Begin
For each (Li, Lj)
```

$$nterest = \frac{Count(L_i, L_j)}{Count(L_i), Count(L_j)}$$

```
End
```

Figure 1. Sequence length derivation of the original algorithm vs. variation one

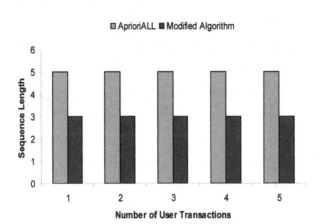

Figure 2. Performance evaluation of the AprioriALL and modified algorithm

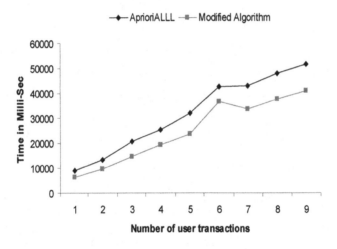

modified algorithm takes less time in comparison to the AprioriALL algorithm. The patterns due to the modified algorithm are only the ones which are really meaningful and interesting. It was also observed that the patterns derived form the proposal is of length three but is of more interest to user requirements.

The main motivation for adding the interest measure in AprioriALL algorithm is due to the patterns obtained from the AprioriAll algorithm. In the original AprioriAll algorithm the change in the candidate generation phase resulted in reduced time and space since the required inter-

ested candidates are generated and passed on for the candidate test phase to qualify the minimum support value. Thus, the user gets only those patterns which qualify the interestingness pattern. The modified algorithm is well when the user transactions are huge in size.

CONCLUSION

Sequence pattern mining is a heavily researched area in the field of data mining with wide range of application areas. One of them is to use find the maximal length pattern from large collection of web log data. Discovering hidden information from Web log data is called Web usage mining. The aim of discovering large sequential patterns in Web log data is to obtain information about the navigational behavior of the users. This can be used for advertising purposes, for creating dynamic user profiles etc.

In this work, we modified the AprioriAll algorithm to obtain the patterns of more interest. We demonstrated that the proposed algorithm generates the only interesting set of patterns as compared over the original algorithm. The proposed algorithm scales well over the large dataset. We also demonstrated the time requirement of the proposed algorithm. The proposed algorithm takes less time as compared to the original algorithm. The viability of our approach was shown over the msnbc web log dataset consisting user transactions.

The Preprocessing pruning of candidates is novel approach and can be extended in the post processing phase to select out the largeitemset sequences generated.

The minimum interest value specification can also be used to get the pruning of candidates is to be given by user who has good domain knowledge about the dataset. This is one area which can be looked in for future enhancement to get the automated interested values by the use of genetic algorithms.

REFERENCES

Aggarwal, C., & Yu, P. (1998). A new framework for itemset generation. In *Proc. of the 17th Symposium on Principles of Database Systems*, (pp. 18-24). Seattle, WA.

Agrawal, R., & Srikant, R. (1995). *Mining sequential patterns*. In 11th Int'l Conf. of Data Engineering, (pp. 3-14). Taipei, Taiwan.

Ayres, J., Flannick, J., Gehrke, J., & Yiu, T. (2002). Sequential pattern mining using a bitmap representation. In *Proc. 2002 Int. Conf. Knowledge Discovery and Data Mining*.

Huang, E., Cercone, N., & Aijun, A. (2002). Comparison of interestingness functions for learning Web usage patterns. CIKM: Proceedings of the Eleventh International Conference on Information and Knowledge Management, (pp. 617-620). McLean, Virginia, USA. New York, NY: ACM Press.

Klemettinen, M., Mannila, H., Ronkainen, P., Toivonen, T., & Verkamo, A. (1994). Finding interesting rules from large sets of discovered association rules. In *Proc. of the 3rd Int'l Conf. on Information and Knowledge Management* (CIKM'94), (pp. 401-407). Gaithersburg, Maryland.

Pei, J., Han, J., Mortazavi-Asi, B., & Pinto, H. (2001). PrefixSpan mining sequential patterns efficiently by prefix-projected pattern growth. In *Proc. of Int. Conf. on Data Engineering*.

Sarawagi, S. (2003). *Sequence data mining techniques and applications*. In the 19th International Conference on Data Engineering.

Srikant, R., & Agrawal, R. (1996). Mining sequential patterns: Generalizations and performance improvements. In *Proc. 5th Int. Conf. Extending Database Technology*.

Tan, P.-N., Kumar, V., & Srivastava, J. (2002). Selecting the right interestingness measure for association patterns. *KDD '02: Proceedings of the Eighth ACM SIGKDD International Conference on Knowledge Discovery and Data Mining*, (pp. 32-41). Edmonton, Alberta, Canada. New York, NY: ACM Press.

Compilation of References

Abe, N., & Warmuth, M. K. (1992). On the computational complexity of approximating distributions by probabilistic automata. *Machine Learning, 9*, 205–260. doi:10.1007/BF00992677

Agarwal, R., Imielenski, T., & Swami, A. (1993). Mining association rules between sets of items in large databases. In *Proc. 1993 ACM-SIGMOD Int. Conf. Management of Data (SIGMOD'93),* (pp. 266-271).

Agarwal, S. (2009). *On finding the most statistically significant substring using the chi-square measure.* Master's thesis, Indian Institute of Technology, Kanpur.

Aggarwal, C., & Yu, P. (1998). A new framework for itemset generation. In *Proc. of the 17th Symposium on Principles of Database Systems,* (pp. 18-24). Seattle, WA.

Agrawal, R., & Srikant, R. (1994). Fast algorithms for mining association rules in large databases. In *VLDB'94: Proceedings of 20th International Conference on Very Large Data Bases,* (pp. 487–499).

Agrawal, R., & Srikant, R. (1995). *Mining sequential patterns.* In 11th Int'l Conf. of Data Engineering, (pp. 3-14). Taipei, Taiwan.

Akhtar, R., & Cochrane, G. (2008). Priorities for nucleotide trace, sequence and annotation data capture at the Ensembl Trace Archive and the EMBL Nucleotide sequence database. *Nucleic Acids Research, 36*, 5–12.

Akleman, L., & Ezekwa, C. U. (2009). *FREQuest: Prefetching in the light of frequent episodes.* Retrieved from http://www.cs.cmu.edu/~lakoglu/classes/arch_paper.pdf

Allwein, E. L., Schapire, R. E., & Singer, Y. (2001). Reducing multiclass to binary: A unifying approach for margin classifiers. *Journal of Machine Learning Research, 1*, 113–141. doi:10.1162/15324430152733133

Altschul, S. F., Gish, W., Miller, W., Myers, E. W., & Lipman, D. J. (1990). Basic local alignment search tool. *Journal of Molecular Biology, 215*(3), 403–410.

Altschul, S. F., Madden, T. L., Schaffer, A. A., Zhang, J., Zhang, Z., Miller, W., & Lipman, D. J. (1997). Gapped BLAST and PSI-BLAST: A new generation of protein database search programs. *Nucleic Acids Research, 25*, 3389–3402. doi:10.1093/nar/25.17.3389

Andersson, J. O. (2005). Lateral gene transfer in eukaryotes. *Cellular and Molecular Life Sciences, 62*(11), 1182–1197. doi:10.1007/s00018-005-4539-z

Andorf, C., Silvescu, A., Dobbs, D., & Honavar, V. (2004). Learning classifiers for assigning protein sequences to gene ontology functional families. In *Proceedings of the Fifth International Conference on Knowledge Based Computer Systems,* (pp. 256–265).

Ayres, J., Flannick, J., Gehrke, J., & Yiu, T. (2002). Sequential pattern mining using a bitmap representation. In *Proc. 2002 Int. Conf. Knowledge Discovery and Data Mining.*

Bairoch, A., & Boeckmann, B. (2003). The SWISS-PROT protein knowledgebase and its supplement TrEMBL in 2003. *Nucleic Acids Research, 31*(1), 365–370. doi:10.1093/nar/gkg095

Bakheet, T. M., & Doig, A. J. (2009). Properties and identification of human protein drug targets. *Bioinformatics (Oxford, England), 25*(4), 451–457. doi:10.1093/bioinformatics/btp002

Bakus, J., & Kamel, M. S. (2002). Document classification using phrases. In *Proceedings of the Joint IAPR International Workshop on Structural, Syntactic, and Statistical Pattern Recognition*, (pp. 557–565). SpringerVerlag.

Baldi, P., Chauvin, Y., Hunkapiller, T., & McClure, M. A. (1994). Hidden Markov models of biological primary sequence information. *Proceedings of the National Academy of Sciences of the United States of America, 91*(3), 1059–1063. doi:10.1073/pnas.91.3.1059

Batista, G., Prati, M., & Monard, M. (2004). A study of the behavior of several methods for balancing machine learning training data. *ACM SIGKDD Explorations: Special Issue on Imbalanced Data Sets, 6*(1), 20–29.

Beigi, M., & Zell, A. (2007). Synthetic protein sequence oversampling method for classification and remote homology detection in imbalanced protein data. In *Proceedings of 1st International Conference on Bioinformatics Research and Development*, (pp. 263-277). Berlin, Germany.

Bejerano, G., Friedman, N., & Tishby, N. (2004). Efficient exact p-value computation for small sample, sparse and surprisingly categorical data. *Journal of Computational Biology, 11*(5), 867–886.

Bejerano, G., & Yona, G. (1999). Modeling protein families using probabilistic suffix trees. In *Proceedings of RECOMB*, (pp. 15–24).

Ben-Hur, A., Horn, D., Siegelmann, H., & Vapnik, V. (2001). Support vector clustering. *Journal of Machine Learning Research, 2*, 125–137. doi:10.1162/15324430260185565

Ben-Hur, A., & Noble, W. S. (2005). Kernel methods for predicting protein-protein interactions. *Bioinformatics (Oxford, England), 21*(1), i38–i46. doi:10.1093/bioinformatics/bti1016

Ben-Hur, A., & Brutlag, D. (2003a). Remote homology detection: A motif based approach. *Bioinformatics (Oxford, England), 19*(1), 26–33. doi:10.1093/bioinformatics/btg1002

Ben-Hur, A., & Brutlag, D. (2003b). Sequence motifs: Highly predictive features of protein function. In *Proceedings of Workshop on Feature Selection, Neural Information Processing Systems*.

Benson, D. A., Karsch-Mizrachi, I., Lipman, D. J., Ostell, J., & Wheeler, D. L. (2008). GenBank. *Nucleic Acids Research, 36*, 25–30. doi:10.1093/nar/gkm929

Berendt, B. A. (2000). Analysis of navigation behaviour in web sites integrating multiple information systems. *The VLDB Journal, 9*(1), 56–75. doi:10.1007/s007780050083

Berger, A. L., Pietra, S. D., & Pietra, V. J. D. (1996). A maximum entropy approach to natural language processing. *Computational Linguistics, 22*(1), 39–71.

Berman, H. M., Westbrook, J., Feng, Z., Gilliland, G., Bhat, T. N., Weissig, H., et al. (2000). *The Protein Data Bank, Nucleic Acids Research, 28*, 235-242. Retrived on January 11, 2011 from *http://*www.rcsb.org

Bhattacharyya, A. (1943). On a measure of divergence between two statistical populations defined by their probability distributions. *Bulletin of the Calcutta Mathematical Society, 35*, 99–109.

Boughanem, M., Chrisment, C., Mothe, J., Soulé-Dupuy, C., & Tamine, L. (2000). Connectionist and genetic approaches to achieve IR. In Crestani, F., & Gabriella, P. (Eds.), *Soft computing in information retrieval techniques and applications* (pp. 173–198). Springer-Verlag.

Boughanem, M., & Dousset, B. (2001). *Relationship between push and optimization subscriptions in documentation centers*. VSST'01, (pp. 239-252). Tome 1.

Boughorbel, S., Tarel, J. P., & Boujemaa, N. (2005). The intermediate matching kernel for image local features. In *Proceedings of the International Joint Conference on Neural Networks*, (pp. 889–894). Montreal, Canada.

Brodley, C. E., & Friedl, M. A. (1999). Identifying mislabeled training data. *Journal of Artificial Intelligence Research, 11*, 131–167.

Bru, C., & Servant, F. (2002). ProDom: Automated clustering of homologous domains. *Briefings in Bioinformatics, 3*(3), 246–251. doi:10.1093/bib/3.3.246

Buchner, A. G., & Mulvenna, M. D. (1998). Discovering Internet marketing intelligence through online analytical web usage mining. *SIGMOD Record, 27*(4), 54–61. doi:10.1145/306101.306124

Buddhakulsomsiri, J., & Zakarian, A. (2009). Sequential pattern mining algorithm for automotive warranty data. *Journal of Computers and Industrial Engineering, 57*(1), 137–147. doi:10.1016/j.cie.2008.11.006

Buehler, E. C., & Ungar, L. H. (2001). Maximum entropy methods for biological sequence modeling. In *Proceedings of BIOKDD*, (pp. 60–64).

Burges, C. J. C. (1998). A tutorial on support vector machines for pattern recognition. *Data Mining and Knowledge Discovery, 2*(2), 1–47. doi:10.1023/A:1009715923555

Büttcher, S., Clarke, C. L. A., & Cormack, G. V. (2010). *Information retrieval: Implementing and evaluating search engines*. MIT Press.

Cai, C. Z., Wang, W. L., Sun, L. Z., & Chen, Y. Z. (2003). Protein function classification via support vector machine approach. *Mathematical Biosciences, 185*(1), 111–122. doi:10.1016/S0025-5564(03)00096-8

Campbell, W., Assaleh, K., & Broun, C. (2002). Speaker recognition with polynomial classifiers. *IEEE Transactions on Speech and Audio Processing, 10*(4), 205–212. doi:10.1109/TSA.2002.1011533

Campbell, W. M., Campbell, J. P., Reynolds, D. A., Singer, E., & Torres-Carrasquillo, P. A. (2006a). Support vector machines for speaker and language recognition. *Computer Speech &. Language, 20*(2-3), 210–229.

Campbell, W. M., Sturim, D. E., & Reynolds, D. A. (2006b). Support vector machines using GMM supervectors for speaker verification. *IEEE Signal Processing Letters, 13*(5), 308–311. doi:10.1109/LSP.2006.870086

Campbell, W. M., Campbell, J. P., Gleason, T. P., Reynolds, D. A., & Shen, W. (2007). Speaker verification using support vector machines and high-level features. *IEEE Transactions on Audio Speech and Language Processing, 15*(7), 2085–2094. doi:10.1109/TASL.2007.902874

Campbell, A. (1999). Genome signature comparisons among prokaryote, plasmid and mitochondrial DNA. *Proceedings of the National Academy of Sciences of the United States of America, 96*(16), 9184–9189. doi:10.1073/pnas.96.16.9184

Campbell, W. (2008). A covariance kernel for SVM language recognition. In *Proceedings of International Conference on Acoustics, Speech and Signal Processing, 2008 (ICASSP 2008)*, (pp. 4141–4144). Las Vegas, Nevada, USA.

Campbell, W. M. (2002). *Generalized linear discriminant sequence kernels for speaker recognition*. In IEEE International Conference on Acoustics, Speech, and Signal Processing, 2002, ICASSP '02, vol. 1, (pp. 161–164). Orlando, Florida, USA.

Campbell, W. M., Campbell, J. P., Reynolds, D. A., Jones, D. A., & Leek, T. R. (2004a). *High-level speaker verification with support vector machines*. In IEEE International Conference on Acoustics, Speech, and Signal Processing, vol. 1, (pp. I–73–76). Montreal, Quebec, Canada.

Campbell, W. M., Campbell, J. P., Reynolds, D. A., Jones, D. A., & Leek, T. R. (2004b). Phonetic speaker recognition with support vector machines. In *Advances in neural information processing systems*, (pp. 1377–1384). Vancouver, Canada.

Campbell, W., Sturim, D. E., Reynolds, D. A., & Solomonoff, A. (2006c). *SVM based speaker verification using a GMM supervector kernel and NAP variability compensation*. In IEEE International Conference on Acoustics, Speech and Signal Processing, 2006. ICASSP 2006, vol. 1, (pp. 97–100).

Chang, C. C., & Lin, C. J. (2001). *LIBSVM – A library for support vector machines*. Retrieved from http://www.cse.ntu.edu.tw/~cjlin/libsvm/

Chao, Y.-H., Wang, H.-M., & Chang, R.-C. (2005). GMM-based Bhattacharyya kernel Fher discriminant analysis for speaker recognition. In *IEEE International Conference on Acoustics, Speech and Signal Processing, 2005, ICASSP 2005*, Vol. 1, (pp. 649–652). Philadelphia, PA, USA.

Chawla, N. V., Bowyer, K. W., Hall, L. O., & Kegelmeyer, W. P. (2004). SMOTE: Synthetic minority over-sampling technique. *Journal of Artificial Intelligence Research, 16*, 324–357.

Chen, E., Cao, H., Li, Q., & Qian, T. (2008). Efficient strategies for tough aggregate constraint-based sequential pattern mining. *Inf. Sci., 178*(6), 1498–1518. doi:10.1016/j.ins.2007.10.014

Chen, Y.-L., & Hu, Y.-H. (2006). Constraint-based sequential pattern mining: The consideration of recency and compactness. *Decision Support Systems*, *42*(2), 1203–1215. doi:10.1016/j.dss.2005.10.006

Chen, Y.-L., & Huang, T. C.-K. (2008). A novel knowledge discovering model for mining fuzzy multi-level sequential patterns in sequence databases. *Data & Knowledge Engineering*, *66*(3), 349–367. doi:10.1016/j.datak.2008.04.005

Cheng, H., Yan, X., & Han, J. (2004). IncSpan: Incremental mining of sequential patterns in large database. *KDD '04: Proceedings of the Tenth ACM SIGKDD International Conference on Knowledge Discovery and Data Mining*, (pp. 527-532).

Cieslak, D. A., Chawla, N. V., & Striegel, A. (2006). Combating imbalance in network intrusion datasets. In *Proceedings of IEEE International Conference on Granular Computing*, (pp. 732-737). Athens, Georgia.

Cooley, R., Mobasher, B., & Srivastava, J. (1999). Data preparation for mining World Wide Web browsing patterns. *Knowledge and Information Systems*, *1*(1), 5–32.

Cortes, C., & Vapnik, V. (1995). Support-Vector Networks. *Machine Learning*, *20*, 273–297. doi:10.1007/BF00994018

Cristianini, N., & Shawe-Taylor, J. (2000). *An introduction to support vector machines and other kernel-based learning methods. The Edinburgh building*. Cambridge, UK: Cambridge University Press.

Cristianini, N., & Shawe-Taylor, J. (2000). *Support vector machines and other kernel-based learning methods*. Cambridge University Press.

Croft, B., Metzler, D., & Strohman, T. (2011). *Search engines: Information retrieval in practice*. Addison-Wesley.

Dalal, N., & Triggs, B. (2005). Histograms of oriented gradients for human detection. *Proceedings of International Conference on Computer Vision & Pattern Recognition (CVPR '05)*, *1*, 886—893.

Darling, A. C. E., Mau, B., Blattner, F. R., & Perna, N. T. (2004). Mauve: Multiple alignment of conserved genomic sequence with rearrangements. *Genome Research*, *14*(7), 1394–1403. doi:10.1101/gr.2289704

Darroch, J. N., & Ratcliff, D. (1972). Generalized iterative scaling for log-linear models. *Annals of Mathematical Statistics*, *43*, 1470–1480. doi:10.1214/aoms/1177692379

Dehak, N., & Chollet, G. (2006). *Support vector GMMs for speaker verification*. In IEEE Odyssey 2006: The Speaker and Language Recognition Workshop, (pp. 1–4).

Dehak, R., Dehak, N., Kenny, P., & Dumouchel, P. (2007). Linear and non linear kernel GMM supervector machines for speaker verification. In *Proceedings of INTERSPEECH*, (pp. 302–305). Antwerp, Belgium.

Delcher, A. L., Phillippy, A., Carlton, J., & Salzberg, S. L. (2002). Fast algorithms for large-scale genome alignment and comparison. *Nucleic Acids Research*, *30*(11), 2478–2483. doi:10.1093/nar/30.11.2478

Denise, A., Regnier, M., & Vandenbogaert, M. (2001). Accessing the statistical significance of overrepresented oligonucleotides. In *Workshop on Algorithms in Bioinformatics (WABI)*, pages 85-97.

Devitt, A., Duffin, J., & Moloney, R. (2005). Topographical proximity for mining network alarm data. *MineNet '05: Proceedings of the 2005 ACM SIGCOMM workshop on Mining network data* (pp. 179-184). Philadelphia, PA: ACM.

Dileep, A. D., & Sekhar, C. C. (2011). Speaker recognition using intermediate matching kernel based support vector machines pairwise classification and support vector machines. In Neustein, A., & Patil, H. (Eds.), *Speaker forensics: New developments in voice technology to combat crime and detect threats to homeland security*.

Ding, C. H. Q., & Dubchak, I. (2001). Multi-class protein fold recognition using support vector machines and neural networks. *Bioinformatics (Oxford, England)*, *17*(4), 349–358. doi:10.1093/bioinformatics/17.4.349

Ding, B., Lo, D., Han, J., & Khoo, S.-C. (2009). *Efficient mining of closed repetitive gapped subsequences from a sequence database*. ICDE 09.

Dkaki, T., Dousset, B., Egret, D., & Mothe, J. (2000). Information discovery from semi-structured sources – Application to astronomical literature. *Computer Physics Communications*, *127*(2-3), 198–206. doi:10.1016/S0010-4655(99)00509-3

Dkaki, T., Dousset, B., & Mothe, J. (1997). *Mining information in order to extract hidden and strategical information*. 5th International Conference RIAO, (pp. 32-51).

Dobrindt, U., Hochhut, B., Hentschel, U., & Hacker, J. (2004). Genomic islands in pathogenic and environmental microorganisms. *Nature Reviews Microbiology, 2*(5), 414–424. doi:10.1038/nrmicro884

Domingos, P., & Pazzani, M. J. (1997). On the optimality of the simple Bayesian classifier under zero-one loss. *Machine Learning, 29*(2-3), 103–130. doi:10.1023/A:1007413511361

Domingos, P., & Pazzani, M. J. (1996). Beyond independence: Conditions for the optimality of the simple Bayesian classifier. In *Proceedings of ICML*, (pp. 105–112).

Dousset, B. (2003). *Integration of interactive knowledge discovery for strategic scanning. Habilitation*. Toulouse: Paul Sabatier University. in French

Dousset, B. (2009). *Extracting implicit information by text analysis from websites in unicode*. Nancy: VSST. in French

Duda, R. O., Hart, P. E., & Stork, D. G. (2002). *Pattern classification*. New York, NY: John Wiley and Sons.

Durbin, R., Eddy, S., Krogh, A., & Mitchison, G. (1998). *Biological sequence analysis: Probabilistic models of proteins and nucleic acids*. Cambridge University Press. doi:10.1017/CBO9780511790492

Dutta, S., & Bhattacharya, A. (2010). Most significant substring mining based on chi-square measure. In *Proc. of 14th Pacific-Asia Conference on Knowledge Discovery and Data Mining*, (pp. 319-327).

Eddy, S. R. (1998). HMMER: Profile hidden Markov modelling. *Bioinformatics (Oxford, England), 14*(9), 755–763. doi:10.1093/bioinformatics/14.9.755

Eichinger, F., Nauck, D. D., & Klawonn, F. (n.d.). *Sequence mining for customer behaviour predictions in telecommunications*.

El haddadi, A., Dousset, B., Berrada, I., & Loubier, E. (2010). *The multi-sources in the context of competitive intelligence*. Paper presented at the Francophone Conference on Mining and Knowledge Management, (pp. A1-125-A1-136). Hamammat, Tunisia.

Eskin, E., Noble, W. S., & Singer, Y. (2003). Protein family classification using sparse Markov transducers. *Journal of Computational Biology, 10*(2), 187–214. doi:10.1089/106652703321825964

Estabrooks, A., Jo, T., & Japkowicz, N. (2004). A multiple resampling method for learning from imbalanced data sets. *Computational Intelligence, 20*(1), 18–36. doi:10.1111/j.0824-7935.2004.t01-1-00228.x

Exarchos, T. P., Papaloukas, C., Lampros, C., & Fotiadis, D. I. (2008). Mining sequential patterns for protein fold recognition. *Journal of Biomedical Informatics, 41*(1), 165–179. doi:10.1016/j.jbi.2007.05.004

Exarchos, T. P., Tsipouras, M. G., Papaloukas, C., & Fotiadis, D. I. (2008). A two-stage methodology for sequence classification based on sequential pattern mining and optimization. *Data & Knowledge Engineering, 66*(3), 467–487. doi:10.1016/j.datak.2008.05.007

Fayyad, U. M., Piatetsky-Shapiro, G., Smyth, P., & Uthurusamy, R. (Eds.). (1996). *Advances in knowledge discovery and data mining*. AAAI/MIT Press.

Ferreira, P. G., & Azevedo, P. J. (2005a). Protein sequence classification through relevant sequence mining and Bayes classifiers. In *Proceedings of EPIA*, (pp. 236–247).

Ferreira, P. G., & Azevedo, P. J. (2005b). Protein sequence pattern mining with constraints. In *Proceedings of PKDD*, (pp. 96–107).

Ferreira, P. G., & Azevedo, P. J. (2006). Query driven sequence pattern mining. In *Proceedings of SBBD*, (pp. 1–15).

Finn, R. D., & Bateman, A. (2008). The Pfam protein families database. *Nucleic Acids Research*, 281–288.

Gao, F., & Zhang, C. T. (2006). GC-Profile: A Web-based tool for visualizing and analyzing the variation of GC content in genomic sequences. *Nucleic Acids Research, 34*, W686–W691. doi:10.1093/nar/gkl040

Garboni, C., Masseglia, F., & Trousse, B. (2005). *Sequential pattern mining for structure-based XML document classification*. Workshop of the INitiative for the Evaluation of XML Retrieval.

Garcia-Vallve, S., Guzman, E., Montero, M. A., & Romeu, A. (2003). HGT-DB: A database of putative horizontally transferred genes in prokaryotic complete genomes. *Nucleic Acids Research*, *31*(1), 187–189. doi:10.1093/nar/gkg004

Garcia-Vallve, S., Romeu, A., & Palau, J. (2000). Horizontal gene transfer in bacterial and archaeal complete genomes. *Genome Research*, *10*, 1719–1725. doi:10.1101/gr.130000

Garofalakis, M., Rastogi, R., & Shim, K. (2002). Mining sequential patterns with regular expression constraints. *IEEE Transactions on Knowledge and Data Engineering*, *14*(3), 530–552. doi:10.1109/TKDE.2002.1000341

Gibbens, R. J., & Saacti, Y. (2006). *Road traffic analysis using MIDAS data: Journey time prediction. (Technical Report, UCAM-CL-TR-676). Computer Laboratory.* England: University of Cambridge.

Girolami, M. (2002). Mercer kernel-based clustering in feature space. *IEEE Transactions on Neural Networks*, *13*(3), 780–784. doi:10.1109/TNN.2002.1000150

Gogarten, J. P., & Townsend. (2005). Horizontal gene transfer, genome innovation and evolution. *Nature Reviews Microbiology*, *3*, 679–687. doi:10.1038/nrmicro1204

Goldberg, R. R. (1978). *Methods of real analysis* (1st ed.). New Delhi, India: Oxford & IBH Publishing Company.

Gouda, K., & Zaki, M. J. (2005). Genmax: An efficient algorithm for mining maximal frequent itemsets. *Data Mining and Knowledge Discovery*, *11*(3), 223–242. doi:10.1007/s10618-005-0002-x

Grauman, K., & Darrell, T. (2007). The pyramid match kernel: Efficient learning with sets of features. *Journal of Machine Learning Research*, *8*, 725–760.

Grauman, K., & Darrell, T. (2005). *The pyramid match kernel: Discriminative classification with sets of image features*. In Tenth IEEE International Conference on Computer Vision, 2005. ICCV 2005, vol. 2, (pp. 1458–1465).

Gribskov, M., Luthy, R., & Eisenberg, D. (1990). Profile analysis. *Methods in Enzymology*, *183*, 146–159. doi:10.1016/0076-6879(90)83011-W

Guan, J. W., Liu, D., & Bell, D. A. (2004). Discovering motifs in DNA sequences. *Fundam. Inform.*, *59*(2-3), 119–134.

Guan, J. W., Bell, D. A., & Liu, D. (2004). Discovering maximal frequent patterns in sequence groups. In *Proceedings of Rough Sets and Current Trends in Computing*, (pp. 602–609).

Guenec, N. (2009). *Chinese scientific information: An essential information source to any business intelligence competitive watch*. Nancy: VSST. in French

Gutierrez, G., Marquez, L., & Marin, A. (1996). Preference for guanosine at first codon position in highly expressed Escherichia coli genes. A relationship with translational efficiency. *Nucleic Acids Research*, *24*(13), 2525–2527. doi:10.1093/nar/24.13.2525

Hajduk, P. J., Huth, J. R., & Tse, C. (2005). Predicting protein druggability. *Drug Discovery Today*, *10*, 1675–1682. doi:10.1016/S1359-6446(05)03624-X

Hamerly, G., Perelman, E., Lau, J., Calder, B., & Sherwood, T. (2006). Using machine learning to guide architecture simulation. *Journal of Machine Learning Research*, *7*, 343–378.

Han, J., & Kamber, M. (1996). *Data mining – Concepts and techniques*. Elesevier Inc.

Han, J., & Kamber, M. (2001). *Data mining: Concepts and techniques*. Morgan Kaufmann.

Han, L. Y., Zheng, C. J., Xie, B., Jia, J., Ma, X. H., & Zhu, F. (2007). Support vector approach for predicting druggable proteins: recent progress in its exploration and investigation of its usefulness. *Drug Discovery Today*, *12*, 304–313. doi:10.1016/j.drudis.2007.02.015

Han, J., Pei, J., & Yin, Y. (2000). Mining frequent patterns without candidate generations. In *Proc. Of ACM SIGMOD Intl. Conf. of Management of Data (SIGMOD 00)*, (pp. 1-12).

Han, J., Pei, J., Asl, B. M., Chen, Q., Dayal, U., & Hsu, M. C. (2000). FreeSpan: Frequent pattern-projected sequential pattern mining. *KDD '00: Proceedings of the Sixth ACM SIGKDD International Conference on Knowledge Discovery and Data Mining* (pp. 355-359). Boston, MA: ACM.

Hanjalic, A., Lienhart, R., Ma, W.-Y., & Smith, J. R. (2008). The holy grail of multimedia information retrieval: So close or yet so far away? *Proceedings of the IEEE*, *96*(4), 541–547. doi:10.1109/JPROC.2008.916338

Haussler, D. (1999). *Convolution kernels on discrete structures* (Tech. Rep. No. UCSC-CRL-99-10). University of California at Santa Cruz: Department of Computer Science.

Haykin, S. (1999). *Neural networks: A comprehensive foundation* (2nd ed.). Upper Saddle River, NJ: Prentice-Hall.

Hennessy, J. L., & Patterson, D. A. (2007). *Computer architecture: A quantitative approach* (4th ed.). Amsterdam, Holland: Elsevier.

Hernandez, N., Mothe, J., Chrisment, C., & Egret, D. (2007). Modeling context through domain ontologies. *Information Retrieval*, *10*(2), 143–172. doi:10.1007/s10791-006-9018-0

Hillisch, A., Pineda, L. F., & Hilgenfeld, R. (2004). Utility of homology models in drug discovery process. *Drug Discovery Today*, *9*, 659–669. doi:10.1016/S1359-6446(04)03196-4

Hitchcock, F. L. (1941). The distribution of a product from several sources to numerous localities. *Journal of Mathematics and Physics*, *20*, 224–230.

Hopkins, A. L., & Groom, C. R. (2002). The druggable genome. *Nature Reviews. Drug Discovery*, *1*, 727–730. doi:10.1038/nrd892

Horn, F., Bettler, E., Oliveira, L., Campagne, F., Cohen, F. E., & Vriend, G. (2003). GPCRDB information system for G protein-coupled receptors. *Nucleic Acids Research*, *31*(1), 294–297. doi:10.1093/nar/gkg103

Hotelling, H. (1947). Multivariate quality control. *Techniques of Statistical Analysis*, *54*, 111–184.

Hsiao, W., Wan, I., Jones, S. J., & Brinkman, F. S. L. (2003). IslandPath: Aiding detection of genomic islands in prokaryotes. *Bioinformatics (Oxford, England)*, *19*(3), 418–420. doi:10.1093/bioinformatics/btg004

Hu, H., Xu, M.-X., & Wu, W. (2007). *GMM supervector based SVM with spectral features for speech emotion recognition*. In IEEE International Conference on Acoustics, Speech and Signal Processing, 2007, ICASSP 2007, vol. 4, (pp. 413–416). Honolulu, Hawaii, USA.

Hua, S., & Sun, Z. (2001). A novel method of protein secondary structure prediction with high segment overlap measure: Support vector machine approach. *Journal of Molecular Biology*, *308*, 397–407. doi:10.1006/jmbi.2001.4580

Huang, J. Y., & Brutlag, D. L. (2001). The EMOTIF database. *Nucleic Acids Research*, *29*(1), 202–204. doi:10.1093/nar/29.1.202

Huang, E., Cercone, N., & Aijun, A. (2002). Comparison of interestingness functions for learning Web usage patterns. CIKM: Proceedings of the Eleventh International Conference on Information and Knowledge Management, (pp. 617-620). McLean, Virginia, USA. New York, NY: ACM Press.

Huiyu, Z., Mabu, S., Shimada, K., & Hirasawa, K. (2009). *Generalized time related sequential association rule mining and traffic prediction*. International Conference on Evolutionary Computation, (pp. 2654-2661).

Huiyu, Z., Mabu, S., Xianneng, L., Shimada, K., & Hirasawa, K. (2010). *Generalized rule extraction and traffic prediction in the optimal route search*. International Conference on Evolutionary Computation, (pp. 1-8).

Icev, A. (2003). *Distance-enhanced association rules for gene expression*. BIOKDD'03, in conjunction with ACM SIGKDD.

Irwin, J. J., & Shoichet, B. K. (2005). ZINC - A Free Database of Commercially Available Compounds for Virtual Screening. *J. Chem. Inf. Model.*, *45*(1), 177-82. Retrieved on January 11, 2011 from http://www.zinc.docking.org

Ishio, T., Date, H., Miyake, T., & Inoue, K. (2008). Mining coding patterns to detect crosscutting concerns in Java programs. *WCRE '08: Proceedings of the 2008 15th Working Conference on Reverse Engineering* (pp. 123-132). Washington, DC: IEEE Computer Society.

Jaakkola, T., Diekhans, M., & Haussler, D. (2000). A discriminative framework for detecting remote protein homologies. *Journal of Computational Biology, 7*(1-2), 95–114. doi:10.1089/10665270050081405

Jaakkola, T., Diekhans, M., & Haussler, D. (1999). *Using the Fisher kernel method to detect remote protein homologies*. In Seventh International Conference on Intelligent Systems for Molecular Biology, (pp. 149–158). Menlo Park, CA.

Jaillet, S., Laurent, A., & Teisseire, M. (2006). Sequential patterns for text categorization. *Intelligent Data Analysis, 10*(3), 199–214.

Jain, A. K., Murty, M. N., & Flynn, P. P. (1999). Data clustering: A review. *ACM Computing Review.*

Jain, R., Ramineni, S., & Parekh, N. (2008). Integrated genome island prediction tool (IGIPT). In *IEEE Proceedings of International Conference on Information Technology* (ICIT2008), (pp. 131-132). DOI: 10.1109/ICIT.2008.42

Janney, P., & Geers, G. (2009). Framework for illumination invariant vehicular traffic density estimation. *Proceedings of Pacific Rim Symposium on Image and Video Technology (PSIVT 2009),* Japan.

Japkowicz, N., Hanson, S. J., & Gluck, M. A. (2000). Nonlinear autoassociation is not equivalent to PCA. *Neural Computation, 12*(3), 531–545. doi:10.1162/089976600300015691

Jayaraman, A. (2008). *Modular approach to online handwritten character recognition of Telugu script*. Master's thesis, Department of CSE, IIT Madras, Chennai-36.

Jenks, P. J. (1998). Microbial genome sequencing beyond the double helix. *BMJ (Clinical Research Ed.), 317*(7172), 1568–1571.

Jerbi, M., Senouci, S.-M., Rasheed, T., & Ghamri-Doudane, Y. (2007). An infrastructure-free traffic Information System for vehicular networks. *Proceedings of Vehicular Technology Conference (VTC-2007).*

Jing, F., Li, M., Zhang, H.-J., & Zhang, B. (2003). Support vector machines for region-based image retrieval. In *Proceedings of the 2003 International Conference on Multimedia and Expo,* (pp. 21–24). Washington DC, USA.

Johnson, M., Zaretskaya, I., Raytselis, Y., Merezhuk, Y., McGinnis, S., & Madden, T. L. (2008). *Nucleic Acids Res. 36 (Web Server issue),* W5–W9. Retrieved on January 11, 2011 from http://blast.ncbi.nlm.nih.gov

Jolliffe, I. T. (2002). *Principal component analysis* (2nd ed.). Springer.

Juhas, M., van der Meer, J. R., Gaillard, M., Harding, R. M., Hood, D. W., & Crook, D. W. (2009). Genomic islands: Tools of bacterial horizontal gene transfer and evolution. *FEMS Microbiology Reviews, 33*(2), 376–393. doi:10.1111/j.1574-6976.2008.00136.x

Jurka, J., Kapitonov, V. V., Pavlicek, A., Klonowski, P., Kohany, O., & Walichiewicz, J. (2005). Repbase update, a database of eukaryotic repetitive elements. *Cytogenetic and Genome Research, 110*(1-4), 462–467. doi:10.1159/000084979

Kailath, T. (1967). The divergence and Bhattacharyya distance measures in signal selection. *IEEE Transactions on Communication Technology, 15*(1), 52–60. doi:10.1109/TCOM.1967.1089532

Kang, D., Silvescu, A., & Honavar, V. (2006). RNBL-MN: A recursive naive Bayes learner for sequence classification. In *Proceedings of PAKDD,* (pp. 45–54).

Kang, D., Zhang, J., Silvescu, A., & Honavar, V. (2005). Multinomial event model based abstraction for sequence and text classification. In *Proceedings of SARA,* (pp. 134–148).

Karacah, B., & Krim, H. (2002). Fast minimization of structural risk by nearest neighbor rule. *IEEE Transactions on Neural Networks, 14*(1), 127–137. doi:10.1109/TNN.2002.804315

Karlin, S. (1998). Global dinucleotide signatures and analysis of genomic heterogeneity. *Current Opinion in Microbiology, 1*(5), 598–610. doi:10.1016/S1369-5274(98)80095-7

Karlin, S. (2001). Detecting anomalous gene clusters and pathogenicity islands in diverse bacterial genomes. *Trends in Microbiology, 9*(7), 335–343. doi:10.1016/S0966-842X(01)02079-0

Karlin, S., & Ladunga, I. (1994). Comparisons of eukaryotic genomic sequences. *Proceedings of the National Academy of Sciences of the United States of America*, *91*(26), 12832–12836. doi:10.1073/pnas.91.26.12832

Karlin, S., & Mrazek, J. (1997). Compositional differences within and between eukaryotic genomes. *Proceedings of the National Academy of Sciences of the United States of America*, *94*(19), 10227–10232. doi:10.1073/pnas.94.19.10227

Karlin, S., Mrazek, J., & Campbell, A. M. (1998). Codon usages in different gene classes of the E. coli genome. *Molecular Microbiology*, *29*(6), 1341–1355. doi:10.1046/j.1365-2958.1998.01008.x

Kaufman, L. (1999). Solving the quadratic programming problem arising in support vector classification. In Scholkopf, B., Burges, C., & Smola, A. (Eds.), *Advances in kernel methods: Support vector learning* (pp. 147–167). Cambridge, MA: MIT Press.

Kay, J., Maisonneuve, N., Yacef, K., & Zaïane, O. (2006). *Mining patterns of events in students' teamwork data*. In Educational Data Mining Workshop, held in conjunction with Intelligent Tutoring Systems (ITS), (pp. 45-52).

KDDCup99. (1999). *Data*. Retrieved from http://kdd.ics.uci.edu/databases/kddcup99/kddcup99.html

Keogh, E., Lonardi, S., & Chiu, B. (2002). Finding surprising patterns in a time series database in linear time and space. In *Proc. of 8th ACM SIGKDD Int. Conf. on Knowledge Discovery and Data Mining*, (pp. 550-556).

Kim, Y. S., Stree, W. N., & Menczer, F. (2003). Feature selection in data mining. In Wang, J. (Ed.), *Data mining: Opportunities and challenges* (pp. 80–105). Hershey, PA: IGI Global. doi:10.4018/9781591400516.ch004

Kleinberg, J. M. (1999). Authoritative sources in a hyperlinked environment. *Journal of the ACM*, *46*(5), 604–632. doi:10.1145/324133.324140

Klemettinen, M., Mannila, H., Ronkainen, P., Toivonen, T., & Verkamo, A. (1994). Finding interesting rules from large sets of discovered association rules. In *Proc. of the 3rd Int'l Conf. on Information and Knowledge Management* (CIKM'94), (pp. 401-407). Gaithersburg, Maryland.

Kondor, R., & Jebara, T. (2003). A kernel between sets of vectors. In *Proceedings of International Conference on Machine Learning, (ICML 2003)*. Washington DC, USA.

Koonin, E. V., Makarova, K. S., & Aravind, L. (2001). Horizontal gene transfer in prokaryotes: Quantification and classification. *Annual Review of Microbiology*, *55*, 709–742. doi:10.1146/annurev.micro.55.1.709

Kotsiantis, S. B., & Pintelas, P. E. (2004). Increasing the classification accuracy of simple Bayesian classifier. In *Proceedings of AIMSA*, (pp. 198–207).

Kressel, U. H.-G. (1999). Pairwise classification and support vector machines. In Scholkopf, B., Burges, C., & Smola, A. (Eds.), *Advances in kernel methods: Support vector learning* (pp. 255–268). Cambridge, MA: MIT Press.

Krogh, A., Brown, M., Mian, I. S., Sjolander, K., & Haussler, D. (1994). Hidden Markov models in computational biology: Applications to protein modeling. *Journal of Molecular Biology*, *235*, 1501–1531. doi:10.1006/jmbi.1994.1104

Krogh, A., Brown, M., Mian, I. S., Sojlander, K., & Haussler, D. (1994). Hidden Markov models in computational biology: Applications to protein modeling. *Journal of Molecular Biology*, *235*, 1501–1531. doi:10.1006/jmbi.1994.1104

Kruengkrai, C., Srichaivattana, P., Sornlertlamvanich, V., & Isahara, H. (2005). *Language identification based on string kernels*. In IEEE International Symposium on Communications and Information Technology, 2005. ISCIT 2005., vol. 2, (pp. 926–929).

Kuang, R., Ie, E., Wang, K., Wang, K., Siddiqi, M., Freund, Y., & Leslie, C. (2004). Profile-based string kernels for remote homology detection and motif extraction. *Journal of Bioinformatics and Computational Systems*, *3*(3), 152–160.

Kubat, M., & Matwin, S. (1997). Addressing the curse of imbalanced training sets: one sided selection. *Proceedings of the Fourteenth International Conference on Machine Learning*, (pp. 179-186), Nashville, TN: Morgan Kaufmann.

Kullback, S., & Leibler, R. A. (1951). On information and sufficiency. *Annals of Mathematical Statistics, 22*(1), 79–86. doi:10.1214/aoms/1177729694

Kum, H.-C., Chang, J. H., & Wang, W. (2006). Sequential Pattern Mining in Multi-Databases via Multiple Alignment. *Data Mining and Knowledge Discovery, 12*(2-3), 151–180. doi:10.1007/s10618-005-0017-3

Kum, H.-C., Chang, J. H., & Wang, W. (2006). Sequential pattern mining in multi-databases via multiple alignment. *Data Mining and Knowledge Discovery, 12*(2-3), 151–180. doi:10.1007/s10618-005-0017-3

Kum, H.-C., Chang, J. H., & Wang, W. (2007). Benchmarking the effectiveness of sequential pattern mining methods. *Data & Knowledge Engineering, 60*(1), 30–50. doi:10.1016/j.datak.2006.01.004

Kuo, R. J., Chao, C. M., & Liu, C. Y. (2009). Integration of K-means algorithm and AprioriSome algorithm for fuzzy sequential pattern mining. *Applied Soft Computing, 9*(1), 85–93. doi:10.1016/j.asoc.2008.03.010

Kuo, R. J., Chao, C. M., & Liu, C. Y. (2009). Integration of K-means algorithm and AprioriSome algorithm for fuzzy sequential pattern mining. *Applied Soft Computing, 9*(1), 85–93. doi:10.1016/j.asoc.2008.03.010

Kyte, J., & Doolittle, R. F. (1982). A simple method for displaying hydropathic character of a protein. *Journal of Molecular Biology, 157*, 105–132. doi:10.1016/0022-2836(82)90515-0

Langille, M. G. I., Hsiao, W. W. L., & Brinkman, F. S. L. (2008). Evaluation of genomic island predictors using a comparative genomics approach. *BMC Bioinformatics, 9*, 329–338. doi:10.1186/1471-2105-9-329

Langille, M. G. I., Hsiao, W. W. L., & Brinkman, F. S. L. (2010). Detecting genomic islands using bioinformatics approaches. *Nature Reviews Microbiology, 8*(5), 373–382. doi:10.1038/nrmicro2350

Lau, A., Ong, S. S., Mahidadia, A., Hoffmann, A., Westbrook, J., & Zrimec, T. (2003). Mining patterns of dyspepsia symptoms across time points using constraint association rules. *PAKDD '03: Proceedings of the 7th Pacific-Asia conference on Advances in knowledge discovery and data mining* (pp. 124-135). Seoul, Korea: Springer-Verlag.

Laur, P.-A., Symphor, J.-E., Nock, R., & Poncelet, P. (2007). Statistical supports for mining sequential patterns and improving the incremental update process on data streams. *Intelligent Data Analysis, 11*(1), 29–47.

Lawrence, J. G. (1999). Selfish operons: The evolutionary impact of gene clustering in prokaryotes and eukaryotes. *Current Opinion in Genetics & Development, 9*(6), 642–648. doi:10.1016/S0959-437X(99)00025-8

Lawrence, J. G., & Ochman, H. (1997). Amelioration of bacterial genomes: Rates of change and exchange. *Journal of Molecular Evolution, 44*(4), 383–397. doi:10.1007/PL00006158

Lawrence, J. G., & Ochman, H. (2002). Reconciling the many faces of lateral gene transfer. *Trends in Microbiology, 10*(1), 1–4. doi:10.1016/S0966-842X(01)02282-X

Laxman, S., Sastry, P. S., & Unnikrishnan, K. P. (2007). A fast algorithm for finding frequent episodes in event streams. In P. Berkhin, R. Caruana, & X. Wu (Eds.), *Proceedings of the Thirteenth ACM SIGKDD International Conference on Knowledge Discovery and Data Mining (KDD-07)* (pp. 410-419).

Lee, K.-A., You, C. H., Li, H., & Kinnunen, T. (2007). A GMM-based probabilistic sequence kernel for speaker verification. In *Proceedings of INTERSPEECH*, (pp. 294–297). Antwerp, Belgium.

Lent, B., Agrawal, R., & Srikant, R. (1997). Discovering trends in text databases. *Proc. 3rd Int. Conf. Knowledge Discovery and Data Mining, KDD* (pp. 227-230). AAAI Press.

Lesh, N., Zaki, M. J., & Ogihara, M. (2000). Scalable feature mining for sequential data. *IEEE Intelligent Systems, 15*(2), 48–56. doi:10.1109/5254.850827

Lesh, N., Zaki, M. J., & Ogihara, M. (1999). Mining features for sequence classification. In *KDD '99: Proceedings of the Fifth ACM SIGKDD International Conference on Knowledge Discovery and Data Mining*, (pp. 342–346).

Leslie, C., Eskin, E., Cohen, A., Weston, J., & Noble, W. S. (2004). Mismatch string kernels for discriminative protein classification. *Bioinformatics (Oxford, England), 20*, 467–476. doi:10.1093/bioinformatics/btg431

Leslie, C., & Kuang, R. (2003). Fast kernels for inexact string matching. In B. Scholkopf & M. Warmth (Ed.), *16th Annual Conference on Learning Theory and 7th Annual Workshop on Kernel Machines*, vol. 2777, (pp. 114–128). Heidelberg, Germany: Springer Verlag

Leslie, C., Eskin, E., & Noble, W. S. (2002). The spectrum kernel: A string kernel for SVM protein classification. In The Pacific Symposium on Biocomputing, (pp. 564–575). River Edge, NJ.

Leslie, C., Eskin, E., & Noble, W. (2002). Mismatch string kernels for SVM protein classification. In *Proceedings of Neural Information Processing Systems*, (pp. 1417–1424).

Li, J., Liu, H., & Wong, L. (2003). Mean-entropy discretized features are effective for classifying high-dimensional bio-medical data. In *Proceedings of BIOKDD*, (pp. 17–24).

Li, Z., Tan, T., Chen, J., & Wassantachat, T. (2008). On traffic density estimation with a boosted SVM classifier. Proceeding *of 2008 Digital Image Computing - Techniques and Applications (DICTA2008)*, Australia.

Li, Z., Zhang, A., Li, D., & Wang, L. (2007). Discovering novel multistage attack strategies. *ADMA '07: Proceedings of the 3rd international conference on Advanced Data Mining and Applications* (pp. 45-56). Harbin, China: Springer-Verlag.

Liao, L., & Noble, W. S. (2003). Combining pairwise sequence similarity and support vector machines for detecting remote protein evolutionary and structural relationships. *Journal of Computational Biology, 10*(6), 857–868. doi:10.1089/106652703322756113

Liao, L., & Noble, W. S. (2002). *Combining pairwise sequence similarity and support vector machines for remote protein homology detection*. In Sixth Annual International Conference on Computational Molecular Biology, (pp. 225–232). Washington, DC, USA.

Lin, N. P., Chen, H.-J., Hao, W.-H., Chueh, H.-E., & Chang, C.-I. (2008). Mining strong positive and negative sequential patterns. *W. Trans. on Comp., 7*(3), 119–124.

Ling, C., & Li, C. (1998). Data mining for direct marketing problems and solutions. In *Proceedings of the Fourth International Conference on Knowledge Discovery and Data Mining*, (pp. 73-79). New York, NY: AAAI Press.

Lio, P., & Vannucci, M. (2000). Finding pathogenicity islands and gene transfer events in genome data. *Bioinformatics (Oxford, England), 16*(10), 932–940. doi:10.1093/bioinformatics/16.10.932

Lipinski, C. A., Lombardo, F., Dominy, B. W., & Feeney, P. J. (1997). Experimental and computational approaches to estimate solubility and permeability in drug discovery and development settings. *Advanced Drug Delivery Reviews, 23*, 3–25. doi:10.1016/S0169-409X(96)00423-1

Lodhi, H., Saunders, C., Shawe-Taylor, J., Christianini, N., & Watkins, C. (2002). Text classification using string kernels. *Journal of Machine Learning Research, 2*, 419–444. doi:10.1162/153244302760200687

Logan, B., Moreno, P., Suzek, B., Weng, Z., & Kasif, S. (2001). *A study of remote homology detection (Tech. Rep. No. CRL 2001/05)*. Cambridge, MA: Compaq Computer Corporation, Cambridge Research Laboratory.

Loubier, E. (2009). *Analysis and visualization of relational data by graph morphing taking temporal dimension into account*. PhD Thesis, in French. Toulouse, France: Paul Sabatier University.

Loubier, E., & Dousset, B. (2007). *Visualisation and analysis of relational data by considering temporal dimension*. International Conference on Enterprise Information Systems, (pp. 550-553). INSTICC Press.

Lowe, T. M., & Eddy, S. R. (1997). tRNAscan-SE: A program for improved detection of transfer RNA genes in genomic sequence. *Nucleic Acids Research, 25*(5), 955–964. doi:10.1093/nar/25.5.955

Lozano, A., Manfredi, G., & Nieddu, L. (2009). An algorithm for the recognition of levels of congestion in road traffic problems. *Mathematics and Computers in Simulation, 79*(6), 1926–1934. doi:10.1016/j.matcom.2007.06.008

Maniez, J., & Grolier, E. (1991). *A decade of research in classification*.

Mannila, H., Toivonen, H., & Verkamo, I. (1997). Discovery of frequent episodes in event sequences. *Data Mining and Knowledge Discovery, 1*(3), 259–289. doi:10.1023/A:1009748302351

Mannila, H., Toivonnen, H., & Verkamo, A. I. (1997). Discovery of frequent episodes in event sequences. *Data Mining and Knowledge Discovery, 1*(3), 259–289. doi:10.1023/A:1009748302351

Manning, G., Whyte, D. B., Martinez, R., Hunter, T., & Sudarsanam, S. (2002). The protein kinase complement of the human genome. *Science, 298*(5600), 1912–1934. doi:10.1126/science.1075762

Manning, G., Whyte, D. B., Martinez, R., Hunter, T., & Sudarsanam, S. (2002). The protein kinase complement of the human genome. *Science, 298*, 1912–1934. doi:10.1126/science.1075762

Manning, G. (2005). Genomic overview of the kinases. In I. Greenwald (Ed.), *WormBook*, The *C. elegans Research Community (pp.* 1-19).

Mantri, Y., & Williams, K. P. (2004). Islander: A database of integrative islands in prokaryotic genomes, the associated integrases and their DNA site specificities. *Nucleic Acids Research, 32*, D55–D58. doi:10.1093/nar/gkh059

Mardia, K. V., Kent, J. T., & Bibby, J. M. (1979). *Multivariate analysis*. Academic Press.

Marsolo, K., & Parthasarathy, S. (2006a). On the use of structure and sequence-based features for protein classification and retrieval. In *Proceedings of ICDM*, (pp. 394-403).

Marsolo, K., & Parthasarathy, S. (2006b). Protein classification using summaries of profile-based frequency matrices. In *Proceedings of BIOKDD06: 6th Workshop on Data Mining in Bioinformatics (with SIGKDD Conference)*, (pp. 51–58).

Masseglia, F., Poncelet, P., & Teisseire, M. (2003). Incremental mining of sequential patterns in large databases. *Data & Knowledge Engineering, 46*(1), 97–121. doi:10.1016/S0169-023X(02)00209-4

Masseglia, F., Poncelet, P., & Teisseire, M. (2003). Incremental mining of sequential patterns in large databases. *Data & Knowledge Engineering, 46*(1), 97–121. doi:10.1016/S0169-023X(02)00209-4

Masseglia, F., Poncelet, P., & Teisseire, M. (2009). Efficient mining of sequential patterns with time constraints: Reducing the combinations. *Expert Systems with Applications, 36*(3), 2677–2690. doi:10.1016/j.eswa.2008.01.021

McCallum, A., & Nigam, K. (1998). A comparison of event models for naive Bayes text classification. In *Proceedings of AAAI-98 Workshop on Learning for Text Categorization*, (pp. 41–48).

McNeil, L. K., Reich, C., Aziz, R. K., Bartels, D., Cohoon, M., & Disz, T. (2007). The National microbial pathogen database resource (NMPDR): A genomics platform based on subsystem annotation. *Nucleic Acids Research, 35*, D347–D353. doi:10.1093/nar/gkl947

Melvin, I., Ie, E., Weston, J., Noble, W. S., & Leslie, C. (2007). Multi-class protein classification using adaptive codes. *Journal of Machine Learning Research, 8*, 1557–1581.

Mendes, L. F., Ding, B., & Han, J. (2008). Stream sequential pattern mining with precise error bounds. *Proc. 2008 Int. Conf. on Data Mining (ICDM'08)*, Pisa, Italy, Dec. 2008.

Mitchell, T. M. (1997). *Machine Learning*. New York: McGraw-Hill Series in CompSci.

Mobasher, B., Dai, H., Luo, T., & Nakagawa, M. (2002). Using sequential and non-sequential patterns in predictive Web usage mining tasks. *ICDM '02: Proceedings of the 2002 IEEE International Conference on Data Mining* (pp. 669-672). Washington, DC: IEEE Computer Society.

Moreno, P. J., Ho, P. P., & Vasconcelos, N. (2004). A Kullback-Leibler divergence based kernel for SVM classification in multimedia applications. In Thrun, S., Saul, L., & Schölkopf, B. (Eds.), *Advances in Neural Information Processing Systems 16*. Cambridge, MA: MIT Press.

Muhlenbach, F., Lallich, S., & Zighed, D. A. (2004). Identifying and handling mislabelled instances. *Journal of Intelligent Information Systems, 22*(1), 89–109. doi:10.1023/A:1025832930864

Nadeem, T., Dashtinezhad, S., Liao, C., & Iftode, L. (2004). TrafficView: A scalable traffic monitoring system. *Proceedings of IEEE International Conference on Mobile Data Management (MDM'04)*.

Nag, S., Chatterjee, R., Chaudhuri, K., & Chaudhuri, P. (2006). Unsupervised statistical identification of genomic islands using oligonucleotide distributions with application to vibrio genomes. *Sadhana, 31*(2), 105–115. doi:10.1007/BF02719776

Needleman, S. B., & Wunsch, C. D. (1970). A general method applicable to the search for similarities in the amino acid sequences of two proteins. *Journal of Molecular Biology, 48*, 443–453. doi:10.1016/0022-2836(70)90057-4

Nicolas, J. A., Herengt, G., & Albuisson, E. (2004). Sequential pattern mining and classification of patient path. *MEDINFO 2004: Proceedings Of The 11th World Congress On Medical Informatics.*

Nigam, K., Lafferty, J., & McCallum, A. (1999). Using maximum entropy for text classification. In *Proceedings of IJCAI-99 Workshop on Machine Learning for Information Filtering*, (pp. 61–67).

Nikolskaya, A. N., & Wu, C. H. (2004). PIRSF: Family classification system at the protein information resource. *Nucleic Acids Research, 32*, 112–114. doi:10.1093/nar/gkh097

Ochman, H., Lawrence, J. G., & Groisman, E. A. (2000). Lateral gene transfer and the nature of bacterial innovation. *Nature, 405*(6784), 299–304. doi:10.1038/35012500

Onder, S. (2008). ADL++: Object-oriented specification of complicated instruction sets and micro-architectures. In P. Mishra and N. Dutt (Eds.), *Processor description languages, volume 1 (systems on Silicon)* (pp. 247-274). Burlington, MA: Morgan Kaufmann (Elsevier) Publishers.

Osborne, A. (1980). *An introduction to microcomputers, vol 1: Basic concepts* (2nd ed.).

Ou, H. Y., He, X., Harrison, E. M., Kulasekara, B. R., Thani, A. B., & Kadioglu, A. (2007). MobilomeFINDER: Web-based tools for in silico and experimental discovery of bacterial genomic islands. *Nucleic Acids Research, 35*, W97–W104. doi:10.1093/nar/gkm380

Ozkurt, C., & Camci, F. (2009). Automatic traffic density estimation and vehicle classification for traffic surveillance systems using neural networks. [MCA]. *Mathematical and Computational Applications An International Journal, 14*(3), 187–196.

Park, K.-J., & Kanehisa, M. (2003). Prediction of protein sub-cellular locations by support vector machines using compositions of amino acids and amino acid pairs. *Bioinformatics (Oxford, England), 19*(13), 1656–1663. doi:10.1093/bioinformatics/btg222

Parthasarathy, S., Zaki, M., Ogihara, M., & Dwarkadas, S. (1999). Incremental and interactive sequence mining. In *Proc. of the 8th Int. Conf. on Information and Knowledge Management (CIKM'99).*

Parthasarathy, S., Zaki, M., Ogihara, M., & Dwarkadas, S. (1999). Incremental and interactive sequence mining. *In Proc. of the 8th Int. Conf. on Information and Knowledge Management (CIKM'99).*

Pavlov, D. (2003). Sequence modeling with mixtures of conditional maximum entropy distributions. In *Proceedings of ICDM*, (pp. 251–258).

Pearson, W. R., & Lipman, D. J. (1988). Improved tools for biological sequence comparison. *Proceedings of the National Academy of Sciences of the United States of America, 85*(8), 2444–2448. doi:10.1073/pnas.85.8.2444

Pei, J., Han, J., & Wang, W. (2007). Constraint-based sequential pattern mining: The pattern-growth methods. *Journal of Intelligent Information Systems, 28*(2), 133–160. doi:10.1007/s10844-006-0006-z

Pei, J., Han, J., Asl, M. B., Pinto, H., Chen, Q., Dayal, U., et al. (2001). PrefixSpan mining sequential patterns efficiently by prefix projected pattern growth. *Proc. 17th Int'l Conf. on Data Eng.*, (pp. 215-226).

Pei, J., Han, J., Mortazavi-Asi, B., & Pinto, H. (2001). PrefixSpan mining sequential patterns efficiently by prefix-projected pattern growth. In *Proc. of Int. Conf. on Data Engineering.*

Perera, D., Kay, J., Yacef, K., & Koprinska, I. (2007). *Mining learners' traces from an online collaboration tool. Proceedings of Educational Data Mining workshop* (pp. 60–69). CA, USA: Marina del Rey.

Piatetsky-Shapiro, G., & Frawley, W. J. (1991). *Knowledge discovery in databases.* AAAI/MIT, 1991.

Pinto, H., Han, J., Pei, J., Wang, K., Chen, Q., & Dayal, U. (2001). Multi-dimensional sequential pattern mining. *CIKM '01: Proceedings of the Tenth International Conference on Information and Knowledge Management* (pp. 81-88). New York, NY: ACM.

Pinto, H., Han, J., Pei, J., Wang, K., Chen, Q., & Dayal, U. (2001). Multi-dimensional sequential pattern mining. *CIKM '01: Proceedings of the Tenth International Conference on Information and Knowledge Management* (pp. 81-88). New York, NY: ACM.

Ponte, J. M., & Croft, B. (1998). A language modeling approach to information retrieval. Proceedings of the 21st Annual International ACM SIGIR Conference on Research and Development in Information Retrieval, (pp. 275–281).

Potter, C., Klooster, S., Torregrosa, A., Tan, P.-N., Steinbach, M., & Kumar, V. (n.d.). *Finding spatio-temporal patterns in earth science data.*

Pradeep, K. M., Venkateswara, R., Radha, K. P., Bapi, R. S., & Laha, A. (2005). Intrusion detection system using sequence and set preserving metric. In *Proceedings of Intelligence and Security Informatics,* (pp. 498-504). Atlanta, USA.

Priya Lakshmanan. 2010. Establishing signature for kinase inhibitors. Unpublished M.Tech dissertation, University of Hyderabad, India.

Pundhir, S., Vijayvargiya, H., & Kumar, A. (2008). PredictBias: A server for the identification of genomic and pathogenicity islands in prokaryotes. *In Silico Biology*, *8*(3-4), 223–234.

Qingda, Z., Qingshan, J., Sheng, L., Xiaobiao, X., & Lida, L. (2010a). *An efficient for protein pattern mining*. International Conference on Computer Science and Education, (pp. 1876-1881).

Rabiner, L., & Juang, B.-H. (1993). *Fundamentals of speech recognition*. United States: Prentice Hall.

Ragan, M. A., Harlow, T. J., & Beiko, R. G. (2006). Do different surrogate methods detect lateral genetic transfer events of different relative ages? *Trends in Microbiology*, *14*(1), 4–8. doi:10.1016/j.tim.2005.11.004

Rahmann, S. (2003). Dynamic programming algorithms for two statistical problems in computational biology. In D. Tsur (Ed.), *Workshop on Algorithms in Bioinformatics (WABI), LNCS 2812* (pp. 151-164).

Raja, G., Sobha Rani, T., & Durga Bhavani, S. (2004). Global feature extraction techniques for identification of secondary structures of a protein sequence. In International Conference on Information Technology (pp.101-108). India: Universities Press.

Rajan, I., Aravamuthan, S., & Mande, S. S. (2007). Identification of compositionally distinct regions in genomes using the centroid method. *Bioinformatics (Oxford, England)*, *23*(20), 2672–2677. doi:10.1093/bioinformatics/btm405

Ramakrishnan, R., Schauer, J. J., Chen, L., Huang, Z., Shafer, M. M., & Gross, D. S. (2005). The EDAM project: Mining atmospheric aerosol datasets: Research articles. *International Journal of Intelligent Systems*, *20*(7), 759–787. doi:10.1002/int.20094

Rani, P., & Pudi, V. (2008a). Repeat based naïve Bayes classifier for biological sequences. In *ICDM* (pp. 989–994). RBNBC.

Rani, P., & Pudi, V. (2008b). *RBNBC: Repeat based naïve Bayes classifier for biological sequences. (Technical report, IIIT/TR/2008/126)*. India: IIIT Hyderabad.

Rani, P., & Pudi, V. (2008c). Repeat based maximum entropy classifier for biological sequences. In *COMAD* (pp. 71–82). REBMEC.

Rani, P. (2008). *Novel Bayesian sequence classifiers applied on biological sequence*s. Masters thesis. IIIT Hyderabad, India.

Rani, T. S., & Bapi, R. S. (2008). *Cascaded multi-level promoter recognition of E. coli using dinucleotide features*. In International Conference on Information Technology (pp. 83–88). Bhubaneswar.

Raskutti, B., & Kowalczyk, A. (2004). Extreme rebalancing for SVMs: A case study. *SIGKDD Explorations Newsletter*, *6*(1), 60–69. doi:10.1145/1007730.1007739

Ratnaparkhi, A. (1997). *A simple introduction to maximum entropy models for natural language processing.* (Technical report, IRCS Report 97-98), Institute for Research in Cognitive Science, University of Pennsylvania.

Ratnaparkhi, A. (1998). *Maximum entropy models for natural language ambiguity resolution*. PhD thesis, University of Pennsylvania.

Rau, B. R., & Fisher, J. A. (1993). Instruction-level parallel processing: History, overview and perspective. *The Journal of Supercomputing, 7*(1-2), 9–50. doi:10.1007/BF01205181

Ravindra Babu, T., Murty, M. N., & Agrawal, V. K. (2007). Classification of run-length encoded binary data. *Pattern Recognition, 40*, 321–323. doi:10.1016/j.patcog.2006.05.002

Ravindra Babu, T., & Narasimha Murty, M. (2001). Comparison of genetic algorithm based prototype selection schemes. *Pattern Recognition, 34*(2), 523–525. doi:10.1016/S0031-3203(00)00094-7

Ravindra Babu, T., Murty, M. N., & Subrahmanya, S. V. (2009). Multiagent systems for large data clustering. In Cao, L. (Ed.), *Data mining and multi-agent interaction, part 3* (pp. 219–238). doi:10.1007/978-1-4419-0522-2_15

Ravindra Babu, T., Murty, M. N., & Subrahmanya, S. V. (2010). *Multiagent based large data clustering scheme for data mining applications.* Intl. Conf. on Active Media Technology, (pp. 116-127).

Ravindra Babu, T., Narasimha Murty, M., & Agrawal, V. K. (2004). Hybrid learning scheme for data mining applications. In *the Proc. Fourth International Conference on Hybrid Intelligent Systems,* (pp. 266-271). Los Alamitos, CA: IEEE Computer Society.

Ravindra Babu, T., Narasimha Murty, M., & Agrawal, V. K. (2005). On simultaneous selection of prototypes and features on large data. In the *Proceedings of PReMI,* (pp. 595-600).

Read, T., & Cressie, N. (1988). *Goodness-of-fit statistics for discrete multivariate data.* Springer.

Read, T., & Cressie, N. (1989). Pearson's X^2 and the likelihood ratio statistic G^2: A comparative review. *International Statistical Review, 57*(1), 19–43. doi:10.2307/1403582

Reddy, A. S., Amarnath, H. S. D., Bapi, R. S., Sastry, G. M., & Sastry, G. N. (2008). Protein ligand interaction database (PLID). *Comp. Biol. and Chem., 32*, 387-390. Retrieved on January 11, 2011 from http://203.199.182.73/gnsmmg/databases/plid/

Regnier, M., & Vandenbogaert, M. (2006). Comparison of statistical significance criteria. *Journal of Bioinformatics and Computational Biology, 4*(2), 537–551. doi:10.1142/S0219720006002028

Reynolds, D. A., Quatieri, T. F., & Dunn, R. B. (2000). Speaker verification using adapted Gaussian mixture models. *Digital Signal Processing, 10*(1-3), 19–41. doi:10.1006/dspr.1999.0361

Roberto, J., & Bayardo, J. (1998). Efficiently mining long patterns from databases. In *SIGMOD '98: Proceedings of the 1998 ACM SIGMOD International Conference on Management of Data,* (pp. 85–93).

Romero, C., Ventura, S., Delgado, J. A., & Bra, P. D. (2007). *Personalized links recommendation based on data mining un adaptive educational hypermedia systems.* Creating New Learning Experiences on a Global Scale. Second European Conference on Technology Enhanced Learning, EC-TEL 2007 (pp. 293-305). Crete, Greece: Springer.

Rubner, Y., Tomasi, C., & Guibas, L. J. (2000). The earth mover's distance as a metric for image retrieval. *International Journal of Computer Vision, 40*(2), 99–121. doi:10.1023/A:1026543900054

Ruping, S. (2001). SVM kernels for time series analysis. In Klinkenberg, R., Ruping, S., Fick, A., Henze, N., Horzog, C., Molitor, R., & Schroder, O. (Eds.), *LLWA 01-Tagungsband der G1-Workshop-Woche Lemen-Lehren Wissen-Adaptivitet* (pp. 43–50).

Russ, A. P., & Lampel, S. (2005). The druggable genome: an update. *Drug Discovery Today, 10*, 1607–1610. doi:10.1016/S1359-6446(05)03666-4

Saigo, H., Vert, J.-P., Ueda, N., & Akutsu, T. (2004). Protein homology detection using string alignment kernels. *Bioinformatics (Oxford, England), 20*(11), 1682–1689. doi:10.1093/bioinformatics/bth141

Salomon, D. (2000). *Data compression – The complete reference.* CA: Springer-Verlag.

Salton, G., Wong, A., & Yang, C. (1975). A vector space model for automatic indexing. *Communications of the ACM, 18*(11), 613–620. doi:10.1145/361219.361220

Salton, G., & Mcgill, M. (1984). *Introduction to modern information retrieval. McGraw Hill Int.* Book Co.

Sanjay, R., Gulati, V. P., & Pujari, A. K. (2004). Frequency- and ordering-based similarity measure for host-based intrusion detection. *Information Management & Computer Security, 12*(5), 411–421. doi:10.1108/09685220410563397

Sarawagi, S. (2003). *Sequence data mining techniques and applications*. In the 19th International Conference on Data Engineering.

Satish, D. S. (2005). *Kernel based clustering and vector quantization for pattern classification*. Master of Science thesis, Indian Institute of Technology Madras, Chennai.

Sauvagnat, K. (2005). *Flexible model for information retrieval in the corpus of semi-structured documents*. Unpublished thesis. Toulouse, France: Paul Sabatier University.

Scholkopf, B., Mika, S., Burges, C., Knirsch, P., Muller, K.-R., Ratsch, G., & Smola, A. (1999). Input space versus feature space in kernel-based methods. *IEEE Transactions on Neural Networks, 10*(5), 1000–1017. doi:10.1109/72.788641

Sekhar, C. C., Takeda, K., & Itakura, F. (2003). Recognition of subword units of speech using support vector machines. In *Recent research developments in electronics and communication* (pp. 101–136). Trivandrum, Kerala, India: Transworld Research Network.

Seno, M., & Karypis, G. (2002). SLPMiner: An algorithm for finding frequent sequential patterns using length-decreasing support constraint. In *Proceedings of the 2nd IEEE International Conference on Data Mining (ICDM)*, (pp. 418-425).

Seno, M., & Karypis, G. (2002). SLPMiner: An algorithm for finding frequent sequential patterns using length-decreasing support constraint. In *Proceedings of the 2nd IEEE International Conference on Data Mining (ICDM)*, (pp. 418-425).

Shang, B., & Si-Xue, B. (2009). *The maximal frequent pattern mining of DNA sequence*. IEEE International Conference on Granular Computing (pp. 23-26).

Sharma, S., Kumar, V., & Sobha Rani, T. Durga Bhavani, & S., Bapi Raju, S. (2004). Application of neural networks for protein sequence classification. In *Intelligent Sensing and Information Processing* (pp.325-328). India: IEEE Press.

Shawe-Taylor, J., & Cristianini, N. (2004). *Kernel methods for pattern analysis*. Cambridge, UK: Cambridge University Press. doi:10.1017/CBO9780511809682

Shen, J. P., & Lipasti, M. H. (2005). *Modern processor design: Fundamentals of superscalar processors*. New York, NY: McGraw-Hill Companies.

Sigrist, C. J. A., & Hulo, N. (2004). Recent improvements to the PROSITE database. *Nucleic Acids Research, 32*, 134–137. doi:10.1093/nar/gkh044

Sikic, M., Tomic, S., & Vlahovicek, K. (2009). Prediction of protein–protein interaction sites in sequences and 3D structures by random forests. *PLoS Computational Biology, 5*(1), e1000278. doi:10.1371/journal.pcbi.1000278

Smith, T. F., & Waterman, M. S. (1981). Identification of common molecular subsequences. *Journal of Molecular Biology, 147*, 195–197. doi:10.1016/0022-2836(81)90087-5

Smith, N., & Gales, M. (2002). Speech recognition using SVMs. In *Proceedings of the 2002 Conference on Advances in Neural Information Processing Systems*, (pp. 1197–1204). Cambridge, MA: MIT Press.

Smith, N., & Gales, M. (2002). Speech recognition using SVMs. In *Proceedings of the 2002 Conference on Advances in Neural Information Processing Systems*, (pp. 1197–1204). Cambridge, MA: MIT Press.

Soujanya, V., Satyanarayana, R. V., & Kamalakar, K. (2006). *A simple yet effective data clustering algorithm*. In Sixth International Conference on Data Mining, (pp. 1108-1112).

Sparck Jones, K., Walker, S., & Robertson, S. E. (2000). A probabilistic model of information retrieval: Development and comparative experiments. *Information Processing & Management, 36*(6), 779–840. doi:10.1016/S0306-4573(00)00015-7

Spath, H. (1980). *Cluster analysis – Algorithms for data reduction and classification of objects*. West Sussex, UK: Ellis Horwood Limited.

Srikant, R., & Agrawal, R. (1996). *Advances in database technology EDBT '96.*, (pp. 3-17).

Srikant, R., & Agrawal, R. (1996). Mining sequential patterns: Generalizations and performance improvements. In *Proc. 5th Int. Conf. Extending Database Technology*.

Stefano, L. D., Milani, I., & Viarani, E. (2000). Evaluation of inductive-loop emulation algorithms for UTC systems. *Proceedings of the Sixth International Conference on Control, Automation, Robotics and Computer Vision (ICARCV 2000)*, Singapore.

Stoicke, A., Kajarekar, S., & Ferrer, L. (2008). *Nonparametric feature normalization for SVM-based speaker verification*. In IEEE International Conference on Acoustics, Speech, and Signal Processing 2008, ICASSP 2008, (pp. 1577–1580). Las Vegas, NV.

Sugawara, H., Ogasawara, O., Okubo, K., Gojobori, T., & Tateno, Y. (2008). DDBJ with new system and face. *Nucleic Acids Research*, *36*, 22–24. doi:10.1093/nar/gkm889

Sun, Y., Castellano, C. G., Mark, R., Adams, R., Alistair, G. R., & Neil, D. (2009). Using pre and post-processing methods to improve binding site predictions. *Pattern Recognition*, *42*(9), 1949–1958. doi:10.1016/j.patcog.2009.01.027

Susheela Devi, V. (2010). *Optimal prototype selection for efficient pattern classification*. VDM Verlag.

Taft, L. M., Evans, R. S., Shyu, C. R., Egger, M. J., & Chawla, N., V., Joyce, A. M., … Michael, W. V. (2009). Countering imbalanced datasets to improve adverse drug event predictive models in labor and delivery. [JBI]. *Journal of Biomedical Informatics*, *42*(2), 356–364. doi:10.1016/j.jbi.2008.09.001

Tan, P.-N., Kumar, V., & Srivastava, J. (2002). Selecting the right interestingness measure for association patterns. *KDD '02: Proceedings of the Eighth ACM SIGKDD International Conference on Knowledge Discovery and Data Mining*, (pp. 32-41). Edmonton, Alberta, Canada. New York, NY: ACM Press.

Tatti, N. (2007). Maximum entropy based significance of itemsets. In *Proceedings of ICDM*, (pp. 312–321).

Tax, D. (2001). *One-class classification*. PhD thesis, Delft University of Technology.

Terai, G., & Takagi, T. (2004). Predicting rules on organization of cis-regulatory elements, taking the order of elements into account. *Bioinformatics (Oxford, England)*, *20*(7), 1119–1128. doi:10.1093/bioinformatics/bth049

Thonangi, R., & Pudi, V. (2005). ACME: An associative classifier based on maximum entropy principle. In *Proceedings of ALT*, (pp. 122–134).

Tiwari, G., Fazio, J., & Baurav, S. (2007). Traffic planning for non-homogeneous traffic. *Sadhna (Special Issue on Transportation Research - Safety and Sustainability)*, *32*(4), 309-328.

Tsuboi, Y. (2002). *Authorship identification for heterogeneous documents*.

Tsuda, K., Kin, T., & Asai, K. (2002). Mariginalized kernels for biological sequences. *Bioinformatics (Oxford, England)*, *18*, S268–S275. doi:10.1093/bioinformatics/18.suppl_1.S268

Tsuda, K. (1998). *Support vector classifier with asymmetric kernel functions*. In European Symposium on Artificial Neural Networks, (pp. 183–188). Bruges, Belgium.

Tu, Q., & Ding, D. (2003). Detecting pathogenicity islands and anomalous gene clusters by iterative discriminant analysis. *FEMS Microbiology Letters*, *221*(2), 269–275. doi:10.1016/S0378-1097(03)00204-0

UCI. (n.d.). *Machine learning repository*. Retrieved from http://archive.ics.uci.edu/ml/

Uniprot: http://www.uniprot.org

Vapnik, V. (1999). *Statistical learning theory* (2nd ed.). New York, NY: John Wiley & Sons.

Vapnik, V. (1998). *Statistical learning theory*. New York, NY: Wiley-Interscience.

Vert, J.-P., Saigo, H., & Akutsu, T. (2004). Local alignment kernels for biological sequences. In Scholkopf, B., Tsuda, K., & Platt, J. (Eds.), *Kernel methods in computational biology* (pp. 131–154). Cambridge, MA: MIT Press.

Vieth, M., Higgs, R. E., & Roberston, D. H. (2004). Kinomics- structural biology and chemogenomics of kinase inhibitors and targets. *Biochimica et Biophysica Acta*, *1697*(1-2), 243–257.

Vilalta, R., Apte, C. V., Hellerstein, J. L., Ma, S., & Weiss, S. M. (2002). Predictive algorithms in the management of computer systems. *IBM Systems Journal, 41*(3), 461–474. doi:10.1147/sj.413.0461

Visa, S., & Ralescu, A. (2005). Issues in mining imbalanced data sets - A review paper. In *Proceedings of the Sixteen Midwest Artificial Intelligence and Cognitive Science Conference*, (pp. 67-73).

Vishwanathan, S. V. N., & Smola, A. J. (2003). Fast kernels for string and tree matching. In Becker, S., Thrun, S., & Obermayer, K. (Eds.), *Advances in neural information processing* (pp. 569–576). Cambridge, MA: MIT Press.

Vrotsou, K., Ellegård, K., & Cooper, M. (n.d.). *Exploring time diaries using semi-automated activity pattern extraction.*

Vu, T. H., Ryu, K. H., & Park, N. (2009). A method for predicting future location of mobile user for location-based services system. *Computers & Industrial Engineering, 57*(1), 91–105. doi:10.1016/j.cie.2008.07.009

Vulpetti, A., & Bosotti, R. (2004). Sequence and structural analysis of kinase ATP pocket residues. *IL Farmaco, 59*, 759–765. doi:10.1016/j.farmac.2004.05.010

Waack, S., Keller, O., Asper, R., Brodag, T., Damm, C., & Fricke, W. F. (2006). Score-based prediction of genomic islands in prokaryotic genomes using hidden Markov models. *BMC Bioinformatics, 7*, 142–153. doi:10.1186/1471-2105-7-142

Walicki, M., & Ferreira, D. R. (2010). *Mining sequences for patterns with non-repeating symbols.* International Conference on Evolutionary Computation (pp. 1-8).

Wan, V., & Renals, S. (2002). Evaluation of kernel methods for speaker verification and identification. In *Proceedings of IEEE International Conference on Acoustics, Speech and Signal Processing*, (pp. 669-672). Orlando, Florida, US.

Wang, Y., Lim, E.-P., & Hwang, S.-Y. (2006). Efficient mining of group patterns from user movement data. *Data & Knowledge Engineering, 57*(3), 240–282. doi:10.1016/j.datak.2005.04.006

Wang, M., Yang, J., Liu, G.-P., Xu, Z.-J., & Chou, K.-C. (2004). Weighted-support vector machines for predicting membrane protein types based on pseudo-amino acid composition. *Protein Engineering, Design & Selection, 17*(6), 509–516. doi:10.1093/protein/gzh061

Wang, J. T. L., Zaki, M. J., Toivonen, H., & Shasha, D. (Eds.). (2005). *Data mining in bioinformatics.* Springer.

Wang, J. L., Chirn, G., Marr, T., Shapiro, B., Shasha, D., & Zhang, K. (1994). Combinatorial pattern discovery for scientific data: Some preliminary results. *Proc. ACM SIGMOD Int'l Conf. Management of Data*, (pp. 115-125).

Wang, J. L., Chirn, G., Marr, T., Shapiro, B., Shasha, D., & Zhang, K. (1994). Combinatorial pattern discovery for scientific data: Some preliminary results. *Proc. ACM SIGMOD Int'l Conf. Management of Data*, (pp. 115-125).

Wang, K., Xu, Y., & Yu, J. X. (2004). Scalable sequential pattern mining for biological sequences. *CIKM '04: Proceedings of the Thirteenth ACM International Conference on Information and Knowledge Management* (pp. 178-187). Washington, DC: ACM.

Wang, M., Shang, X.-Q., & Li, Z.-H. (2008). Sequential pattern mining for protein function prediction. *ADMA '08: Proceedings of 4th International Conference on Adv Data Mining and Applications* (pp. 652-658). Chengdu, China: Springer-Verlag.

Watkins, C. (1999). *Dynamic alignment kernels* (Tech. Rep. No.CSD-TR-98-11). Royal Holloway, London, UK: University of London, Department of Computer Science.

Weka. http://www.cs.waikato.ac.nz/~ml/

Wen, Y.-H., Lee, T.-T., & Cho, H.-J. (2005). Missing data treatment and data fusion toward travel time estimation for ATIS. *Journal of the Eastern Asia Society for Transportation Studies, 6*, 2546–2560.

Westbrook, J. D., & Berman, H. M. (2000). The protein data bank. *Nucleic Acids Research, 28*(1), 235–242. doi:10.1093/nar/28.1.235

Weston, J., Leslie, C., Ie, E., Zhou, D., Elisseeff, A., & Noble, W. S. (2005). Semisupervised protein classification using cluster kernels. *Bioinformatics (Oxford, England), 21*(15), 3241–3247. doi:10.1093/bioinformatics/bti497

Wishart, D. S., Knox, C., Guo, A. C., Cheng, D., Shrivastava, S., Tzur, D., et al. (2008). DrugBank: a knowledgebase for drugs, drug actions and drug targets. *Nucleic Acids Res., 36 (Database issue),* D901-6. Retrieved on January 11, 2011 from http://www.drugbank.ca

Witten, I., & Frank, E. (2000). *Data mining: Practical machine learning tools and techniques with Java implementations.* Morgan Kaufmann Publishers.

Wong, P. C., Cowley, W., Foote, H., Jurrus, E., & Thomas, J. (2000). Visualizing sequential patterns for text mining. *Proc. IEEE Information Visualization, 2000* (pp. 105-114). Society Press.

Wu, M., & Eisen, J. A. (2008). A simple, fast, and accurate method of phylogenomic inference. *Genome Biology, 9*(10), R151. doi:10.1186/gb-2008-9-10-r151

Wuu, L.-C., Hung, C.-H., & Chen, S.-F. (2007). Building intrusion pattern miner for Snort network intrusion detection system. *Journal of Systems and Software, 80*(10), 1699–1715. doi:10.1016/j.jss.2006.12.546

Xia, X., Maliski, E. G., Gallant, P., & Rogers, D. (2004). Classification of kinase inhibitors using bayesian model. *Journal of Medicinal Chemistry, 47,* 4463–4470. doi:10.1021/jm0303195

Xing, Z., Pei, J., & Keogh, E. (2010). A brief survey on sequence classification. *SIGKDD Explorations Newsletter, 12*(1), 40–48. doi:10.1145/1882471.1882478

Yan, X., Han, J., & Afshar, R. (2003). CloSpan: Mining closed sequential patterns in large datasets. *Proceedings of SDM,* (pp. 166-177).

Ye, N., & Chen, Q. (2001). An anomaly detection technique based on chi-square statistics for detecting intrusions into information systems. *Quality and Reliability Engineering International, 17*(2), 105–112. doi:10.1002/qre.392

Yoon, S. H., Hur, C. G., Kang, H. Y., Kim, Y. H., Oh, T. K., & Kim, J. F. (2005). A computational approach for identifying pathogenicity islands in prokaryotic genomes. *BMC Bioinformatics, 6,* 184–194. doi:10.1186/1471-2105-6-184

Yoon, S. H., Park, Y. K., Lee, S., Choi, D., Oh, T. K., Hur, C. G., & Kim, J. F. (2007). Towards pathogenomics: A Web-based resource for pathogenicity islands. *Nucleic Acids Research, 35,* D395–D400. doi:10.1093/nar/gkl790

You, C. H., Lee, K. A., & Li, H. (2009b). An SVM kernel with GMM-supervector based on the Bhattacharyya distance for speaker recognition. *IEEE Signal Processing Letters, 16*(1), 49–52. doi:10.1109/LSP.2008.2006711

You, C. H., Lee, K. A., & Li, H. (2009a). A GMM supervector kernel with the Bhattacharyya distance for SVM based speaker recognition. In *Proceedings of IEEE International Conference on Acoustics, Speech and Signal Processing,* (pp. 4221–4224). Taipei, Taiwan.

Yu, C. Y., Chou, L. C., & Darby, C. (2010). Predicting protein-protein interactions in unbalanced data using the primary structure of proteins. *BMC Bioinformatics, 11*(1), 167..doi:10.1186/1471-2105-11-167

Yun, C. H., & Chen, M. S. (2007). Mining mobile sequential patterns in a mobile commerce environment. *IEEE Transactions on Systems, Man, and Cybernetics,* 278–295.

Yun, U. (2008). A new framework for detecting weighted sequential patterns in large sequence databases. *Knowledge-Based Systems, 21*(2), 110–122. doi:10.1016/j.knosys.2007.04.002

Yun, U. (2008). A new framework for detecting weighted sequential patterns in large sequence databases. *Knowledge-Based Systems, 21*(2), 110–122. doi:10.1016/j.knosys.2007.04.002

Yun, L., Yunhao, Y., Yan, S., Xin, G., & Ling, C. (2008). *Mining self-adaptive sequence patterns based on the sequence fuzzy concept lattice.* Second International Symposium on Intelligent Information Technology Application (pp. 167-171).

Zaki, M. J. (2001). SPADE: An efficient algorithm for mining frequent sequences. *Machine Learning, 42*(1-2), 31–60. doi:10.1023/A:1007652502315

Zaki, M. J., Lesh, N., & Mitsunori, O. (1999). PlanMine: Predicting plan failures using sequence mining. *Artificial Intelligence Review, 14*(6), 421–446. doi:10.1023/A:1006612804250

Zaki, M. J. (2001). SPADE: An efficient algorithm for mining frequent sequences. *Machine Learning, 42*(1-2), 31–60. doi:10.1023/A:1007652502315

Zaki, M. J. (2000). Sequence mining in categorical domains: Incorporating constraints. *CIKM '00: Proceedings of the Ninth International Conference on Information and Knowledge Management* (pp. 422-429). New York, NY: ACM.

Zaki, M. J., Parthasarathy, S., Ogihara, M., & Li, W. (1997). New algorithms for fast discovery of association rules. In *Proceedings of KDD*, (pp. 283–286).

Zhang, S.-W., Pan, Q., Zhang, H.-C., Zhang, Y.-L., & Wang, H.-Y. (2003). Classification of protein quaternary structure with support vector machine. *Bioinformatics (Oxford, England)*, *19*(18), 2390–2396. doi:10.1093/bioinformatics/btg331

Zhang, C. T., Gao, F., & Zhang, R. (2005). Segmentation algorithm for DNA sequences. *Physical Review E: Statistical, Nonlinear, and Soft Matter Physics*, *72*, 041917. doi:10.1103/PhysRevE.72.041917

Zhang, H. (2004). The optimality of naive Bayes. In *Proceedings of FLAIRS Conference*.

Zhang, M., Kao, B., Cheung, D., & Yip, C. (2002). Efficient algorithms for incremental updates of frequent sequences., In *Proc. of the 6th Pacific-Asia Conference on Knowledge Discovery and Data Mining* (PAKDD'02).

Zhao, X. M., Li, X., Chen, L., & Aihara, K. (2008). Protein classification with imbalanced data. *Proteins: Structure, Function, and Bioinformatics*, *70*(4), 1125–1132. doi:10.1002/prot.21870

Zhou, P., & Onder, S. (2008). Improving single-thread performance with fine-grain state maintenance. In A. Ramirez, G. Bilardi, & M. Gschwind N (Eds.), *Proceedings of the 5th Conference on Computing Frontiers (CF-08)* (pp. 251-260). New York, NY: ACM.

About the Contributors

Pradeep Kumar obtained his PhD from the Department of Computer and Information Sciences, University of Hyderabad, India. He also holds an MTech in Computer Science and BSc (Engg) in Computer Science and Engg. Currently, he is working as an Assistant Professor with Indian Institute of Management, Lucknow, India. His research interest includes data mining, soft computing and network security.

S. Bapi Raju obtained BTech (EE) from Osmania University, India, and his MS and PhD from University of Texas at Arlington, USA. He has over 12 years of teaching and research experience in neural networks, machine learning, and artificial intelligence and their applications. Currently he is a Professor in the Department of Computer and Information Sciences, as well as Associate Coordinator, Centre for Neural and Cognitive Sciences at University of Hyderabad. He has over 50 publications (journal / conference) in these areas. His main research interests include biological and artificial neural networks, neural and cognitive modelling, machine learning, pattern recognition, neuroimaging, and bioinformatics. He is a member of ACM, Society for Neuroscience, Cognitive Science Society, and a Senior Member of IEEE.

P. Radha Krishna is a Principal Research Scientist at Software Engineering and Technology Labs, Infosys Technologies Limited, Hyderabad, India. Prior to joining Infosys, Dr. Krishna was a Faculty Member at the Institute for Development and Research in Banking Technology (IDRBT) and a scientist at National Informatics Centre, India. His research interests include data warehousing, data mining, and electronic contracts and services. He authored five books and has more than eighty publications.

* * *

Ilham Berrada currently serves as the Professor of Data Mining and the pedagogic director at National Graduate School of Computer Science and System Analysis in Rabat, Morocco. She is member of scientific committee of the Conference of Strategic Information Scanning System, Technological and Scientific Watching. She has established himself as one of the leading academic experts on data mining in both the public and private sector in Morocco.

Arnab Bhattacharya is currently an Assistant Professor at the Department of Computer Science and Engineering at the Indian Institute of Technology, Kanpur, India. He received his undergraduate degree, Bachelor of Computer Science and Engineering (BCSE), from Jadavpur University, India in 2001. He then worked in Texas Instruments (India) Pvt. Ltd. as Software Design Engineer for one year in Bengalooru, India. He received his Master of Science (MS) and Doctor of Philosophy (PhD) degrees in Computer Science from the University of California, Santa Barbara, USA in 2007. Since then, he has been working at the Indian Institute of Technology, Kanpur. His current research interests are in databases, data mining, and bioinformatics.

S. Durga Bhavani obtained her PhD in Mathematics from University of Hyderabad, Hyderabad, India. She has over 10 years of teaching and research experience. Her areas of interest are fractals and chaos theory, computational modeling of biological systems, and analysis of algorithms. She has over 20 publications in major journals and conferences. She is a member of IEEE and Computational Intelligence Society.

C. Chandra Sekhar received his B.Tech. degree in Electronics and Communication Engineering from Sri Venkateswara University, Tirupati, India, in 1984. He received his M.Tech. degree in Electrical Engineering and Ph.D. degree in Computer Science and Engineering from Indian Institute of Technology (IIT) Madras in 1986 and 1997, respectively. He was a Lecturer from 1989 to 1997, an Assistant Professor from 1997 to 2002, an Associate Professor from 2004 to 2010, and a Professor since 2010 in the Department of Computer Science and Engineering at IIT Madras, India. He was a Japanese Society for Promotion of Science (JSPS) Post-Doctoral Fellow at Center for Integrated Acoustic Information Research, Nagoya University, Nagoya, Japan, from May 2000 to May 2002. His current research interests are in speech processing, handwritten character recognition, artificial neural networks, kernel methods, Bayesian methods, and content-based information retrieval of multimedia data. He has published 11 papers in refereed journals and edited volumes, and 84 papers in the proceedings of international and national conferences. He has supervised 2 Ph.D. and 12 M.S. theses. He is currently supervising 4 Ph.D. and 2 M.S. students. His main research contributions are related to acoustic modeling of subword units of speech in Indian languages using a constraint satisfaction neural network, acoustic modeling and handwritten character recognition using support vector machines, and hybrid Gaussian mixture model and support vector machine model based classifiers for speech emotion recognition. He has reviewed papers for the *IEEE Transactions on Speech and Audio Processing, Neurocomputing Journal, Pattern Recognition Letters,* and *Electronic Letters.* He has organized the First and Second International Conference on Intelligent Sensing and Information Processing at Chennai, India in 2004 and 2005, respectively. He also organized the Indian National Academy of Engineers (INAE) Workshop on Image and Speech Processing in 2006 and the Winter School on Speech and Audio Processing in 2008 at Chennai. He is a member of IEEE.

Dileep A.D. received his B.E. degree in Computer Science and Engineering from Gulbarga University, Karnataka, India, in 2000. He received his M.Tech. degree in Computer Science and Engineering from Indian Institute of Technology Madras, Chennai, India, in 2006. Since 2006, he is pursuing the Doctoral degree at Indian Institute of Technology Madras, Chennai, India. He was a Lecturer in the Department of Computer Science and Engineering at Nitte Mahalinga Adyantaya Memorial Institute of Technology, Nitte, Karnataka, India from 2001 to 2004. He published 8 papers in the proceedings of international and national conferences. His current research interests include kernel methods and support vector machines, artificial neural networks, pattern recognition, speech technology, and image processing.

Bernard Dousset currently serves as the Professor of Data Mining at Paul Sabatier University in Toulouse, French. He is the Founding Editor of the Conference of Strategic Information Scanning System, Technological and Scientific Watching, and the chairman of scientific committee. He has established himself as one of the leading academic experts on competitive intelligence system in both the public and private sector. He has been an active consultant, a qualified expert witness, and an invited speaker on the competitive intelligence to both trade and academic audiences.

Sourav Dutta is currently working as a Software Engineer at IBM Research Lab, New Delhi, India. He obtained his undergraduate degree, Bachelor of Engineering (BE) in Information Technology, from Jadavpur University, India in 2008. In 2010, he received his Master of Technology (M.Tech.) degree in Computer Science and Engineering from the Indian Institute of Technology, Kanpur, India. His current research interests span algorithms, data structures, databases, data mining, and cloud computing.

Manish Gupta, http://www.cs.illinois.edu/homes/gupta58/, is currently a Ph.D. candidate under Dr. Jiawei Han in the Department of Computer Science in the University of Illinois at Urbana-Champaign. Previously, he worked at Yahoo!, Bangalore, India. His research interests lie in data mining and information retrieval. Recently, he has been working on a variety of topics in data mining related to evolution in graphs.

Anass El Haddadi is currently a PhD student of Data Mining at Paul Sabatier University in Toulouse, French, co-supervised with National Graduate School of Computer Science and System Analysis in Rabat, Morocco. He is member of program committee and organizing committee of the Conference of Strategic Information Scanning System, Technological and Scientific Watching. He is Member of the French Research Group in Competitive Intelligence.

Jiawei Han is a Professor of Computer Science at the University of Illinois. He has served on program committees of the major international conferences in the fields of data mining and database systems, and also served or is serving on the editorial boards for *Data Mining and Knowledge Discovery, IEEE Transactions on Knowledge and Data Engineering, Journal of Computer Science and Technology,* and *Journal of Intelligent Information Systems.* He is the founding Editor-in-Chief of ACM *Transactions on Knowledge Discovery from Data (TKDD).* Jiawei has received IBM Faculty Awards, HP Innovation Awards, ACM SIGKDD Innovation Award (2004), IEEE Computer Society Technical Achievement Award (2005), and IEEE W. Wallace McDowell Award (2009). He is a Fellow of ACM and IEEE. He is currently the Director of Information Network Academic Research Center (INARC) supported by the Network Science-Collaborative Technology Alliance (NS-CTA) program of U.S. Army Research Lab. His book "Data Mining: Concepts and Techniques" (Morgan Kaufmann) has been used worldwide as a textbook.

Rudra Narayan Hota is a Ph.D. Scholar at Frankfurt Institute for Advanced Studies, Frankfurt. Prior to joining this, he has few years of industrial research experience after completing MTech in Computer Science from Indian Statistical Institute, Kolkata, India, in 2005. He worked in Software Engineering and Technology Labs, Infosys Technologies Limited, Hyderabad, as a Research Associate and Honeywell Technology Solutions Lab, Bangalore for couple of years. During his academic and industrial research, he published few papers in international conferences and journals, and also holds couple of patents on his name. His research interests include computer vision, pattern recognition, machine learning, and neuroscience.

Kishore Jonna is a Senior Software Engineer at Software Engineering and Technology Labs(SETLabs), Infosys Technologies Limited, Hyderabad, India. He completed Bachelor of Engineering in Electronics and Communication Engineering from Anna University, Chennai, India. His research interests include computer vision and image analytics.

Engin Maden received his BS degree from Hacettepe University and MS degree from METU Computer Engineering Department. He studied on the use of sequence mining on architectural simulation for his MS thesis. Currently he is working in the IT department at Turkish Central Bank.

Hui Meen Nyew is a PhD candidate at Michigan Technological University's Computer Science Department. He received his BS degree from MTU, MS degree from MTU Computer Science on the use of machine learning techniques for the Foreign Exchange Market. His research interests include artificial intelligence, machine learning, and computer architecture.

M. Narasimha Murty is a Professor at Department of Computer Science and Automation, Indian Institute of Science, Bangalore, India. He obtained B.E., M.E., and Ph.D. from Indian Institute of Science, Bangalore. He guided more than 21 Ph.D. students, 18 of whom awarded Ph.D., and guided 60 M.Sc.(Engg) or ME theses. He has 71 journal papers and 60 conference papers to his credit. His survey paper on "Pattern Clustering: A Survey" in ACM Computing Surveys is cited more than 5000 times as reported by Google (www.google-scholar.com). The paper was reported to be most frequently downloaded article in 2004, 2005, and 2006 from ACM publications. He received "Alumni Award for Excellence in Research for Engineering" from the Indian Institute of Science, Bangalore, India in March 2007. He was elected as a Fellow of the Indian National Academy of Engineering (FNAE), awarded in 2009. He is consultant to many Industry sponsored projects and undertook projects sponsored by Ministry of HRD, Govt. of India, DST (Indo-US project), and AOARD (Tokyo).

Nilufer Onder is an Associate Professor of Computer Science at Michigan Technological University (MTU). She received her BS and MS degrees from METU Computer Engineering Department and her PhD degree from the Computer Science Department at the University of Pittsburgh. Her research interests include planning under uncertainty, contingency planning, applications of planning in construction project management, and machine learning.

Soner Onder is an Associate Professor of Computer Science at Michigan Technological University (MTU). He received his BS degree from METU Chemical Engineering Department, MS degree from METU Computer Engineering Department, and PhD degree from the Computer Science Department at the University of Pittsburgh. His research interests include computer architecture, micro-architecture, optimizing compilers and domain specific languages. He is a recipient of NSF CAREER award in 2004.

T. Maruthi Padmaja received M.Tech degree from Tezpur University, India in 2004. She is currently pursuing the PhD degree with University of Hyderabad. Her research interests include machine learning and data mining.

Nita Parekh is a currently Assistant Professor at the Center for Computational Natural Sciences and Bioinformatics, International Institute of Information Technology, Hyderabad. She obtained her PhD from School of Physical Sciences, Jawaharlal Nehru University, New Delhi in 1995 involving study of phase ordering dynamics of binary systems in presence of disorders and external fields. Her post-doctoral work at NCL Pune (1994-1997), and CCMB, Hyderabad (1997-1999) focused on synchronization and control of spatiotemporal chaos and patterns with applications to chemical and biological systems. While at NIST, Maryland, USA (2000-2001) she worked on the computational analysis of mechanical properties of spatially segregated polymer systems. She worked in the industry as a domain specialist at iLabs Ltd., Hyderabad (2001 – 2003). Her role at iLabs was to identify important areas and develop algorithms for software products in the area of sequence analysis, pattern recognition, and structure-based comparison methods. She has been at IIIT from 2003 onwards and her current research interests are pattern recognition in biological sequences, applications of graph theoretic approaches to the analysis of biological systems, and complex systems theory.

S. Prasanthi completed M.Tech Bioinformatics from School of Life Sciences in 2010 from University of Hyderabad.

Vikram Pudi graduated from J.N.T.U, Hyderabad in Computer Science and Engineering, in 1997. He immediately pursued his PhD at the Indian Institute of Science, Bangalore and completed it in 2003. His PhD topic of research was on the efficient discovery of concise association rules from large databases, and his advisor was Prof. Jayant Haritsa. After completing PhD, he worked for a short duration (8 months) in Yahoo! Inc., Bangalore as a senior software engineer. He then decided to take up an academic career and joined IIIT, Hyderabad in December 2003 as an Assistant Professor. At IIIT Hyderabad, he has taught courses on Data Mining, AI, and Computing Tools. His research interests primarily include data mining, artificial intelligence and database systems. He has published in top quality international conferences (e.g. ICDE) and journals (e.g. *Information Systems*). He is currently working on applying association rule mining for classification and on privacy issues in data mining. More information regarding Vikram Pudi and his research may be obtained from http://www.iiit.ac.in/~vikram.

Pratibha Rani graduated from M.A.C.E.T., Patna in Computer Science and Engineering, in 2004. She joined MS (by Research) program at International Institute of Information Technology, Hyderabad in 2006 under the guidance of Dr. Vikram Pudi and completed it in March 2009. Her MS thesis topic was classification of biological sequences. She worked on the problem of predicting the family of a newly discovered biological sequence, using the collection of available sequences. This problem comes in the category of classification problems, which is one of the widely studied problems in the data mining and machine learning fields. In her thesis she presented two data mining based effective solutions for this problem. Currently she is pursuing PhD at International Institute of Information Technology, Hyderabad under the guidance of Dr. Vikram Pudi. She has published in top quality international conferences ICDM 2008 and COMAD 2008 and recently one paper is to appear in DASFAA 2011. She is currently working on extracting knowledge from medical journals and finding unusual pattern behaviour from language specific annotated texts.

T. Sobha Rani obtained her M.Tech from Jawaharlal Nehru Technological University and PhD in Computer Science from University of Hyderabad, Hyderabad. Her PhD thesis dealt with the problem of promoter recognition for both prokaryotes and eukaryotes, and this work is published as a chapter in Wiley book series. She has over 15 journal and conference publications. She has been involved in teaching and research for the last 10 years, primarily in the area of bioinformatics. She is a member of IEEE and Computational Intelligence Society.

T. Ravindra Babu has been working as Principal Researcher, E-Comm. Research Laboratories, Education and Research Group, Infosys for the last 2 years. He leads a team of researchers working in the areas of image processing, and pattern recognition. He had earlier served ISRO for over 24 years as a Scientist. He obtained his Ph.D. and M.Sc.(Engg) from Department of Computer Science and Automation, Indian Institute of Science, Bangalore under the guidance of Prof. M. Narasimha Murty. Dr. T. Ravindra Babu was awarded Seshgiri Kaikini medal for best M.Sc.(Engg) thesis in the Division of Electrical Sciences, Indian Institute of Science. The areas of his interest include image processing, biometrics, pattern recognition, data mining, evolutionary algorithms, large data clustering and classification, and spacecraft orbital dynamics. He has a number of international journal/conference publications and book chapters to his credit in the above areas.

Pinar Senkul is an Assistant Professor in the Computer Engineering Department of Middle East Technical University (METU). She received her BS, MS, and PhD degrees from METU Computer Engineering Department. She conducted part of her thesis research as a visiting researcher at SUNY Stony Brook. Her research interests include web service discovery and composition, workflow modeling and analysis, data mining, and Web mining.

S.V. Subrahmanya is working at Infosys Technologies Limited as Vice-President, Research Fellow, and Head of E-Commerce Research Lab, Education and Research Group. He obtained his M. Tech from IIT Kharagpur. S.V. Subrahmanya has authored more than 20 papers that are published in journals, international conferences, and book chapters. He co-authored 3 books, titled, "Web Services," published by Tata McGraw-Hill (2004), "J2EE Architecture," published by Tata McGraw-Hill (2005), and "Enterprise Architecture," published by Wiley (2006). He has one granted patent from US PTO. His areas of interest include software architecture, mathematical modeling, and data and information management.

Veena T. received her B.E. degree in Bio-medical Engineering from Mangalore University, Karnataka, India, in 1998. She received her M.S. degree in Medical Software from Manipal Academy of Higher Education, Manipal, India, in 2000. Since 2006, she is pursuing the Doctoral degree at Indian Institute of Technology Madras, Chennai, India. She was an Assistant Professor at Manipal Center for Information Sciences, Manipal, Karnataka, India from 2000 to 2003. She was a Senior Lecturer in the Department of Computer Science and Engineering at Sri Siva Subramania Nadar College of Engineering, Chennai, Tamilnadu, India form 2003 to 2006. She published 5 papers in the proceedings of international and national conferences. Her current research interests include kernel methods and support vector machines, artificial neural networks, pattern recognition, speech technology, and image processing.

Index

A

aerosol time-of-flight mass spectrometer (ATOFMS) 18
AGP 14
Alignment-Based Methods 168, 173
All-Pair Refined Local Maxima Search (ARLM) 79-81
Amino acid (AA) 54, 60, 65, 67, 70, 78, 112-114, 118, 141, 156, 158, 160-163, 167-168, 170-171, 176-177
Amino Acid Bias 171
AMPHORA 174
Anti-monotonicity 142-143
APPEND 146-147
Approximate Greedy Maximum Maxima Search (AGMM) 79-81
ApproxMAP 150
Apriori 2, 11-12, 14, 17, 123, 137-140, 142, 236
AprioriALL 19, 237-240, 242-243
Apriori with Subgroup and Constraint (ASC) 2

B

bioinformatics 1, 9, 19, 22-24, 51, 68-71, 82, 91, 93, 111, 114, 132-135, 153, 157, 162, 164, 166, 177-181
Biosequence 9
Block 54, 77-79, 96-97, 101-102, 104, 107, 189, 199, 207
blocking algorithm 77-78, 80
Boolean method 3
branch prediction 216-217, 225, 236

C

cache 116, 216-218, 221, 224-226, 234
candidate set 220, 238-241
centroid 170, 181

Chi-square 73, 75-77, 81-82
CI 8, 31, 80, 195-196, 208, 241
CloSpan 144-145, 152
clustering 15, 24-26, 32-36, 45-47, 49-52, 66, 92, 94-95, 98, 103, 106-110, 116, 132, 180, 213, 225-226, 228
Clustering-Based Approach 168, 174
Codon Usage Bias 170
command-line mode 230
Comparative Genomics 168, 173, 175-176, 178, 180-181
ComputeProb 127-131
conditional branch instructions 216
Contiguous sequential patterns (CSPs) 6
control speculation 216
Correspondence Analysis (CA) 195-196, 198, 207
CROSS-FMSM 150
CSP model 6-7
cumulative density function (cdf) 74
Cycle-accurate simulators 218
cycles per instruction (CPI) 214-215

D

Data Mining 1, 3, 5, 7, 9, 14-15, 17-25, 48, 81-82, 84, 92-95, 100, 107-112, 133-135, 137, 142, 151-153, 184, 195-196, 198, 204, 208, 210, 213, 217-219, 223, 225-226, 228-229, 233-239, 242-243
Data pre-processor 229
Decision Making 190, 196, 205, 210-211, 237
digital library (DL) 206
Dissimilarity Threshold 96
Diversified 197
dNTP 167
Druggability 155-156, 159-161, 163-165
Drug-Target 165